Simon Martin is the author of *Football and Fascism: The National Game under Mussolini* which was awarded the Lord Aberdare Literary Prize for Sports History in 2004. He holds a PhD from University College London and has taught there, as well as at the University of Hertfordshire, the University of California Rome programme and New York University in Florence. He currently teaches at the American University of Rome and is a Research Fellow at the University of Hertfordshire and the British School at Rome. He appeared in the BBC2 documentary 'World Cup Stories' and is an FA qualified coach.

Dedicated to my Mum

and in memory of my Dad. . .

whose love of Arsenal was his only fault

SPORT ITALIA

★ ★ ★ ★

THE ITALIAN LOVE AFFAIR WITH SPORT

Simon Martin

I.B. TAURIS

LONDON · NEW YORK

Published in 2011 by I.B.Tauris & Co Ltd
6 Salem Road, London W2 4BU
175 Fifth Avenue, New York NY 10010
www.ibtauris.com

Distributed in the United States and Canada Exclusively by Palgrave Macmillan,
175 Fifth Avenue, New York NY 10010

ISBN: 978 1 84511 820 4

A full CIP record for this book is available from the British Library
A full CIP record is available from the Library of Congress

Library of Congress Catalog Card Number: available

Designed and typeset by 4word Ltd, Bristol, UK
Printed and bound in Sweden by ScandBook AB

Contents

List of figures

Acknowledgements

When I first stumbled into Florence in the autumn of 1998, with two bags and even fewer words in Italian the odds on me still being in the *bel paese* some ten years later were long. My first introduction to *calcio* (football) *Italiano* couldn't really have been better, soaking up the autumn sun in the curva Marione and the talent of a team containing Toldo, Batistuta, Rui Costa and Edmundo. But it wasn't love. A move to Bologna in 2001 confirmed that I was heading in the wrong direction at totally the wrong time, just as Roma took the *scudetto*. Garbatella's walls, street lights and pedestrian crossings were still painted red and yellow when I reached Rome the following year. There I found love... and hate. Love of a city never fails to stagger with its beauty, chaos and capacity to turn up the unexpected and frequent hatred of the fact that it could surely be so much better, but then would it be the same? Considering myself an adopted Roman, with all of the personal faults that entails, I am indebted to the city and Italy for all that it has given me, how it has changed me and for being my home from home. During the production of this text I have naturally accrued enormous debts without which things would have been very different and this project would never have got out of the starting blocks. Financial and personal, they are priceless.

With this project clear in my mind, the Leverhulme Trust placed its faith in me, demanding little more than commitment. I hope this meets its expectations and counts as a good return on its investment during a two-year Studentship Abroad. Many thanks to Jean Cater for her endless, patient support and her team's deciphering of my expenses. Beyond the time this award gave me to begin the enormous task of researching this book, it also enabled me to live in Rome, which enriched the text and my life enormously. The support was picked up by a nine-month Fellowship at the British School at Rome. My thanks to Andrew and Jo Wallace-Hadrill, current Director Christopher Smith and Sue Russell. Beyond an environment tailored to selfish academic needs, the BSR became my daily reference point and mother-ship of humanity. Thank you to all the domestic, catering and administrative staff, plus the library *veline* who all make it what it is. From the BSR, a one-year Fellowship at the University of Hertfordshire included a generous period of time to begin the writing process.

Research remains a soul-destroying business at times and thankfully I never appreciated the scale of what I had undertaken or quite how long it would require, until it was too late. That it has eventually been completed is in no small measure due to the efforts of library and archival staff across Italy. Suffering a funding crisis, the *Biblioteca Nazionale di Firenze* deserves better, as do its staff in the reading and microfilm rooms where I occasionally caused confusion with duplicate requests, as my mind began to boggle. Roberto Gollo and his team in the *sala microfilm* of the *Biblioteca Nazionale Braidense* in Milan were equally available and friendly, as was the staff of Rome's *Biblioteca di Storia Moderna e Contemporanea*, where I spent much time. The search for one particular text took me to the *Biblioteca di studi meridionali Giustino Fortunato*, within the *Associazione Nazionale per gli Interessi del Mezzogiorno d'Italia*, where the staff's enthusiasm uncovered maps from the *Touring Club Italiano* that were graciously provided for reproduction free of charge. CONI's library in Rome was also of enormous help in providing free use of its material for reproduction. Many thanks to the Director and Olga Colazingari for her help, which has embellished this book.

The list of those who have got me this far through the jungle of academia is long, but bracketed by the input of Roger Mettam from day one and Jonathan Morris, whose advice continues way beyond PhD supervision. I also thank Paul Corner for his thoughts and taking on the dubious role of my mentor, with the administration that entailed. With morale low, Chris Young injected much enthusiasm during the final year or so. I also owe a debt of gratitude to the numerous scholars whose work on Italy developed my interest and inspired this project. With specific reference to Italian sport Angela Teja has always shown enthusiasm for my work and a permanent will to help. Sergio Giuntini has also been an inspiration in his productivity, while his enormous source of information and advice was invaluable. Besides producing Italy's excellent sport history journal *Lancillotto e Nausica*, thanks to Paolo Ogliotti for finding me a personal copy of a text without which life would have been considerably more awkward.

No book is produced without enormous debts to equally important friendships. Richard and Sharon Thomas continue to fund my research trips to Milan: their door and fridge remain open, their support and friendship unceasing. M18743 thanks you for getting him in the garden! Having failed to enlighten me on football, John Pitonzo has continued to teach me many things about the important issues in life and has always been there when it mattered. John, Paola, Marianna and Romy are my Florentine family. Antonio Palmieri and Giuseppe Pellegrino became brothers too. Besides constantly keeping me up to date on Roma, *calcio* and popular culture, when life got complex, just as this project ground to the end and almost to a halt, Peppe pulled me out of a large hole. *Ti ringrazio di nuovo*. There when it mattered were also Bjorn Thomassen, Francesca Cantarella, Maria and Stella. Thank you. Ed Nadalin has also remained a great friend and a huge source of help and support when either technically or personally challenged. Thanks dude. A thanks also to Pino Coccia, Gianfranco Novelli and everybody associated with *Podistica Solidarietà*; an example of Rome at its best.

This book would also have been seriously different, and not for the better, had I not met the Bellisaris, who welcomed me with no questions asked about just what the hell this quiet *Inglese* was doing, when would it be finished, and then what? The answer to all three was I didn't know, but thank you. Around their table I ate like a king, and rapaciously drew on lessons in Italian life that an eternity's reading could never have achieved or demystified. This was thanks to Barbara, who also lived this book. Contributing to its conception and nursing its growing pains, her thoughts, advice, corrections and translations cover every page. Thank you.

To all of my friends who took the trouble to remain in touch (and to Roberta Alunni who joined the fray in time added on for stoppages), thank you.

Above all, this book is dedicated to my parents who always backed me beyond the call of duty: to mum who remains my rock and to dad who barely let a day pass without asking for a progress report during the years of research and writing. It is to my great regret that he never got to read it; he would have enjoyed the subject matter. Not only did he stimulate and encourage my love of sport from day one, it was his work ethic and belief in the merits of education that made it possible for me to consider and reach university. A devotee of all things Italian, his love of architecture, high-quality Italian bicycle parts (Campagno-low – *Campagnolo* – as we called it), coffee and Italian tailors in 1960s East London first exposed me to the myth and reality of the exported 'Made in Italy' brand. Although unable to share our football teams in London, we were united on the Curva Sud behind Roma and Er Capitano, while Rino Gattuso's memories of his front room as Marco Pantani stormed the Galibier were incredibly familiar. Thanks for everything dad, this one's for you.

Abbreviations

AIA	*Associazione Italiana Arbitri* (Italian Referees' Association)
APEF	*Associazione Proletaria per l'Educazione Fisica* (Workers Association for Physical Education)
DC	Christian Democratic Party
CCI	*Confederazione Calcistica Italiana* (Italian Football Confederation)
CONI	*Comitato Olimpico Nazionale Italiano* (Italian Olympic Committee)
ENEF	*Ente Nazionale per l'Educazione Fisica* (National Body for Physical Education)
FASCI	*Federazione delle Associazioni Sportive Cattoliche Italiane* (Federation of Catholic Sporting Associations)
FIDAL	*Federazione Italiana di Atletica Leggera* (Italian Athletic Federation)
FIFA	*Fédération Internationale de Football Association* (International Football Federation)
FIGC	*Federazione Italiana Giuoco del Calcio* (Italian Football Federation)
FGSI	*Federazione Giovanile Socialista Italiana* (Italian Young Socialist Federation)
La Gazzetta	*La Gazzetta dello Sport*
ONB	*Opera Nazionale Balilla* (Balilla Youth Movement)
OND	*Opera Nazionale Dopolavoro* (After-work Movement)
PCI	*Partito Comunista Italiano* (Italian Communist Party)
PNF	*Partito Nazionale Fascista* (Fascist Party)
PSI	*Partito Socialista Italiano* (Italian Socialist Party)
UOEI	*Unione Operaia Escursionisti Italiani* (Italian Workers Excursionists Union)

Map 1: *Map of Italy showing locations of major cities*

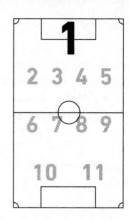

Introduction

Theoretically Italy

'Generally in Italy, he said, the great majority of kidnap victims survive. But when the Sards are involved, that's not necessarily so. The victims disappear. "They feed them to their pigs."'[1] The *Il Giorno* war correspondent quoted in Pete Davies' marvellous account of the 1990 football World Cup Finals held in Italy, warned of what might await English hooligans based in Sardinia for the tournament's group stage. The barren and rocky island in the Tyrrhenian Sea has not always been as hospitable as its cobalt waters, spectacular beaches and ports for Europe's glitterati suggest. Having been invaded from all angles, Sardinians are not to be underestimated, their resolute character evident in the region's flag: the red cross of St George on white background with the silhouetted, turbaned head of a Moorish king in each quarter.[2]

As the Sardinian Giovanni Pinna discovered in 2006, banditry and hostage-taking occasionally still occur. Abducted and a €300,000 ransom demanded for his release, he escaped after eight months and ten days of incarceration. Interviewed by police, the emaciated and bearded Pinna's first questions were reportedly: 'Who won the *scudetto*?'(league title) and 'Were Cagliari relegated?'[3] While news that Inter had broken its 15-year jinx was reason enough to voluntarily return to the bubble of captivity, Cagliari's last gasp salvation must have eased the blow. Pinna's story seemed to be a scene from the soap opera of Italian life starring a disaffected people, lawless rogues and a bedraggled hero expressing deep concern for his family, having first been assured of the football results. Understanding just why the majority of accounts focussed first upon his *calcio* quip is effectively the aim of this book. How did football and sport manage to usurp such a serious crime? How and why did this originally bourgeois, minority interest become an all-consuming national passion worthy of a place on Italy's podium of national stereotypes, alongside pizza and the Mafia? Just how did Italy get here?

✪ ✪ ✪ ✪

Even before Italy's formation, Giuseppe Mazzini, one of the national movement's leading thinkers and activists, proposed the need for a strong state with a capital that would encourage unity and cohesion; namely Rome. His thoughts were indicative of a nation that needed creating rather than one whose identity was already strong. Although Liberal Italy failed to generate national patriotic fervour before collapsing under the weight of its weaknesses and paralyses, Fascism chose to maintain and build upon many of its foundations. Similarly, in the post-war Republic, the restoration of democracy did not involve a complete dismantling of the Fascist state.[4] Thus, in its development and transition from Liberal Italy through to Fascism, the Republic and beyond, considerable continuities exist,[5] which the analysis of sport further confirms.

Rather than striding from a bloodstained battlefield united in triumph like Germany, Italy was a dislocated collection of people sharing little more than a dislike of each other and the new state that was now interfering in their lives, or not. Following unification in 1861, many of the issues and debates that had driven it persisted: questions over Italian character, education and patriotism; the burden of former greatness; the search for a common past; regional identities; the role of the Catholic Church and the rise of Socialism; all within the dislocating experience of Italy's transition from a primarily agricultural economy into a modern industrial nation. These issues were intensified by the new, weak state that remained desperately short of legitimacy and popular support.

Just who and what were Italians was a valid question that unification posed, failed to resolve, and even complicated with the establishment of borders that excluded many Italian speakers. Italian identity has thus featured prominently in the various accounts of the country's history that *Sport Italia* is intended to complement. Each chapter's brief summary of the principal events and issues of the period provides the bare minimum without which the sport would have no context. Readers wishing to know more will be well served by Christopher Duggan's entertaining and detailed recent work or the established texts of Denis Mack Smith and Paul Ginsborg, from the many in existence.[6]

The issue of the Italian nation has been one of considerable interest and difficulty for many historians who, John Foot suggests, 'often seem to adopt very stringent models to which Italy, inevitably, has failed to adhere'.[7] This apparent lack of national identity was often the justification for the numerous wars in which Italy became involved from 1860 onwards, spurred on by

Risorgimento myths and the memory of Giuseppe Garibaldi's heroic unification campaign. Unfortunately, the impact of these conflicts upon patriotism was minimal. With Italians rarely wanting to die for their country, such assessments added to its impoverished reputation, which varies according to the interpretation of Italy's history.[8] The reality is, of course, very different. Having created and overthrown Fascism before supporting the largest Communist Party in post-war Western Europe, Italy has had an extraordinary impact upon modern Europe. 'Italians matter and so does their history.'[9]

Having established this, it is even more inconceivable that the national passion of sport has commanded so little interest. Engaging with Italian history at macro and micro levels, sport provides unrivalled snapshots of the large and small picture, of central government policies and devolved regions, of national dreams and everyday lives, of a proud nation fractured by the myriad of local identities within its DNA.

In a country whose borders have shifted, expanded and occasionally contracted and whose people have not always shared a language, rigid concepts of nationhood do not always apply. While Italian sport has been exploited by regional, political or religious forces whose identities have exposed the nation's fissures, on several occasions sport has been one of Italy's greatest successes, one of the few occasions in which Italians could freely unite and be proud.

Sport and society

For the unconverted or plain uninterested, sport can appear an incomprehensible means of passing or wasting time. Even if there is little consensus as to its meaning or definitive role in modern life, theorists have argued that there is more to it than simple recreation.[10] That said, most attempts to explain or understand it are flawed and many arguments highly speculative.[11]

Among a number of twentieth-century theories regarding play and recreation, the Dutch historian Johan Huizinga proposed in *Homo Ludens*, in 1938, that play was the primary formative element in human culture, present in all areas of life, from work to leisure, literature, music, religion, war and naturally sport.[12] In essence, many of man's great accomplishments could be attributed to the innate desire to run, chase, wrestle and simply play. Identifying the construction of order, rules and conventions as one of play's principle characteristics, he nonetheless failed to address just why people play – what stimulates this most basic desire? The combination of sport as an escape or release from everyday life and its role in establishing order has particular relevance in Italy where sport, leisure and free time were seized upon by political opportunists.

In their classic 'civilizing process' theory Norbert Elias and Eric Dunning also connected sport with evolutionary development, proposing its fulfilment of man's need for challenges once obstacles in the struggle for survival had been overcome. As order and stability developed in society, so sport provided an outlet for man's now redundant survival qualities and animal instincts.[13] The need for risk, danger and uncertainty was thus experienced vicariously through sportsmen in stadiums that were interpreted as metaphorical killing fields. A central plank of their theory related to the development of modern states in which the need for control, the imposition and acceptance of rules, acceptable behaviour and the settlement of disputes became more pressing. As the state's monopolization of the legitimate use of force increased, so acceptable levels of violence theoretically reduced as members of society chose or were forced to modify their behaviours. Deterministic in its vision of humanity's relentless progress, it still highlighted the simple human pleasure gained from sport.

Sport has also been interpreted politically. While Karl Marx made no reference to it, the left's appreciation of sport's capacity to attract and mobilize large sections of society resulted in its politicization in the early 1900s. In 1920, a Workers' Sport Movement was established to connect Soviet sport with various European organizations. Promoting class loyalty, the movement held Workers' Olympics and had a Europe-wide membership, with the majority coming from Germany, Austria and Czechoslovakia.[14] Italy did not feature among the member nations, which certainly wasn't due to the left's lack of interest; too much interest, in fact. From 1910, the Italian left fought an ideological civil war over sport's relevance to Italian society and its campaign for Socialist change.

The enduring Marxist interpretation of sport was as a bourgeois/middle class tool that distracted workers from the class struggle and thereby contributed to the preservation of the status quo.[15] Rejecting the idea that political developments could be totally attributed to economic factors, such as employment, wages and the relationship between capital and labour, Antonio Gramsci indentified a fundamental role for culture in the elite's domination, which was achieved through a combination of coercion and consent.[16] In effect, sport trained workers to accept rules, discipline and hard work, theoretically in return for shared success, while physically equipping them to meet the demands of the industrial age and increase production. Exhausted at the end of a long working day, any remaining energy for radical thought would be drained by sport.

Consequently, it was interpreted as both a means of repressing the working class and maintaining its servility, while also promoting solidarity and mobilization that could potentially challenge the existing order. Far from meritocratic, however, the apparently equal chance of victory that sport offered replicated capitalism's structural inequalities that maintained the poor in poverty while encouraging them not to question why. Lacking money, facilities and opportunity, the working class' capacity to challenge the social order through sport was limited. This increased with the growth of national sporting bodies, international organizations and tournaments, such as the Olympic Games, as sport became an essential component of the modern state. In her analysis of its globalization, Barbara Keys observes how:

> in the twentieth century sports became an important way to instill a sense of belonging to a nation, to solidify loyalty, to create a bond of attachment to an abstract entity...
>
> For the great powers it became a matter of urgency to win more medals or more championships than rival powers. For the smaller nations it became critical not so much to win but to show up, to perform respectably, and to be seen as a member of the club.[17]

Almost as soon as tournaments like the Olympic Games became major international events, so the original ideals of fraternization and brotherhood wilted under political and commercial pressures. Commodified and sold off for profit, athletes and their events were woven into a repressive system controlled by the elite. Encouraging victory at all costs, promoting extreme individualism and elitism, classifying individuals by success and gender, and generating nationalism, this particular interpretation interested Italy's left in the politically charged 1970s.

In this period, according to Elis Cashmore, Paul Hoch developed 'one of the most acerbic Marxist critiques of sport, which he likened to the mainstream religions about which Marx himself wrote so much'.[18] His ideas have particular relevance for Italy where the Catholic Church meddled in sport almost from day one, in an attempt to create religious solidarity that would compete with the class-based identity of its secular rivals, Socialism and Communism. Initially unsure of how and if sport should be used for religious propaganda, its politicization by the Fascist regime convinced the Church of its merits as a communication tool and a means of forming an alternative counterculture. Despite coming to rival the Church as a new, secular religion itself, sport proved highly effective in the Vatican's penetration of post-war Italian society.

Sport has thus provided huge opportunities to mobilize working-class, bourgeois or religious groups, which indicates one of its primary roles in society. Otherwise, why would the nation's various democratic and dictatorial administrations have gone to so much trouble trying to shape it? Consequently, it is even harder to fathom how historians have unpicked modern Italy through art, architecture, food, music, marriage, mafia, opera and theatre, with few deeming sport worthy of even a mention.

Sport and modern Italy

Many studies of modern Italy have taken a chronological approach, with 1860 the logical starting point. A 'critical moment of rupture in the history of a country characterised by centuries of political fragmentation, with profound repercussions on Italian economic and social life',[19] the date also corresponds with modern sport's boom as Europe industrialized. The risk, however, of such a clear watershed moment is disconnection from previous epochs that continue to resonate.

In ancient Rome sporting and athletic culture held great importance in preparation for war, while the construction of amphitheatres, baths and arenas for the masses evidence a concept of leisure.[20] Consumed as well as practised, mass leisure, recreation and spectacles bore a striking resemblance to contemporary arenas.

> Romans of all classes attended and enjoyed the games. For the state, the provision of great spectacles symbolized power, leadership, and empire...
>
> Attentive and knowledgeable, some spectators, including some emperors, were true fans – or even fanatics, some arguably were sadists, some went for the crowd and the gambling as well as the violence, and many perhaps went to simply escape their deplorable living conditions. Indeed, as social functions, spectacles were occasions... for seeing performances of skill and courage, and for being seen – as producers and patrons of games sitting at prominent vantage points, as citizens of status in seats of privilege, as citizen-spectators participating and sanctioning the rules and rulers of Rome.[21]

Following the fifth-century collapse of the Roman Empire, the next injection of impetus into Italian sport came from the fourteenth- to sixteenth-century Renaissance. In this period of artistic rebirth and creativity that spread through Europe from Italy, racket and ball games emerged along with events like the Florentine football-type game of *calcio Fiorentino*.[22] Local celebrations or mediaeval pageants that engendered civic pride also often involved sport or some form of athletic, combat-based activity, such as Arezzo's *Giostra del Saracino* (jousting) and Siena's famous Palio horse race. Primarily entertainments, they became enduring events in the peninsula's calendar. Unable to stop Renaissance liberalism's encouragement of pleasure-seeking among the public that began to increasingly drink, gamble and enjoy blood sports, Church resistance waned and events were permitted on holy days.

Catholic corruption, however, contributed to the early sixteenth-century Protestant Reformation that established man's capacity to save his own soul without the clergy. Emphasizing religion and idealizing work over leisure, Protestantism promoted ambition, austerity, abstinence and determination. Putting labour at the heart of everyday life, it encouraged the metamorphosis of games into pragmatic pursuits that developed health and character, which led to a reinterpretation of sport from a frivolous pursuit into a useful activity that forged disciplined bodies and minds dedicated to labour.

As Italy industrialized and huge numbers of people moved into city centres and factory jobs, the need for discipline and labour grew. Responding to social injustice and long working hours in tough conditions, pioneers proposed reform and increasingly unionized workforces demanded time off for rest, which became leisure. In addition to factory-based teams and activities organized by enlightened or philanthropic employers, the introduction of the five-and-a-half-day week boosted sport enormously. From its leisurely origins as an alternative to work, sport was transformed into something that totally reflected it.[23]

The development of international competitions that associated pride with sporting achievement also created a demand for permanent improvement. This was particularly true in nineteenth-century Italy where the national question, even after unification, saw an increase in sporting festivals, events and activities. An eclectic mix, they raise the debate about just what constitutes sport, and I confess to having always found a friend's theory of the necessity of a ball highly appealing, if theoretically flawed. But as Richard Holt has persuasively argued, 'narrow semantic distinctions' offer little other than restriction, while 'it may be possible to turn this ambiguity to our own advantage by using the conflict itself as a defining feature of modern European physical culture'.[24] This explains *Sport Italia*'s brief forays into leisure and manufacturing to consider tourism, the Vespa and cars. The space dedicated to particular sports was also questioned in this project's early stages, with specific reference to an apparent lack of fencing coverage. As will be seen, fencing was important in the construction of a nationalist culture in the Liberal period. However, it has always been and remains a minority sport, which reduces its importance in terms of this study, that focuses on those sports with the greatest social, economic and political impact.

More justifiable might be to question the space given to motor sport. While the impact of the motor car and racing is far from ignored, it has been restricted to its contribution to the development of the Italian identity and economy. With the salient points of the Ferrari story applying equally to Ducati and motorcycles, there was no need for repetition. Moreover, as 'sports' that have increasingly become engineering contests, they failed to hold my research or personal interests. Accepting the considerable scope for debate over the various sports included, 1860 remains the unquestionable moment from which to fire the starting pistol. While it was not year zero in the peninsula's athletic history, it clearly marks Italy's entry into the international arena.

Thereafter, sport was fundamental in the standardization of life and the forging of Italians. Influenced by German physical culture, Piedmont's gymnastic societies were the crucibles of Italian minds and bodies, which is where *Sport Italia* begins. As Chapter 2 discovers, it was from these clubs that sport flourished, primarily in the major metropolises of the industrial north. Although Italy's entry into the First World War, in 1915, exposed the considerable work still needed to create an intensely patriotic nation, the decimation of its sportsmen on the battlefields along the Austro-Hungarian border indicated sport's already significant contribution. Although Italy emerged victorious with an enlarged territory, the First World War nonetheless created the conditions for Fascism's semi-constitutional takeover that quickly became dictatorship. Obsessed with Italy's weakness and intent on restoring the nation to former glories, Mussolini set about regenerating Italians. As Chapter 3 unveils, sport and physical education were fundamental in the creation of Fascist bodies, minds and the illusion of power.

Politicizing sport to previously unknown levels, Fascism's medals and international victories were almost certainly enjoyed by a vast number of Italians. But sporting success could not buy support, hide the loss of civil liberties and ever-decreasing standards of living, or create the rabidly patriotic race that the *Duce* demanded. Fascism did, however, demonstrate sport's potential to reach out and mould the masses, and following the regime's collapse in 1943 it was seized upon by the Catholic Church and Socialism, which contested the power vacuum. Reconstituting their recreational groups that were dissolved by Fascism, each exploited sport to impose their vision of society on post-war Italy. As Chapter 4 reveals, Fascism's demise did not end the politicization of sport, which was intensified by Italy's strategic Cold War importance.

The Marshall Plan and an enormous pro-Christian Democratic Party (DC) and anti-Communist Party (PCI) publicity campaign assisted the Catholic right's 1948 electoral victory that fixed Italy's political path for the next 40 years. Creating stability, the economic boom from 1958 to 1963 saw the country make its great leap forwards, producing new wealth and the desire for quick riches. Chapter 5 follows Italy's sporting resurgence from the ashes of war and disaster until Rome's triumphal Olympics in 1960, in which the confident, cool nation introduced the world to *la dolce vita*.

Beyond the veneer and bright lights, however, not all Italians surfed the crest of the economic wave and serious tensions grew within a society desperate for change, which became extremely politicized and violent from the late 1960s onwards. Chapter 6 explores sport's role in the conflict between the polarized political extremes. Politicians of all persuasion began encroaching onto the field of play, a major actor that no aspiring leader could ignore. Following the de-regulation of the state broadcasting monopoly, money also began to pour into sport, the implications of which are explored in Chapter 7. A barometer of Italian society, serious sporting corruption reflected the downward spiral of the morally bankrupt First Republic, which collapsed in 1992. Ending the old political order, the space was filled by Silvio Berlusconi's *Forza Italia!* Party that used football to make politics.

As Chapter 8 reveals, sporting scandals dogged the nation that continued to punch above its weight in terms of success. But with the rise of the Northern League and increasing demands for regionalism, sporting achievements began stimulating groans of protest and pleasure. In summarizing and drawing conclusions as to how and why sport has become such a fundamental aspect of Italian life, consideration will be given to its future role. With race both a contentious and potentially constructive area in which sport might influence Italy's future, it is with some irony that elements of the deeply divided nation have only found their 'Italian' voices under the pressure of immigration.

It is inevitable that with such a broad timescale *Sport Italia* owes much to existing work, the bulk of which is in Italian and focuses upon the Liberal and Fascist periods or specific sports.[25] Felice Fabrizio's *Storia dello Sport in Italia*, Patrizia Ferrara's *L'Italia in Palestra*, Adolfo Noto and Lauro Rossi's *Coroginnica*, Remo Bassetti's *Storia e Storie dello Sport in Italia*, plus Nicola Porro's *Identità, Nazione, Cittadinanza* provide the launch pads for any investigation into sport in modern Italy.[26] In addition to making an enormous contribution to the study of female sport under Fascism,[27] Angela Teja has also outlined the labyrinthine organization of Italian sport in the edited collections of Pierre Arnaud, Arnd Krüger and James Riordan.[28]

Since the ground-breaking collective work *Atleti in Camicia Nera*,[29] Fascist sport has generated the most research and interest. Maria Canella and Sergio Giuntini's collection of essays, *Sport e Fascismo*, has significantly advanced knowledge of sport in the period, as does Alessio Ponzio's commendable investigation of the regime's sport university.[30] Complementing Victoria De Grazia's seminal study of leisure time, *Sport Italia, Football and Fascism*, plus Gigliola Gori's analysis of women and physical culture – *Female Bodies, Sport, Italian Fascism* – stand more or less alone as studies of Fascist sport in English.[31]

There are also a number of important sport-specific studies in Italian, with Daniele Marchesini's three notable works on boxing, motor racing and cycling coming immediately to mind.[32] As one of the best researched areas, Stefano

Pivato's various works on cycling have unveiled the sport's intense politicization in the twentieth century.[33] Football coverage is naturally not lacking, with Antonio Papa and Guido Panico's two volumes the yardstick in an ocean of contemporary and commercial accounts of clubs and individuals that include two recent studies in English.[34]

Sport Italia seeks to connect and develop all of these, to establish how and why different forms of government and leadership in Italy have consistently interacted with sport. In the process, it is hoped that this new look at sport's capacity to reveal change will offer a new means of analysing and viewing the histories of nation-states, while interesting the general and academic reader alike, and even non-sport fans. It is what sport reveals about Italian society, politics and its economy that interests, rather than the goals, medals, records and statistics that have sometimes suffocated sport history in a sweaty fug.

Various histories have already established Italy as a special case, which sport appears to confirm. As one of the few historians to have given even minimal consideration to its importance in Italian society, Paul Ginsborg's telling observation explains *Sport Italia*'s *raison d'être*:

> The sort of game that football is... makes for difficult arbitration... the rules exist, but they are not easy to interpret. In these circumstances, the referee's authority is perforce uncertain, but it is made much more so in Italy by the almost universal climate of suspicion, if not derision, that accompanies his decisions. The referee is the butt on to whom the spectators can project all their fury and disdain, as well as their oft-repeated conviction that he has been corrupted. It is not difficult to discern here a series of emotions – suspicion, contempt, cynicism, even hatred – that characterize the relationship between Italians and their state.[35]

The Italian factory

The process of unification is referred to in Italian as the *Risorgimento*, a revival or reawakening. Implicitly suggesting a nationalist campaign among a united people intent on throwing off repressive shackles and restoring glories of old, it is somewhat misleading. How and why this disparate group of people came together in 1861 has a variety of explanations, none of which can demonstrate a peninsula-wide demand for unity. Certainly, Napoleonic rule (1792–1814) and the Austrian restoration governments (1814–60) were contributory factors to insurrections in 1820–1, 1831 and 1848, in which local sentiments were put aside in the pursuit of a shared goal. But this was not necessarily a common identity.

Making Italy

Unlike Germany, forged under the leadership of the Kaiser and Bismarck, and fuelled by Prussian ambitions in the crucible of a nationalist war, Italy effectively emerged from the victory of French and Piedmontese forces over Austria, in 1859. Piedmont thus provided the nucleus of the Italian nation-state, even if Rome, Naples, Milan or the Grand Duchy of Tuscany might have made more logical centres of Italian nationalism than a kingdom that contained vast French-speaking areas.

One of the driving forces behind Italian unification was the Savoy Count Camillo Cavour. He envisaged a primary role for Piedmont in an independent nation-state in the north of the peninsula; his French mother-tongue indicating one of the major difficulties in forming any common bond among 'Italians', the majority of whom would not have understood him. Even when Giuseppe Garibaldi's redshirts launched their assault on Sicily in 1860, Cavour did much to impede the operation. It was only Garibaldi's arrival on the Italian mainland that finally forced him to illegally annex the Papal territories with Savoy troops in an effort to save Rome and neuter the fear of a democratic, republican revolution.

The legendary figure of Italian unification, Garibaldi was inspired by Giuseppe Mazzini, arguably the great theorist of the Italian nationalism who envisaged the nation as a spiritual entity. Insurrections were key in his patriotic programme, with Garibaldi's 'voyage of the thousand' and conquest of the southern Kingdom of the Two Sicilies exactly the type of action that he had been preaching. Arguably the greatest General in modern Italian history, Garibaldi was almost a saint in southern Italy and respected across the world. More tactician than politician, the single-minded patriot immediately ceded his territorial gain to King Victor Emmanuel II, the first King of Italy. With his title affirming the continuity of the dynasty rather than the creation of a new state, the 1861 parliament was also officially named the eighth legislature. Italy had been made, but this Piedmontese 'passive revolution' proved a long-term weakness.[1]

The Austrian Chancellor Prince Clemens von Metternich and Piedmont prime minister Massimo d'Azeglio provided two of the most enduring clichés in Italy's modern history, and they have been well-quoted for good reason. While the peninsula's diverse regions and people certainly had enough in common to refute Metternich's reduction of Italy, in 1847, to a mere geographical expression, the centuries of division left their mark. With Italians alienated from themselves and the state by regional histories, traditions of government, law, culture and language, plus geographical, social, economic and linguistic impediments, there was good reason for D'Azeglio's assertion that having made Italy, the same now had to be done with Italians.

Despite the considerable regional differences within the newly created Italy, the nation-state's philosophy was uniformly nationalist. The Savoy royal family provided the Head of State, who could declare war, appoint the prime minister, and select ministers without parliament's approval. Parliamentary majorities were based upon regional rather than ideological groupings, which contributed to the politics of *trasformismo*: bargaining or changing sides. The dominant political class came from the agricultural elite that worked with a small, educated, professional electorate to preserve their own interests. This limited democracy was further weakened by Pope Pius IX's *non-expedit* decree, in protest at the loss of the Papal States and the seizure of Rome, which discouraged Catholics from participating in national politics.

With the vote restricted to literate males over 25 years old who paid a minimum of 40 lire per annum in taxes, the electorate represented only two per cent of the population, in 1870, of which almost 50 per cent abstained. Incredibly, some 50 seats went uncontested in the 1874 election, while one quarter of all deputies elected in Italy's first 20 years did so unopposed.[2] A limited expansion of the franchise, based upon literacy and property, was introduced in 1882. Including many shopkeepers and skilled workers, it saw the Radical and Republican parties grow and the Socialist movement emerge. Yet, even the formation of the Socialist Party (PSI), in 1892, did little for the universal suffrage campaign, with both left and right suspicious of the peasantry's reactionary or revolutionary nature.

Italy's end-of-century crisis brought a wave of state repression. Including the banning of the PSI, it divided the political class and worried industrialists, so contrary did it seem to the rest of Europe where the extension of political rights was linked with economic progress. Terrorist/anarchist activities culminated in the assassination of King Umberto I, on 29 July 1900, as he left a gymnastics display by the 'Forti e Liberi' (Strong and Free) association in Monza. When the consequent repression ended later that year, there was general consensus that the base of the political system had to widen. Dismayed by the results of unification so far, many intellectuals turned away from the *Risorgimento*'s ideals and looked to the new faith of Socialism.

In 1871, almost 60 per cent of the population worked on the land. The wars of unification and the post-1860 repression of the south had left huge public debt. Principally paid for by heavy taxation on agriculture, this debt further punished and alienated the disenfranchised, impoverished peasantry. Further pressure from free trade and the loss of previous price protections, high taxation, unemployment, falling living standards and starvation, combined with agricultural recession, increasingly affordable trans-Atlantic fares and the potential for relatively well-paid work in South and North America, led to mass emigration. Between 1900 and 1915 over eight million Italians left for America, half of whom came from the agricultural south. What investment there was tended to benefit northern agriculture and industry, thereby exacerbating class and regional inequality.

Compared with other major European nations, Italy's industrialization was late and seriously hampered by limited raw materials and the introduction of tariffs in 1878. It was only during the first economic boom, from 1896 to 1908, that Italy's economy grew significantly. While industry shifted from textiles to steel, much growth still came from agriculture, especially in the northern Po valley, where new techniques were introduced and the labour force reorganized. Although these changes represented progress, Italy remained far from a modern industrial nation, with most workers occupied in artisan businesses and small factories. The major increases in the factory population were limited to the industrial triangle of Genoa, Turin and Milan, which, along with Venice and Palermo, were still among the most populous in Europe at the turn of the century.

Thus from 1860 to 1914, Italy experienced major shifts in economic, religious and social power that produced tension between dominant interest groups, new industrial and agrarian entrepreneurs, the political class and the regions, which was reflected in the end-of-century crisis. Nonetheless, at no point prior to 1918 did the leaders of industry and agriculture feel the need to intervene directly in the political process to defend their interests. This occurred only with the apparent threat of revolution.

The middle class was also growing and producing a huge number of highly educated people within a society that still possessed relatively low economic development and significant illiteracy. Resulting in a chronic surplus of high-school and university graduates who created great competition for white-collar positions, the middle class sought to control the political system to defend its interests and repel those of the increasingly organized mass workforce. There were also ominous tensions in agriculture, where rapid economic growth had disrupted traditional peasant society. The emergence of a stratum of entrepreneurs introducing new agricultural techniques drew opposition from landless day labourers and sharecroppers in the Po valley, where Catholic peasant leagues and Socialist peasant unions began to organize.

These political, economic and social differences, inequalities and traditions resulted in a country and nation in desperate need of means and reasons to discover just what, if anything, citizens from Milan, Bari and Palermo actually had in common; just what made them Italian? Yet, as Christopher Duggan suggests, any encouragement was minimal:

> the state did little in the way of celebrations or festivals to etch the reality of the new Italy into the hearts and minds of the public... For those many Risorgimento patriots who had imbibed the central lesson of Mazzini that the nation, to be strong, needed to become the focus of a secular religion, the failure of the liberal state to capture the popular imagination through spectacle, imagery and display was a source of deep disappointment.[3]

This identity crisis was worsened by the education system. Governed by the Catholic Church, it refused to teach *Risorgimento* history and gave an unbalanced portrayal of the regime that had removed much of the Pope's temporal power and sequestered the Vatican's land. It was not until the late 1880s and the nationalizing zeal of Francesco Crispi that the *Risorgimento* began to assume a strong presence within the school curriculum. Thus, the elitist nature of the Piedmont-led unification, the non-participation of the Catholic Church, plus inefficiencies and corruption, resulted in the state suffering a permanent crisis of legitimacy.

Some attempts to address these widely recognized problems were made. In 1912 Giovanni Giolitti's progressive reform package extended the vote to all male literates over the age of 21 and all male illiterates over 30, or as soon as they had completed military service. The electorate rose immediately to 8.6 million, representing 24 per cent of the population. Keen to reconcile the people with the regime, Giolitti welcomed the Church's recommendation of tactical voting against the Socialist threat, from 1904 onwards. He also sought to neuter the left by co-opting trade unions and Socialist groups into the political system, in return for recognizing the labour movement. Welfare measures were introduced, along with compulsory accident insurance in the workplace, a non-compulsory national insurance fund for industrial workers, the outlawing of child labour, working-day limits and, most importantly for Italian sport, the introduction of a compulsory rest day into the working week.

Although 1901–14 was a period of unprecedented prosperity and growth, the 1907–8 economic depression, the 1911 Libyan war, and the introduction of universal manhood suffrage left both working and middle classes disgruntled. While left-wing parties grew, so did aggressive nationalist movements advocating strong imperialism to revitalize Italy. Along with pro-war Socialists, who saw conflict as a route to revolution, by the outbreak of the First World War there were strong forces in favour of military intervention which, far from finally uniting the country, enlarged the fractures.

War games and the citizen soldier

Gabriele D'Annunzio fought his first duel in 1885 against a local journalist who mocked his poetry. In Italian society, virile, athletic, combative sports, such as fencing, shooting and gymnastics, were encouraged to 'repair the historical hiatus between the real nation and the legal nation, between North and South, to construct national manifestations for national unity... [and]... to introduce, prepare, and conserve the military preparation of all Italians'.[4]

Sport was a key aspect of the state's use of culture to nationalize and strengthen Italian society.[5] In 1882, the Neapolitan sociologist and former Garibaldi follower Pasquale Turiello proposed 'the building of gymnasia, the introduction of compulsory fitness programmes in every town and village, and the promotion of group and military activities among children', to foster social and political cohesion.[6] While sport's potential to unite was recognized, it remained an exclusive pastime for those with disposable time and income. Gymnastics was thus an exclusive prerogative of the well-to-do that bored the middle class and excluded the poor, most of whom had little reason to take an interest in sport. With their days occupied in unmechanized agriculture and with serious food shortages, there were few overweight peasants with excess calories to burn. For the agricultural and urban working class, sport was as irrelevant as it was impossible, and only following small increases in leisure time and disposable income, in the early 1900s, did it begin to penetrate society.

Modern warfare demanded enormous supplies of well-trained, patriotic citizen-soldiers to defend the nation in times of need before returning to their civilian roles at the end of the conflict.[7] Pre-military instruction was therefore vital, and most popular in nations that were yet to unite, such as the German states following the Napoleonic occupation. Founded in 1811, Friedrich Ludwig Jahn's *Turnen* gymnastic movement introduced gym equipment, such as parallel bars, to merge militarism and physical education within the national movement. After witnessing the impact of gymnastics upon the Prussian military, in 1831 King Carlo Alberto invited the Swiss grammar school teacher Rudolf Obermann to introduce basic gymnastics into the Royal Artillery of the Savoy army. Inspired by a former student of Jahn, Obermann's method included free and supported floor exercises, collective rhythmic activities, plus gym apparatus.

Complementing army drills and training exercises while developing public/civic spirit, the extension of gymnastics to the entire Savoy force, in 1839, began the military's long association with sport. Modifying mechanical and militaristic exercises, and adapting them to the age, sex and strength of students, Obermann's gymnastics had mass appeal. After giving private lessons to sons of Turinese aristocrats and group instruction to high-ranking army officials in 1839, his desire to extend physical education throughout society saw the foundation of the Turin Gymnastic Society (*Società Ginnastica Torinese* – SGT), in 1844. Italy's first gym club was open to all social classes, with free lessons given to 60 elementary school children and a limited number of poor. With its raison d'être to form a generation of state-school gymnastics teachers and citizen-soldiers, a free course of instruction for male teachers also began in 1861, which left the SGT conducting what would normally have been a state activity.

Despite its 300 graduates from 1861 to 1869, the expansion of this model of gymnastics throughout Italy was a pressing concern. Schools were crucial and in 1861 Francesco de Sanctis, the Minister for Public Instruction (1861–2, 1879–81), appointed a commission to draw up a programme for its introduction. Emphasizing the importance of the citizen-soldier, Obermann's pre-military model entered the elementary and secondary school curriculum in 1862. Non-compulsory, its effect was minimal, with around one third of enlisted soldiers still failing to meet minimum physical requirements from 1866 to 71.[8] Enforced in 1879, its effect was still limited by difficulties in training teachers, professional apathy, a lack of equipment and no national supervision. In the 1880s, 28 per cent of army recruits were still being rejected on the basis of height or illness.

In 1909, the Daneo Law addressed some of the problems by demanding that: all trainee teachers undertook a course in PE before obtaining their diploma; all middle schools had a gymnasium or sports field nearby; and all primary-age children undertook half an hour of activity per day, with three hours per week for those in middle school. Giving state-school sport a fundamental role in the creation of patriotism, discipline and national awareness, its impact was limited by the failure to address the economic and legal disparity between PE teachers and those of more traditional subjects, plus a lack of funding, equipment and security of tenure for staff.

Clubs wishing to receive what limited government support existed had to embrace and promote the official, national ideology, which was evident in the names of the early gymnastic societies: *'pro-patria'*, *'pro-Italia'*, *'Libertates'*, *'Forza e Coraggio'* (Strength and Courage), *'Garibaldi'* and *'Cavour'*. Officially politically neutral, they were strongly infused with the regime's dominant lay, monarchist, patriotic, liberal principles. As one contributor to the bi-monthly *La Educazione Politica* argued, in 1902: Gymnastics

> is a part of Republican education that we have neglected too much... A gymnasium in which our young can exercise their muscles as they previously did their brain and heart in schools, would give tomorrow's Italian citizens a healthy courage to kill for the freedom of the nation.[9]

In 1869, these individual societies were united within the Italian Gymnastic Federation (*Federazione Ginnastica Italiana* – FGI), a type of 'super federation with a large protectorate over various sporting disciplines: from swimming to weight lifting, athletics, etc'.[10] Effectively ending Turin's monopoly of gymnastics and teacher training, this was formalized during the 1874 Federation congress when a debate over the methods of Obermann and Emilio Baumann resulted in a schism and the breakaway Federation of Italian Gymnastic Societies

N. 1.   Venezia 1. Ottobre 1868.   Anno II.

LA GINNASTICA

GIORNALE DI EDUCAZIONE FISICA.

Si pubblica il 1. ed il 15 di ogni mese.

n° inv. 19669

La SALUTE e la LIBERTA' sono i supremi beni dell'uomo,
La RAGIONE la NATURA' scrutando, ce li acquista e conserva.

Direttore COSTANTINO REYER Maestro brevettato dalla scuola Normale di ginnastica di Torino nel 1. corso magistrale 1861.

	Un Anno
Italia.	L. It. 2
Estero	» 3
Venezia un numero separato	Cent. — 5
» arretrato	» 20

Per le associazioni dirigersi con vaglia alla Amministrazione del Giornale la Ginnastica Venezia. Calle della Bissa N. 5471.
Richieste di associazione non accompagnate dal relativo importo non si accettano.
Le lettere non affrancate vengono respinte.

I numeri seguenti si spediranno soltanto a chi avrà inviato la sua quota di associazione.

AVVISO AGLI ANTICHI ASSOCIATI.

Questo giornale ebbe vita in Livorno col 1. gennaio 1866; dopo 11 numeri si dovette sospenderne la pubblicazione per diverse ragioni. Crede la direzione suo dovere di inviare agli antichi associati che pagarono la quota di associazione, tutti i numeri da oggi a tutto Decembre 1869.

PROGRAMMA

La scuola in generale istruisce miseramente l'intelletto, educa male il morale, punto il fisico; essa perfino ignora assolutamente l'esistenza di quella scienza suprema che è l'educazione fisica. Fatto desolantissimo che però subito si spiega riflettendo che la società mantiene ancora una base mitologica e non naturale, che l'ignoranza ed i pregiudizi non la scienza la reggono. È però giunta agli estremi di vita la Mitologia. Matematica, Chimica, Fisica, Astronomia, Anatomia, Fisiologia, Igiene, smantellano coi colpi irresistibili dei fatti il funesto edifizio di antiche credenze.

Sappiamo che ogni funzione dipende da un organo; dobbiamo logicamente con ogni premura coltivare la materia perché la forza sia ottima. Vogliamo sviluppato al massimo il pensiero e perciò ci occorre un perfettissimo cervello, ma per avere questo ci vuole un ottimo apparecchio vegetativo — respirazione — circolazione — assimilazione — e per questo un ottimo appa-

recchio locomotore. Vogliamo la ginnastica obbligatoria ma innalzata al grado di scienza dell'educazione fisica. Molto *declama* il volgo e plebeo e gentilizio sul ritornello di progresso e libertà, ma *non fa* nulla - per quello che solo può darci la vera libertà-per l'*educazione.*-

Ci narra Senofonte nella Ciropedia: « le leggi persiane sembra che incomincino ad avere cura del pubblico » bene, né come il più delle città incominciano già. Perciocché la più parte delle città concedendo a ciascuno di » educare come gli piace, i figliuoli suoi, e anche a quelli, di più età sono, di vivere come lor pare, comandano di non rubare, di non rapire, di non isforzar casa, » di non battere alcuno ingiustamente, di non commettere » adulterio, di non disubbidire al magistrato, ed altre cose » a questi somiglianti; e se vi ha chi in alcune di esse » trasgredisca, gli ordinano delle pene. *Ma le leggi dei* » *Persi col prevenirvi hanno da principio cura, che tali* » *non siano i cittadini che appetiscano mai cosa alcu-* » *na trista o vergognosa; e così lo procurano ecc.* »

Lo stesso vogliamo noi, prevenire le malattie, conservare il vigore e la salute, che perdute quasi sempre per l'ignoranza delle più elementari nozioni del proprio corpo, di rado e difficilmente si riacquistano.

Svolgeremo più ampiamente nei seguenti numeri le nostre idee ed indicheremo ancora i mezzi da noi più efficaci reputati e specialmente ci occuperemo dell'educazione fisica della donna perché più negletta e più importante.

Invochiamo poi il soccorso di tutti gli intelligenti in questa materia perché colla loro penna possa acquistar questo modesto giornaletto, quella forza ed influenza che un individuo isolato non può esercitare.

Figure 1: La Ginnastica: *taking sport to the literate*

(*Federazione delle Società Ginnastica Italiane* – FSGI). Although the FSGI had more member societies and encouraged the expansion of gymnastics, the duplication of activities and the silent war fought within the education ministry were unsustainable and severely damaging. In 1887, the gymnastics movement was reunited within the National Gymnastic Federation (*Federazione Ginnastica Nazionale* – FGN),[11] and its headquarters established in the new capital of Rome. With the Ministry for Public Instruction taking responsibility for school gymnastics, the Federation was left to prepare young people outside of school and adults. Hang on, it's important this!

Obermann's pre-military methods failed to excite the masses and clubs began exploring ways of broadening their appeal, with one of the champions of change the University of Turin physiology teacher and SGT President, Angelo Mosso. Concerned by bourgeois disinterest in existing military gymnastics, Mosso's experience of Britain and the USA led him to propose non-apparatus-based gymnastics and games, such as football, rugby, swimming, running and tennis. Encouraging individual expression and competition, with the incentive of prizes, they were significantly more appealing to the young than regimented gymnastics with the sole purpose of fitness. Conflicting with government repression in the 1890s, his desire to extend this programme to all social classes was restricted.

Following De Sanctis' limited introduction of gymnastics into schools, in 1878, many clubs introduced swimming, running, wrestling, skating, horse riding, canoeing and cycling. Yet, with many adults joining societies principally for the free lessons given to their children, once these became available in schools membership lists quickly declined, and societies were forced to attract adults with games and sports, in which the state had already declared its disinterest. With many clubs formed within gymnastic societies, by default the FGN found itself governing the rules, coaching, discipline and organization of various championships.

Physical education still held a clear nationalistic role nonetheless, which intensified as Italy's confidence and ambitions grew. When King Umberto's Ethiopian campaign (1889–96) failed disastrously, PE and selected sports were identified to strengthen patriotism, nationalism and militarism. The high demand for citizen-soldiers competent in the use of firearms saw the encouragement of target shooting in pre- and post-unification, military and civilian life, with Piedmont again founding the first clubs. Formed in 1848, the National Shooting Society was placed under the control of the Interior Ministry, in 1861. Competitions with significant prize money were organized, with the first national tournament held in Turin, in 1863, the second in Milan the following year, the third in Florence to celebrate its new status as Italy's capital, in 1865, and the fourth in Venice, in 1866, to mark the city's return to the motherland.

Garibaldi was a zealous propagandist for the sport and proposed the novel idea of establishing training camps along one hundred of Italy's rivers, where in times of need members would come to Italy's defence.[12] To maximize the number of citizens ready for war, clubs were encouraged to use the same rifles as the National Guard, with SGT members offered significant discounts to join Turin's Target Shooting Society.

Within parliament, the former military General Oreste Baratieri promoted the sport's military-educational role and the economic benefits of reducing military training and service.[13] Denouncing the limitations of the old shooting organization, he instigated a parliamentary commission that laid the foundations for a new law, in 1882. 'Preparing the young for military service, promoting and preserving the use of weapons by all who are in the permanent and voluntary army',[14] it assigned technical and administrative control of the clubs to the Ministries for War and Interior. Shooting thus became increasingly militarized: 'Order, discipline, obedience: these are the cardinal virtues that target shooting had to infuse. No pastime, no pleasurable sporting practice, rather a means of introduction to military life.'[15]

Fencing completed the trinity of sports dedicated to Italian militarism. A defensive weapon, a chivalrous duel and a sporting discipline, it had a long and prestigious history within the peninsula, and had been practised in Roman times. 'Italians' reigned supreme in the sport's sixteenth-century golden age.[16] Unification prompted its renaissance, with the four main schools of Naples, Caserta, Capua and Gaeta united in 1865. Following the formation of further centres in Parma, Modena and Milan, in 1868, a dispute over teaching methods was resolved by a national competition to rationalize teaching practice, in 1882. Won by the Neapolitan Masaniello Parise, he took charge of the military teaching school in Rome and launched a fencing programme that became the army standard. Similar to gymnastics in its militarist aims, it was highly elitist.

Well funded, Italian fencing was unsurprisingly successful. Providing Italy with its first Olympic gold medal in any sport, in 1900, the Rome school won the sabre team silver at the 1908 London Games. The sport's symbol was the Livornese fencer Nedo Nadi. Following the formation of the Italian Fencing Federation (*Federazione Italiana Scherma* – FIS) in 1909, Nadi made his Olympic debut in Stockholm, in 1912. His success in the individual foil was followed by an incredible 72 victories that culminated in five gold medals at the 1920 Antwerp Olympics: the individual foil and sabre, plus the team épée, sabre and foil events. Nadi's performances were acclaimed as close to perfection, while his brother's individual silver in the sabre plus three team golds, made this an Olympic record for any one family.

Voluntary groups also played a significant role in creating the citizen-soldier, and following a diplomatic crisis with Austria–Hungary over the annexation of Bosnia, in 1908, these paramilitary-type organizations developed a corps skilled in specific sports. Along the coastline and on the great lakes, rowing and water sport groups were launched, while in the mountains, on the Austrian border, alpine volunteers were recruited. The Alps were a particular focus that connected and bonded Italians within and beyond the border. Formed in 1863 by Quintino Sella, the Italian Alpine Club's (*Club Alpino Italiano* – CAI)[17] work was supported by the Italian Cycling Touring Club (*Touring Club Ciclistico Italiano*, 1894) and the *Audax Italiano* (1898). Organizing long rides and marches, they provided the core of the National Voluntary Body of Cyclists and Motorists (*Corpo Nazionale Volontari Ciclisti Automobilisti* – 1897), whose members were trained in logistics, military tactics and target shooting.[18]

While the corps occasionally conducted military exercises, most of its time was devoted to communicating in remote areas of the country and establishing groups for cycling enthusiasts. Contributing to the nationalist-irredentist campaign, cycling excursions took the nation's heritage and identity into the borderlands, as Giuseppe Monti, the director of Turin's Physical Education Teaching Institute, explained, in 1915: 'Gymnastic societies were always the fear and terror of Austria that pursued, oppressed and suppressed them with every means. The gymnastic instructors were among the strongest defenders of Italian identity.'[19]

With Italian-speaking minorities across the border, the *Club Alpino* was highly effective in Italy's nationalist campaign. Aiming to 'acquaint Italians with the mountains' and provide guides, rules and training courses that would ease their exploration,[20] this non-elitist, democratic, Turin-based club welcomed anybody. Forming sections across the country, most notable was Bologna's, which produced the first guide book in 1881. Alpine tourism was further stimulated by the early railway connections with Brenner (1867) and Pusteria (1869). This was supplemented by the First World War legacy of a narrow-gauge railway, built by the enemy nations of Austria and Italy for strategic motives, which became the Dolomite railway and opened Cortina to a new period of prosperity. Winter sports were already established, however: the Turin Ski Club formed in 1899; bobsleigh's pioneers first launched themselves down the Dolomite road in 1905; with ice hockey appearing in 1911, some 13 years before a national team entered international competition. It lost 12-0 to France.[21]

Educated in national defence and ideas of a community and destiny that extended far beyond the established borders, members of the Alpine Club's University Station (*Stazione Universitaria del Club Alpino* – SUCAI)[22] contributed to the development of a force experienced in the Alps and its conditions. Unlike most army regiments that deliberately mixed troops from across Italy's regions in an attempt to minimize provincial loyalties, the Alpini consisted almost entirely of troops from the northern mountain regions. One of the army's most effective forces in the First World War, they were evidence of the strength of local identities and the difficulty in nationalizing Italians through compulsory army integration.

Dedicated to defending Italy and developing the citizen soldier, sport in this period was primarily for men. Towards the end of the nineteenth century, however, eugenicists began prescribing physical activity for women too, in preparation for motherhood. A Central Women's Committee was formed within the FGN that began to develop physical education opportunities. Archery, tennis and golf were recommended, swimming accepted, so long as no men were watching, with gymnastics and hiking the preferred options. In 1897, Rome held a tournament for English women that included an eclectic mix of sack, egg and spoon, and cake races along with marches and a concert performed with bicycle bells.[23] Although limited and restricted, these exercises began to develop a culture of women's sport which, by the beginning of the First World War, was accepting activities for fun as well as preparation for childbirth.

Industrialization and urbanization: the birth of sporting nation

Economic growth during the late-nineteenth-century boom brought technological advances plus increases in leisure time and disposable income that stimulated sport and recreation. Between 1896 and 1913 the economy grew at an average of 2.8 per cent per annum, one of the highest rates in the world. As the production of cheaper iron and steel climbed,[24] modernization of the electricity, metal and rubber industries, plus factory line production techniques, saw the motor industry take off, with almost 14,000 cars and 10,000 motorbikes in circulation by 1912. Modernization made some sports possible and shaped others, with cycling a major beneficiary of the reduced production costs.[25] As the bicycle became increasingly affordable, its loss of exclusivity stimulated the bourgeoisie's interest in motor cycling, with the *Moto Club d'Italia* formed in 1911.

Restrained by technology and the sparse road network, motor-cycle racing was limited prior to the war. With the early city–city events highlighting the desperate need for roads, it was the integration of existing local rail networks that first 'stitched the Boot together'.[26] Doubling in size from 1861 to 1866, the railway began to unite the country and encourage a national market, reaching as far south as Foggia, on the Adriatic coast.

As a result, beach tourism developed among wealthier classes.[27] 'The fashion for bathing ran with the engine, the nineteenth century symbol of affluence and civilization, of progress and sometimes even solidarity. The successes of big and small spas and seaside resorts depended upon the existence of the railway.'[28]

Italy's numerous commercial ports had well-established marine traditions, with beach and sea-based festivals often culminating in mass dips. From 1830 to 1880, however, Italians began to demand the health benefits offered by the sea and sun.

> The first seaside tourism was part of bathing-therapy and was based on medical science and, in the same way, the coastal towns trusted the statements of illustrious professors who were always ready to declare that one area was more healthy and valid than another.[29]

From the 1880s, resorts grew in Venice, Livorno, Naples, Genoa and Rimini, where the first bathing pier with changing cabins was within a medical centre for sea cures. If the development of beach culture was restrained by the vogue for pale skin and mass society's limited leisure time, the bourgeoisie's enjoyment of the sea's therapeutic effects stimulated the development of hotels, tourist infrastructure and publicity, as Italians discovered the beach.

Continuing a tradition of water-based activities since ancient Rome's establishment of thermal baths, swimming was promoted in the eighteenth century for physical training. With such huge lengths of coastline to defend, it was a recognized military skill, with an 1864 Ministry for War instruction manual recommending lessons for all troops, especially bridge and pontoon builders. The first official competitive race was the 1893 Rome Championship; a 7.5 kilometre swim along the Tiber. The first clubs also came from the capital, with the *Società Rari Nantes* and *Società Romana di nuoto* based on the river just beyond the Porta del Popolo. Developing the sporting dimension of what had long been considered a health-related activity, their affluent members – engineers, lawyers, doctors, artists and accountants – turned their pastime into a competitive event to display their physiques and establish their social visibility, thereby differentiating themselves from the lower classes and escaping from the anonymity of mass society.[30]

While the establishment of clubs throughout the country led to a national federation in 1900, the sport's development was impaired by minimal international competition and a total lack of pools. With military barracks rarely near the sea and most civilians unable to regularly reach it, swimming possibilities were limited. Even Fascism, which built a huge amount of sports facilities but few indoor pools, barely raised the quality of Italian swimmers and it was not until the 1960s and the injection of funds to improve Olympic results that Italian swimming really made strokes.

✪ ✪ ✪ ✪

As *the* urban game, football's spread was directly related to Italy's industrialization. Introduced by English sailors on their way to and from India, with injections of enthusiasm from Switzerland and across the Italo-Austrian border, there is no officially documented year zero in the history of Italian football (*calcio*), but consensus of opinion blasts the first whistle in 1893 with the formation of the Genoa Cricket and Football Club. Established by British consular officials, the club's immediate ban on Italians was soon reduced to a quota system, the first of many in *calcio*'s protectionist history.

Formed in March 1898, the Italian Football Federation (*Federazione Italiana del Football* – FIF) was dominated by Turin's football community. The *Ginnastica Club* was a founder member and one of three Turin teams to contest the first championship, a one-day tournament won by Genoa, in May 1898. Three months later, the SGT held another competition in Turin, against teams from gym clubs in Udine and Ferrara. With gymnastics the only mass sport to have spread throughout the country, its societies were fundamental in football's expansion. Following Angelo Mosso's recommendation that Italy embrace British-style team games, football was included in the National Gymnastics Federation statutes, in 1903. By 1906, of the 15 clubs affiliated to the Football Federation, six came from gymnastics societies.

As enthusiasm for the game grew, the championship was expanded to run over three days in 1899, and 20 in 1900 and 1901. The majority of clubs were concentrated in the northern urban centres of Piedmont, Lombardy, Liguria, Veneto and Friuli, plus Trieste's Black Star FC in Austria–Hungary. By 1908 Juventus, Milan and Internazionale had all made their debuts, with 262 clubs affiliated by 1914. One of the most successful was Pro Vercelli. Formed in 1903 within the pioneering gymnastics club, Pro Vercelli were national champions seven times from 1908 to 1921.

Blending modern tactics with core fitness from gymnastics, Pro Vercelli players ran harder, further and faster than any other team. They were also all Italian. Reflecting gymnastics societies' campaign to nationalize football, this culminated in a ban upon foreign players in 1908. Suspecting it was an attempt to restrict their growing economic power, Genoa, Milan, Torino and Juventus withdrew in protest, creating *calcio*'s first major crisis. Won by Pro Vercelli, the Italian-only championship was a poor imitation of the real thing and football was reunited in 1909 under the auspices of the new federation, the *Federazione Giuoco Italiano del Calcio* (FIGC).

An 'Italian' representative team had met Switzerland in 1900, but consisted primarily of foreign players from Genoa and Milan. With 'nationality' determined by residency rather than country of birth, gymnastics clubs protested against

Italians being forced to play alongside foreigners with no concept even of the Italian language.[31] Italy's official debut, in 1910, further developed interest in the game while forming an early sense of common, shared identity among football fans.

With private, middle-class clubs and state-sponsored, bourgeois, nationalist and militarist institutions providing the bulk of Italy's sport, its mass diffusion was still some way off. A perfect opportunity for the labour movement and the Church to exploit, their establishment of sporting societies had the potential for considerable success.

Suspicious Socialists

By the turn of the century the Italian Socialist Party (PSI) was a growing force, with its parliamentary deputies increasing from 32 in 1902 to 79 in 1913, when it claimed almost one quarter of all votes cast. Possessing its own daily newspaper, *Avanti!*, and a local organizational network for the working/peasant class, it was aided by the late-nineteenth-century economic boom that stimulated trade unionism and the formation of the General Confederation of Labour (*Confederazione Generale del Lavoro* – CGL), in 1906. Intellectuals set about mobilizing and educating the working classes, the faith of the future, with a missionary-like zeal:

> Socialist activists staged public meetings, debates, conferences and lectures wherever they could: in clubs, halls, cafés and Chambers of Labour, or out in the open air. They wrote pamphlets and contributed articles to the countless local Socialist newspapers that sprang up across northern and central Italy from the 1890s... They encouraged school attendance... and promoted 'popular libraries' to make books accessible to workers.[32]

If their overall impact was questionable, there was no mistaking the Socialists' aim: the establishment of an alternative culture and parallel faith. Within this, sport was a potentially strong source of interest, unity and community.

The roots of Socialist sport in Italy lay in mid-nineteenth-century mutual-aid associations. Often individual philanthropic initiatives that defended and promoted working-class cultural and educational activities, they expanded to include physical exercise and military training. Formed in 1866, one of the most significant was the Workers Gymnastic Society (*Società Ginnastica Operaia* –

SGO), based in Genoa. Promoting gymnastics, fencing and target shooting, the movement spread throughout Liguria and Piedmont, before being restricted by Francesco Crispi's mid-1890s repression.

The PSI's interest in the physical education of the proletariat was ostensibly from the traditional perspective of its contribution to the nation's armed forces. Equally, its bourgeois leadership was unaware of the real needs of its supporters. Not only would the Party's few sportsmen have been involved in what were essentially middle-class activities, most intellectuals were highly diffident towards it. Seen as a luxury or time-wasting mania, sport, they argued, was unable to represent Socialist ideals and certainly came below malnutrition and illiteracy in terms of importance. Suspicious of its impact upon recruitment, the Federation of Young Socialists' weekly, *L'Avanguardia*, encouraged readers to debate sport's potential use and whether the paper should cover it.[33] In 1910, Giovanni Zibordi reiterated the suggestion that physical exercise was a capitalist weapon that distracted and diverted workers from political activity, prioritizing team loyalties over those of class:

> The generation under 20, entering a world of relatively good conditions, finding the way paved by the older citizens, ignores our organization, associations and papers, giving itself excessively, uniquely and madly to sport... undoubtedly, the bourgeoisie intends to spread the contagious microbe of feverish sporting infatuation through its newspapers, an illness far from the healthy sport practised as an aspect of human existence and vigorous youth.[34]

With many societies emerging thanks to the benevolent sponsorship of company and factory owners, the argument appeared to have some basis.

While some on the left hoped sport's flame of enthusiasm would soon extinguish itself, the more critical hoped to snuff it out immediately. Radical publications like *Avanti!*, of which Benito Mussolini was the editor from 1912 to 1914, advocated direct action, inviting readers to sabotage cycle races by littering the streets with nails.[35] Popular among the working classes, the Tour of Lombardy (1905), the Milan–San Remo (1907) and the *Giro d'Italia* (1909) provoked the Socialist anti-sport campaign. Reaching its apex in 1910, the third national congress of the Federation of Young Socialists (*Federazione Giovanile Socialista Italiana* – FGSI) in Florence, established three principle positions towards sport.

The revolutionaries argued that far from developing physical fitness, sport debilitated and destroyed the human body and contributed to the degeneration of the species, while encouraging nationalism and discouraging class unity. A softer version was proposed by Zibordi, who suggested that Socialism should embrace and exploit sport rather than reject it as a bourgeois evil. 'If we want to copy those skilful maestros of organization and astuteness, the priests, we mustn't oppose it in general but divert it according to our needs.'[36] More positively, the future prime minister Ivanoe Bonomi argued that the FGIS' rejection of sport was a major mistake, indicating an inability to appreciate the opportunities that sport and cycling, in particular, provided for social change.[37] Identifying physical exercise as both the cause of and solution to working class subjugation, it stimulated a reappraisal of sport within the party.

While little change appeared likely within the PSI, some independent initiatives were launched. In 1907, the Socialist Sports Union was formed as a branch of the Workers International, with the more effective Italian Workers Excursionists Union (*Unione Operaia Escursionisti Italiani* – UOEI) following in 1911. Organizing working-class trips to the countryside and mountains, it tried to improve workers' mental and physical health and educate on the effects of alcohol.[38] By 1914 the UOEI had over 40 sections with over 10,000 members, but its proletarian character was compromised by the admission of non-working-class members and support from establishment organizations, such as the Italian Alpine Club, the Touring Club and *La Gazzetta dello Sport*.

In 1912, the first group of 'red cyclists' was formed. Wearing the association's emblem plus a distinctive red shirt or armband bearing their group's name, 'red cyclists' were particularly useful during election campaigns, strike action, demonstrations and political agitations, when they provided a safe and reliable means of communication.[39] Often anti-nationalist, anti-war and opposed to national service, 'red cyclists' were attacked in the liberal press. When *Avanti!* reported a parade of more than 700 cyclists at the 1912 Young Socialist convention,[40] the more conservative *Corriere della Sera* described the rally transforming 'into an anti-militarist demonstration' that 'provoked a brawl outside a bar frequented by nationalists'.[41]

To mobilize mass support, spread Socialist ideals and principles of solidarity and working-class emancipation, 'red cyclists' organized excursions across the plain of Padania in the north of Italy, distributing pamphlets, newspapers and news of discussions and debates. They were also encouraged to ride the 'Avanti' bicycle. With latter models blessed by 'Carl Marx' wheels, it was designed for low-income workers, with a favourable discount for 'red cyclists'. Previously disliked by left-wing intellectuals as a bourgeois symbol, the bicycle was transformed into a tool of propaganda, action and politics that further encouraged Socialism's re-examination of sport. As Antonio Lorenzini explained in *Avanti!*:

> The *aim* of the 'red cyclists' is propaganda: their *means* is the 'sport' of
> the bicycle, if it can be called that, contained within human and *dignified* limits.

> Our cyclists don't want their or other people's physical education to be
> at the detriment of intellectual and moral education, and neither do they see
> it as this.[42]

As with many Socialist initiatives, while the 'red cyclists' did not enter competitions, in their commitment to represent and spread their ideals they bore a striking resemblance to their rival Catholic and nationalist sporting bodies.

Catholic action

Catholicism's relationship with sport was established in the mid-nineteenth century. It provided physical education within its schools, colleges and oratories, or parish youth clubs, the most renowned of which was Turin's Valdocco oratory, where Don Giovanni Bosco encouraged the physical and spiritual development of youngsters through running, jumping, exercise, music and theatre.

Under the Pontificate of Leo XIII (1878–1903) oratories expanded to provide a network of recreational services that included pre-military training, excursion groups, choirs and gymnastics sections, some of which broke away to form the first Catholic gym clubs. One of the founders of Church-sport ideology was the Barnabite priest Giovanni Semeria,[43] who proposed gymnastics as a way of life, a release from the servitude of work, a means of creating stronger and disciplined Catholics, and a highly patriotic service that prepared civilians for combat.[44] Reconciling traditional Catholic culture with the modernizing country, he identified the gymnasium as a breeding ground for a Catholic youth physically and morally schooled in Christian ideals.

Sport also impacted upon the Church's changing relationship with the state, which came thanks to their mutual fear of Socialism rather than any rapprochement. Having refused to recognize Italy since its formation, Catholicism more or less withdrew from state activities until 1904 when Pope Pius X relaxed the *non expedit* decree. A tactical error that had severely limited the Church's potential to shape Italy, its re-entry into national politics saw a number of conservative, Catholic deputies elected to parliament. Yet, while participating in national life, the Church continued to try to establish an alternative culture around its spiritual and social values.

Competing with nationalist and patriotic societies, by the turn of the century a large network of Catholic gymnastic clubs had 'positioned themselves as alternatives to the state's control over physical education in schools that tended to socialize youngsters according to laic and liberal ideals and values'.[45] Having posed little initial threat, the National Gymnastics Federation (FGN) expressed growing concerns about this challenge to its monopoly, in its official publication:

> A great danger threatens the freedom and safety of our country: the black danger. The party that hates Italy and its unity, has now also eaten away at youth gymnastics and... not lacking the means, it will take control of it wherever, multiplying its gymnasia.[46]

When, in 1903, the FGN refused to affiliate two Catholic societies – *Fortitudo* of Bologna and *Voluntas* of Milan – due to their confessional and political nature, which was incompatible with its laic and supposedly apolitical structure, plans were made to create a Catholic body. The Union of Italian Catholic Sports Associations (*Unione delle Associazioni Sportive Cattoliche Italiane*) was formed in 1906 within the Church's cultural wing, Catholic Action (*Azione Cattolica* – AC). A response to Catholic sport's exclusion from the FGN, it also demonstrated the Vatican's desire to rein in the movement.

Uniting Catholic sport, the Union launched its own magazine, *Stadium*, and received a 3,000 lire subsidy from the Catholic Youth Society (*Società della Gioventù Cattolica*) on the basis that: its centre was in Rome, its associations were confessional, and half of its board of control was nominated by the Church's Superior Council. With the majority of societies coming from Turin and Milan, its Roman base provoked a parochial dispute that encapsulated one of Italy's greatest problems.

Considering the role of physical exercise at the conclusion of the first Italian Catholic Sporting Convention in Rome, in 1905, Pope Pius X heaped praise upon the athletes:

> Not only do I approve of all your work in Catholic Action, but I admire and bless all of your games and pastimes from my heart: gymnastics, cycling, alpinism, sailing, running, walking... as the material exercise of the body has a wonderful impact upon the spirit; because these entertainments that require effort deter idleness, which is the father of all vice.[47]

A growing number of member societies elected the Rome-based body's committee at its 1907 conference, before renaming it the Italian Federation of Catholic Sporting Associations (*Federazione delle Associazioni Sportive Cattoliche Italiane* – FASCI). Responsible for guaranteeing that 'sporting conduct conformed to Catholic morals', it organized competitions and opportunities to demonstrate the quality of Catholic Italian athletes.[48]

In 1908 the Vatican hosted the First International Gymnastics Tournament (*Concorso Internazionale al Vaticano*) for around 2,000 competitors from France,

Belgium, Ireland and Canada, with the majority coming from Italy. Reflecting the internationalist Church, the event led to the formation of the International Federal Union of Catholic Physical Education (*Unione Internazionale delle Opere Cattoliche di Educazione Fisica* – UIOCEP), in 1911, which was naturally based in Rome.

By 1910, there were 204 FASCI groups with over 10,000 members. With its base of support moving towards the centre and south of the country, where there was less competition from lay groups, it soon surpassed the FGN's membership. But as Catholic sport grew so did anti-clericalism, with Socialism correctly fearing a 'pact' between the Church and liberals against the working class. Incidents of intolerance between lay and Catholic groups began to occur, as during the Second International Gymnastics Tournament in Rome, in 1913. Including a strong educational element and injury insurance for athletes, the event demonstrated progressive thinking, most notably with the inclusion of events for the visually impaired and deaf. One of the earliest examples of disabled sport, this expanded, post-1918, as physiotherapy for the war-wounded.

With 168 societies and over 4,000 competitors, the 1913 event's opening procession from San Giovanni in Laterano to St Peter's was cancelled due to anti-clerical and nationalist protests following the repression of a pro-Italy demonstration in Trieste, some days earlier.[49] Among the many incidents registered by the *Corriere della Sera*, which included chants of 'Long live Giordano Bruno' and 'Down with the Vatican' at a public concert, there was the molestation of 'gymnasts of the "Virtus Unitus" squad, from San Remo... in Via Arenula, by a number of anti-clericalists leaving a trattoria. They grabbed and broke the placard they were carrying. There was a brief exchange of punches' before the police arrived.[50] With the Trieste incident having provoked national outrage, the presence of an Austrian team was considered outright provocation.[51] While the lay press gave little or no coverage to the incidents, Catholic dailies, such as *L'Italia*, were more forthright: 'in the innocent act of the gymnasts, they [the anti-clericalists and nationalists] chose to see a trap or provocation that Austria wanted to inflict upon Italy. The hot nationalist spirit rose and remembered the governor of Trieste's measures.'[52]

Indicative of the opposition that Catholic sport faced in the more nationalist, anti-clerical regions of northern Italy, the FASCI became more defensive in its activities there and more expansive in the country's centre and south. By 1914, Catholic sport had become a mass, national organization, an alternative to the FGN, and a fundamental part of Christian-democracy's participation in Italy's political and social life. While promoting its own brand of repetitive, group-style gymnastics, FASCI competitions also replicated those of the mainstream Gymnastics Federation, with a focus upon results, prizes, and the classification of athletes into merit-based categories.

While support for team games was growing, some activities were still frowned upon, such as football, which was considered Anglo-Saxon and thus Protestant; boxing and rugby, which were too violent; and cycling. Although deeply suspicious of cycling's competitions, embryonic professionalism, and the personal freedom that it brought, even the Pope was unable to combat the bicycle boom.

The bicycle boom

> Cycling isn't simply a sport, but it is a social benefit and, like sport, it is also democratic.[53]

✪ ✪ ✪ ✪

By the beginning of the twentieth century the bicycle's growing diffusion was stimulating a consumer thirst. With its cost still prohibitive, some bought individual parts to construct their own machines over time, while instalment schemes enabled those on modest incomes to buy outright. As modernization transformed and standardized modes of production, the practicality and efficiency of essential parts, such as frames, tyres, brakes, cables, chains and handlebars, improved, and the manufacturers of cars (Opel, Peugeot) motorbikes (Ganna), heaters and other household goods (Singer) diversified. Creating a national market, modernization also saw the emergence of an industrial class that was key in the development of Italian sport. One of the many examples was Edoardo Bianchi, who rose from a modest worker to producing one of Italy's most internationally known brands.[54]

From a luxury item, the bicycle quickly became one of the great instruments of equality and by 1928 there were 4,935,019 in circulation.[55] Turning the bourgeoisie's interest towards more elitist cars and motorcycles, the bicycle's diffusion stimulated a spirit of adventure that saw the Italian Cycling Touring Club's (TCCI) membership grow from 784 in 1894 to 157,897 in 1915. Initially acting as a cycling pressure group, fighting the prohibition and taxation of bicycles and providing cheap insurance, the inclusion of motorists saw it become the Italian Touring Club (*Touring Club Italiano* – TCI) that fought for road improvements and produced maps that led to guide books.[56]

One of the Club's founders, and president from 1917 to 1926, was the Milanese businessman, alpinist and passionate cyclist Luigi Vittorio Bertarelli. At a time when many saw the bicycle 'as little more than a devilish contraption, good only for grotesque cycling races', Bertarelli promoted cycle tourism by undertaking an extraordinary tour of Italy's deep south, riding from Reggio Calabria to Eboli, in 1897.[57] Unknown territory to Italians from the north and

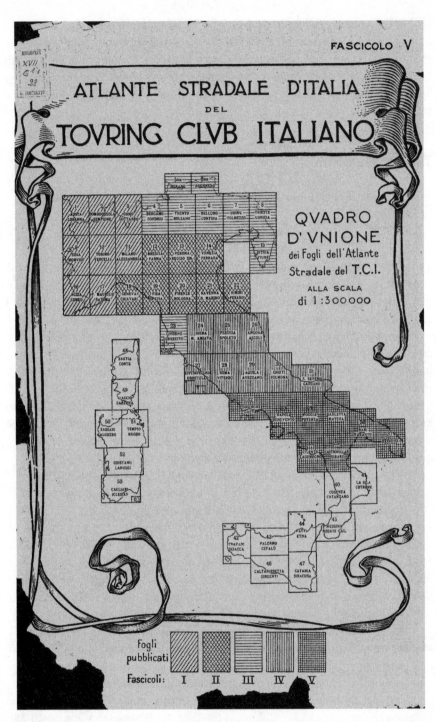

Figure 2: *The* Touring Club Italiano: *introducing Italians to Italy*

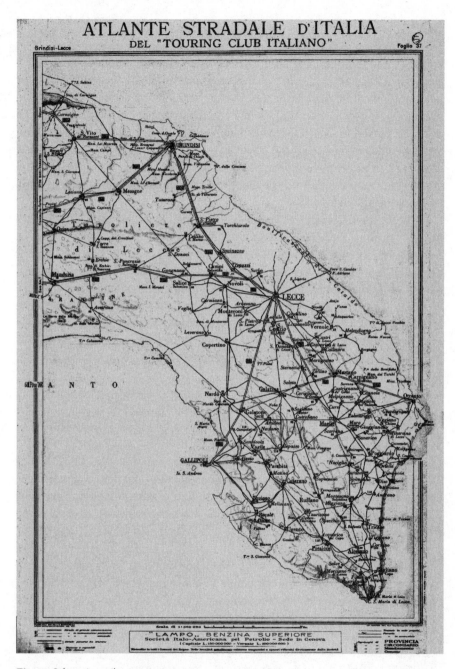

Figure 2 (continued)

even Naples, Bertarelli's journey challenged common-place stereotypes about the south, which was renowned for its reported violence and brigandage: 'who knows if this might be the sting that takes the air from your prejudices?'[58] Reflecting the patriotic spirit of the times and the *Risorgimento* dream of national unification, it was the Touring Club's motto in action: *far conoscere l'Italia agli Italiani* – make Italy known to the Italians. First published in *La Bicicletta*, Bertarelli's journey provided an alternative account of perceived crime and violence, while noting the generosity and curiosity of the people, their poverty, terrible hygiene and social conditions. Above all, he introduced the albeit small readership to the beauty of the countryside, mountains, rivers, earth, birds, animals; to Italy.

The demand for bicycles was also stimulated by racing, with early events mostly individual time trials over short distances or contests against buses or trams. More organized, competitive track racing began in 1893 and attracted a dedicated paying public that almost immediately created professional cyclists. As the early manufacturers of Bianchi, Pinarello, Campagnolo and the tyre producer Pirelli became household names and their interests linked to the expansion of competition, road racing provided the perfect stage to advertise the efficiency, durability and value for money of their products. As Carlo Doglio proposed in a revealing inquiry into Italian sport in 1952, it was

> the production of bicycles and tyres that soon made the sport of cycling a slave to industry. In the sense that... the concrete background to racing... is the competition between the bicycle manufacturers, the battle to impose their brand on the public rather than another.[59]

Run over inhuman distances, races were sometimes fatal due to accidents or illnesses associated with inhaling road dust during extreme physical exertion; Giovanni Brunero, Ernesto and Luigi Azzini and Libero Ferrario all died young from tuberculosis.[60] Punishing city–city races, such as the Milan–Turin (1876), the Tour of Lombardy (1905) and the Milan–San Remo classic (1907), commanded huge interest as endurance and survival tests for man and machine. The tougher the race the better for those manufacturers whose bikes made the distance, which sometimes exceeded 400 kilometres and required 18–20 hours in the saddle. Workers who toiled 10–15 hours per day, six days per week, could sympathize with their heroes who laboured, sweated and pedalled hard for their livelihoods.

Highly visible publicity machines, the big races were often created by newspapers keen to self-publicize and increase the demand for advertising. Inspired by the French daily *L'Auto-Vélo*'s *Tour de France* in 1902, and aware of the political daily *Corriere della Sera*'s similar plan, in collaboration with Bianchi and the Touring Club *La Gazzetta dello Sport* announced its organization of the *Giro d'Italia* on 24 August 1908.

> Without excessive noise... we have serenely brought great honour back to Italian cycling... [and]... we now launch the appeal that shakes and stirs the sporting spirit.
> We cry. Italians, get ready! [61]

Formed in 1896, from the fusion of three cycling publications, the twice-weekly *La Gazzetta dello Sport* added another day in 1909 before becoming a daily in 1913. As its editor and race founder Armando Cougnet later explained, in contrast to the traditional political journalism of information, sports journalism was new and didn't just describe what had happened. It also invented, created and determined events in order to continually develop a greater readership.[62]

A watershed in Italian sport, the *Giro* was the premier event in *La Gazzetta*'s calendar, until the 1920s when Italy's Olympic and international football fortunes improved and the *Mille Miglia* motor race began. Generating excitement and publicity for the newspaper, the *Giro* captured the nation's imagination with reported acts of endurance and heroism. As one Socialist lamented, in 1909: 'I was in Forlì one day... and with pain I saw a newspaper man sell 500 copies of *La Gazzetta dello Sport* in little more than half an hour, while in 15 days only 10 copies of *Giovine Italia!*'[63]

Riders first left Milan on 13 May 1909 and were welcomed back by 500,000 fans along the final leg from Turin.[64] Twenty thousand people in the Milan Arena saw only 49 of the initial 127 cyclists reach the finish, after 17 days covering 2,400 kilometres at an average of 300 kilometres per stage. Luigi Ganna was the first winner. A bricklayer who cycled over 100 kilometres per day to and from work, he demonstrated the bicycle's conquest of Italy. Covering enormous distances in such a short period of time, the race began to shrink the country's perceived size while marking history, local traditions, dialects, values and reference points, all within a nationally shared event. With riders nicknamed according to their region, *La Gazzetta*'s illustrated descriptions of each stage acquainted Italians with their country, such as Abruzzo's Gran Sasso mountain:

> the giant that sleeps, the giant that protects, there, where everything is new, where the earth has a strange language and the sky a pure blue; where our Italy boasts unknown beauties, the idea of watching the finish of the second stage must be irresistible... Like so, for the spectator, the *Giro d'Italia* can be a tour through our greatest beauties.[65]

Pursuing a different route each year, the race often commemorated particular dates and events in Italian history, with first *Giro* passing the battlefields of the mid-nineteenth-century wars of independence with Austria. In 1911 it left from Porta Pia in Rome, 40 years after it became Italy's capital; in 1928 it began in Mussolini's home village of Predappio; in 1960 from Rome, to celebrate the hosting of the Olympic Games; while the following year's 'centenary' *Giro* marked Italy's 100th anniversary.

Despite the bicycle's mass appeal, from its early days Italian authorities viewed it with diffidence at best and often with outright hostility. As the first machines appeared on the streets of northern Italy, many local authorities only permitted their use far from city centres or on ramparts to protect public safety. Fearing its insurrectionary potential, Milanese authorities completely banned it. With contraventions considered akin to an act of war, suspects were forced to appear in a military court. The Catholic Church was equally wary, with the Vatican's newspaper *L'Osservatore Romano* declaring cycling:

> a true global, transport anarchy... as anarchy is fast moving in global society... The cyclist isn't a pedestrian, a coachman, a train driver, he isn't an animal to be hunted or a pack animal: he is like a hermaphrodite, indefinable, unclassifiable, who evades every law of the road.[66]

The criminologist Cesare Lombroso didn't help by identifying the bicycle as a major source of concern: enabling delinquents to quickly escape crime scenes, creating materialistic desires that could stimulate violent theft, even cyclists themselves could provoke attacks from unruly youngsters and con men.[67] As *ciclofobia* grew, *La Bicicletta* offered subscribers the chance to buy a 'Bulldog' revolver to protect against dogs and even more dangerous men. 'Given the actual state of public security in Italy, a good revolver is indispensable for cyclists.'[68] Lombroso did see some positive health-inducing aspects to cycling, however, while news of his apparent conversion was greeted by *La Bicicletta* as a sign of his understanding of the laws of progress and future needs.[69]

Besides crime, fears also surrounded the bicycle's potential to destabilize society and threaten decorum. Increasing their mobility, women could travel longer distances unaccompanied, sweating and wearing what they chose rather than what was deemed appropriate. In turn, this raised fears about the bicycle's facilitation of sexual indiscretions, which didn't even require a guilty partner for those who thought the combination of the saddle and peddling could induce illicit orgasms. Others feared that cycling might compromise a woman's virginity, while riding during menstruation was discouraged due to fears of its effect upon the reproductive system. Responding to an 1894 report from Paris that suggested the bicycle had become a means of abortion, *La Bicicletta* agreed that its

> excessive use can produce grave dangers in pregnancy, like riding, work and excess with the sewing machine; but from this to accusing the poor bicycle of such a serious crime as abortion, is a bit much. For the honour of the bicycle, we believe that the news from our Parisian colleague is no more than a *fin de siècle* fantasy.[70]

Such ideas were apparently expanded upon by Doctor Ludovic O'Followell in his 1900 niche market publication, *Bicyclette et organs génitaux* (The bicycle and genital organs),[71] which contributed to calls for saddle modification.[72] While there were some male-specific concerns, the majority of fears regarded the bicycle's physical and sexual emancipation of women more than the bicycle itself.

Despite the enormous possibilities that cycling offered priests to reach more parishioners, the Church retained serious concerns about compromising their dignity and religious authority. Applauding the Archbishop of Milan's annulment of a cycling ban on priests, *La Bicicletta* hoped the example would 'be followed by other bishops who had also believed in the prohibition of the bicycle, when its use was less widespread'.[73] Its appeal was lost on the hard-line Cardinal Giuseppe Sarto of Mantua who, having banned it among clerics, vowed:

> If, however, somebody might find the yoke of this rule unbearable and thinks about following his whim, he might know that in disobeying the Bishop, in what I retain to be a very serious matter, he risks incurring ecclesiastical punishment to which, with displeasure but equal firmness, I will give a hand.[74]

Sarto's thoughts came in direct response to *La Bicicletta*'s supplement, *I Preti in Bicicletta* (Cycling Priests). Promoting responsible cycling among the clergy, it claimed:

> The priest can ride a bike just like any other human, but he needs composure so as not to offend appearances and decency. For this reason the *Levita* bicycle was designed; a replica of a woman's bike... The priest sits composed, his cassock falls naturally and covers his legs.[75]

Compiled by two priests in the Milan diocese, the selection of previously published articles on cycling and the Church was removed from circulation by ecclesiastical authorities after one edition.[76]

Austrian Italians

In its suspicion of the bicycle the Church certainly wasn't alone, with the left also wary and the gymnastic movement slow to appreciate its value to the nationalist campaign. Cycling clubs spread quickly, as far down the Dalmatian coast as Split but principally in the Italian-speaking areas of the Trentino and Friuli-Venezia across the Austro-Hungarian border, where Italian cycling patriots awakened public opinion to the issue of independence. In response, Austrian police strictly controlled cycling clubs, such as the *Società Ginnastica Triestina*. Founded in 1863, in Austrian Trieste, this strong focus for Italian nationalism was dissolved six times by 1916. Began as a gymnastic society, it opened a cycling section in 1865 that disseminated propaganda with increasing guile and secrecy. With its publications frequently seized, it used the green, white and red of the Italian flag to make direct political statements: bouquets of flowers were given to tournament winners while one cycling event included a triplet ridden by three girls, each wearing one of the flag's colours.[77] Organizing exchange visits and day trips to Italy, its connection of the city with the motherland drew Fascist praise in 1929:

> We cannot but recognise the patriotic good-service of those Giulian institutions which, during the dark period of foreign servitude, admirably forged the spirit and bodies of our youth... In fact, in all of the provinces subjected to Austria at the time, while youngsters bodies were strengthened with healthy physical exercise, their consciences were inspired with fervent love for Italy and implacable hate for the foreign tyranny.[78]

Dedicating his youth to patriotic Italian activities and wrestling, Giovanni Raicevich symbolized Triestinan sport. At just 16 years of age he celebrated becoming Austrian wrestling champion by brawling with Habsburg officials, while his defeat of a strong Viennese athlete in Pola, in 1902, aroused Istrian Italians. Born within Austria–Hungary in 1881, Raicevich never disguised his Italian identity. Called up for military service, he refused to wear the 'enemy' uniform and fled the country. On the outbreak of the First World War he was one of the region's sportsmen who, having received a virile education in Italian gymnasiums, according to *Lo Sport Fascista*, 'were among the Giulian volunteers fighting in the name of that ideal for which our heroes gave their blood'.[79] Joining the Italian army to fight for Trieste, Raicevich risked execution as an Austrian deserter. A member of the National Voluntary Corps of Cyclists and Motorists, he miraculously escaped death on the retreat from Caporetto.

At his peak during professional wrestling's golden years from the end of the nineteenth century until the First World War, when iron men with handlebar moustaches tested their strength in circuses, fairs and theatres across the globe, tournaments were frequently contested over weeks, with daily bouts often lasting hours. Winning his first World Title in Paris, in 1907, Raicevich sent a telegram to *La Gazzetta dello Sport*'s director, Eugenio Costamagna, declaring: 'Victory! Now delighted in triumph, an embrace thinking of adored Italy, my Trieste.'[80] Avenging a disputed defeat in Paris in 1908,[81] Raicevich's World Title victory the following year, after 47 minutes of combat against the legendary Frenchman Paul Pons, confirmed him as one of the greatest all-time wrestlers and pushed *La Gazzetta*'s sales through the 100,000 barrier for the first time.

Celebrating the national triumph, the daily attributed the success to his mixed genes: 'It's true that within him there is a mixture of Teutonic calm and reason, with Latin genius and fighting spirit.'[82] Like many Italian athletes, however, Raicevich was smaller than many of his opponents and after winning one bout it was noted: 'Many fans... ask themselves, with surprise, how that little man (relatively speaking) might have had the *chance* of beating the colossus.'[83] Yet, this was no new phenomenon for, since the London 1908 Olympic Games, the triumph of mind over muscle was a celebrated Italian speciality.

National heroes, irrational identities and a glorious defeat

Positive and negative; little method and great intelligence; minimal preparation and great inventiveness; a lack of organization and great spirit: Riccardo Grozio's description of the Italian sporting psyche is persuasive.[84] Forced to accept its role as the 'poor cousin', Italy overcame malnourishment, minimal facilities and disorganization to exceed realistic expectations in an appealing manner. The idea stuck too with legendary journalist Gianni Brera making the point in 1970, in his personal campaign against footballer Gianni Rivera:

> In Rivera you find talent but no character. Like in the Italians in general. The Italian is crafty, sly and intelligent, with no commitment: thus Rivera is a beautiful Italian example. It is the reason why he is so loved by the crowd that recognizes itself in him.[85]

Impoverished, famished, chaotic and frequently corrupt, Italy could easily have developed a large inferiority complex. Indicative of the divided, repressed nation is its anthem the *Inno dei Mameli*, adopted in 1946. Written by the patriotic poet/student Goffredo Mameli, on the eve of the war with Austria in 1847, it was a rallying cry for a downtrodden, disunited people rather than an exuberant, confident, rising nation. This mentality was reflected in Italian sportsmen up until the late 1970s. From a background of poverty, hardship, minimal education, and sacrifice, it was often hunger that drove them on and their tough lives that made them strong. Known as 'the troublemaker' for his aggressive style, the cyclist Vito Taccone confessed in the mid-1960s: 'I need to be a wolf because I'm hungry, my family has always been hungry. Every victory is a robbery.'[86]

The Gymnastics Federation's bid to host the 1908 Olympic Games was welcomed by its founder, Baron Pierre de Coubertin, King Victor Emmanuel III and Rome's Mayor Prospero Colonna. With their approval in principal, the FGN secretary Fortunato Balerini began preparing for the event even prior to de Coubertin's visit to assess the venues. The adaptation of Roman facilities, such as the ancient Roman Baths of Caracalla for fencing and wrestling, guaranteed atmosphere and few problems, with the Tiber proposed for swimming.

Among the sceptics was Angelo Mosso, one of the founding fathers of modern Italian sport. Afraid that Italy's facilities were not up to scratch and the country yet again risked embarrassment, his opposition was supported by Giovanni Giolitti, prime minister from 1903 to 1905. The Games were eventually awarded to London, where Italian sport came of age in what *La Gazzetta* triumphantly declared as a 'demonstration of a race that has, in itself, the essential elements – moral, intellectual and material – for a superb resurrection, for a wonderful return to ancient times'.[87]

The first to make his mark in London was the wrestler Enrico Porro. A former seaman, at just over 1.5 metres tall he was well short of the minimum army recruitment height and weighed a paltry 62 kilos. Countering generations of malnourishment, he demonstrated great tactical, technical and physical strengths, in the lightweight category, to take gold from a Russian weighing seven kilos more. As *La Gazzetta* declared:

> Porro's victory makes each of us proud, as it shows that even without possessing gigantic, Herculean, huge-chested men, Italy is first, as in the times of ancient Rome...
>
> In spite of their methodical and diligent preparation, a memory and muscular intelligence is within us, which often makes us superior to northern peoples.[88]

Revelling in Porro's style as much as the victory, the comment highlighted one of the great pleasures that Italians would take from the successes of their sporting heroes: the skill and occasional craftiness (*furbizia*) that separated them from their adversaries and often compensated for what may have been physically lacking. As Beniamino Placido questioned in a newspaper polemic with Alberto Asor Rosa, in 1984, just because Italians were not physically built like northern Europeans should they renounce winning? 'No, if we know how to develop a tactic that builds on our qualities and neutralizes our defects.'[89] The idea was shared by Romano Guerra, editor of the National Gymnastic Federation's monthly *Il Ginnasta*, as early as 1902, who viewed it in terms of Italy's economic productivity:

> Guglielmo Ferrero... puts in clear light this difference in collective production by comparing Latin people with Germans. In the former he recognizes more intelligence, intuition, artistic tendency than in the second, but the work produced together by the Anglo-Saxons is infinitely greater than that of Latins because they are more tenacious, controlled and coordinated.[90]

Another Italian star of the London Games was the gymnast Alberto Braglia, who adapted his background in military-inspired gymnastics to the demands of competitive sport. He had already made his name at the unofficial Intercalated Athens Games, in 1906, where he won Italy's first gold medal. To the applause and cries of '*Viva Italia*' the Greek crowd added '*Viva Garibaldi*' in honour of a legion of red-shirted Garibaldian troops that had fought for Greek independence against Turkey at Domokos, some ten years earlier.[91] Lacking a coordinating body and government financial support, Italy had sent no athletes to the previous modern Games. For the 1906 tournament an Italian Commission for the Olympic Games was formed, much to the chagrin of the Turin Gymnastic Society. Opposed to records and selection, the SGT was also concerned about this obvious threat to its control of Italian sport. After initially refusing to join, its resistance collapsed through fear of alienation, but its former worries were confirmed by the formation of the Italian Olympic Committee (CIO) in 1907. On becoming the Federation of the Federations in 1914, the SGT's monopoly of Italian sport was over.

Selected by the CIO for the 1908 London Games, Alberto Braglia won the combined individual gymnastics event, or athletic pentathlon. Had there been medals for each of the specialities, he would have swept the board. Like Porro, Braglia was also nationalized by *La Gazzetta*, which referred to his small stature and connected modern Italy with ancient Rome: 'His body is shaped in perfect equilibrium... He demonstrates and recreates the harmonious, classic system; that of the Greeks, the most elegant and civilized people, and the Romans, the most powerful in the world.'[92]

Braglia repeated the trick four years later, while leading Italy's gymnasts to their first ever gold in the team event. The achievement was all the more impressive given the multiple fractures he had suffered when, soon after his 1908 success, he briefly joined the circus as a human torpedo. Launching himself from a chair mounted on a primitive ski-slope-type contraption, Braglia overshot the safety net on his first 'successful' attempt. Worse still, having been paid for his act, he was suspended for two years from the Gymnastics Federation, for professionalism.

Undeterred from using his extraordinary talent to escape poverty, Braglia entered the theatre in 1913, playing the piano with one hand while balancing with the other on a pommel-horse. His real money-making idea, however, was bringing to life the cartoon acrobats 'Fortunello e Cirillino', from the Corriere della Sera's children's supplement, Corriere dei Piccoli. Entering the stage with a briefcase from which his young assistant emerged, Braglia attempted to sweep up the boy who, supported and guided by his maestro, performed a series of acrobatics around the broom handle. Warmly received in Buckingham Palace, the pair commanded huge fees in America for a number of years. On returning to Italy in the mid-1920s, Braglia trained the national Olympic team before attempting to coach a new Cirillo, but was banned by the Fascist regime. Investing his savings into an unsuccessful bar that was destroyed during the war, Braglia was almost destitute by 1948. He finished his working life polishing his trophies in a Modena gymnasium named after him.

Born in Carpi, near Modena, Dorando Pietri's 1908 Olympic marathon failure was the first sporting press sensation, turning him into an overnight star. Still championed as a plucky loser, in 2008 his home town held a marathon to celebrate the one-hundredth anniversary of what is one of the great 'chokes' in history. Inspired by Italy's champion marathon runner Pericle Pagliani, in 1903 Pietri began training beneath the porticoes of Carpi, where he was a baker's apprentice. He was an outsider in the 1908 Olympic marathon, behind the South African favourites and the native-American Canadian, Longboat, who collapsed mid-race after gulping down a bottle of champagne. While the recommendation of alcohol to combat dehydration seems absurd, marathon runners occasionally used strychnine as a performance enhancer, which, legend has it, may have contributed to Pietri's crisis.

Having led from around the 30 kilometre mark he entered the stadium in first place, turning left rather than right before falling and being helped to his feet. Bent almost double and encouraged by a delirious crowd, he took ten minutes to stagger the last lap before reaching the finishing tape and collapsing. 'Since the glory of imperial Rome declined and the huge Coliseum fell into ruins, never had a bigger crowd applauded the triumphal arrival of a winning athlete,' reported the Corriere della Sera.[93] Much to the crowd's annoyance Pietri's victory was short-lived, and he was disqualified for the assistance received. To make matters worse, he reportedly entered a coma, with some evening newspapers even announcing his death.

Recovering miraculously, he emerged 24 hours later to enjoy a triumph greater than he might have expected in victory. Flowers, gifts, and an invitation of marriage rained down during a lap of honour, after which he received a trophy from Queen Alexandra. *La Gazzetta* published its

> greatest thanks to the worthiest Pietri who, even if he doesn't bring first place in the marathon... does win one of the greatest and most illustrious trials: that of brilliantly affirming in front of the admiring eyes of the world, the immortal heritage of Latin strength and virtue.[94]

The drama prompted the Italian press to dedicate significant column inches to a sporting event for the first time. Small, with a handlebar moustache, wearing a baggy vest, red shorts and a knotted handkerchief, Pietri encapsulated Italian poverty while becoming the country's first, internationally recognized sporting hero. Sharing *La Gazzetta*'s pride in Pietri's 'indomitable courage and ancient Roman energy',[95] Sir Arthur Conan-Doyle's claim, in the *Daily Mail*, that 'no ancient Roman had known how to accept the laurels of victory better than Pietri', was gleefully reported. 'The great race still isn't extinct. In fact, Dorando is worthy of the ancient victors of the Coliseum.'[96] So impressed was Conan-Doyle, and perhaps guilt-ridden for his apparent involvement in Pietri's disqualification, that he opened a fund for the athlete in the same newspaper. One Italian worker gave Pietri his last five shillings, while a French collector offered him 12,500 francs for the Queen's trophy. His refusal said much about Italy and its sportsmen, according to the *Corriere della Sera*: 'This young man, who knows how much effort it takes to earn money, refused what for him is an enormous sum that he couldn't dream of earning in years of work in Italy.'[97]

Yet, coming at the height of their angst over the merits of sport, Young Socialists criticized Pietri's 'victory' and the attention it commanded. Not only was he working class and the representative of an athletics club with strong links to the left, his activities were fuelling the sport mania. As Giovanni Rinaldi explained in *L'Avanguardia*, the Federation of Young Socialists' weekly:

> We feel that we have to speak up to defend our youngsters from this now general malaria that degenerates them and tears them away from our organizations and circles... We neither want nor feel like associating ourselves with these shameless events. Our people, our youth has something better to do, which isn't sport.
>
> We must energetically fight what constitutes, for the bourgeoisie, one of the practical means of attracting our young, thus taking them away from our organizations.[98]

Pietri's achievement and efforts lasted longer in the memory of Britons, who invited him as a guest of honour to the 1948 Games. While his death had passed almost unnoticed some six years earlier, he remained a plucky 'champion' with character and spirit to whom Italians warmed far more than others whose sweat and dedication brought greater returns. 'Porro, Pietri [and] Braglia', *La Gazzetta* proudly proclaimed, 'have solemnly confirmed to the entire world that the ancient Roman race still isn't finished, and is marching wonderfully towards a superb resurrection of Italy. Long live Italy!'[99]

The sporting war

There was little sense of resurrection in Italy's unheroic, pragmatic foreign policy, however. Despite conscription remaining one of the Italian male's greatest fears,

> there was a growing feeling in many quarters from the 1870s that the best hope for the army and for Italy lay in a great military victory that would expunge the past, heal the rift between government and the governed, cement the prestige of the monarchy and the institutions, and finally secure the moral unity of the nation.[100]

Having returned empty-handed from the 1878 Congress of Berlin and seen France occupy Tunis in 1881, Italy signed the conservative, defensive, Triple Alliance with Germany and Austria in 1882, which lasted until 1914. Intent on forging an empire, the 1893–6 Abyssinian campaigns ended in defeat at Adua, leaving Francesco Crispi's government to collapse and Italian prestige to sink even further. Nursing a sense of shame and a thirst for revenge, Italian Nationalists were buoyed by the 1911 invasion of Libya, while the Socialist split over the issue enabled the revolutionary wing to seize control of the party and appoint Benito Mussolini as editor of *Avanti!*

Adopting an openly interventionist position, Italian gymnastics developed new competitions and military training.[101] But unimpressed by the products of its zeal thus far, the government made the War Ministry responsible for physical education, which restricted many societies to benefit and fundraising activities. Thereafter, Baumann's traditional, aristocratic school of gymnastics was replaced by a democratic, bourgeois model that encouraged physical exercise, vigour and extreme individualism/heroism as an end in itself.

No longer feasible to deny soldiers the vote, in 1912 suffrage was extended to all men who had completed military service, those over 21 who were literate, plus all men over 30. The electorate rose from 3.5 million to 8 million overnight.

Mass politics had arrived. Unable to resist the Socialist rise or strengthen the state with unprecedented welfare changes, Giovanni Giolitti's government collapsed in 1914. On the eve of war, Italian democracy was in chaos.

Supporting intervention, Benito Mussolini became a rallying figure for revolutionary Socialists. Ousted as *Avanti!* editor and expelled from the party, with the support of industrialists he launched another daily, *Il Popolo d'Italia*. Despite the majority of Italians preferring neutrality, Prime Minister Antonio Salandra took Italy into the conflict on 24 May 1915, swayed by a violent nationalist campaign and the Treaty of London that promised territorial expansion. It was time, preached *La Gazzetta dello Sport*, to 'take up arms for the oldest, hardest and truest sport; war',[102] 'the hour to remember' and avenge the nation's suffering and humiliation:

> Remember every offence, every insult, every contempt... Remember the fallen in Adua ...
> We must remember!... A people that forgets, is a people defeated. And, brothers, we have never wanted to win more than today!
> Italy's organ grinders, lazzaroni, maccheroni, polentas... [and]... brigands have changed. On the battlefields, on earth or sea, in the trenches and in the vanguard of the sky's streets, the enemies will find the new generation: your, people of sport!
> And you will be the vendicators!... Sportsmen of Italy! Your time has come![103]

Over five and a half million Italians were mobilized, with the majority coming from the peasantry and joining the infantry that sustained 95 per cent casualties.

✪ ✪ ✪ ✪

World War One changed European sport. Introduced by officers to ease boredom and maintain fitness, sport became an important part of wartime and civilian life thereafter. With initial celebrations soon neutered by what quickly became clear would be a long and painful campaign, *La Gazzetta* advised those heading off to the 'big match' of battle: 'Calm, as at the start of your biggest game.'[104] After the kick-off, sport was reduced to almost nothing, the *Giro d'Italia* postponed and the 1915 football championship suspended one week from its conclusion. Replaced by regional leagues, it did not recommence until the war was over. Short of events to cover, the sport's press worked the war into a marketing opportunity. *La Gazzetta*'s fortnightly wartime photo-reportage magazine held a competition challenging troops to arrive as close as possible to the front line. Offering a 25 lire prize for each advance, soldiers needed to produce a photograph with a copy of the magazine, authenticated by an official.[105] *La Gazzetta* also sent 'free' copies to the trenches while encouraging readers to make subscriptions. As one anonymous troop returning from the front line reportedly wrote:

> Today, after two months in the trenches, I stepped back into Italy and found *La Gazzetta*. If you only knew how much pleasure I got! I was truly moved when devouring the news on its pink pages that brought back memories of many friends and sport that was dear to me. Believe me, in that moment, *La Gazzetta* was a treasure that I wouldn't have swapped for anything in the world.[106]

As Liberal Italy had envisaged, sportsmen provided the army with a huge source of disciplined, fit young men, with Fascism later celebrating how clubs lost around 50 per cent of their members on the declaration of war, with the remainder swallowed up by full mobilization.[107] Inter and Italy national team captain Virgilio Fossati, who died at Montefalcone on Christmas Day 1916, was joined by Carlo Oriano, one of the first winners of the *Giro d'Italia*, the champion rower Giuseppe Sinigaglia, plus numerous weightlifters, athletes, mountaineers, cyclists and gymnasts. 'Italian sportsmen no longer count the medals, mutilations and injuries... [Death]... chose the youngest, the strongest and the most beautiful.'[108]

Sport nonetheless continued preparing troops for combat. The Genoese Gymnastic Society ran a free, fast-track weapons training course, while *La Gazzetta* proposed the adaptation of discus and shot-putt techniques towards the launching of hand grenades,[109] within its fervent backing of the war:

> Sport will not march alone: it will be followed by sports journalism that must not cease to enthusiastically drive as many events as there can be... Get ready – sport's journalism's clearest and most pressing mission, a mission to which, from today, this paper... is ready to dedicate all of its strength.[110]

Publishing long, daily lists of the nation's sporting soldiers, their clubs and the regiments to which they had been assigned, the paper trumpeted sport's rush to defend the motherland with a gruesomely portentous analogy: 'Sport empties itself. Like a huge wounded body, blood and life flow from open veins... All sportsmen, are leaving.'[111] Some days later, it continued: 'We'll put away our flag for now, that of the sporting battle, as the other big, beautiful, bright one of national battles unfolds in the Italian sky.'[112]

Bianchi bikes unfolded too, with some light enough to be carried on a soldier's back or quickly converted into temporary beds or stretchers. Championed by *La Bicicletta* as early as 1885,[113] a special company of cycling riflemen was formed in 1898. Joining the National Voluntary Corps of Cyclists and Motorists, in 1908, it was open to all Italians over 16 in possession of a bike or motorcycle. Often working at night, moving quickly in front of or alongside the marching cavalry, conducting reconnaissance, carrying messages and occupying key advanced positions, cycling infantrymen were among the war's heroes.[114]

The conflict brought millions of peasants into the cities to serve production needs, which accelerated and concentrated Italy's industrial revolution. Aided by armament contracts and favourable tax breaks that encouraged reinvestment in plant, the steel and engineering industries grew along with car production. By 1907 there were six different manufacturers in Turin alone, employing over 6,500 people. Aware that the exclusive end of the market was limited, FIAT (*Fabbrica Italiana Automobili Torino*) began diversifying into lorries, buses and more affordable cars in 1912, long before the era of mass motoring. Formed in 1899 by a group of ex-cavalry officers, which included Giovanni Agnelli Snr, by the 1920s his family owned 70 per cent of the company that was producing 90 per cent of Italy's cars.[115] It was, however, lucrative government contracts for submarine engines and military transport that saw its output rise from 4,500 vehicles in 1914 to 25,000 in 1918.

The major beneficiary of FIAT's new-found wealth was Juventus Football Club, formed as the Sport Club Juventus by a group of Turin students in 1897. FIAT's financial backing enabled it to heavily invest in the emerging transfer market in the 1920s, and launch the club's domination of *calcio*. Their relationship came from a dispute over the left-sided *terzino* (wing-back) Antonio Bruna. Unable to train due to his factory duties, fellow FIAT employee and Juventus fan Sandro Zambelli took Bruna to Giovanni Agnelli Snr's house to plead for his release. Agnelli's permission confirmed his *Juventino* (Juve fan) status and sealed a historic deal. His son Edoardo was the first of the dynasty to become Juventus president, on 24 July 1924, after which the club won its first *scudetto* (league title) in 1926, before claiming five consecutive championships from 1930 to 1935.

✪ ✪ ✪ ✪

In August 1917, Turin's radical factory workers were at the centre of bread riots that developed into the potentially revolutionary Red Week. Following the army's disastrous defeat at Caporetto on the Austrian border, in November 1917, which left 11,000 dead, 30,000 wounded, 300,000 captured, and 350,000 in 'disorderly retreat', the government was forced to offer land reform in an effort to maintain discipline and boost morale among peasant troops.

Italy exited the conflict with many of its traditional structures in crisis: the parliamentary system had collapsed; 600,000 primarily peasant troops had died, creating a rural labour shortage, while urban mass unemployment, following de-mobilization, was worsened by inflation. Hitting middle-class savers, their anger was intensified by government attempts to buy off the proletariat. Italy was more divided than ever: combatants against shirkers; peasants against workers; patriots against defeatists. The 1918–19 Spanish flu epidemic killed another 600,000 Italians, as many as the conflict itself.

Having won the war, Italy appeared to have lost the peace. Crusading against the 'mutilated victory', in September 1919 the romantic poet Gabriele D'Annunzio occupied Fiume (Rijeka) with 2,000 'legionaries' of mainly army deserters or mutineers. Fuelling the ideals of patriotic fervour and youthful vitality, they remained until 20 December 1920, when Giolitti sent in the navy. Despite D'Annunzio's surrender, the episode showed the Italian government's weakness, undermined the authority of the state, and questioned the loyalty of the Armed Forces. Convincing many Italians that they had been robbed, such daring activism appeared a route to regaining what had been lost and left the country ripe for takeover by an extreme nationalist group.

✪ ✪ ✪ ✪

Pre-empting what would happen on a grander scale after 1945, the immediate post-war years saw sport gradually open up to all social classes. *Calcio* began its slow march south, with clubs forming in Palermo, Naples and Bari. Reflecting the south's limited industrial and urban development, its expansion was still modest. Italy's rebirth was signalled by the 1919 *Giro d'Italia*. With 42 military cyclists among the 87 competitors, the race crossed the north-eastern battlefields to reach the disputed Italian-speaking regions where 'populations along the roads and the same soldiers still armed to defend the new border, welcomed the Giro as the symbol of the motherland.'[116]

Yet nothing could detract from the lack of sporting facilities that was accentuated by the conflict. As if to prove the Communist objection to sport as a proletarian pacifier, the response to Red Week saw the National Gymnastic Federation build workers gymnasiums and schools, while FIAT, Lancia, Alfa Romeo and Pirelli created gyms and fields for their newly formed clubs. But there was an element of subjection in accepting such benevolence and, most damagingly, 'from a "neutral" and free institution, the company sports group became an ideal recruitment reservoir for "white guards" and an efficient propaganda instrument for the concepts of Fascist sport.'[117]

A sporting chance? The routine death of Liberal Italy

In 1919 the vote was extended to men over 18 who had served in the army and to all men over the age of 21. With a new system of proportional representation and sport commanding a 'principal and prevailing part in the educational and economic movement of society', *Il Giornale dello Sport* proposed four candidates, in 1921:

> we do not need to ask the politics of the candidate involved in sport, it doesn't interest us. Instead, we must demand that the candidate is a man who has given and wants to give his time to sport... [and we need to]... analyse if his position among the parties might enable him to aspire to reach the highest levels of government so that... he might have the power to carry out the wishes of the sporting class.[118]

One of those elected was Luigi Gasparotto[119] who, as Minister for War, set about reforming physical education. Intent on improving the quality of military recruits, his proposed coordinating body for gymnastic and sporting activity was a potentially pivotal moment for Italian sport. Committing the government to providing facilities, equipment, tax breaks and subsidies for all societies that signed up to this patriotic initiative, parliament rejected the proposal through fear of funding and arming groups of undetermined political persuasion in a time of civil conflict.

Once again sport was left to civil society and exposed to the vision, ethics and morals of those providing it, principally the Catholic Church and Socialism. While *Avanti!* defended sport, to prepare red soldiers, strengthen workers and spiritually improve the human race,[120] Marxism could only see it as a distraction from politics. As the Milan Socialist weekly *La Battaglia Socialista* maintained, in 1921:

> 'Healthy in mind healthy in body': everybody agrees.
> But 'sport' in the healthy body, too often creates the brain of an imbecile.[121]

Others, such as Giacinto Serrati,[122] supported physical recreation so long as it was directed towards mass society. His recommendations were made in *Sport e Proletariato*,[123] the Milan-based weekly that he co-founded for the proletarian sporting movement. But with Socialists and Communists finally close to consensus on 10 December 1923, *Sport e Proletariato*'s printing offices were destroyed by Fascist squads and the newspaper closed down. Drastic action against a four-page publication with a circulation of nine to ten thousand, it demonstrated Fascism's awareness of sport's importance. One by one the premises and centres of workers' sporting organizations were either violently attacked or destroyed by Mussolini's squads, or quietly coerced into the Fascist system. But as late as 1934, with the dictatorship in place for almost a decade, the sport debate still wracked the left. Writing under the pseudonym of Ettore Bianchi, the author Carlo Levi argued that sport had depoliticized the masses and 'reduced [them] to interesting themselves, like babies, in the gratuitous bounce of a ball'.[124]

The Workers Association for Physical Education (*Associazione proletaria per l'educazione fisica* – APEF), formed in 1920, provided an alternative viewpoint. One of the last bastions of resistance, it won both the respect and ire of its Fascist adversaries. The self-declared breeding ground of proletarian strength provided PE facilities and instruction for workers only, while allowing its members to participate in competitions organized by bourgeois national bodies. Contravening the left's stance on class fraternization, the APEF demonstrated previously missed opportunities to voice and demonstrate the left's alternative.[125] Besides creating champions, it developed bicycle tourism, mountaineering, hiking, mass excursions, cultural activities, plus health education. However, Italian Socialism still proved too ideologically rigid to embrace and profit from sport.

Catholicism was equally inflexible and just because the majority of Italians were Catholic did not guarantee their automatic involvement in FASCI activities. Engaged in a long, unwinnable battle with the mainstream federations, the Catholic leadership ploughed on regardless in its attempt to create an alternative national culture. While the FASCI was unquestionably successful, it contributed to the creation of a strong but disunited national sporting culture. Its ultimate contradiction, however, was the participation of Catholic gymnasts in the defence of the nation:

> Moderately intense gymnastics will provide strong, gallant sons upon which, our beloved motherland will be able to count in the moment of danger. Governed according to the principles of all of our societies, gymnastics will provide an army of citizens that will form the strongest bastion for the institutions.[126]

Thus, the Church defended the principles and values of Liberal Italy, with which it had been in conflict since its formation.

From 1923, the FASCI concentrated on surviving growing Fascist pressure and the Church's increasingly warm relationship with the regime, which encouraged it to avoid any incidents that might have upset the *Duce* and de-railed their ongoing dialogue. Equally, rather than brutally and decisively repress the FASCI, the regime slowly eroded it via its own organizations before its effective liquidation in 1927.[127] Nonetheless, it did delay the Fascistization of sport and physical education and certainly helped the Church extend deeper roots into Italian society than its Socialist rival.

But while both groups opposed the liberal state, in terms of sport they offered little of tangible difference. While neither supported the nationalist goal of strengthening bodies and creating patriotism through sport, each used it to create their own proletarian and religious armies. Worse still, having identified but failed to secure these groups, they were exposed to conquest by a political ideology with a greater appreciation of sport's ability to mobilize and create community. Unwittingly, from the angst-ridden years of interminable debate, Catholicism and the Italian left's most enduring contribution was a virtual blueprint for Fascist sport.

Mussolini's boys: athletes of fascism, soldiers of sport

Since the Fascist Party came to power in 1922, historians have tried and failed to agree upon why it happened. There is, perhaps, only one factor that all might accept: the impact of the First World War. The conflict produced an exasperated sense of nationalism, intensified Italy's inferiority complex, and caused severe economic crises, all of which further delegitimized the already tarnished democracy. Threatened by the political left and right, almost any attempt to create order in post-war Italy was doomed.

The rise of a regime

Fascism emerged from the *Fascio di Combattimento*, an ex-combatants' organization that mobilized various discontented elements, including officers, students, professionals, farmers and estate managers, intent on defending Italy against revolution while sweeping away the old political class. Launched in 1919, support for the Fascist movement took off in the winter of 1920–1 following a campaign of terror against Socialists and their local institutions by its violent squads (*sqadrismo*). Winning support and new recruits with its successful use of violence, Fascism's breakthrough came in the 'red' provinces of central Italy, most notably Tuscany and Emilia Romagna.

Following the May 1921 elections, parliament contained a wide mix of Socialist, Communist, Popular Party, Radical and Reformist deputies, in addition to 35 Fascists. Unable to form a stable administration Giolitti dissolved parliament, with the succession of brief coalitions that followed only strengthening anti-democratic forces, which included the formation of the Fascist Party (PNF) in the autumn of 1921. A failed general strike in mid-1922, further discredited the left, confirmed Italy's political paralysis and made Fascism's entry into government seem inevitable. As Mussolini conducted statesmanlike negotiations, playing all parties off against each other to preserve the political impasse, a rally of 40,000 Fascists at Naples, on 24 October, was followed by the March on Rome, on 27–8 October 1922 when Mussolini's blackshirted-supporters threatened to seize power by force.

While doubts about the army's loyalty to the King may have existed, the March on Rome could easily have been stopped along with the mythology of the Fascist Party's seizure of power. Remaining in his office in Milan, Mussolini acted like a true Italian politician, or one afraid of being in Rome at such a critical moment. He need not have worried. This limited threat of violence was enough for the King to invite him to form a government, in November 1922.[1] His cabinet contained only four Fascist ministers and the Party a mere seven per cent of parliamentary deputies. Having bluffed its way into power, the Fascist Party spent its first four years in government containing its own radical, unruly elements. Only when relatively secure would it seek to establish dictatorship.

Its weakness was evident in June 1924 when, in a courageous parliamentary speech, the Socialist leader Giacomo Matteotti detailed violence and corruption in the May elections. Following his disappearance on 10 June, Mussolini's government was in real danger. Although Matteotti's body was not found until mid-August, it was clear that a serious crime had taken place, which was traced very close to Mussolini. As an indication of how the working class had already been coerced into submission, there were almost no protests or strikes. With the Vatican daily, *L'Osservatore Romano*, preaching forgiveness and the King impotent, opposition deputies withdrew from parliament until the government resigned.

What became known as the Aventine Secession proved a huge mistake. De-politicizing the opposition, the walkout enabled Mussolini to survive a confidence vote. At his greatest moment of weakness, it bought him the necessary time to establish the illusion of moderacy and subservience to the King, while ending any chance of consensus politics. In crisis, he fell back on his more thuggish followers, who demanded harsh measures against the opposition. Having narrowly avoided the resignation of his cabinet, Mussolini, in a speech on 3 January 1925, challenged his opponents to impeach him. Nobody did, and by the end of the year opposition parties had been banned, liberties and press freedoms removed and dictatorship established, the final blow coming after an apparent assassination attempt against the *Duce* following his opening of the Littoriale Stadium in Bologna, in October 1926.[2]

Lo sport fascista

With the Fascist Party's early years in government focussed on survival, the regime's interest in sport only began in 1925, following the appointment of Lando Ferretti as President of the Italian Olympic Committee. Renamed the *Comitato Olimpico Nazionale Italiano* (CONI), the 1928 Charter of Sport (*Carta dello Sport*) made the body responsible for centrally planning and directing sport towards the regime's needs.

Having come to power following another military failure, the Fascist Party was embarrassed by Italy's modest international status at a time when national strength, virility and honour were determined by imperial exploits. The takeover of sport, as Ferretti clarified, was thus a means of distinguishing the regime from its Liberal, laissez-faire predecessor:

> The laudable attempts of the pioneers... were nothing more than scarce oases in a desert of general indifference and incomprehension. The Liberal state was uninterested in the problem... the war, in which the individual heroism of sportsmen glowed, showed the lack of physical preparation of many Italians: entire generations had been left to ossify.[3]

But with Fascism unable to restore Italy's embarrassing military reputation to health, unprecedented international sporting success was joyously converted into domestic and diplomatic propaganda. As the Bolognese daily *Il Resto del Carlino* reminded athletes leaving for the 1928 Amsterdam Olympic Games: 'Victories are valued as clear signs of racial superiority that are destined to reflect in many fields outside of sport.'[4] By 1940, according to *La Gazzetta*'s *bellicose* scribe Bruno Roghi, it had become much more:

> No longer a frivolous entertainment, even if it's exciting... Sport has become a weapon. It is way of being and becoming a warrior race. It is a weapon with exceptional powers of conquest and education. Who does sport is a military power in waiting.[5]

Sport thus expressed Fascism's demand for individual dedication to the greater collective need. As the 1927 Labour Charter (*Carta del Lavoro*) explained:

> The Italian nation is an organism having ends, a life, and a means of action superior in power and duration to the single individuals or groups of individuals that compose it. It is a moral, political, and economic unity that is integrally realized in the fascist state.[6]

Redefining individuals as cells of the Fascist social organism obliged them to improve their health and fitness while making formerly private behaviours state interests. Motivated by disastrous military conscription statistics, widespread illness and early mortality, Mussolini, in his 1927 Ascension Day speech, launched the 'battle for births' and a national health campaign. 'Men that get a belly are certainly not the Fascist "model". Palid, sedentary, bespectacled, clumsily awkward, they constitute the absolute antithesis of the Mussolinian ideal.'[7]

A sports medicine and training unit was established in Bologna, where physicians conducted anthropometric and eugenic research, plus more mainstream inquiries into biomechanics, biometrics and the effects of nutrition, tonics, stimulants and hormones.[8] Inspired by the physician Giovanni Pini, the Italian Federation for Sports Medicine (*Federazione Italiana dei Medici Sportivi* – FIMS) assessed 'physical stamina among adolescents and adults that train in... gymnastics and sport, with the aim of getting a pedigree, robust mass, physically and morally ready to serve the Motherland'.[9] Intended to maximize performance and prevent injuries, the Institute's work had spin-offs for general medical science that was protecting Fascist society.

Hampered by minimal and antiquated sports facilities, the Party Secretary Augusto Turati demanded a stadium in every commune of the country and by 1930, over 2,000 were either built or under construction. Directed through public works programmes, this massive investment provided thousands of jobs and stimulated the economy as Fascism fought the Great Depression. Promoting an organized, modernized Italy capable of hosting big sporting events, stadiums were a vital part of the regime's creation of spectacle, income and propaganda. Monolithic or tiny, they addressed the needs of the common man. As the head of the Italian Football Association (FIGC) Leandro Arpinati stated sport was not just 'athletic competition between champions, but an indispensable physical education of the masses... For the physical improvement of the race, nothing is as useful as sport that teaches everybody discipline and moulds muscles with character.'[10]

The encouragement of mass society to take up sport increased participation and produced Italy's great Olympic leap forward. At the four Games from 1924 to 1936, Italy won 36 gold, 29 silver and 28 bronze medals in mass sports like athletics, and traditionally elitist events, such as fencing. Primarily representing the achievements of Fascism's male elite, the 1936 Olympic team also included a small nucleus of women. Unable to produce ideologically 'trained' coaches overnight, the Fascist Party pragmatically employed the likes of Alberto Braglia, Giovanni Raicevich and Nedo Nadi. Products of Liberal Italy, their backgrounds were irrelevant when 'Mussolini's boys' finished second behind the USA, in Los Angeles in 1932. Four years later in Berlin, hampered by the absence of many Italian athletes fighting in Abyssinia, an increase in the number of Olympic nations, plus the athletic rise of Nazi Germany, third place was another impressive performance.

Appealing to wider sectors of the population and penetrating more households than arguably any other social activity, sport was a propaganda opportunity, a political tool, and a means of expressing and imposing just what Fascism was about. As Bruno Roghi wrote after Gino Bartali's success in the 1938 *Tour de France*: 'since the health of a people is the fundamental coefficient of its progress and achievement, this is why sport is politics in the most noble and generous sense of the word'.[11] Inserted into everyday life, it educated in the new national spirit, with almost every sport imaginable becoming a political football in its own right; from golf, rugby, swimming and greyhound racing, to pigeon fancying and hunting. With sport for all, it developed a sense of commonality that would theoretically be converted into a strong, unifying nationalism. As the Milan newspaper *L'Ambrosiano* proclaimed after Giuseppe Campari's 1924 World Title motor race victory at Lyon: 'The supremacy of the Italian man, of the Italian machine and of Italian work was repeated yesterday, at Lyon, in the face of the entire world.'[12]

Glorified in the press, mythologized athletic battles and victories created the image of an energetic and virile nation capable of fighting and winning, as Arpinati declared in parliament, in 1933:

> The champion is a safeguard against the tendency towards mediocrity. He is the flag that stirs the passions of the crowd and rouses enthusiasm, he is the happiest expression of a race and a generation, he is a symbol in which the young recognize and rediscover themselves...
>
> The champion is thus indispensible not only as an athletic act but as a social fact. The champion is the advanced sentry who represents the motherland and holds the flag's prestige high in international competition.[13]

Mussolini ordered all athletes: 'Remember... when you compete abroad, the honour and sporting prestige of the nation is entrusted to your muscles and above all your spirit.'[14]

Champions also embodied the 'new Fascist man' – the *Italiano nuovo* – that the regime was striving to create. Putting national and collective interests above his own, more than just physically honed, the new man had to be mentally strong: 'If force dominated over intelligence, physical beauty over moral, we wouldn't have an army of athletes but a multitude of removal-men; and from our sporting centres it wouldn't be heroes that rise for every occasion but ugly spivs.'[15]

But even if sport shaped and honed the Fascist man, women still had to give birth to him, and sport prepared them for their patriotic duty. Expected to push rather than play for the *patria* (motherland), women's physical exertions were directed towards the home and childbirth rather than sporting records.[16] Yet some women did play and were remarkably good too, their achievements and victories stimulating national pride, while heightening Fascism's fear of sport as distraction from their primary reproductive roles.[17]

For these reasons, the regime was compelled to take control of the nation's leisure time, with children from 8 to18 attending the Youth group *Balilla*[18] and 18–21 year olds joining the Militia. 'Ten years of incessant, meticulous and progressive work, to equip the Fascist call-up of youngsters in spirit and muscles.'[19] Most adults then joined their local 'afterwork' club (*Opera Nazionale Dopolavoro* – OND), which was supposed to physically and morally elevate the masses rather than create champions. Mixing light education and recreation, the OND still identified and encouraged talent through provincial and national competitions. By 1930, as CONI's annual publication made clear, the key question was no longer if but why people should partake in sport.[20] Yet beyond the myths and propaganda, sport had difficulty in achieving the regime's goals, and frequently landed short of its high expectations.

Blackshirts on bikes?

Cycling wasn't among Mussolini's favourite sports and during his 20 years of rule he never attended the start or finish of any stage of the *Giro d'Italia*. Rarely seen in the saddle, he did occasionally ride a curious machine with a back wheel larger than the front and a rudder-type steering mechanism, around his Villa Torlonia garden.[21] Such was his apparent dislike of cycling, however, it was probably the only sport in which he wasn't Italy's 'Number One', and was perfectly happy not to have been.

With Fascism obsessed by cults of speed, virility, strength, heroism and courage, the bicycle appeared an unlikely candidate for the regime's attention and investment. Cycling was still relatively slow, while the huge levels of fitness and courage that racing demanded could not distract from the attention the sport drew to the terrible state of Italy's roads. Already difficult for cyclists to demonstrate the combative characteristics of the citizen-soldier, the individual nature of the sport also countered Fascism's team ethos. Moreover, coming from very humble backgrounds and speaking a variety of Italian dialects, professional cyclists tended to highlight Italian diversity rather than unity. Unsurprisingly, cyclists were not among the 25 champions of Italian sport selected to form a guard of honour at the 1934 Exhibition of the Fascist Revolution.[22] Since cycling was hugely popular, however, the regime was forced into an accommodation with it.

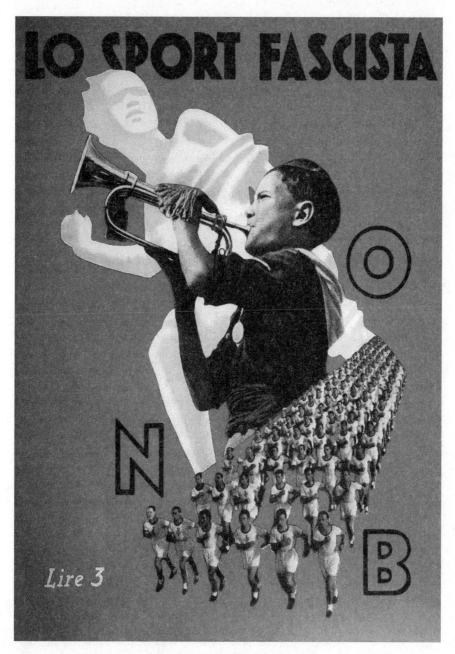

Figure 3: *A bugling* Balilla *calling the nation's youth to exercise*

Ottavio Bottecchia was one of Fascist Italy's earliest cycling champions. A bricklayer who volunteered as a cavalryman in the advanced cycling assault corps in Italy's northern Alto Adige region during the First World War, he escaped from brief imprisonment and was decorated for his efficient machine-gunning and calm under enemy fire. As *La Gazzetta* recalled, in 1943:

> Mindless of the danger, while his captain refused him permission to go back, crawling along the ground he managed to cover the one hundred metres from the zone of fire to return with his bicycle, while all around him was an infernal crackling of bullets.[23]

Finishing far behind the 1923 *Giro d'Italia* winner, Bottecchia was still first among the so-called *isolate*; riders with no team, who survived on prize money and benevolence. It secured him a *domestique* (support rider) role in the French 'Autoloto' team for that year's *Tour de France* where, after leading the race for some time and apparently terrorizing the team captain, he finished second, a feat never previously achieved by an Italian. Returning to great acclaim, Bottecchia confessed his motive for racing: poverty.

Leading the 1924 *Tour de France* from start to finish, he returned to a hero's welcome in his home town of Pordenone. More importantly, he was financially able to support his extended family, which included 37 nieces and nephews. After winning the *Tour* again in 1925, his career began to decline. Continuing to train, on 3 June 1927 Bottecchia was found on the roadside with a fractured skull and collar bone, and blood coming from one ear and his nose. He died 12 days later. The simplest explanation was a fall, and he certainly wouldn't have been the first cyclist to have died in what was a high-risk sport. However, with his grave condition not matching his scratch-free bike, conspiracy theories were stoked by the regime's hastily concluded inquest.

Some years later a peasant's death-bed confession to an altercation with a cyclist supported rumours of Bottecchia having been struck on the head with a stone after stealing grapes from a vine. But the story left too many doubts, most notably the lack of vines in that particular area and the immaturity of grapes in June. Fifty years later another death-bed confession, this time from a priest, talked of a murder.[24] Like Matteotti, Bottecchia was apparently a militant Socialist and thus a strong Fascist adversary. But while he had certainly paraded in Socialist rallies with his bike, he also joined the local Vittorio Veneto branch of the Fascist party in 1923, neither of which were conclusive evidence of his affiliation either way. Many athletes publicly supported the regime, and it is difficult to determine their true political beliefs given that all sportsmen, as members of a federation affiliated to CONI, were automatically members of the Party. With doubts surrounding the theory of a political murder, the true reason behind his death remains unknown.

Fascism's suspicion of cycling was nonetheless real, arguably explicable by the bicycle's role as *the* working class means of transport. Not only was it inherently simple, it was a continual reminder of the Liberal era, when it first flourished. Consequently, riding the bicycle's wave of popularity would have risked the regime's revolutionary identity. Two wheels simply weren't Fascist enough, and cycling was marginalized. Never among the recommended events for students of the regime's sport university in Rome, cycling also failed to make it into the *Balilla* or *Dopolavoro* programmes. It was only really encouraged in the form of non-competitive, group excursions. But even then there was a catch, with *Lo Sport Fascista* promoting 'the joy of the bicycle' while demanding the reintroduction of its taxation to pay for necessary road improvements.[25] Nonetheless, the sport's lack of politicization by Fascism was good for Italian cyclists, who appear to have been treated with far more neutrality than other sportsmen. In 1938, while the national football team was being whistled and insulted in Paris, French fans gave a warm welcome to Italians competing in the *Tour de France*.[26]

Hugely popular, cycling could not simply be ignored by the regime, as *Lo Sport Fascista* noted through gritted teeth, in 1929: 'The Giro d'Italia is such an event that it cannot be ignored by our magazine even if, for some of its professional aspects, it seems quite removed from the spirit that guides Fascist sporting education.'[27] Nonetheless, racing's potential to market Fascist modernity was recognized, with the Padua–Venice stage of the 1936 *Giro* run along the smooth carriageways of the brand-new motorway connecting the two cities. Despite Mussolini's reservations, since 1926 he had ensured that riders were encouraged by significant contributions to the race prize money,[28] while other Fascist leaders publicly supported it. In 1929, the Party Secretary and CONI President Augusto Turati launched the *Giro* in Milan, and in 1933 Achille Starace greeted the riders at the end.

Appropriating all victories, whether an individual openly supported the regime or not, the Fascist Party made ambassadors out of its cyclists, with 10,000 *Dopolavoro* members parading in the Milan Arena before the conclusion of the 1936 race.[29] One of the regime's greatest stars was Gino Bartali, who, in 1938, was ordered to leave the *Giro d'Italia* in order to concentrate on the internationally more important *Tour de France*. Celebrating his subsequent victory, Bruno Roghi declared: 'toughened in the Fascist gymnasium of race, for which the athlete is a soldier and the soldier is a winner, Gino Bartali has completed a venture that globally honours Italian sport'.[30] His bicycle manufacturer – Legnano – also published an advertisement caricaturing Bartali as a steam-roller flattening his opponents on the road: 'An order from the

DUCE's Italy: "Win". Bartali, champion on a Legnano, has obeyed!'[31] Although Bartali never made a Roman salute or appeared in a blackshirt, his image and achievements were exploited by the regime, which deemed the chaste, pious Catholic an appropriate example of the new Fascist man.

With Bartali absent from the 1938 *Giro*, Giovanni Valetti secured a second, consecutive victory, which fuelled their apparent duel. Real or otherwise, such sporting rivalries were positively encouraged by the regime, the strongest of the era being between Learco Guerra, affectionately known as the 'human locomotive', and Alfredo Binda, 'the nasty one'. As a member of the militia and with a surname that translated as war, Guerra was naturally popular with the regime, while his impulsive, daring style won him national adoration, particularly among women. A naturally attacking rider, he was vulnerable and generous in defeat.

By contrast, Binda left the regime and crowds cold. More calculated, he was disliked for the ease with which he destroyed his opponents, winning the *Giro d'Italia* five times from 1925 to 1933. Well prepared, shrewd, tactically aware, and lacking pro-Fascist sound bites, he contrasted strongly with Guerra. Having won 12 out of the 15 stages of the 1927 *Giro d'Italia* and claiming the first of three world titles by 1930, his domination was such that *La Gazzetta* begged him not to enter that year's *Giro* in order to maintain interest. His agreement netted him 22,500 lire, the same as the winner.

While splitting cycling's fan base between two individuals may have appeared divisive and anti-nationalist, such duels and rivalries gave Italians the freedom to disagree and argue among themselves, without fear of reprisals and without threatening the regime. Thus, through the cultivation and differentiation of mythical sportsmen, Italians were able and encouraged to take sides and let off steam, in unthreatening, non-politicized ways, within the increasingly repressive atmosphere of the one-party police state where dissent was totally unacceptable. Generated and stoked by the sports press there was one 'sportsman', however, who was beyond all rivalry and comparison.

Italy's number one

> Face of Caesar and the body of a gladiator: this is how Mussolini appeared to the sporting legionaries after the March on Rome when he crossed the threshold of our time, our era that is sun and air and has victory as its god.[32]

For all of sport's attractions, the regime's creation of spectacle was heavily reliant upon the censored media. While it is impossible to establish the truth behind the stories, myths and legends, so much were they politically driven, analysis of the sports press still reveals what the regime wished to portray to society. Crucial sources of Fascist power, newspapers were initially controlled by a combination of informal partnerships with owners and financiers, plus outright intimidation by the Party. Once secure, Fascism's control became more systematic. Combining intimidation, violence and large fines with the threat of suspension and forced closure, there was no need to introduce strict censorship laws until 1925.

The Press Censorship Law established the Order of Journalists to which all had to belong, even if the regime was in no position to purge the profession of all who had trained within the liberal free press. For many, even membership of the Order did not initially restrict their work, but from 1926 to 1928 they were increasingly supervised and standardized by Mussolini's Press Office. Initially concerned with news censorship, from 1933 to 1935 radio, motion pictures, tourism, music, theatre and literature were added to its brief. Renamed the Ministry of Fascist Propaganda, it became the Ministry of Popular Culture (MINCULPOP), in 1937.[33] Giving often imprecise instructions on what newspaper editors should and shouldn't publish, such as not criticizing football referees,[34] the Ministry expected the press to publish only positive news. While promoting the regime's achievements it played down negative stories, such as natural disasters, train crashes and sporting defeats.[35]

The mass media was naturally key in creating mythical and legendary sportsmen, especially through the Istutito LUCE's newsreel images and state radio. Following a huge programme of investment in the late 1920s, one in ten families had a radio subscription by 1938, with bars and *Dopolavoro* centres providing collective listening opportunities for those without. With sporting transmissions some of the most followed in the period, the commentator Nicolò Carosio became the voice of Fascist sport.[36] Above all, it was print journalism that aided and benefited the most from the sport boom, the sports press expanding to over one hundred different publications by the mid-1930s. In addition to the enlarged *La Gazzetta dello Sport* and the launch of the Rome-based *Il Littoriale* in 1929, which became CONI's official daily, a huge number of new, sport-specific and specialized magazines emerged, including CONI's monthly *Lo Sport Fascista*.

Encouraging literacy, the sports press socialized and united the masses around national successes, which were appropriated by the regime. As Benedict Anderson proposes in his study of the origins and spread of nationalism, print languages laid the bases for national consciousnesses by creating awareness of commonality and thereby stimulating an embryonic imagined community.[37] For this, the sports press was perfect. Not only was there an apparently endless source of victories and good news, it also had an enthusiastic, receptive, mass readership to repeatedly bombard with metaphors equating sporting struggles with real and imaginary Fascist battles. For the 'Soldiers of sport', 'Athletes of Fascism', 'sporting armies', 'squads', 'legions' and 'Mussolini's boys' there were 'battles', 'wars' and 'mobilizations'. As *Il Littoriale* informed, journalists needed: 'to uphold sport's role in the physical and moral improvement of the race, to penetrate the masses with propaganda and belief in the merits of sport, making... [it]... not an instrument of dissent but the cement of a national unity'.[38] Reporting in standardized Italian also assisted the spread and acceptance of the national language over dialect. Encouraging a means by which Milanese, Romans or Sicilians could communicate, the sports press increased awareness of their fellow countrymen with whom they shared a language while, at the same time, limiting this group to a finite figure and thereby, largely unconsciously, connecting readers to an imagined community.[39] Naturally, within this, the stellar athlete was Mussolini:

> I dedicate 30 to 45 minutes of the day to physical exercise and practise almost everything. I prefer swimming in the summer, skiing in the winter and horse-ride every day.
>
> I am familiar with all mechanical sports, from the bicycle to the motorbike, to the car and the aeroplane. Marching is also among my favourites. While my duelling is in the past, fencing is a perfect exercise to keep the body sharp.
>
> ...I have organized my activities from the perspective of the division of work, the struggle to avoid wasting energy and time. This explains my amount of work and lack of tiredness. I made my body a controlled and monitored engine that runs with absolute reliability.[40]

'We don't fear the accusation of servile homage if we say that Mussolini is Italy's first and most complete sportsman,'[41] asserted Lando Ferretti in 1930.

Embodying all that was supposedly Italian, Mussolini was photographed skiing, fencing, swimming, horse riding, motor cycling, flying or simply spectating. 'Let's look again at our Duce in the cockpit, at the wheel, on the springboard, riding, swimming: he is impetus, energetic, audacious,' implored Adolfo Cotronei. 'His thoughts remain sharp, his morale strong, his faith intact... despite giving his all as a superb athlete.'[42] The former *squadrista* (Fascist squad member) Nino Macellari was equally impressed: 'Muscles, nerves, respiratory system etc on one hand; intelligence and technical ability on the other; these are the elements that make the perfect sportsman.'[43] For others, such as Carlo Dall'Ongaro, Mussolini didn't even have to practise sport: 'He would have been a sportsman of thought, a sportsman of spirit.'[44]

Figure 4: *No sport troubles the* Duce

The image of Italy's number one was part of a wider development of his personality cult and the leadership principle. 'Elasticity. Speed. Strength. Courage. That is to say Mussolini! Exactly so! Italian sportsmen are worthy of their leader.'[45] Cementing their 'relationship', athletes often came to Mussolini's Rome residence – the Villa Torlonia. Eraldo Monzeglio, former captain of the national football team, coached tennis to his sons while, in 1932, the Grand Prix driver Tazio Nuvolari brought his Alfa Romeo, at the *Duce*'s request. As Filiberto, the protagonist in architect Pier Maria Bardi's 1936 motoring novel, *La Strada e il Volante*, described:

> It is our vow to always think of Mussolini... Pilots call him the first airman, motorcyclists the first motorcyclist, the cyclists that come to Rome in their thousands raise their bikes beneath the Palazzo Venezia's balcony and demand Mussolini the cyclist: everybody wants Mussolini as one of their own, with them, in the midst of them. It is the force of common spirit, the correspondence between the heart of the collective and heart of the leader.[46]

Mussolini's enthusiasm for being seen and photographed in athletic pose, often stripped to the waist, demonstrated his virility, plus that of the regime and the

Figure 5: *Tazio Nuvolari casts an admiring eye over the* Duce's *technique at the Villa Torlonia*

race. Introducing a new style of politics that John Hoberman terms 'political athleticism',[47] he contrasted with his democratic predecessors and other leaders, such as Austria's, thin, formally dressed Chancellor Dolphus, who Mussolini greeted on the beach at Ostia, near Rome, in 1933, dressed only in a pair of swimming trunks.

Even if the photographic evidence wasn't always that convincing, his virility was never questioned. Not only was Mussolini apparently never ill and his head shaved to avoid the issue of greying hair, neither his birthday nor his grandchildren were ever mentioned, in order to protect the vigour of the 'Prince of Youth'.[48] In fact, there was no mention of either his family life or his numerous affairs, the light burning permanently in his Palazzo Venezia office due to his incredibly long hours, rather than late-night liaisons. 'It's necessary to make way for the young', he said. 'Nobody is as old as he who is jealous of youth.'[49]

Football and fascism

Tie carefully knotted and trousers belted securely over an expansive midriff, it is difficult to assess the *Duce*'s dribbling in one of the few photos of him with a ball at his feet.[50] Strangely for Italy's number one sportsman, photos of Mussolini the footballer are almost non-existent. Given that *calcio* was a perfect metaphor for Fascism's idealized society, the *Duce*'s dislike of the game is unexpected. With a weekly calendar of matches drawing enormous crowds for two-thirds of the year, football was a Fascist marketing dream and its stadiums tailor-made for the diffusion of propaganda and the cultivation of strong myths and nationalism.

✪ ✪ ✪ ✪

In its 1930s golden era Italy played 63 matches, winning 45, drawing 12 and losing only six. It hosted and won the World Cup in 1934 before retaining it in France in 1938, with a team of university students winning the Olympic football tournament in Berlin, in 1936. At club level Bologna twice won the Central European Cup, before claiming the 1937 Paris Exhibition Tournament, where it crushed Chelsea and, apparently, 'shook the world'.[51]

The basis for this success was laid in 1926, when the Fascist Party reorganized, nationalized and politicized the game that had been lurching from one crisis to another since 1900.[52] With results regularly disputed, players and officials threatened by crowds, fan violence on the rise and the FIGC almost bankrupt, a referees strike forced the regime to take control of the nation's paralysed passion. The Viareggio Charter (*Carta di Viareggio*) revolutionized *calcio* by imposing a Fascist hierarchy upon the Football Federation (FIGC) that was now led by the former head of Bolognese Fascism, Leandro Arpinati.[53] Establishing a new statute, the most notable change was the formation of a national league, in 1929 – Serie A. Intensifying competition and raising standards, the improvement was almost immediate, with the emergence of teams like Juventus and Bologna dominating European competition. What the regime failed to appreciate, however, was how national competition would actually strengthen city-based, local identities built around their clubs. But if football was to unite Italy, there could be no place for such divisive rivalries, as the Florentine Fascist daily, *Il Bargello*, explained in 1929:

> Every football match between squads of nearby cities or from the same province has the seeds of an incident waiting to happen... Fascism and sport cannot tolerate this... In sport one can be an adversary but one must not be an enemy. We already have enough of this at the border.[54]

1930s Italian football demanded the characteristics that the regime wanted to build among Italians and display to the rest of the world, most notably the ability to battle and resist. The approach and image of Italy's coach or *commissario unico*, Vittorio Pozzo, reinforced Fascism's aggressive militarism and the leadership principle upon which Mussolini's rule was based. As Pozzo explained: 'The norms that govern the game impose the principle of authority, without which order cannot exist.'[55] An autocratic leader, his selection of a group of players that was stronger than the sum of its individual parts reflected Fascism's organic society in which talented individuals would selflessly dedicate themselves to the team.[56]

Blending survivors from the previous two triumphs with a number of debutantes, the victorious 1938 squad was living proof of Fascism's Futurist-inspired theory of racial regeneration through conflict, permanent change and the consistent introduction of new blood. Although Fascism was not driven by the desire to biologically purify the race, the exact nature of this new blood became an increasingly awkward issue. With five first-generation Italians from South America in the victorious 1934 squad,[57] these *oriundi* raised questions about the meaning and implications of joint nationality. When, in 1935, World Cup winner Enrico Guaita and two other AS Roma *rimpatriati* were stopped trying to leave the country with their considerable earnings, it wasn't so much their defection but their evasion of military service that offended, with a clear demonstration of patriotism considered more important than any biological 'purity'.

While footballers weren't necessarily expected to die for the nation, the will to confront death was the ultimate commitment for all Italians. On the way to Budapest in 1936, for a fixture against Hungary that Italy had never beaten away from home, Pozzo's team stopped off at the Redipuglia war cemetery on the Austrian border. Among the thousands of Italian war dead, speeches outlining the sacrifices of their forefathers and the responsibilities of the current generation to defend the nation's honour were said to have focussed the team. A 5-0 destruction of the Magyars duly followed

International competition and victories were naturally important, both domestically and abroad. If hosting the 1934 World Cup provided the opportunity to show the world how Fascist hard work and creativity had transformed Italy, its athletic elite would leave no doubt about the rejuvenation of the race, and its stadiums would demonstrate a genetic artistic and engineering genius. 'An event as colossal as this', *Lo Sport Fascista* declared, 'could only have been organized by Benito Mussolini's Italy.'[58]

With the chance to be the perfect host and send visiting teams and their supporters home with positive experiences, Italy enticed fans with subsidised travel to and within the country, while special stamps, match tickets, posters and cigarette packets, all featuring easily identifiable Fascist symbols, made it one of the first international sporting events to be seriously marketed, or propagandized. The second World Cup tournament and the first to be held in Europe, countries battled it out not just for the Jules Rimet trophy and the honour of being world champions, but also for the *Coppa del Duce* (The Duce Cup). A gaudy, huge bronze sculpture of footballers in action in front of the symbol of the regime – the *fasces* – it completed Fascism's highjacking of FIFA's tournament.

Mussolini's presence at matches, accompanied by his sons and various members of the hierarchy, only added to the excitement of Italy's progress towards the final, which was far from inevitable. Following the 1-1 quarter-final draw with Spain, Pozzo compared the dressing rooms to an infirmary, with only 11 of the original 22 players fit for the replay the following day. The final against Czechoslovakia was contested in the Fascist Party stadium in front of 50,000 spectators, including approximately 2,000 Czechoslovaks.[59] As the teams entered the stadium, the crowd waved handkerchiefs to the cries of '*Duce, Duce*', while the Militia band played a selection of Fascist hymns, which created the atmosphere of a political rally more than a sporting contest.

There is no evidence to support the conspiracy theories that Italy's victory was fixed. Home advantage has always had a heavy presence in the World Cup with Brazil, in 1950, the only host nation to reach and lose the final. The physically and tactically strong Italian side was also urged on by the fervent atmosphere and the *Duce*'s presence, naturally. A goal in extra time from Angelo Schiavio secured the title, after which the Italian players paid homage to the Fascist leadership in the stand. For their efforts, they were rewarded with the World Cup, the *Coppa del Duce*, a signed photograph of

Figure 6: *Fascist football sent to the world*

Mussolini and the Fascist *medaglia d'oro* (gold medal), one of the highest honours available. With the press reporting the triumph in the language of national struggle and football patriotism, the FIGC head General Vaccaro declared it an expression of the national will and the merits of collective organization and discipline, an indication of just what could be achieved if all Italians worked together.[60]

Crowds outside of Italy, however, were less enthralled by Fascism's political football. With Italian teams seen as representing the regime, playing abroad became an increasingly risky business as European political tensions rose. Coming soon after the collapse of Léon Blum's Popular Front government, towards which Mussolini had registered his disapproval by withdrawing Italian cyclists from the 1936 *Tour de France* and its footballers from an international match in 1937,[61] defending the nation's honour at the 1938 World Cup in France was a tense affair.

Arriving in Marseilles, squad member Ugo Locatelli recalled 3,000 or more French and Italian anti-Fascists being controlled by baton-wielding mounted police,[62] which contrasted with Italian accounts of a courteous reception by dignitaries.[63] Encountering protests throughout the tournament,[64] Italy were unpopular favourites. Drawn against Norway in the opening match, the Italian national team, nicknamed the *azzurri* (the blues) also took on an estimated 10,000 anti-Fascists and political exiles in the terraces. With all Italian teams compelled to give the Fascist Roman salute prior to kick-off, Pozzo recalled:

> As Commander, I knew exactly what was my, our duty... I enter the field with the squad militarily organised... as predicted, we were greeted by a solemn and deafening barrage of whistles and insults... We had just put down our hands when the violent demonstration started again. Straight away: "Team, be ready. Salute." And we raised our hands again, to confirm we had no fear... Having won the battle of intimidation, we played.[65]

Italy scraped a 2-1 victory and a place in the quarter-final against the hosts. The team were required to change shirts due to a colour clash, and the regime, apparently enraged by the reception in Marseilles, ordered them to play in all-black rather than its traditional change of white. The only occasion when the infamous *maglia nera* (black shirt) was worn, it was a clear two-fingered salute to the protestors. Thereafter, Italy's traditional blue shirts eased into the Final, where they gave one of the great displays in World Cup history to defeat Hungary 4-2 and retain the title. Celebrating the triumph, *Lo Sport Fascista* cast a greedy eye towards a third victory in 1942, but the golden generation was denied by war.

Standardizing sport

The class of 1938 was the first generation to have had an entirely Fascist education, with one of the regime's earliest reforms that of the education system, in 1923, as it sought to impose rigorous uniformity upon the nation's youth. Moving the provision of physical education from schools to the newly created National Body for Physical Education (*Ente Nazionale Educazione Fisica*), by 1926, Fascism had an almost complete monopoly over physical education with all non-Fascist sporting bodies for children disbanded, other than those belonging to the Catholic Church.

Although these were also repressed the following year, their survival indicates the delicate relationship between the two. For the Church and Pope Pius XI, Fascism's rise to power was both interesting and alarming, with Mussolini's declared will to negotiate substantial concessions in return for the Church's benevolence off-set by his anti-clericalism. The Vatican was thus cautious about openly declaring its support for the regime, especially while doubts about its longevity remained. Years in the making, the 1929 Lateran Accords were the final step in building a stable relationship between the two, which lasted until 1943.

Despite tightening its grip over society's health and bringing all sporting and physical education under its wing, Fascism's changes had limited success and, in 1927, the ENEF was absorbed by *Balilla*. With health and fitness now state concerns, the training of PE teachers assumed increasing importance and, in 1928, the ONB Farnesina Academy for Physical Education was opened in Rome. Despite the growth in graduates from 1,034 in the first year to 14,038 by 1936, there were still not enough to serve all elementary and middle schools whose rolls expanded dramatically. Nonetheless, 'it was the first link in a long chain, the engine in an entire totalitarian, technical-political educational system for the control of Fascist youth... If it had reached its most extreme ends it would have guaranteed the regime a block of educational experts motivated by one objective: to totally transform, in the Fascist sense, Italian youth.'[66]

Trainee teachers were either selected from the Fascist Party's youth ranks that had already met strict criteria, or from candidates that had passed the middle school leaving exam, a medical, and a technical assessment of their sporting ability. No expense was spared in the education of PE teachers, who studied Fascist mysticism, militarism, politics and law, in addition to medicine and sport science. Their teaching methods were based upon strict but enjoyable sport and physical education that would form strong, calm and audacious men. Uninterested in preparing sporting champions, which were only sought at a later stage, sport and physical education were mass pursuits for all. Following their three-year, total immersion, Farnesina graduates were sent to mould the 'new men' and citizen soldiers within the Party's youth groups, the armed forces and schools across the country.[67]

Inspired and driven by its patron Renato Ricci, the head of the *Opera Nazionale Balilla*, the construction of the Foro Mussolini complex, which included Farnesina, saw a completely new zone rise in Rome's periphery. Architecturally linking the regime with the Roman imperial past while establishing a vision of the new Fascist civilization, Mussolini's name was cut into a 400 tonne white marble obelisk that marked the entry to the Forum at the via Piazzale dell'Impero. The walkway was decorated with mosaics of classical and Fascist sporting and military scenes, with huge blocks of marble along each side recording the key events in Italy's modern, primarily Fascist history. Built at the foot of the Monte Mario hill where some blackshirts had rested during the March on Rome, the complex's centrepiece was the *Stadio dei Marmi*. Crowned by 60 statues of ancient and contemporary sporting figures that were designed to inspire, the stadium blended *romanità* (Romaness or Romanism) and modernism to form a distinct style that encapsulated the Fascist present.

While the *Duce* was portrayed as the embodiment of the idealized, national figure, the reality was that Italian Fascist identity was often a complex, contradictory mix. But so long as loyalty towards Fascism was not compromised, different identities and ideas were permitted and even encouraged. Preferring not to deal with the inevitable consequences of strict policies that excluded, the regime chose to be inclusive where and when possible. In this sense, sport and the diversity that it permitted and encouraged acted as a cultural safety valve by allowing the release of pressure and tensions that accumulated within society.

Sexual confusion

In 1932 an Academy was also launched for women, in Orvieto.[68] Trained in housework, health, hygiene, home economics and social discipline, graduates were similarly sent to schools across the country. Considered important preparation for motherhood, sport and physical exercise were included among their disciplines, even if Fascism was torn between directing women towards childbirth and its fear of international sporting embarrassment. This was one of the regime's toughest dilemmas: how to reconcile the idealized woman with the modern female athlete.

Convinced that size equalled domestic and international power, Mussolini demanded a large population. Financial assistance and tax reductions encouraged men to marry early and father numerous children, with taxes

Figure 7: *New Fascist Men,* Stadio dei Marmi *style*

Figure 7 (continued)

imposed upon bachelors. With motherhood of national importance, women became heroic Fascist figures, awarded medals of honour and incrementally increasing cash prizes from the fifth to the twentieth child. Unsurprisingly, Fascism's idealized woman was round, rural, and prolifically fertile.

✪ ✪ ✪ ✪

The regime's initially liberal approach to female sport is therefore surprising. With sport considered solely an expression of male strength and virility, those few female athletes who competed at international level received no financial support whatsoever. Despite this discrimination, it was impossible to completely exclude them. Pavia's young gymnasts won a higly impressive silver medal at the 1928 Antwerp Olympic Games,[69] after Alfonsina Strada had provided a striking example of a woman bucking the trend, in 1924, by completing the *Giro d'Italia*. Competing in road races and time trials since 1910, Strada experienced suspicion, misunderstanding and insults. An apparition from heaven or hell, a woman on a bicycle, in shorts, couldn't fail to draw attention. As the 1923 *Almanac for the Italian Woman* clarified: 'Sport... must be nourished solely to preserve, improve and perfect and not to "force" the body to dangerous excesses and ridiculous exaggerations.'[70]

Cycling was one of the few sports to continue during the First World War, with the 1917 Tour of Lombardy even running a few days after the calamitous defeat at Caporetto. A 'show of the country's calm and serenity',[71] according to *La Gazzetta*, the predominance of amateurs in what had been an entirely professional race, indicated how Italy's war was going. Intuitively sensing extra publicity for the event, race director Armando Cougnet welcomed Strada's request to ride. She completed the 204-kilometre tour, one-and-a-half hours after the Belgian winner Philippe Thys.

Despite finishing the race again in 1918, just one week after the end of the war when entrants were again minimal, Strada's big break didn't come until 1924, when she became the first woman to complete the *Giro d'Italia*. But while her entry was significant, the decision was purely commercial, with Cougnet and *La Gazzetta*'s editor Emilio Colombo exploiting her appeal after a number of bicycle manufacturers had withdrawn from the race following a dispute with the paper. Either a genuine mistake or a deliberate attempt to disguise Strada's entry in the hope of creating even more attention, few eyebrows were raised by the unknown amateur Alfonsin Strada of Milan. The missing 'a' on the end of her name would have established her gender immediately and helped the Bolognese newspaper *Il Resto del Carlino* avoid listing her as male competitor Alfonsino.

Beginning on 10 May 1924, Silvio Zambaldi noted 'a lively little woman' in the pack with a short baby-haircut and even shorter shorts, from which the hems of her jumper impertinently protruded. She pedalled with self-confidence and cheer, like a schoolboy playing truant. The public that lined the streets in the passing villages immediately noted her with exclamations of wonder, the women in particular, perhaps scandalized to see her like this... hardly representing their sex.[72]

Ending almost three weeks later on 1 June, the race covered 3,613 km along terrible roads, over 12 stages, in which time *La Gazzetta*'s publicity around the foreign body grew. 'In only two stages this little lady's popularity has become greater than all the missing champions put together.'[73] Intrigued observers awaited her often considerably late arrival, to applaud, encourage and insult her bare legs, which were banned by several prefectural orders under normal circumstances but permissible in the name of sport.[74]

Travelling deep into southern Italy, the riders encountered pot-holed, rock strewn roads and a passionate public that was increasingly enamoured by Strada. At the departure of the Rome–Naples stage: 'There was the usual hullaballoo around Alfonsina who arrived at the checkpoint in a new, bright outfit. This woman is becoming... famous. Yesterday some receptions were held in her honour. The good Romans gave her flowers, a new jersey and even a pair of earrings. She is radiant.'[75] Following that gruelling fourth stage, the heat, dust, and terrible roads worsened as the race went further south.

Planning to retire due to physical stress following her 15-hour completion of the Foggia–L'Aquila mountain stage, on 22 May, Strada was visited by Colombo, who gave her the small fortune of 500 lire, an apparent contribution from her fans.[76] Having persuaded her to continue, race rules were bent to avoid her disqualification for exceeding the maximum time allowed on one stage. From there onwards, such was her value to the paper that Colombo personally met Strada's hotel bills and provided her with a masseur. Of the 90 riders that started, only 30 officially finished, plus three that had exceeded the maximum time limit, including Strada, who arrived 28 hours behind the winner. It was a feat never previously attempted by a woman. Collecting cups, medals and donations, Strada is estimated to have earned up to 50,000 lire,[77] plus the affection of a previously hostile press.

In addition to a proposed meeting with Mussolini and an official communication from King Victor Emmanuel III, Strada was fêted by the Italian public and foreign journalists. The fruits of her labour, however, amounted to little more than some decent earnings and short-lived fame. Considering herself a 'professional' cyclist, Strada mistakenly believed that her success would secure her entry into other races. In 1925, with the dispute between the bicycle manufacturers and *La Gazzetta dello Sport* resolved, there was no need for publicity stunts. Colombo personally refused Strada's entry. So much for the paper's bold support the previous year:

> Alfonsina doesn't challenge anybody for victory, she just wants to show that even the weak sex can do the same as the strong sex. Might she be a vanguard for feminism that demonstrates its stronger capacity to demand the rights to vote in local or national elections?[78]

❂ ❂ ❂ ❂

Indicative of a changing wind in Italian sport, female athletes were increasingly discriminated against. 'Late to appreciate the importance of women's consent for the regime and the propagandistic support they could offer,'[79] Fascism's conservative about-turn was influenced by sport science and Church disapproval, with Pope Pius XI firmly opposed to Rome hosting a women's gymnastic competition, in 1928.[80] It was supported by the regime which, in 1930, asked CONI to 'review and organize female sporting activity... so as to avoid whatever might dissuade women from their fundamental mission; maternity'.[81] Luigi Gedda, who became the leading figure in the re-launch of post-war Catholic sport, added: 'A trial of strength between women is no less absurd than a beauty contest between men. The woman, if she really is one, will never seriously take up sport with the aim of breaking records.'[82]

Despite making the Orvieto Academy available to Italy's female athletes during their preparations for the 1936 Berlin Olympics, *Balilla* head Renato Ricci thought it ridiculous that 'women have to be called to defend the colours of a nation as strong and civilized as ours... Thus, I believe that women should be eliminated from the international sports field more than... they should be restricted to more modest limits on the sports field.'[83]

For average women, recommended physical exercise involved moderate gymnastics, tennis, roller-skating and dance, with swimming considered optimum as they apparently floated better and possessed a 'natural' obedience that made them more likely to follow instructions.[84] There were also cosmetic benefits, according to Goffredo Barbacci: 'Swim, go the pool... You will gain fitness and beauty, becoming statuesque women and then healthy mothers. Feel this need towards yourselves, towards us, towards the race that makes us proud and that we are proud to serve.'[85]

Lighter in their demands, such sports were considered helpful in developing physically robust girls who would become strong and courageous mothers. Citing an American educationalist, the regime's pre-eminent sports physician Giovanni Pini asserted that 'the intent of women's sport should not be to create champions and representative teams, but to complete, broaden and consolidate the physio-biological achievements of pre-athletic education.

Champions and those at representative level will be the exceptions.'[86] The remark, however, indicated Fascism's growing confusion. While attempting to restrict women to motherhood and the family home, it was pragmatic enough to realize that their involvement in sport could not be stopped.

Losing the 'battle for births', women's physical exercise was repackaged into a means of strengthening the body and spirit in preparation for childbirth which, by 1934, even the Church supported:

> It is absurd to think that sport might damage athletes' roles as mothers. There are many learned, foreign and Italian medical contributions to the argument; but what better documentation of these than the photos published here that show our athletes who have become good mothers, proud of their children that surround them? With this, we hope to have conquered at least some of the diffidence surrounding women's sport.[87]

The argument wasn't new, with the champion golfer, distinguished skier and swimmer, Isaline Crivelli-Massazza, having also espoused the merits of sport and exercise for pregnancy, in 1929:

> How many women have been unable to support the weight... [of the unborn child]... because of constitutional and growth weaknesses... when sport and the open-air life would have strengthened and prepared them for their divine function: maternity!
>
> Whoever says that sporting exercise for women strengthens the abdominal muscles that will support the weight of the baby, is right; it is extremely useful and advisable. Between a woman who has developed a strong and balanced body through sport, since childhood, and one that is too in love with salons or cities, it will always be the first that is more likely to bring a strong and robust creature into the world.[88]

Crivelli-Massazza's comments were a lightly disguised attack upon new, glamorous images of women appearing in US-influenced, commercial cultures of cinema and mass circulation magazines. Contrasting with round, rural, prolific mothers, these thin, single and desirable women were condemned as socially useless *donne crisi* (crisis women). Possessing a dangerous mass appeal, they required managing, which gave the glamorous Mimì Aylemer's participation in the *Mille Miglia* potentially serious implications. But, as she explained: 'Naturally, just because she likes motoring, there is no reason to forget that... [a woman]... is a woman. Let's leave the layers of clothing under leather jackets to the men. Even when driving, we must remain women, with all of the attractions we have.'[89]

Despite such opposition, a new and different woman emerged in the 1930s and not totally to the regime's disapproval: 'not necessarily a wife or mother but one inserted in social work and labour and not subordinate, at the service of Fascist womens organizations *alone*, as an apostle of the same regime'.[90] Another 'new woman' was the fit, healthy, *donna sportiva* and, with Fascism at the height of its popularity/consensus in 1936, Trebisonda 'Ondina' Valla became an inspiration for Italian women and a symbol of Fascist Italy at the Berlin Olympics.

Her participation with seven other female athletes was something in itself, given that no Italian women had gone to Los Angeles in 1932. As Valla later recalled: 'The crossing was expensive and as the only woman on a boat full of men, the Vatican did not approve.'[91] But Valla did more than just turn up in Berlin, she also won. Most embarrassing for the regime that had invested heavily in the male squad, her 80m hurdles world-record-equalling victory was Italy's only athletics gold of the Games. Having dedicated her victory to the Motherland and female Italian sport, she was congratulated by the Pope, photographed with Mussolini and awarded the Fascist Gold Medal.

The regime was still pragmatic enough to appreciate that a number of select, successful sportswomen marketed a strong Fascist Italy abroad. Even better news was the birth of Valla's first child, which removed the question marks that appeared to have been deliberately placed over her sexuality[92] while further demonstrating the compatibility of sporting competition and maternity, not just in terms of the physical fitness of mother and child but also in patriotic spirit. As Valla's coach Marina Zanetti had rhetorically asked: 'Who can say what sense of patriotism will be infused in the children of a young mother, by the memory of her blue-shirt and sporting adolescence that throbs with nostalgia and enthusiasm?'[93]

Yet the success of Valla and her team mates, who also claimed fourth place in the 4×100m relay, drew moderate press coverage. CONI's official report on Italy's 1936 tournament failed to mention her gold medal, while one journalist hoped to see her at the next Games in Tokyo, purely on honeymoon.[94] If successful women athletes were good for the regime, the risk of excessive liberation was too high to let them run unchecked. Fascism's snubbing of Valla's achievement indicated its uncomfortable relationship with women in general.

While Valla projected an idealized Superwoman, for ordinary women little changed, as Dedy Baldi unwittingly demonstrated in *Lo Sport Fascista*, in 1939:

> First and foremost, the woman has to maintain harmonious feminine proportions, look after her health and remember that more than breaking a record or deserving sporting admiration, she has been entrusted with the

mission of being healthy and beautiful, to give healthy and beautiful children to the Motherland.[95]

She was backed in 1940 by the physician Giuseppe Poggi-Longostrevi, whose support for women's sport was still based upon its reproductive benefits. 'Physical exercise is one of, if not the only efficient means of protecting... [the reproductive organs]... contrary to those who accuse it of diminishing the capacity for procreation.'[96]

If Valla had become an ambassador for the regime, promoting an apparently healthy and emancipated society, the vast majority of Italian women remained restricted to basic physical activities that preserved their Latin female grace and modesty. Even if sport did create the occasional wonderwoman, she was still playing by the old rules.

Primo Carnera: man superman or fascist fraud?

The obvious Fascist superman was heavyweight boxer Primo Carnera. Standing 6'7" (2.01m) tall and weighing nineteen-and-a-half stones (125 kg), Carnera's career began in American fairgrounds, where he was hugely popular among expatriate Italians. As much as his punch, it was his capacity to connect with the Italian diaspora and entertain in depression-era America that interested Fascism in the 1930s. Examined by *Lo Sport Fascista*'s favourite physician Giovanni Pini, in 1930, rumours of Carnera's enormous appetite were refuted. Instead, his apparently parsimonious diet and discipline of character were an example to the nation:

> The other side of Carnera is that he is docile, observant of the rules drawn up for him, he appreciates and loves his instructor and obeys him in all of the minor details because he has faith in him or because he has seen the benefits he has given him and has a profound belief in attaining the best results. He doesn't thus think it illogical that from their collaboration... comes an exceptional success.[97]

In austerity Italy it reflected the *Duce*'s apparently meagre diet that theoretically kept the mind sharp and the body in shape:

> In the morning, a cup of milk.
> At 14.00 a steak, an omelette or a little boiled fish and some vegetables...
> Sometimes an apple or a pear. Never dessert.

La Domenica Sportiva

Lo Sport Illustrato

Settimanale illustrato de "La Gazzetta dello Sport"

ANNO XX - N. 28 - MILANO, 9 LUGLIO 1933-XI - CENT. 60 - C. C. POSTALE

LO SPORT E LA BANDIERA.

Primo Carnera, campione del mondo di pugilato dopo la clamorosa vittoria per k. o. su Sharkey, ha dichiarato di aver vinto per l'Italia fascista e per il Duce. Primo Carnera leva in alto il tricolore d'Italia. - *A lato*: Le... buone disposizioni atletiche di Primo Carnera prima dell'incontro con Sharkey.

Figure 8: *Primo Carnera, in happier times*

The evening, at 22.00, some fruit and a glass of milk. Nothing more. No concession to gluttony...

But Mussolini is not only habitually frugal; once or twice a month he undertakes a complete fast for 24 hours in which he drinks nothing but sugar water...

If all Italians followed the Duce's example – with exception made for manual labourers that need solid nourishment – the country would suddenly rejuvenate and gain enormously in intellectual production.[98]

Following a politically and biologically healthy lifestyle and performing the Roman salute more often and vigorously than necessary, Carnera appeared an obvious figure for Fascist exploitation. His first big win, in 1933, created huge fame and highlighted his marketing potential. After being knocked out in the thirteenth round, in New York, his opponent, Ernie Schaaf, entered a coma before dying three days later. Although absolved of all blame by the New York state governor – Schaaf's autopsy indicating brain damage from a previous bout, six months earlier – the devastated Carnera attained an element of freak-show appeal.

In the build up to his world heavyweight title fight with Jack Sharkey later that year, Carnera became a Fascist flag bearer, with newspapers and newsreels capturing him with the Party hierarchy, keen to cash in on his popularity. The effect was significant, according to the weekly *l'Illustrazione Italiana*:

He returned to America to meet Sharkey with a renewed spirit, transformed in some way that you don't see but always counts a lot: in spirit. Here among us, he breathed the air of his country, illuminated by enthusiasm and rich in strength and youth, as it is today... This is why Carnera came back to America transformed. He brought with him a promise made to the leader... He won due to his vigour, the strength of his muscles, his increased experience, but he also won because he bore in his heart a symbol that does not admit defeat: the sign of the Littorio.[99]

Knocking out Sharkey in the sixth round, Carnera became Italy's first and only world heavyweight champion. Despite Fascism having done almost nothing for him, Carnera celebrated the victory with a Roman salute. The first telegram he sent was to his mother and the second to Mussolini: 'Delighted to have kept the promise, bringing the heavyweight title to Fascist Italy, we send your Excellency unlimited feelings of devotion...' Hungry for national triumphs, especially in a sport that suggested Italians could finally fight, the regime devoured Carnera's dedication. Mussolini replied: 'Express my deep pleasure to Carnera and tell him that all of Fascist and sporting Italy is proud that a Blackshirt is a world boxing champion.'[100] Echoing the reporting of Enrico Porro's victory in 1908, Adolfo Cotronei recalled: 'Carnera has confirmed our skill, definitively consecrating the esteem of the Latin athlete. And in the country of ultra powerful and outstandingly strong champions, he was the unbeatable giant... [who]... surprised experts and the ignorant with his intelligent aggression.'[101]

Carnera's return to Italy was fully exploited by the regime. Exultant after one of many interviews conducted by radiophone with Carnera at sea, *La Gazzetta* connected the heavyweight's success with 'the genius of Marconi that has accustomed us to the feats of the human voice that is stronger than space, which crosses seas, mountains, continents'.[102] Conquering the elements and the earth was a familiar Fascist claim, through aviation, mountaineering and motor racing. Between 1929 and 1936 Carnera travelled between Europe, the USA and South America over 20 times, his voyages tapping into an escapist fascination in travel while further cementing his mythical status. His embarkations and arrivals attracted huge crowds and, on reaching Naples in 1933, his dockside press conference, in which he dedicated his belt to the regime, was followed by a bout with a kangaroo.

His title defence in Rome was Fascism's first great sporting propaganda opportunity; not just to associate itself with a success story and create a national, collective experience, but to demonstrate its modernization of Italy and capacity to organize big events. For the bout with the Spaniard Paulino Uzcudun, the Piazza di Siena equestrian showground, in Rome's Villa Borghese, was transformed into an arena for 70,000 spectators, who came from across the country on subsidised trains. The *Duce* arrived ten minutes before the start, accompanied by his sons and Party Secretary Starace. *La Gazzetta* recorded the moment:

> Bareheaded, with skin bronzed by the sun, agile, athletic, Mussolini is an image of strength, of youth, he is truly the first sportsmen among all Italians...
>
> The applause that greets him, and gets confused among the hymns and shouts, erupts uncontrollably at the highest level. The clear shout from 70,000 mouths, Du-ce, Du-ce!... lasts for minutes and becomes almost frenetic when the Head of Government responds by repeatedly raising his arm in a Roman salute.[103]

With the crowd whipped into frenzy, Carnera entered the ring and removed his dressing gown to reveal a military blackshirt, before turning to salute Mussolini. Winning in the 15th round, he donated his prize money to the '*Pro Opere Assistenzitalia*', which organized Fascist welfare projects. It was, according to Emilio Colombo, 'a noble sporting gesture, a Fascist gesture'.[104]

A technically limited boxer whose main assets were his size and force, Carnera's time as champion was brief. A few days after Italy won the football World Cup in 1934 he was battered by Max Baer in New York, knocked out in the 11th round. With Carnera on his back, the image of a vigorous, combative new nation took a body blow too, the defeat shattering the myth of the Fascist Superman and creating domestic shock at what many had been encouraged to believe was impossible. Worse came on 25 June 1935 when he lost to boxing's rising black star Joe Louis. With Mussolini contemplating the invasion of Abyssinia, the last thing he needed was defeat to a black man when war was justified by the superiority of the white race.

The issue had already been flagged by Fascist Italy's own black champion, Leone Jacovacci.[105] Born in the Congo to an Italian father and Congolese mother, Jacovacci grew up in Rome, and so strong were his roots that his bout with the Milanese Mario Bosisio, on 24 June 1928, for the national and European middleweight titles, provoked a spat between the cities' newspapers. The first black Italian to win a sporting title of any sort, his victory was questioned as suspect by the Fascist press before a more outright racism emerged. 'He is perhaps far from my Latin spirit', wrote Adolfo Cotronei, 'even if I know he is precisely and uncontestably Italian. I am a diehard fanatic of my race and for a peculiarity of my spirit I can't see or love it other than with the lightest of colours, and my psyche doesn't appreciate all the shadows and black.'[106] He continued the following day: 'Neither is revoking his nationality in question. Instead, it appears a purely spiritual issue: our reluctance to put white and black on the same level. It is a passion of the race. The athlete, with his virtues, competitive style, his values, is beyond discussion.'[107] Following two defeats in 1928, in his article titled 'Jacovacci, the imperfect boxer', Beppi Negri was quick to identify his weakness. 'The sluggishness and laziness that he demonstrates in life never leave him, not even in the ring.'[108]

With Jacovacci's story indicating the stirrings of racism, Carnera's later defeat to Louis was so devastating that Minculpop ordered no photos be published of him on the canvas.[109] So serious was the loss that any previous concerns about Baer's Judaism were forgotten. 'Max Baer the last standard bearer of the white race against the threat posed by the negro Louis,' *La Gazzetta* warned.[110]

Carnera continued to contest minor bouts, but was increasingly restricted by the regime. On 13 December 1937, 'given the results of recent bouts contested by the boxer Primo Carnera, in Paris and Budapest, the Italian Boxing Federation has forbidden... [him]... from carrying out his activity outside of Italy until further orders.'[111] Despite the almost blanket ban on press coverage, his defeat to a Yugoslav gypsy was another huge embarrassment, after which newspapers gave him no further space.

Boxing for free in the Piazza di Siena, in front of Mussolini and the Fascist hierarchy, Carnera made even short, still undernourished Italians feel like supermen; one short bald one, in particular. Yet, referring to doubts that had dogged Carnera since his earlier naturalization as a French citizen, which he later relinquished, *La Gazzetta*'s Adolfo Cotronei argued on more than one occasion that Carnera really didn't represent the archetypal Italian athlete:[112]

> We admire his courage, loyalty, patriotism. If he brings such virtues into the *ring* he will be world champion. But the ex-lumberjack couldn't really be one of ours, he couldn't be Italian: he was too big, too round, too much in the body and too little in the mind. So mentally lacking that he chose France as his country, ignoring the beauty and grace of the Latin race.[113]

His image did, however, suit the idealized Italian male, whose masculinity was measured in strength and virility. But having surpassed the 'standard', within four years the Man Superman became a Fascist flop. Unable to serve the regime's needs, he was unceremoniously discarded. Yet closer consideration might have questioned whether he really constituted the *Italiano nuovo*, and it is hard to imagine that signs of gigantism, flat feet and visible varicose veins featured in the ideal. His dwarfing of the average Italian might also have prompted reflection as to whether such a figure was an appropriate and realistic example to aspire to. Yet, as Aldo Santini suggests, he was in fact a perfect symbol for a nation that puffed out its chest to intimidate adversaries and a regime that deluded itself as a great power, embodying the myth of strength which, at the decisive moment, Italy showed it didn't possess.[114]

Ferrari

More than just physical power, Fascist supermen required tactical and moral strength too. Battling opponents and the elements in conjunction with machines on land, sea and air, Fascism loved the cocktail of speed, risk and danger. In July 1933, Italo Balbo led a squadron of 25 sea-planes on the 'cruise of the decade', crossing the Atlantic from Rome to New York, Chicago and back again. Recorded by LUCE, it was one of many epic voyages in which Fascism conquered ocean and space. In 1925 Francesco De Pinedo flew Rome–Tokyo–Melbourne–Rome; Francesco Agello set a new air-speed record in 1933; the steamer *Rex* claimed the blue riband for the fastest Atlantic crossing; and on terra firma, racing drivers pushed Italian engineering to the limit.

The prancing horse that became the symbol of Ferrari was originally painted on the plane of First World War fighter pilot Francesco Baracca. Shot down over Montello, northern Italy, legend has it that Baracca's mother suggested that Enzo Ferrari put her son's emblem on his cars, for good luck, after he won his first race in 1923. While the horse remained black, Ferrari claimed to have added Modena's yellow to the background. True or otherwise, it became a powerful symbol of post-war Italian manufacturing.

❂ ❂ ❂ ❂

The 1920s saw a huge increase in the interest in motor racing, as Alfa Romeo, Maserati and Bugatti overtook the sport's former leaders of Sunbeam, Peugeot, Renault and FIAT. While ordinary roads were still hosting city-to-city races and tours like the *Mille Miglia*, new tracks were also being built, such as Monza's Royal Park, which created a demand for cars that outstripped supply. Demobilized after working as a driver during the First World War, Ferrari had few skills and little employment experience. Rejected by FIAT's racing programme, he worked for a small garage in Turin testing reconditioned Lancia truck chassis being prepared for conversion into passenger vehicles.

His racing career began in 1919, contesting hill climbs in his own CMN touring car before participating in the *Targa Florio*, a hair-raising time trial around the villages of Sicily's Madonie Mountains. Employed as a junior member of the Alfa Romeo team, he mixed with the drivers and mechanics that would shape the sport in the inter-war years. Expanding his involvement with Alfa Romeo into the entrepreneurial side of the business he launched his first enterprise, the *Carrozzeria Emiliana*, in 1923. Effectively an Alfa salesman, Ferrari established his business roots in the Modena region, exploiting his local fame as a driver to sell sports cars to the affluent. As his racing career dwindled he made plans to form his own team, securing financial backing from two customers over dinner in Bologna's Fascist Headquarters. On 1 December 1929, the *Società Anonima Scuderia Ferrari* was born.

Based in Modena, with its skilled metal workers, Ferrari's early masterstroke was involving the tyre manufacturer Pirelli and Alfa Romeo in its production. Fully aware of the impact such a racing team could have upon its sales, but uninterested in maintaining one itself, the deal was perfect for Alfa – it could maintain its racing profile through Ferrari (which was never considered a commercial rival) in return for shares in the Ferrari business along with Pirelli. For the *Scuderia*, there was a small injection of capital from each company plus their tools, technical cooperation and know-how. Ferrari developed further successful deals with other essential parts providers, such as Bosch, Weber and Shell in an early experiment with trade sponsorship.

With a passion for fast, flamboyant drivers, Ferrari attracted Tazio Nuvolari to the team in 1930. Not content with victories and press coverage alone, he proactively publicized the team's achievements through lavish dinners and what became a tradition of brochures, which began with the stylishly photographed *Due Anni di Corse* (Two Years of Racing), in 1931. Sent to sponsors, customers and associates, the innovation grew to include advertisements and endorsements. In 1933, it also began using the Italian Fascist calendar, which declared 1922 as year one. As the regime became more militaristic and the Great Depression bit into Alfa's profits, Ferrari was forced to focus on government demands for military vehicles before being taken over by the state's Institute for Industrial Reconstruction, a type of nationalization scheme to protect companies in danger of bankruptcy. After suspending its racing involvement, Alfa refused to let Ferrari compete with its cars, leaving him to continue with his own, ageing fleet.

Encouraged by Fascism's desire to compete with state-assisted German manufacturers, Alfa returned to racing in 1937. Resuming its previous working relationship with Ferrari, Alfa bought 80 per cent of the company's stock and sent one of its most experienced engineers to manage the team. Italian manufacturers remained uncompetitive, however, and on 1 January 1938 the *Scuderia Ferrari* was wound up by Alfa Romeo. Taking control of its own racing affairs, Enzo Ferrari moved to Milan to run the new Alfa Corse team. Well remunerated, his contract dictated that on leaving Alfa he would be unable to form a new company under his own name for four years.

Sacked in 1939, Ferrari returned to Modena and used his compensation to form *Auto-Avio Costruzioni*. With a staff that quickly expanded to 40 employees, the company manufactured primarily aircraft parts. Italy's entry into the war was a real opportunity for the new business, which began making grinding machines for the manufacture of ball-bearings which were stamped with the *Scuderia Ferrari* name and logo. A contract with the Milanese Breda factory that made guns, military vehicles and aircraft saw the Ferrari coffers swell. As the war and bombings intensified, the factory left central Modena for safety. Eighteen kilometres south of the town, Ferrari bought a farm where the new factory was built. Few of the Maranello's 6,000 inhabitants could have imagined that a global legend had arrived.

Planes, bikes and autarchy-mobiles

According to Lando Ferretti, there was more to the regime's obsession with machines and speed than simply sport and adventure:

> Think about... the war of tomorrow, not a war that we want but one that may be forced upon us by destiny: transport lorries, motorbikes to deliver orders behind the front lines... torpedo boats on the sea... engines

that roar in the sky and take the slaughter to the enemy far from our homes. Thus, engines on the ground, in the air and on the sea... that are perfected in sporting competition... These engines, however, are also of use in peace: in the battles for grain and quicker transport for all, and in the noble effort to raise the tone of our economic life and to multiply the fruits of labour.[115]

The *Coppa della Mille Miglia* (One Thousand Miles Trophy) was a motor race from Brescia, near Milan, down to Rome and back again. The course changed annually and covered roughly 1,600 kilometres or one thousand miles. Run over 24 hours, the regular deaths of drivers and spectators as cars hurtled along muddy or dusty, pot-holed, untarmaced roads that were open to the public and occasionally blocked by livestock, conjures the image of a Fascist 'Canonball Run' or 'Wacky Races'. With the curious Italian habit of driving on the left in towns and on the right in the countryside only abandoned in 1926, when Turin and Milan came into line with the rest of country, it is perhaps surprising that the race was as organized as it actually was.

Conceived in 1926 by four racing enthusiasts who wanted to restore Brescia's reputation as a centre of motor sport, the race stimulated government and industry into action. Just like the *Giro d'Italia*, motor racing demonstrated car reliability, with manufacturers and drivers vying for glory, money and markets. It was, as *La Stampa*'s correspondent noted in 1923:

> a curious disguise of business... More than the exponents of a given amount of human energy, today's champions are the representatives of a given industrial formula, a fact of commercial shares.... You go onto the track not so much to enjoy yourself as to work, to establish the excellence of a brand of tyres, of an engine, of a wheel, of a wheel hub.[116]

Although not a Fascist creation, the *Mille Miglia* ran thanks to the regime, which duly exploited it: 'In no country in the world', proclaimed *Lo Sport Fascista*, 'does motor sport offer such a great spectacle of passion, courage and enthusiasm, as the *Mille Miglia* trophy. It is Fascism that has made this wonder possible.'[117] Party Secretary Achille Starace was the race's patron, with some Fascist leaders even participating: Leandro Arpinati retired from the 1927 event with a broken arm, following a crash at a level crossing; Mussolini's driver, sons and nephew also took part, while the *Duce* was member number one of the Italian Automobile Club.

No other sport contained so much risk and danger. Demanding bravery, resolution, cold blood and a will to face death, motor racing offered a direct route to Fascist glorification.[118] An epic event, heroic in scale and execution, with villagers lighting flares at the approach to their communities and Fascists holding flaming torches on dangerous bends, it captured the public's imagination and honed the new Fascist man. As the journalist Emilio De Martino wrote in *Mille Miglia*, one his many sport-based novels published during the Fascist era: 'Racing in a car was a decisive trial. The fearful and timid cannot test themselves. Who takes the wheel in a race is a man, a true man able to confront all the responsibilities and risks of life with his head held high.'[119] Amidst the race's furious progress the novel's hero Giorgio Ratti matured:

> Now I am a man... now I begin to understand. Now there's a completely different horizon ahead of me. My life... starts right now, in the decisive moment. Giorgio Ratti is no longer the same person, and do you know why? Because the test we overcame has shown us our strength and our true value as men and drivers, it has created a new faith based on a confidence in ourselves.[120]

Soon after, Ratti left to support Franco's troops in the Spanish Civil War, reflecting how De Martino regularly used his sporting novels to impart a moral education for readers of all ages.

With death often closer than victory, champions such as Tazio Nuvolari and Achille Varzi were easily repackaged into heroes. 'Nuvolari is a young-mature, very brave Mantovan Blackshirt... Fascist bravery. Fascist heart. Fascist courage. Tazio! We Roman salute with complete fraternity, this brother who goes at 133 kph! Towards all tests. Towards all victories.'[121] 1933 was a disastrous year for the sport with nine driver deaths, including four Italians who took the nation's post-1918 tally into double figures.[122] Yet, according to *Lo Sport Fascista*, progress required sacrifices.[123] 'When misfortune strikes, however serious or painful, it must be accepted, with solid heart, as a necessity that cannot be removed.'[124] There was, however, no way of glorifying the deaths of ten members of the public, including seven children, after a Lancia ploughed into a crowd of spectators at a popular viewing point near Bologna, in 1938. Too grave for even the compliant media to suppress, the incident forced the government to suspend and then ban the *Mille Miglia*. With neither the state nor the event organizers able to claim road reliability, it was the end of the race's pre-war era.

Often seen on the victory podium with his arm aloft in a Roman salute, it is frequently presumed that Nuvolari was a Fascist, despite the gesture's compulsion for all sportsmen. Unlike Carnera, however, Nuvolari was no one-hit wonder but a consistently successful driver whose rivalry with Varzi divided the nation, just as the regime liked. Nuvolari's fans were more numerous and strangely working class given his aristocratic landowning roots, with the bourgeoisie tending to back Varzi.[125]

Nuvolari's reputation and national appeal were built around skill, courage and myths. As a driver in the First World War he was rebuked by an officer for his fearless negotiation of mountain roads. Graduating from Bianchi motorcycles, he drove his first *Mille Miglia* in 1927. At the peak of his powers he was said to have completed one race with no steering wheel, controlling the car with a spanner, and another in Berlin with one leg in plaster. One of the greatest legends was his 1930 night-time pursuit of Varzi, without lights, only to dramatically turn them on as he overtook his rival. Occurring at 6.30–7a.m., in good weather, in April, it is unlikely that Varzi was unable to see Nuvolari behind him or that either of them had needed lights for some time. Equally, with the *Mille Miglia* a time trial, Nuvolari was already ten minutes ahead. Truth, however, was never enough to spoil a good story. The first driver to win with an average speed of 100kph, despite technological advances making this inevitable, he still smashed a great psychological barrier. Capturing headlines and hearts, Nuvolari was a national hero.

Celebrating Italian victories, the motor industry was presented as an organic body. Recalling Giulio Masetti's debut race, Lando Ferretti described how: 'In that moment [he] was not the representative of a single industry; he was the representative of the entire nation, of all Italian passions.'[126] Creating the National Fascist Union of Professionals and Employees in the Sporting Industries (*Unione Nazionale Fascista dei Professionisti e Addetti alle Industrie Sportive*), workers were included in this organic enterprise, 'no longer disperse and amorphous elements but well-defined cells of a healthy and powerful organism'.[127] Fundamentally anti-working class, Fascism was keen to give the illusion of including factory workers, whose support or benevolent neutrality was critical in increasing production. Regularly praised for their part in the construction process, in 1922 over 100,000 went to the Monza Grand Prix to celebrate the opening of the new track, with a further 200,000 attending the following year. With motor racing representing Italy's organic potential, even the presence of only three foreign competitors, in 1934, could not dent Emilio Colombo's pride in Varzi's victory, in an Alfa on Pirelli tyres:

> They triumphed together: athletes, engines, wheels, the most Italian accessories. And the *Mille Miglia*, a genuine expression of organizational maturity, of discipline, of the undisputable maintenance of the road network, the ingenuity of industry and the undeniable bravery of Fascist Italy's drivers, has reconfirmed its highest technical value, strength of appeal, the propagandistic esteem that distinguishes and characterises it from any other event.[128]

This organic ethos was also how Enzo Ferrari ran his factory, even if his management techniques occasionally resembled those of the *Duce*.

Ferrari, however, did not contest the *Mille Miglia* in the pre-war period, when the race became a hugely important feature of the Italian sporting calendar. With cars roaring through villages and historic cities, crossing mountains, passing basilicas, paddy fields and olive groves, single-issue magazines, maps and timetables contrasted the ancient landscape with modern Fascist machinery and encouraged the public to recognize and embrace the regional differences that had been century-long sources of division. It also encouraged Italian car owners to use the new road network and not travel abroad, as Filiberto proposed in Bardi's 1936 motoring novel:

> Enjoy the road: the Italian road is the most beautiful theatre in the world. When you have the strange idea of travelling abroad, ask yourself what are the Italian regions that you don't already know and head for those parts. The car must help you to work and when you need it for pleasure, it can be your companion in visiting Italy. Previously, Italians went red if they were forced to confess that they had never seen Paris: today... he who blushes is forced to confess to having never visited the Bonifiche.[129]

As originally intended, the Italian Touring Club's annual *Guide to Italy* showed 'the role that the various localities. represented and represent in [Italian] history and life', from its geology, agriculture and industry to the various costumes of the people. It was equally important that this was done in-house:

> One is talking of 'freeing Italians... from visiting their country, guided by foreigners, which is to say... substituting Baedeker that ruled uncontested'. Always keen on generating tourist income, 'the Guide to Italy naturally couldn't remain to the exclusive benefit of Italians. It also needed an Italian inspired... [version]... for the numerous foreigners that come to admire our country.'[130]

French, English and German editions duly appeared. Making its contribution to tourism, the 1931 *Mille Miglia* added the Marche coastal resorts of Porto Recanati and Ancona to the route.

Developing an awareness of the country's vastness and complexity, the increasing speed with which the race was completed also reduced Italy's perceived size, thanks to the developing road network upon which collective life was based. Road improvements, the close involvement of the ministries with the local organs of the state in its organization, plus the 1927 creation of a street police, also enabled Fascism to extend its machinery of control deep into society. As the foreign motorist unwittingly noted in Bardi's novel:

> Do you think that your old prime ministers knew Italy as well as Mussolini? I am an automobile fanatic, but I tell you, the car is an instrument of good government. Mussolini travels around more of Italy in one month... than his predecessors did in ten years.[131]

As *Lo Sport Fascista* concurred, Fascism's enthusiasm for cars related to their pacifying potential:

> One of the most reassuring factors... for social order in France is the number of cars on the road: almost a million... [second behind]... America. It is admirable! Because whoever buys a car, even the smallest one available, immediately becomes antirevolutionary... There will not be a revolution in America because each worker drives his Ford. One million cars on the road represent a social guarantee.[132]

Thus, if the affordable car brought the embourgoisement of the working class, its popularization was the key to a more direct collaboration with the masses. In effect, the 'right to buy' a car would bring motorists behind the regime. 'Rather than a sign of American affluence', Mussolini argued, 'we need to see the motor car as the reagent of American society, the disinfectant that protects against Bolshevik intoxication.'[133] As Filiberto explained to the foreign visitor in Bardi's novel: 'Italian motorists are among the happiest of all, because they lack nothing: great factories, race victories, a continually growing spread of cars, great streets, a mechanical spirit, traffic police and whatever else the man travelling by road might hope for.'[134]

The regime's road-building programme was huge in ambition and scale. Motorways connecting the north and south were spanned by impressive arched bridges that provided jobs and showcased Italian engineering. Directly alluding to the *Vie Consolari* that connected the entire peninsula from the ancient capital, the Fascist network continued the regime's self-association with the Roman Empire. Opening the Milan–Laghi autostrada, Mussolini stated: '"Motorways are a great Italian advance and a certain sign of our constructive power, not unworthy of the ancient sons of Rome".'[135]

It was also hoped that improved roads and exciting races would translate into car sales. Despite popular memory recalling the *Mille Miglia* being contested by great drivers in Ferraris and Maseratis, in most years the vast majority of entries were small FIAT saloons and specials driven by amateurs, exactly as Nando Minoia, the winner of the inaugural race, suggested:

> I am of the opinion that all races should be on the road and the cars equipped as they would be when consigned to clients. In this way... important lessons can be learnt to help eliminate all of those faults that clients often complain about.[136]

Representing Fascism in duels with Porsche and Mercedes, Italian engineering struggled to keep pace with its German rival, with Nuvolari's win in the 1935 German Grand Prix, at the *Nürburgring*, the pinnacle of Fascist Italy's motor racing success. Driving an Alfa, he not only passed his rival Varzi, who had earlier moved to Mercedes, but did so in front of a Nazi hierarchy anticipating a German victory. With the Italian motor industry unable to compete long-term, Nuvolari also moved to German manufacturers in the search of success.

Foreign entrants to the *Mille Miglia* continued to be encouraged and, in 1933, the driver, engineer, journalist and Count of Calvezano, Giovanni 'Johnny' Lurani, persuaded the British MG team to enter, which was received by the King, Mussolini and the British Ambassador after its victory in the 1100cc class. Despite such enthusiasm, few foreign teams entered and from 1935 the race became an almost entirely Italian event.

Contributing to the image of national sporting and industrial superiority, the *Mille Miglia* held importance in the regime's battle for self-sufficiency, which gained a real purpose after the League of Nations imposed sanctions following Italy's invasion of Abyssinia, in 1935. While these did not extend to coal or petrol, the regime's anxiety about its oil supplies was already stimulating the exploration of alternative energy. Welcoming cars running on substitute fuels, the *Mille Miglia* included an Alfa powered by a charcoal burner, as early as 1933. Producing a form of gas, the car stopped ten times during the 1,650km race, which it completed in twenty-five-and-a-half hours, some ten-and-a-half behind the winner. Spun into a great success and with a special class for substitute fuelled cars introduced in 1936, the reality was they remained uncompetitive. Some were put on the mass market, but this primitive, alternative energy never rivalled petrol. Despite the experiments not continuing much beyond 1936, the *Mille Miglia* maintained its reputation as a race of 'national resistance' and 'anti-sanctions'.

Camouflaging and distracting from reality, in many respects the *Mille Miglia* represented much of what Fascist sport was about and how, despite its huge range of success, this was still never enough. While the regime's propaganda drive was unquestionably boosted by its athletes, cars and stadiums, the only significantly enduring feature of its politicization of sport, beyond the bricks and mortar, was its demonstration of arguably the easiest easy route into the hearts, minds and homes of Italian society. Unable to paper over a failing economy, destroyed civil liberties and reduced standards of living, sport was already identified as a key battleground in the fight to control post-war Italy.

From the **Duce** *to De Gasperi*

Despite Fascism drilling an entire generation, Italians refused to become military-minded. With the armed forces also woefully equipped, Mussolini entered the Second World War only after the Nazi blitzkrieg of northern Europe and the invasion of France, in May 1940, intensified his fear of missing out on the spoils. An opportunity to gain control of the Mediterranean, there was the prospect of doing so in the glorious, aggressive style that Fascist ideology and rhetoric demanded. Repeating its message from 1915, *La Gazzetta* called its readers to arms:

> A large and stupendous multitude of sportsmen already have the honour of the first line of battle. Others are preparing to reach their comrades. They went... and they will go with the flame of resolution, serenity and enthusiasm in their blood that erupts from the breeding ground of sport.[1]

The reality, however, was different, with only one and a half million volunteering for mobilization.[2]

War, resistance and liberation

The outbreak of war had a limited impact upon Italian sport and with perfect timing, the young conscript Fausto Coppi's *Giro d'Italia* victory, on the day that Italy joined the conflict, inspired Bruno Roghi's patriotic pen:

> The twenty-eighth edition of the Giro d'Italia... put corporal's stripes on the shirt of a conscript. Fausto Coppi... has won the Giro d'Italia at the first attempt... The Giro d'Italia hasn't been won by a professional rider... it has been won by a twenty-year-old boy... a young soldier, just called up. The Italy of sportsmen in grey and green has named its twenty-eighth race of the people after a young athlete from the first draft.[3]

Eight days before Italy dropped its non-belligerent status, Ambrosiana-Inter won the last peacetime football championship, on 2 June 1940. With a quick conclusion to the war expected, the 1940–1 football season kicked off on time, with the national team also playing a number of matches against Axis allies and the neutral countries of Spain and Switzerland. With British aerial bombardments of strategic Italian cities having begun in the summer of 1940, the Hungarian national team's visit to Genoa that December still attracted 35,000 spectators. Eighteen months later, in Milan, the match with Spain drew a further 55,000 fans, close to the national record. Somehow, the *Giro* also continued until 1943, despite the gradual destruction of roads that stimulated a boom in velodrome racing. In total, 21 different sports remained active in some form or other, with the hunting federation seeing an extraordinary growth of 50,000 members.[4]

After landing in Sicily on 10 July 1943, the Allies made slow progress up the peninsula. Days later, on 25 July 1943, the King asked Mussolini to resign as head of government and replaced him with the army's Chief-of-Staff Marshall Badoglio. *La Gazzetta*'s front-page coverage of the regime's collapse was shared with that of 'the millionaire blonde' Danao's trotting win in the Monte Rosa Cup, in Milan.[5] From the fall of Fascism until the armistice, on 8 September, was the only time that football was totally paralysed. Coinciding with the summer break, 'avoiding the bombs and finding something to eat was everybody's daily objective'.[6] Conducting secret negotiations with the Allies while, at the same time, promising not to desert Germany, the new regime was despised by both. As the King hesitated, Hitler's troops poured into central Italy. In an effort to maintain the façade of normality *La Gazzetta* continued publishing a two-page, twice-weekly broadsheet that implored young men to maintain their fitness, should they be required to fight.[7]

The 'forty-five days' interregnum ended on 8 September 1943. With an armistice signed with the Allies, who were poised to attack the mainland, the royal family and government abandoned Rome for Brindisi, where they hoped to launch a Kingdom of the South. The army also dissolved and while many soldiers streamed out of the barracks before Nazi forces could stop them, over

500,000 were made prisoners and deported to Germany. Passing from one side to another in the same war, the country's division 'provoked the definitive collapse in the idea of the nation and the state'.[8] By mid-September 1943, Italy south of Naples was controlled by the Allies and the King, who finally declared war on Germany on 30 October. In the north, Mussolini was installed as Head of the Nazi puppet-state, the Italian Republic of Salò (RSI), where partisan Resistance groups began to emerge.

By the end of 1943, there were in the region of 9,000 partisans, which rose to around 100,000 by the spring/summer of 1944, and over 200,000 at the height of its activity.[9] As the war dragged on it became clear that three forces would dominate Italy's future – the Allies, Communism and Catholicism. But despite the Resistance's considerable assistance and sacrifices, the Allies were concerned about this large, growing, armed, left-wing force.

Led by Palmiro Togliatti, the Communist Party's (PCI) immediate aim was to unite anti-Fascist forces in the fight for liberation, leaving Italy's future to a free, popular vote. In the process of formation, the Christian Democratic Party (DC) had a much reduced role in the Resistance, with often only a token presence on the Committees of National Liberation.[10] The Vatican declared its support for the DC, led by Alcide De Gasperi, following the liberation of Rome, after which Catholic Action lined up its two million members behind the party.[11]

✪ ✪ ✪ ✪

Italian sport was also divided and in 1944 the northern branch of the football federation organized its national championship. This was the most prestigious sporting event run in the Salò Republic, and stadiums were often full for what were regional tournaments. Concluding with a play-off, all Serie A and B teams could enter and were free to replace any players lost through war commitments with whoever was available. The *Vigili del Fuoco Spezia* (La Spezia Fire Brigade) proved a particular case, inheriting the majority of La Spezia's formerly strong Serie B side.

With the town under heavy bombardment, La Spezia played their home matches in Carpi, near Modena, and reached the play-off in Milan. After an unexpected draw with Venezia, certain defeat beckoned against Torino. Facing such strong opposition, coach Barbieri positioned one player between the defence and the goal-keeper, in one of the earliest versions of what became known as *catenaccio*. An incredible 2-1 win, followed by Torino's defeat of Venezia, made La Spezia Alta Italia champions.

The city's mutilation made it shine it like a light in the dark of the enormous tragedy immersed in the barbarities of Italians fighting and killing

Italians. It's true that the title cannot be recognised as a national trophy by the Federation, but for history it has no price. Because it is the proof that even the most merciless war [could] not stop this 'phenomenon football'.[12]

Wherever the situation allowed, sport survived, with a physical education programme also published for prisoners of war.[13] Even in the midst of the occupation of Rome, from September 1943 to June 1944, during which the *Fosse Ardeatine* massacre saw 335 civilians shot after partisans killed 33 German military police, the Nazi command and the Fascist authorities still organized a football tournament between ten of the city's squads, which was won by Lazio.[14] Finally, on 29 August 1944, the Ministries of the Interior and Popular Culture suspended all sporting activity in northern Italy.

The winter of 1944–5 saw massive partisan losses of life and conditions deteriorate in the large northern cities gripped by severe cold, illness and food shortages. In the factories, fears of the deportation of men and machinery to Germany were worsened by the threat of mass unemployment. In the spring of 1945, with Nazi Germany squeezed by Russia in the east and the Allies in the west, liberation became a real prospect and, contrary to Allied wishes, on 24–6 April, Resistance-led risings in Genoa, Turin and Milan ended the Nazi occupation.

Fleeing towards Switzerland, Mussolini's SS escort was stopped by a partisan brigade that arrested him and his lover, Clara Petacci. Ignoring Allied orders, they were tried and executed before being hanged by their ankles in Piazza Loreto, Milan. Some members of the Fascist hierarchy fled Italy for South America, while others, such as Leandro Arpinati and PE devote Achille Starace, were tracked down and killed. By 1 May northern Italy was free, with the popular insurrection making a deep impression upon its participants. Never before had the 'ordinary' Italian been so actively involved in national life. The Resistance's sacrifices did much to restore Italy's tarnished image, unite some Italians, and create a lasting anti-Fascist tradition. The price of the vicious conflict, however, was the collapse of authority and the destruction of any concept of national or collective identity.

Republican Italy

Italy's first post-war government was an anti-Fascist coalition led by the Action Party head and Resistance leader Ferruccio Parri. With both Socialists and Communists confident of emerging from the scheduled elections as the major force in Italian politics, neither pushed for immediate social and institutional reforms to ensure there was no delay in the vote. Exploiting their disunity, the DC leader Alcide De Gasperi gained concessions and delayed the elections, thereby giving time for the post-war radical fervour to dissipate. An early sign of the left's moribund policy of cooperation with the DC, it also indicated the direction of post-war political power. Remarkably, when Parri was forced to resign in November 1945, the Communists and Socialists were already planning to replace him with De Gasperi, who somehow managed to inspire them while denying their objectives.[15] Thereafter, no attempt was made to reform central government administration that had grown massively under Fascism, or the judiciary that had been tailored to the regime's needs. The left was equally impotent in directing economic and social policy towards the needs and demands of the labour movement, while peasant land occupations and cooperatives failed to secure desperately needed agrarian reform.

On 2 June 1946, Italians went to the polls in free elections for the first time in over 20 years, choosing the new Assembly and the country's monarchical or republican future. By voting day King Victor Emmanuel III had already abdicated in favour of his son Umberto, in a desperate attempt to save the monarchy. His efforts were in vain, with 12,717,923 opting for a republic against 10,719,284 supporting the monarchy.[16] Having tried to stall the process, Umberto eventually fled into exile on 13 June. The Constituent Assembly elections showed the Christian Democrats to be the strongest party, with 35 per cent of the vote and 207 seats, followed by the Socialists (20 per cent – 115 seats) and Communists (19 per cent – 104 seats), who had expected to emerge as the strongest party within the left.

The Assembly designed the new Constitution based upon two houses of parliament – the Chamber of Deputies and the Senate – with the former elected every five years by proportional representation (PR) and the latter every seven years by a mixture of PR and single-member constituencies. Once every seven years members of both houses would also elect the President of the Republic, whose duties were strictly limited. Most controversial was the renewal of the Concordat with the Church, which maintained Catholicism as the official state religion, with marriage declared irrevocable by the narrowest of margins.

De Gasperi was happy to continue the coalition while it suited, especially with the Concordat yet to be written into the Constitution and the Peace Treaty, which needed Soviet approval, still to be signed. The arrangement was also acceptable to the PCI, which was intent on maintaining its alliance and remaining within government as long as possible. But in early 1947, which saw the rising strength of the left, America's anti-Communism drive in Italy, plus the

DC's collapsing popularity after signing the Peace Treaty that cost Italy money, colonies and the city of Trieste, De Gasperi broke with the left to form a centre-right government that excluded the PCI. Ending the anti-Fascist coalition and polarizing Italian politics, this division was reflected in the rebirth of Italian sport which, once again, became a political battleground.

CONI and continuity

> The importance of sport in the life of our country, grows every day... Since the fall of fascism... the mass parties have begun competing to exploit this frantic passion: the DC through the CSI, the PCI via UISP... the government, in the meantime, appears uncertain, caught – as elsewhere – between the tendency to become a regime through the state bureaucracy or the apparatus of Christian Democracy.
>
> Today, rejecting sport is as ridiculous as opposing electric lights or cinema.[17]

❁ ❁ ❁ ❁

On 25 July 1943, the former international tennis player, ice skater, journalist and sports administrator Count Alberto Bonacossa became head of CONI. Compromised by his close relations with Fascism, his appointment by Badoglio's government was indicative of continuity after the fall of the regime. With the war still to reach its conclusion, sport was a low priority for the government of national unity. When Bonacossa abandoned his position after little more than a month, it was not until the liberation of Rome, in June 1944, that any successor could be found.

With the various partisan groups dividing up the regime's administrative structures, CONI was given to the Socialist Party and Giulio Onesti appointed its regent on 28 June 1944, with the limited brief to oversee its dissolution and preserve its minimal assets.[18] As the political class returned to its traditional dislike of sport, which it now labelled a creature of Fascism, CONI was the only body capable of saving it from total collapse. In October 1944 Onesti's limited powers were expanded when he became Extraordinary Commissioner and three vice commissioners were appointed – two in the south and another, Alessandro Frigerio, in the north (Alta Italia).

First saving and then strengthening CONI, Onesti worked completely against his brief. Sacking around 75 per cent of existing employees, he surrounded himself with 30 or so loyal replacements and launched six commissions,[19] one of which paid 'particular attention to relations between the Allies' to create 'an atmosphere of reciprocal friendship'.[20] Before the war was over, football matches were taking place between 'civilian representatives, partisans or regulars within the Italian and Anglo-American armed forces',[21] with Rome also hosting an inter-Allied boxing championship.

Restoring autonomy to the various federations and re-launching Italian sport, Onesti was criticized for running CONI like a personal fiefdom and appointing personnel tainted by Fascism.[22] One notable example was the former leader of Florentine Fascism, Luigi Ridolfi, who continued as president of the Football Federation. Justifying his appointments by the need for honesty and talent, some accused CONI of being more oligarchic than under Fascism. Former CONI head Lando Ferretti saw it differently: 'The political faction has been overcome by the hunt for the best men because with everybody's collaboration Italian sport's problems, which are certainly not easy, can be overcome.'[23]

While Ferretti's objectivity is questionable, the extent to which such criticisms were merited was debatable given the total destruction of democracy. The issue reflected the broader problem of former regime activists remaining within the government administration and state apparatus. While those that had fought within the Resistance or suffered under the regime wanted justice for Fascist sympathizers and collaborators, their complete eradication from the civil service where Party membership had been mandatory, might well have paralysed the state's functioning. In effect, the only 'cleansing' achieved was of those partisans or anti-Fascists that entered the administration immediately after the national insurrection.[24] With government ministries unable to address this issue, was it realistic for CONI to have achieved anything different?

Onesti's freedom to do more or less as he pleased was huge and would almost certainly have been less so had he not been appointed on the eve of liberation. Among his strongest critics was CONI's Milan-based Alta Italia section, led by the Christian Democrat Alessandro Frigerio. Resuming north–south hostilities that would continue to grow, he demanded that all sporting organizations move to Milan,[25] the CONI bureaucracy be streamlined, its statutes and rules modified, and all bureaucrats and federation heads with Fascist links be purged. By also refusing to allow the repatriation of CONI funds to Rome, Onesti was forced to seek bank credit and Frigerio went beyond impeding the unification of Italian sport to forming a separate, dualistic entity.[26] A unification agreement was brokered on 21 July 1945,[27] but cancelled within months. It was, as *La Gazzetta* lamented, a position from which there appeared no escape: 'Rome makes itself legitimately strong by decree, Milan by its athletic potential. Rome rules, Milan disobeys. It is something more impassable than the Gothic line. It's anarchy.'[28]

Although democratically elected as CONI president by the national council, in July 1945, Onesti's position still required the sanction of the new DC Prime

Minister Alcide De Gasperi. Fully appreciating the importance of Italian sport, he proceeded with care to maintain political balance within CONI and prevent its Socialist domination. Besides Onesti's position, CONI's role also needed defining. Was it right for the former organizing body of Fascist sport to continue exerting complete control in the new democracy? After eliminating its leader's authoritarian potential, CONI was retained as the Federation of federations and, most importantly, a state/public body. With the independence of individual sports guaranteed, the Christian Democrats finally opened the road to Onesti becoming president.

In February 1946, the Milan and Rome branches were reunited. Reducing the bureaucracy in Rome and outlining a purge of ex-Fascists, Onesti was elected CONI president by the various federation heads. The following year, the Palazzo Barberini schism saw him resign from the PSI, thereby finally depoliticizing CONI. Freed from his Socialist ties he sought a more concrete agreement with the DC, which offered better protection of his position. Forming an unofficial 'holy alliance' with the future seven-times prime minister of Italy, Giulio Andreotti, Onesti remained in his post until 1978. A born politician, Andreotti understood the potential for shaping Italian sport from the outside, thereby avoiding the need to bring it directly under his or the DC's control.

CONI's complete autonomy and separation from the state was encompassed in its slogan, 'sport for sportsmen'. Reorganized and further democratized in 1947, all member associations, societies and sporting groups now elected their federation heads, who selected the national board that elected CONI's managing executive.[29]

Apparently transparent, the reality was that the federations were still rigidly controlled by CONI, upon whom they were reliant for funding. Moreover, the federation heads were chosen by councils comprising representatives from the richest sports societies, which were usually immersed in a strong patronage system involving industry and the armed forces. Consequently, programmes, budgets, rules and plans were established to serve their interests rather than mass sport.[30]

Onesti's restructure of CONI thus failed to create a mass diffusion of sport. While maximizing opportunities within schools and local communes might have weakened CONI's centralized structure, its widening participation among Italian citizens would have empowered it further. There was also a definitive rupture in the ideal of sport as pre-military training. Adults began to see exercise more as a relaxant and medicinal cure for the frustrations and ills of modern life, while school PE was shaken up by a decree, in May 1947, that created a special office for physical education within the Ministry for Public Instruction. With education no different from any other institution, schools were still staffed by teachers 'formed in the Fascist period, strongly indoctrinated by the former regime and with an evident military mentality. Or, alternatively, a scratched-together, demotivated and absolutely unprofessional personnel that had accepted the job as a stopgap or an easy opportunity.'[31]

While the closure of the Farnesina and Orvieto institutions removed Fascism from PE, the lack of any alternative only worsened the already drastic lack of qualified teachers and forced the reappointment of Farnesina graduates. In 1952, the Higher Institute for Physical Education (ISEF) was reopened in Rome, running separate three-year courses for men and women. Originally private, even the establishment of state ISEF institutions across the country, from 1959 onwards, could not produce enough staff, who would have had minimal facilities anyway. The ramifications of these problems would be felt in the 1960s.

'Favouring the sport-show to hide the lack of gymnasiums, buildings, facilities, swimming pools... Italians remained a nation of fans, while the practice of sport remained a privilege of the few.'[32] Primarily considered spectacle, sport was structured and directed towards identifying, selecting and developing potential champions who would embellish CONI's reputation, and an elite programme established in partnership with schools, universities and the military. Through its physical exercise programmes, the armed forces sifted the mass of conscripts for talent, with each force assigned to different disciplines: the army covered athletics, skiing, horse riding and boxing; the navy, swimming, diving, sailing and canoeing; and the air force shooting, fencing and judo.

The obvious contradiction in CONI's control of Italian sport was its exclusive interest in the competitive elite, with even school PE designed to identify the most able. The result was a 'strengthening of the national federations, the encouragement of the most efficient and best organized sporting societies... [and]... the construction of Pharaonic sporting structures... to the disadvantage of the spread of basic, multisport facilities.'[33] As Andreotti lamented in 1954: 'Unfortunately in Italy, sport has little popularity when it is amateur and is never thought to reach the heights of other public spectacles when it is professional.'[34] Worse still, despite exceptional results that culminated in the triumphal 1960 Rome Olympic Games, the policy disguised the real nature of Italian sport. The creation of new champions, matches and contests only developed the sport 'business' that now actively stimulated what had originally been spontaneous. Yet, in a cash-strapped country concentrating its resources on material rebuilding, Onesti's elite programme had a major problem: funding. His solution not only secured CONI's political independence while maintaining its monopoly of Italian sport, it also seized the spirit of the era and appealed directly to Italians' love of sport and debate. It was *Totocalcio*; the football pools.

'Normalization'

Some days after the Allied landings in Sicily, between 9 and 10 July 1943, I left from Serradifalco as I'd no news of my father for 20 days, who was at Porto Empedocle.

In my uncle's basement I found a bike which... was the only possible means of reaching the coast along a destroyed road, the scene of clashes between German, Italian and Allied troops.

I embarked on a journey that immediately promised to be full of difficulty as I was going in the opposite direction to an uninterrupted flow of Allied lorries, jeeps and tanks that often flung me from the road.

Straight away the bike gave me a sense of solidity, of confidence... For the longest 50km of my life the bike never let me down!... A spoke didn't bend, the chain didn't jump, nothing broke.

I reached Porto Empedocle, found my father safe and sound, and took that street once more, this time less worried. And again, the bike never let me down.

It was a Montante, a wonderful bike made by the Calogero Montante company at Serradifalco. What a great bike.

The bike of liberty, the bike of legality, a wonderful Montante bike. (Andrea Camilleri).[35]

✪ ✪ ✪ ✪

Sport's hiatus during the war was incredibly brief and its speedy resumption welcomed by all as a distraction from the realities of a shattered society, destroyed infrastructure and economic crisis. Although desperately short of paper the sports press began printing again in July 1945, taking sport's rebirth into homes and bars across the country. Having been renamed *Il Littoriale* under Fascism, the Rome-based *Corriere dello Sport* reappeared only a few days after the city's liberation in 1944. Less positively, there was little change in *La Gazzetta dello Sport*'s administrators, leaders and thinkers. Afraid of paying for his Fascist enthusiasm, the paper's proprietor Alberto Bonacossa offered to sell the daily to the Socialist Party. Its rejection of the offer showed its gross underestimation of sport's importance, yet again. The Church was wiser and the archbishopric of Milan snapped up the paper and its mass readership in 1945, placing it first under the editorship of Bruno Roghi and then Emilio De Martino, in 1947; two of Fascist sport's most hyperbolic scribes.[36]

Part of a cultural rebirth that included the launch of the state broadcaster RAI, the development of a prototype Vespa and the first Miss Italia beauty pageant, the re-emergence of a free press and sport contributed to restoring national pride and hope. According to *La Gazzetta*, triumphs like Gigi Villoresi's in the first international motor race of the post-war period, on 23 April 1946 in Nice, had significance beyond sport: 'After this victory in France they will appreciate us all the more, and to the brilliant "Gigi" we must be grateful for having restored our pride in being Italian.'[37]

The swimming, athletics and boxing federations organized national championships as soon as possible, while cycling sought to limit the impact of the destroyed road network with a number of regional tours: 100,000 spectators witnessing the Tour of Lombardy's conclusion, in Milan, in October 1945. With Italy still divided, football quickly resumed across the country to aid and assert normalization. In Genoa, in late spring 1945, the Liberation Cup (*Coppa della Liberazione*) was contested between groups of British troops and the Andrea Doria club, which merged with Sampierdarienese in 1946 to form Sampdoria. For Serie A, Italians had only to wait until 14 October 1945.

Logistical problems determined that the tournament be divided into Upper-Italy and Centre-South divisions, with the first four teams in each contesting a playoff to decide the national champion. In the first week's matches, the Turin derby drew 40,000 spectators, with another 30,000 flooding into the Milan Arena, the following week, for AC's clash with Juventus.[38] The terraces also contained the daily struggle for survival in the immediate post-war years, from the selling of drinks and home-made flags to 'an improvised black market of consumer goods and... a small industry of cons and theft'.[39]

Clubs generally retained their pre-war colours and traditions, which aided the rediscovery of temporarily lost identities. Fascist symbols in the stadiums were torn down and Genoa and Ambrosiana-Inter reassumed their original names – Genoa Cricket and Football Club and Internazionale – having being forced to abandon them in 1929. The small shield on the shirts of the champions of Italy, which had been introduced in 1924, was retained along with numbered shirts and the tradition of the home team changing colours in the event of a clash. While there was not the same grave loss of life among football's community as in the First World War, the line-ups of all Serie A sides had changed considerably. Some stadiums were in ruins and totally unsafe for the crowds that poured in, but with many pitches having been requisitioned or the sites of violence and death, their restoration to use aided the healing process.

In the immediate post-war years sport became a diplomatic olive branch, *La Gazzetta* reporting in April 1946 how 'official Italy [wa]s doing its utmost to open the road to the solidarity of sporting internationals'.[40] Italy's re-entry into the international sporting community was aided by football matches against the former enemies of England and France, in 1948, and its participation in the 1948 London Olympics when Germany, Japan and the USSR were excluded. 'In CONI, sport has its own Foreign Ministry', *La Gazzetta* proclaimed.[41] Italy's fifth-place finish was an impressive achievement built on its cycling, fencing and wrestling strengths. The ultimate performances were discus gold and silver medals for Adolfo Consolini and Beppe Tosi, who projected the perfect image at the time: 'substantial bonhomie, rustic strength and mildness'.[42] Equally important was a totally unexpected water polo gold medal. The first gifted swimmer to enter the sport that usually attracted the pool's misfits, Ermenegildo Arena went on to launch a range of swimwear that remains an internationally recognized brand. And neither was he alone in moving into fashion, with the designer Ottavio Missoni reaching the final of the 400m hurdles before making an even greater contribution to 'Made in Italy''s global development.

Italy's welcome back into the international sporting community was neither immediate nor universal, however. During the first post-war meeting of football's world governing body (FIFA), on 10 November 1945, France led the arguments to exclude Italy. Recognizing the work of the Resistance and Italy's co-belligerence under Badoglio, the motion was rejected.[43] In 1950, simmering French antagonism spilled over into the *Tour de France*, where Italian cyclists were threatened and roughed up. Gino Bartali retired from the race in protest along with the entire Italian squad. Not lacking in irony, it was Italy's military athletes that rectified the situation:

> In September our armed forces concluded the brief but important and successful series of international sporting events at Pau, where the woes of Bartali and his companions occurred on the Tour... Among everything else our soldiers, who were admired and celebrated wherever they went, can boast of having repaired the painful fracture that took place during the Tour.[44]

During international cycling's golden age from 1945 to 1960, the bicycle became an increasingly affordable and indispensable means of transport, with approximately three million in circulation and 400,000 produced per year, by 1946.[45] Cycling was also a spectacle that fans and casual bystanders could watch for free, occasionally from outside their front doors, schools, offices, factories, or fields. Waiting for hours to catch a fleeting glimpse of their hero, fans also participated by cheering vociferously, passing prepared bottles or buckets of water to cyclists on hot days, or providing newspapers that were stuffed down shirts to protect against cold on the mountain descents.

Italian cyclists also consistently won the most prestigious tours, track events and world titles. Gripping the nation with popularized rivalries and duels, racing boomed and amateurism wilted under the pressure of prize money. As the secretary of the Italian Association of Professional Cycling Racers explained in 1952, it was impossible for local races, such as the Tour of Emilia, to attract top names like Fausto Coppi with only 500,000 lire of prize money, when he could take 350,000 in a less-demanding track meeting.[46]

The mass popular spectator sport of the era, cycling's importance was evident in the almost immediate relaunch of the *Giro d'Italia*, in 1946: 'the mistral that puts the wind in the sails of young and free Italy... A Giro d'Italia for all Italian athletes, for all of Italy's sportsmen.'[47] In a devastated country in which the average per capita calorie consumption had dropped to the lowest level since 1860, where only 25 per cent of factories were operational, and transport capacity had been reduced by 35–40 per cent, with 2,972 bridges destroyed and over 60 per cent of the road network damaged,[48] the 'race of rebirth' recommenced only 14 months after the end of the war, 13 days after the national elections for the new constituent assembly, and one year earlier than its rival the *Tour de France*. At the end of the first stage Bruno Roghi declared:

> the Giro d'Italia is not an organizational machine made by streets and bicycles, results and prizes. The Giro has its own mysterious spirit. It slept for six years. Today it reawoke and released the song of Resurrection, of hope, of faith and of victory.[49]

One of the personalities to emerge from the 1946 race was Luigi Malabrocca, who won national fame for his unstinting effort, commitment and toil that never took him beyond last place but symbolized how Italy would recover. Developing a common identity around the simple, understandable values of work, sweat and endurance, the verb '*pedallare*' – to pedal – came to signify unstinting effort, without complaint. The *Giro* also evidenced Italy's physical reconstruction, with each stage stitching together areas and regions separated and isolated by the war:

> You see, or better, you guess the secret language of our good Italian people. With your unrivalled charm – sport, sport – you understand that something is rising again... the certainty of tomorrow, united and brothers, visibly sick but free from Turin to Naples, Florence to Trieste, Trento to Milan. The stages are not measurable in kilometres but in recognition. The athletes are the messengers of this good news. For this, the 1946 Giro d'Italia will never be forgotten.[50]

The race reached Naples in 1946 and Bari in 1947, before finally crossing the Straits of Messina into Sicily in 1949, where the *Corriere della Sera*'s correspondent Dino Buzzatti referenced Garibaldi's voyage to the island almost a century earlier:

Who will be tough, oh Garibaldians without bayonets? Who will become your Garibaldi? You still don't have Generals, you are simple soldiers up until now. The stripes will need to be won. You start from scratch, tomorrow morning. Victory, with its inscrutable face, smiles indifferently at you all.[51]

Cold War games

US troops, barracked in Italy following the 1918 armistice, introduced a number of new sports to the nation. Baseball teams debuted in 1919, but the sport's growth was slow. Sponsored by individuals, club competition only began in 1945 after American troops again boosted its popularity with raucous, improvised games in Italy's streets and piazzas. 'During the Allied invasion of 1943–5, Italy had had its first direct experience of the American way of life – violent in many ways, but also incandescent with its bonhomie, benevolence and jazz.'[52] With almost 1,500 teams in their ranks, as US forces moved up the peninsula they took their sporting culture with them.

A version of basketball had been played at the 1907 National Gymnastics Tournament (*Concorso Ginnastico Nazionale*) in Venice, but it was American YMCA instructors in north-eastern Italy during the First World War that diffused it among Italian troops. The first major competitive match was between the Second Monza Company of Motorists and the Malpensa Pilots, in 1919. Contested in the Milan Arena in front of a crowd of 30,000 – a figure the sport never came near to repeating in Italy – the spectators had actually come to see the arrival of Girardengo and the culmination of that year's *Giro d'Italia*. Formed in Milan in 1921, the *Federazione Italiana del Basket-Ball* was too English for Fascism and became the *Federazione Italiana della Palla al Cesto*, in 1926.[53]

Post-1945, US army Captain Elliot Van Zandt stayed on to improve the Italian national team, while the establishment of permanent US military bases in Italy saw Puglia, Campania, Tuscany and the Veneto become Italy's principal basketball regions, around the hub of Bologna's Virtus club. Aided by the Harlem Globetrotters' visit in 1952, the national team's fourth place in the 1960 Olympics, and TV's coverage of a women's match in 1961 – a cunning ploy to circumvent the moral code and show bare legs – basketball entered its boom years.[54]

As the Second World War concluded and the Cold War began, America invested heavily in the ideological and practical defence of Italy's border with Communist Yugoslavia. While Italy was liberated on 25 April 1945, the conflict continued in the primarily Italian-speaking city of Trieste as Allied forces tried to secure it before Marshall Tito's forces. In 'The Race for Trieste', New Zealand troops arrived only hours after their Yugoslav adversaries had annexed the city, on 9 May 1945. The 42-day occupation that followed saw reprisals against Fascists and Italians before Yugoslav troops were forced to withdraw.[55] Established on 9 June 1945, the Morgan line divided Venezia-Giulia, putting Trieste, Gorizia and the area around the Isonzo river under Allied control in Zone A, while leaving the remainder in Zone B under Yugoslavia, in a similar arrangement to Berlin. After the Paris Peace settlement declared Trieste a free city under international supervision, pro-Italian demonstrations and violent incidents made war between Italy and Yugoslavia seem a distinct possibility. Finally, in 1954, the Memorandum of Understanding ratified the existing border, Zone A being given to Italy and Zone B to Yugoslavia.

A nationalist cause since Italian unification, the conflict over the unredeemed lands and Trieste was evident in the region's sport. Following the formation of the national football championship in 1926, Venezia-Giulia's principal clubs (*Unione Sportiva Triestina* and *SBS Ponziana*) 'officially enter[ed] the Italian football family'.[56] The seriousness of the recruitment of Ponziana, the team of the old Trieste port (a key Cold War frontier), into the Yugoslav first division in 1946[57] was exacerbated by AS Triestina's relegation from Serie A, in 1947. Provoking an official FIGC congress, Triestina was readmitted into an expanded league of 21 teams.[58] This was officially for 'sporting merit', but the reality was that the political implications of the club's relegation were too great, which was underlined by the silence with which the relegated teams accepted their fate. Supported by government investment, Trieste finished second in Serie A the following season, an achievement it never repeated.[59]

In an 'attempt... to counter Soviet championships',[60] the US Department of State sent a number of university teams to compete in summer Olympic-type activities, but it was cycling and the 1946 *Giro d'Italia* that really put Trieste on the map. As *La Gazzetta*'s editor Bruno Roghi and race director Armando Cougnet declared, it was a race of solidarity towards a city that wanted to be Italian but couldn't: 'Purely and simply, we wanted to come to Trieste because the "Giro d'Italia" without Trieste was like a decapitated statue, a river with no source, a venture with no goal.'[61]

One day prior to the race launch on 15 June 1946, the Rovigo–Trieste stage, on 30 June, was cancelled. Allied Command had refused it transit of Zone A after secret services uncovered a Yugoslav plot to stop the race and prevent organized Italian celebrations in the city. With the *Giro*'s mission to unite Italy, Roghi thought the Trieste cyclist Giordano Cottur's first-stage victory was predestined:

> An obsessive idea seizes the mind. This: that the benign gods of sport,
> well aware that the race of the people has been given a role that goes beyond
> sport, have chosen in Giordano Cottur the prophetic protagonist for the job.[62]

With Cottur angered by the cancellation of the Trieste stage and intent on drawing attention to his city's plight, Franc Štoka, the leader of the Yugoslav Liberation Front, realized the plot to stop the race had been counter-productive. Fearing potential reaction within the city, the Allied command also revoked its decision. But as the race approached it became increasingly political.

After entering the Allied controlled Zone A on 30 June, near the small town of Pieris the *Giro* was stopped by blocks of concrete, nails and barbed wire, reportedly laid by Yugoslav Communists who threw rocks at the cyclists and exchanged shots with the police.[63] With damage only to some bikes after the shoot-out that lasted in the region of five minutes, some of the cyclists continued at walking pace towards Trieste, symbolically led by Cottur. Entering the city, they passed 'phantasmagorical scenes of a crowd in delirium':

> Every house, every building was fluttering with tricolour flags and curtains, frantically waved from the windows. The crowd launched itself towards the walking procession with open arms, shouting its infinite and uncontainable love, a love for which it was crying with unrestrained emotion.
>
> ...the widest of streets is darkened by the crowd shouting I-T-A-L-I-A, I-T-A-L-I-A, I-T-A-L-I-A... The acclamations grow in intensity. It is no longer a Sabbath as hot as hell, it is an Italian Sabbath.
>
> Then, we see no more. The swarming hippodrome of Montebello swallows the brave boys that have reached the sporting and national finish line of Trieste. Sport, in this instant, was a flame. The god of the just, must have seen it.[64]

As news of the attacks broke, the celebration became a general strike, with reprisals taken against Yugoslav businesses and agencies that resulted in one death and over 30 injuries. Italian and Yugoslav press coverage appeared to inflame the situation, with further incidents leaving a police officer dead on 1 July,[65] before the *Giro* sheepishly left for Udine. Concluding on 7 July, Roghi lauded its success:

> The Giro d'Italia did its duty. It went to find the Italians. It went to tell the Italians that we must stay united and love each other. Without unity and love Italy would perish and decay...
>
> The Giro d'Italia kept all of its promises.
>
> It had to go to Naples to show the brotherhood of Italians in the north and south. It went to Naples.
>
> It had to go to Rome because Italians see themselves in the capital and interpret it as a symbol of national unity. It went to Rome, the Holy Father blessed it.

It had to go to Trieste, in precisely the extreme days of intense pain, to bring evidence of a desperate solidarity of all Italian brothers to a sister in danger. It went to Trieste.[66]

Coming from Bruno Roghi, who had ferociously hammered his typewriter in the name of Fascist sporting nationalism, the demand for a new, moderate Italian patriotism[67] rang somewhat hollow prior to the race. By the time it left Trieste, it positively echoed.

The 'Tour of rebirth' has given a great lesson of humanity to all sporting Italians... They welcomed it as a flag that didn't need the blood of battle to be feared, but demanded dedication of spirit to be honoured. Honoured by everybody, because whoever thinks of humiliating a flag of peace, of pride... throws away the seed of regret and perhaps, even remorse.[68]

✪ ✪ ✪ ✪

Gino Bartali was the race winner, whose very public and devout Catholicism now made him a key figure in the Church's post-war propaganda. With the Holy See giving special consideration to sport and cycling in particular, Bartali was among the selected riders and sporting dignitaries invited to the Vatican in 1947, to be blessed by Pope Pius XII.

You struggle in the race of life towards the eternal glory, not to earn a prize that is corruptible or that you can pass to others, but with the hope of an imperishable crown that doesn't expose any of you to the delusion of not winning, so long as you faithfully follow the laws of this sublime contest of spirit and never give in to tiredness or any obstacle before reaching the goal....

Go brave riders of the earthly and eternal race. Our wishes and prayers are with you while, with great affection, we give you and all who follow you, our Papal blessing.[69]

Seeking to maintain its freedom while ensuring Christian democracy's strong presence in Italy's reconstruction, Pope Pius XII launched the Church's re-entry into national politics on Christmas Day 1942.[70] In addition to the embryonic Christian Democratic Party, the Church's lay cultural organization Catholic Action became another weapon in the battle against Communism. On 11 August 1943, Catholic Action's head Luigi Gedda offered its assistance to Badoglio's government. While there was no mention of sport,[71] Gedda later revealed he had proposed that 'AC simply take over the buildings and the activities of the Fascist organisations'.[72] Although rebuffed and never repeated, the attempt to position Catholicism at the centre of post-Fascist national sport indicated the 'intuition of the Catholic world, and Gedda in particular, for the importance of sport as a unifier of mass youth'.[73]

Seeking to control what it considered the principle issues of birth, sex and death in post-war Italy, 'the Vatican sought to discipline the human body by setting norms for clothing, by censoring love scenes in the cinema, and by discouraging dancing'.[74] Equally committed to the fight against Communism, on 5 January 1944 Catholic Action's director-general, Monsignor Evasio Colli, approved the formation of the Italian Sporting Centre (*Centro Sportivo Italiano* – CSI). Uniting ecclesiastical and lay organizations, the CSI established sports groups at parish, local and national levels to create a strong, mass Catholic body.

It was encouraged by speeches, broadcasts and support from the 'sportsmen's Pope', Pius XII. On 20 May 1945, in front of 10,000 Catholics, which Gedda described as the baptism of sport, the pontiff declared that '*sport* can and must be at the service of God'.[75] While Pius X and Pius XI had supported sport, Pius XII now endorsed the merits of competition. Creating an adversary to be defeated around which Catholicism could unite, Catholic athletes and their opponents were crucial in its sporting campaign.

Catholic sport was also supported by the Christian Democratic Party (DC), most notably in the shape of Giulio Andreotti who, with no government ministry for sport, was its Under-Secretary. Representing the DC in all sporting contexts he also backed CONI president Giulio Onesti, who reciprocated by assisting the CSI. As Gedda noted:

> we have had... the continuous and loving support from the government that we sincerely thank, with a special thought for the honourable Andreotti to whom national sport was and is trusted, as we equally profess our dutiful recognition of Onesti with whom we have had, in these ten years, an uninterrupted tie and collaboration.[76]

The DC also launched its own sporting organization, the Libertas Sporting Centre (*Centro Sportivo Libertas* – CSL), to penetrate central and southern Italy by encouraging sporting initiatives within businesses, local groups and committees. Five hundred disconnected groups in 1945 became 19 regional inspectorates with 92 centres and 411 multi-sport clubs by 1952.[77] Contributing to the anti-Communist campaign, particularly prior to the 1948 election, CSL groups were often the nuclei of the DC political body.

By the beginning of the 1950s, the CSI and CSL had in the region of 110,000 members in regular sporting activity,[78] which was supplemented by spiritual meetings, religious education, plus the words of Gedda and the Pope, who declared sport: 'an efficient antidote against weakness and the easy life, it awakens the sense of order and educates in challenging and controlling oneself'.[79]

⚙ ⚙ ⚙ ⚙

Exclusive by nature, Catholic sport alienated those who did not share its devotion to the Church, many of whom joined the Union of Workers Sport (*Unione Italiana Sport Popolare* – UISP). But, while the Catholic reorganization of sport was rapid and directed, the left's was slower, more fragmented and generally troubled. With its structures completely dismantled under Fascism, sport's post-war development was hampered by a leadership that had cut its political teeth in the pre-Fascist era when the left was almost doctrinally opposed to sport. There was, however, a definite appreciation of its merits and political potential among some, which made UISP's formation not just an effort to rival the CSI but a means of fighting the class struggle through mass popular culture.[80] Early evidence was the Communist Finance Minister Mauro Scoccimarro's tax reduction on sporting events which, according to Sergio Giuntini, was 'one of the most significant, as well as final measures to benefit sport, taken by the anti-fascist coalition'.[81]

The PCI's formation of the Youth Front and the Socialist Party's launch of its Sporting Associations (*Associazioni Sportive Socialisti Italiani* – ASSI) in 1946, were important in the left's modernization but equally indicative of a desperate lack of unity. Worse still, the Palazzo Barberini schism in January 1947, which saw 52 of 115 Socialist deputies leave for the Italian Social Democratic Party (PSDI), was a 'major tragedy for Italian Socialism' that saw the rump of the party subordinated to the PCI, while condemning 'the social-democratic minority to a sterile future, in the shadow of the DC and constantly susceptible to Cold War American pressure'.[82] This paralysing of the PSI's organizational structures impacted upon workers' sport, which was further wounded by the 1948 electoral defeat and the collapse of the Popular Front. When the left finally got back to politics after the shocking defeat there were few defenders of sport and mass popular culture, with 'the traditionalism of PCI chief Palmiro Togliatti and many other officials ma[king] them somewhat aversive to films and other forms of mass entertainment'.[83]

Some, however, defended film and sport as efficient means of forming a national workers' culture. The 1948 National Workers' Sport Conference, in Rome, evidenced the left's long overdue change of heart and its desire to establish an alternative mass culture. Viewing sport as neither a private affair, nor a question of improving individual physiques, or an issue of local, regional or national prestige, the conference defined it as a social problem to be integrated into the broad struggle for reform.[84] Targeting areas of society untouched by CONI, UISP was key in the left's resistance to Catholicism's incursion into Italian life. It was, however, hampered by hostility from the CSL and the various national federations. As its first secretary-general Gennaro Stazio explained, in 1948: 'Nobody gave us anything, everybody sabotages our organization... telling the newspapers not to publish our bulletins. For UISP there are no fields, no money and no words of encouragement.'[85]

This division of sporting provision and the conflict between the CSI and UISP reflected post-war Italy's left–right split. Rivalling each other for the control/support of mass society, both poles stressed their difference and superiority to the world around them, while opposing consumer society and offering alternative cultures and utopian visions of the future. But, as Ginsborg notes, their relationships with authority were very different:

> The Church... was the very essence of institutional authority, both political and moral. The culture it preached *vis-à-vis* authority was fundamentally that of submission and docility...
>
> For the Communists on the other hand, contesting authority, often against the councils of their more prudent leaders, organizing the 'masses', leading strikes, seeking collective solutions to collective problems, was the very heart of the matter. They were the form and sense that the Communists gave to the word 'solidarity'.[86]

During the next 30 years, these approaches to politics were played out in their exploitation of mass culture and sport to direct Italy's future.

Gino Bartali, 'saviour' of Italy

Cycling further agitated this political division, most notably in the rivalry between the fraternal 'enemies' of Gino Bartali and Fausto Coppi. With his reputation built under Fascism, Bartali was associated with the past, while Coppi's post-war achievements represented a new, modernizing country. As Curzio Malaparte described, in 1949:

> in some ways they represent the two main currents of contemporary Italian thought. Bartali belongs to those who believe in tradition and their changelessness, Coppi with those who believe in progress. Gino is with who believes in dogma, Fausto with those who refute it in politics and sport as in every other sphere.[87]

Bartali's image was that of a devout Catholic whose capacity for silent suffering won him the moniker of the 'iron man'. In contrast, Coppi was almost inevitably portrayed as a Socialist, Communist or infidel.

Figure 9: *The Bartali blade: 'This is my edge'*

> Bartali prays pedalling. He lifts his head only to look at the sky. He smiles at invisible angels. Fausto Coppi, instead, is a mechanic. He only believes in his machine, that is to say his body. For all of the stage it's he who leads: only he guides the machine, his body... Coppi doesn't fear hell, he fears second place. He knows that Bartali will probably arrive first in paradise. But what does he care? Fausto Coppi wants to arrive first on earth.[88]

Few, however, recalled Coppi's support for the DC in 1948, unlike Bartali's wartime contribution to partisan activities in his native, traditionally Communist Tuscany. As press coverage exaggerated their apparent differences, support for either became a political and sporting choice.

Pope Pius XII's relationship with cycling was close, and in the six years after 1946 he granted *Giro d'Italia* riders three audiences.[89] Coppi was one of the cyclists whose attendance publicly reaffirmed their Catholic identities while ratifying to the Church's association with the sport. The following year, he also starred on the cover of the CSI's fortnightly publication *Stadium*:

> FAUSTO COPPI, 'everybody's champion', completely shares the Centro Sportivo Italiano's ideals. Without speculation and without particular interests... he freely adheres to our movement and is happy to send... his warm greeting to all CSI members. And we return the greeting even more strongly.[90]

The Cold War's impact upon the Church, with its teachings and practices the antithesis of Communism, was profound. Thus, the struggle between Coppi and Bartali was 'represented as a fight between Christian good and evil... Catholic forces were represented pictorially as the Archangel Michael or other figures of strength and purity, Communism by the Angel of Death, masked devils, demons and animals.'[91] In the Italy of 'Don Camillo and Peppone', the Catholic priest and Communist mayor of the post-war small, northern town in Giovanni Guareschi's novels that became nationwide film hits, Bartali was repackaged as cycling's De Gasperi. Publicly devout, he confessed to Padre Pio during the Foggia stage of the 1947 *Giro*,[92] which further contributed to the construction of the Communist tag that was later attached to Coppi. As the journalist Vito Pratolini argued, the *Giro d'Italia* 'gives an unmistakable census of the political opinions of Italians that is more valid than those expressed in the referendum and the elections because it is spontaneous and unrestrained'.[93]

In one of the most politically charged periods of Italian history, Bartali was practically canonized for his 1948 *Tour de France* victory. Further differentiating him, the strength of his reputation as the 'angel of the mountains' encouraged the left to mythologize Coppi's Communist credentials:

In a period in which the Catholic Party had cast left-wing parties out of political life, the popular imagination may have interpreted the defeats that Coppi inflicted on Bartali as a symbolic victory over one of the most popular symbols of Catholic Italy.[94]

The 1948 election was fiercely contested amid growing Cold War tensions and American fears of a Communist Party victory. Crucial in determining Italy's future, the Church exploited every opportunity available to ensure a DC win: priests urged their parishioners to vote for the Cross, a network of 'civic committees' ran a huge propaganda campaign, while 36 Madonnas wept in Naples at the prospect of a Communist majority.[95] Much of its efforts were conducted through Catholic Action. Massing DC supporters into St Peter's Square in September 1947, Pius XII implored the throng:

> The time for reflection and plans has passed: now is the time of action. Are you ready?
>
> The tough contest that St Paul spoke about is underway; it is the hour of intense effort. Even a few moments can decide the victory. Look at your Gino Bartali, member of Catholic Action; he has won the longed-for 'jersey' the most. Now you run... so that you can win an even nobler palm of victory.[96]

The first time a Pope had officially cited a sportsman as a behavioural model, it indicated his appreciation of sport's capacity for mass communication. Furthermore, voters were also 'encouraged' to do the right thing by the threatened withdrawal of the sacraments. A conservative man of his word, even after the conclusive DC victory Pius XII collectively excommunicated millions of Communist voters.[97]

The US government also dedicated $176 million of 'interim aid' to Italy, in the first three months of the year. Money, food and medicines arrived in ports across the country, with every hundredth ship greeted with fanfares of publicity and political speeches. With goods often distributed by a friendship train, the US Ambassador James Dunn attended the opening of schools, hospitals and bridges, built with American money in the name of freedom. On 20 March 1948, however, George Marshall warned that such aid would immediately cease in the event of a Communist victory. 'The most widespread image of America was that of "ships loaded with food, coal and medicines for the sick" that would continue to arrive in Italian ports or would be sent elsewhere depending upon the outcome of the elections.'[98]

With the Popular Front coalition having anticipated a close contest at worst, the DC's significant parliamentary majority was a crushing blow. Worse was to follow when a neo-fascist from Catania shot and gravely injured the PCI leader Palmiro Togliatti, on 14 July. As one worker described: 'Everybody felt the blow; by hitting him they had tried to destroy the party, the working class, its ideals and liberty, only recently reconquered from Fascism.'[99] A general strike was proclaimed and violent confrontations with police, which left 16 people dead and over two hundred injured, heightened fears of an imminent insurrection that might encourage a Soviet incursion into Western Europe.

As Togliatti's condition improved 24 hours later, the strike was suspended and the PCI implored workers to return to the factories. The same day, Bartali won the first of three consecutive *Tour de France* mountain stages that effectively sealed him that year's race. As the situation calmed, the Catholic publicity machine launched the legend that Bartali had saved Italy from civil war, with Prime Minister De Gasperi said to have called him, on 14 July: 'Try to do it if you can. You know it would be important for all of us. There's a lot of confusion here.'[100] Four years later, Carlo Doglio recalled Milan,

> where after two days of silence, brooding and deserted streets, you found a flood of people in front of *La Gazzetta dello Sport*, in Viale Galilei... 'Bartali has left them all behind', the small groups of people grew and the abuse and deviant cries of joy merged, inexorably veering towards the Bartali-Coppi, Coppi-Bartali argument.[101]

As the first huge, post-war international sporting success for Italy, Bartali's victory was of unquestionable national importance and would certainly have interested many insurrectionists, with even Togliatti asking about his progress having been reassured of the domestic situation. Fully appropriated by the Catholic establishment, De Gasperi, President Luigi Einaudi and Pope Pius XII all granted Bartali personal audiences, but his victory as pacifying Italy is a myth: 'That resistant figure of the collective imagination corresponds, in reality, to one of the first mass-media campaigns knowingly made in post-war Italy.'[102] With the strike already over, it was the PCI and CGIL trade union's management of the crisis, plus efficient policing, which prevented its escalation.[103] Nonetheless, the Bartali myth was propagated thereafter by the Catholic right and its media. As the Catholic Youth publication *Gioventù* recorded: Bartali 'minimized the insurrection by pushing down on the pedals'.[104] Furthermore, the recuperation of his 21 minute deficit in three stages appeared miraculous,[105] as Lucio Villari recalled almost 60 years later:

> Bartali's victory seemed almost a sign from above in favour of Christian Democracy and its government. Gino transformed into an icon of emergency. Not only, but the Tour victory contributed to giving a religious and conservative

dimension to the myth of the champion... thus a new contradictory aspect between Bartali and Coppi was born. On the one hand the believing Catholic who was close to the DC, on the other the layman, hostile to that world. For Coppi, in reality, it wasn't so, but it worked journalistically.[106]

A perfect example was Giordano Goggioli's 1951 account of the events in a children's book, which neither referred to the assassin Pallante, Togliatti nor the PCI and CGIL:

> In those days ugly things were happening in Italy. A young man tried to kill an important politician, we don't know if he was more wicked or mad, and after all of the pain and the destruction of the war, our country avoided the horrors of revolution by the skin of its teeth...
>
> Groups of people with worrying faces and behaviour were on the streets...
>
> Women shook in their houses at the thought of seeing their sons, brothers and husbands with weapons in their hands again...
>
> But one evening the radio announced that Gino Bartali had reclaimed the Tour de France yellow jersey...
>
> The people smiled: a great sigh of liberation rose from the cities to the countryside. Once again, in the joy of a great Italian sporting victory, we felt the same and looked at each other with love.
>
> In the hospital bed... even the politician, struck by that young lunatic's bullet, knew of Bartali's victory... Peace had returned, the danger was over.[107]

As the Cold War in Italy intensified, the polemic continued and the gulf between each cyclist's supporters widened. Most memorably, on 6 July 1952 Coppi and Bartali exchanged a water bottle during a *Tour de France* climb over the *col du Galibier*. An apparently innocuous act, it stimulated one of the most enduring arguments in Italian sport. When *Lo Sport Illustrato* published a photo of the exact moment in which both riders had one hand on the bottle, fans demanded to know just who had given it to whom? That there were numerous other examples of their mutual assistance failed to pacify the clamour to know just who was the generous giant.

Still debated, the iconic and deeply controversial image exposed just what little it took to reopen Italian society's inherent divide.[108] Although Bartali later claimed to have passed the bottle,[109] more constructively the event represented two rivals uniting to reach a shared goal. Whereas the political ambitions and ferocious campaigning of the DC and Popular Front drove a huge wedge into Italian society in 1948, the message for all citizens on either side of the political chasm was made apparent in a way that perhaps only sport could achieve.

Figure 10: *How controversial can a bottle be?*

Moreover, even prior to the arrival of television, the combination of sport and media had stimulated greater debate and interest than politics could ever have dreamed of.

Superga: the end of the post-war party

After claiming the 1943 *scudetto* and the first post-war title in 1946, Torino proved unstoppable, winning the next two football championships. When the squad left to play a friendly in Lisbon, on 1 May 1949, the club was on the verge of a fifth consecutive title. Three days later, terrible weather on the team's return led its plane to crash into a wall at the back of Turin's landmark, eighteenth-century Superga basilica.[110] There were no survivors and the national football team was decimated. The greatest sporting disaster in Italian history, its impact was enormous:

> Work stopped at FIAT for one minute's silence, and shops closed all over the city... A 38-year-old woman in Bologna committed suicide on hearing the news. The tragedy united left and right, at the height of the cold war... In Rome, Parliament suspended its sitting once the news came through.[111]

At least half a million people attended the funeral service, which was broadcast live on national radio, with over thirty thousand making the pilgrimage to Superga to leave flowers that day. A huge number of conspiracy theories abounded, but three separate inquiries attributed the accident to human error, induced by bad weather and a plane with no radar. The club sued the airline for the value of its players, but its action was rejected by the High Court, which ruled that damages could be only awarded for people and property.[112]

Superga has remained a pilgrimage site for Torino supporters in the club's occasionally good times and the frequently bad. Each year on 4 May, fans and family connected to the victims attend a mass at which the current Torino captain reads out the names of those lost. As John Foot proposes, remembering the 'team that never died' became an industry in itself, a 'kind of civic religion'.[113]

Despite its World Cup triumphs in the 1930s, Italy's frustrating inability to defeat England continued in the following decade. A 4-0 defeat in Turin, in May 1948, underlined the unabated English strength while questioning the wisdom of basing the national team so completely upon that of Torino and its scheme of play. Although its system represented progress from that which had been so successful in the 1930s, by 1944 La Spezia had already demonstrated the value of an extra defender, undoing the great Torino in the process. A defensive system coined *catenaccio* (padlock), it was almost perfected by Nereo Rocco when leading Triestina to its incredible Serie A second place, in 1948.

While tactics were changing, from 1946 to 1947 Torino players still provided the majority of the national team. On 11 May 1947, ten out of eleven players for the match against Hungary came from the club, with only the Juventus goalkeeper preventing the 'perfect XI'. The wisdom of this 'policy' was apparently confirmed by the 5-1 defeat by the Austrian 'Wunderteam' in September 1947, which was blamed upon the use of players from other clubs that failed to adapt to Torino's style of play. Besides crediting the club with Italy's international success, the heavy presence of its players gave Torino an identity that began to blur the boundaries between city and nation.

With Torino's success having represented hope for the future and the new political order, the Superga tragedy, which effectively condemned *calcio* to international failure for the best part of a generation, contributed to a growing national introspection following the jubilation of the immediate post-war years. As *La Gazzetta* noted at the time: 'Sporting and non-sporting Italy is in mourning: national mourning for the incredible loss of our dearest and most celebrated athletes: the heirs to the squad that won three world titles.'[114]

IN RICORDO DELLA SQUADRA DEL TORINO,
TRAGICAMENTE PERITA IL 4 MAGGIO 1949

Figure 11: *A reminder of the wreckage*

Coming at the beginning of a period of social, economic and political reconstruction that ran concurrently with one of the darkest periods in Italian football's history, the national gloom that was intensified by the disaster was only lifted by the economic miracle, in the late 1950s. As Carlo Doglio predicted as early as 1952: 'For whoever might have different ideas, it is truly painful to have to say it: but only making football spectacular can cure it of the sores, apparently at least.'[115]

La Dama Bianca: the 'scarlet' woman

Valentino Mazzola was captain of Torino and Italy when he lost his life at Superga. In the ensuing national mourning, the players or *caduti* (fallen) were revered irrespective of any unpleasant details in their lives. An attacking midfielder remembered as one of the greatest players in Italian history, Mazzola was a 1940s icon: his 'blond curly hair, strong-running, muscular upper body and his smile symbolized the rebirth of Italy after the horrors and privations of war'.[116]

Only ten days before he died, Mazzola remarried in Vienna after obtaining a divorce in Romania. Contested in Italy where divorce was still illegal, Valentino was awarded care of his son Sandro, whose brother Ferruccio went to their mother. In April 1948 after Turin's appeal court validated the divorce, the state appealed the decision and sent the case to the high court in Rome. Still unresolved at the time of his death, the divorce was annulled, thereby invalidating Mazzola's second marriage.[117] With no regard for the impact upon the lives of the individuals involved, the family's breakup was fodder for the moralist press.

On a hot evening in July the following year, Edith Mingoni Toussant was dining with friends in a Roman restaurant, wearing a dress revealing her shoulders and upper back. Four months later, the evening commanded three columns on *La Stampa*'s front page, in which Mingoni Toussant's name was cited and her picture published. As the daily recalled, scandalized by her outfit 'three DC deputies... impulsively confronted a woman who was quietly having dinner with some men, reproaching her for wearing a morally unsuitable dress'.[118] In the ensuing argument, Mingoni Toussant was reportedly slapped across the face. Her lawsuit for injuries was sustained and an Interior Ministry inquiry launched to establish if the three deputies had 'acted within the law and their mandate'. They, in turn, questioned what actions the Ministry would take 'to check a fashion that offended the morals and dignity of citizens, even in the city'.[119] One of the three deputies was Oscar Luigi Scalfaro, the future ninth president of the republic from 1992 to 1999, who stated: 'when a woman goes too far in a public display, she ceases to be a private woman'.[120] Defended in the Catholic press, Scalfaro's moralistic bigotry was slammed by lay publications and the PCI.

In 1953, the body of Wilma Montesi[121] was found on the beach at Tor Vaianica, on the Lazio coastline, near Rome. The subsequent case against Piero Piccioni, son of DC Deputy Prime Minister and Foreign Minister Attilio Piccioni, was one of the Republic's first infamous crime stories. The titillating cocktail of sex, an unexplained death, politicians and members of Roman high society was intensified by rumours of orgies and black masses. With Roman drawing rooms already filled with tales of the night-time arrival of rafts loaded with naked Tunisian women eager to please the rich, in 1958, an impromptu strip by a Turkish dancer, Aiché Nanà,[122] during a private party of personalities and VIPs that included Anita Ekberg, drew comparisons with Sodom and Gomorrah.[123]

As the print media sought to address its falling readership with a combination of hero-worship and scandal, 'it was the great season of magazines which, with the most precision possible, recorded the sexual, loving, married, procreational relationships of all known men and women in Italy... actors, actresses, princes, princesses and singers.'[124] Within De Gasperi's moralistic Italy, the DC, the Church and their media army established and reinforced a Christian-based society in which immoral, scandalous behaviour was mercilessly judged and publicly punished.

In this atmosphere, Fausto Coppi's extramarital relationship with Giulia Occhini was explosive material, despite him having been a darling of the Catholic media: 'Everybody knows Coppi the champion. And everybody loves to imagine themselves like him, even in their private lives, safe and strong, flexible and rigid: decisive and quick; just like when he pushes on the pedals with feline softness and force.'[125] The Communist Coppi was apparently forgotten until he offended Catholic morality.

A well-known secret for some time, the affair broke when Occhini appeared at Coppi's side following his world championship victory, in August 1953. What the couple hadn't fully taken into consideration was how scandalized religious, hypocritical Italy would be, despite affairs being regularly forgiven on the basis of penitence in order to save the marriages upon which the well-regulated society was based.[126] With Christian Democratic Italy highly moral and sex-phobic towards both procreational and recreational activities, their affair was grave enough alone. With the added dimensions of Coppi's public adoration and his slight downturn in form, which was attributed to his extra expenditures of energy, it became a national scandal.

It was yet another stark comparison with Bartali, whose longevity, success and vigour were attributed to his 'pious religious life that enabled his moral and physical fibre to work like a clock', because 'a Christian life lived in a Christian way is the ideal means of gaining earthly successes'.[127] The virtuous, chaste, family-oriented, Catholic hero contrasted with Coppi's pantomime villain. Transgressing morality and expectations about top-class athletes, he was publicly spurned for succumbing to the not-so-original sin.

With the law punishing women for even the most occasional case of adultery and men only in the event of the husband 'keeping a concubine in the marital home or somewhere else well-known',[128] the trial of Coppi and Occhini commanded national attention. Publicly rejected by her father and accused of gold-digging, Occhini was forced to live under house arrest in Ancona. With the moral current considering women more responsible than men for the upkeep of sexual morality, Occhini was seen as having committed the greater crime, especially having left her two children to whom she was denied access. Spending four days in prison in the autumn of 1954, her fellow detainees, a thief and a prostitute, were pressed for revelations. Apparently too vulgar to publish, their accounts only added to moralistic titillation and speculation.[129]

Reinforcing the gravity of their offence, their eldest children were called to give court evidence as 'injured parties', with Occhini unable to attend due to her advanced pregnancy. As Mario Cervi reported, the judge asked nine-year-old Loretta Locatelli if she had met Coppi. 'Yes. Once, I saw him at Gardone. We followed the race by car. That night I went to sleep with a woman who was with mum.'[130] Gripping the nation and selling huge amounts of newspapers and magazines, the trial conveniently distracted from the Wilma Montesi case. 'Fausto Coppi, dismissed by the judge, went towards the exit. He turned to look at the crowd that filled the court-room, but didn't see one friendly face.'[131]

Having denied the charge of adultery, claiming to have been Coppi's secretary, Occhini was found guilty and given a three-month suspended prison sentence.[132] The extreme punishment was unfortunately necessary, according to De Gasperi's spokesperson Vincenzo Cecchini: 'Coppi is the idol of our innocent children and for that, we cannot and must not make good his sins.'[133] Charged with abandoning the marital home and conduct contrary to family order, he received a two-month suspended sentence. His passport withdrawn, Coppi was also impeded from racing abroad. With his name tarnished, Coppi's sins and guilt added lustre to Bartali's halo.

Some doted on Bartali, others on Coppi. 'The old and the young... the white and the red... the chatterbox and the reserved, the iron man and the man of crystal.... The faithful one until the death of his wife Adriana, the adulterer that leaves his wife Bruna and daughter Marina for Giulia Occhini... the Dama Bianca'[134]

Symbolizing Italy's division between left and right, good and evil, past and progress, Coppi and Bartali were used to collectively and socially recreate or re-imagine Christian democracy's desired vision of post-war Italy; a traditional, patriarchal society that prioritized the family. Even in 1993, *La Gazzetta*'s coverage of Occhini's death, following 18 months in a coma after a car accident, reflected the residual ire: 'That woman who robbed the great champion's heart' and 'the affair that shook and scandalized Italy'.[135] It also raised a number of awkward questions about Italian society, most notably after Occhini gave birth to Coppi's son in Argentina. Born in Italy, Faustino would have been forced to take the surname of Occhini's legal husband, who she could not divorce.

That year, *Noi donne*, the Italian Communist Party's women's magazine, ran a series of articles detailing extreme cases resulting from Italy's lack of a divorce law, the need for which Luigi Sansone proposed to parliament, in 1954. The Coppi–Occhini case only underlined his argument about the harmful effects of indissoluble marriages.[136] Within the general liberalization of society and erosion of Catholic control, sporting personalities were arguably the only Italians with the necessary finance and social capital to mount the challenge. Following Coppi's premature death from malaria, in 1960, few wanted to think beyond the 'exceptional athletic personality of the deceased champion... admired and loved by the sporting public that was removed from the shameful, disrespectful atmosphere of his familial, sentimental and material affairs, on which certain newspapers that boast of being educational, speculated.[137]

A Cold War and hot economy

Soon after the 18-year-old Giampiero Boniperti gave Juventus a ninth-minute lead against Roma, in December 1947, the 26-year old Juventus president's watch began to ring, to the amusement of all around. Following Juventus' 3-2 victory, Gianni Agnelli went to the dressing room where, immersed in the celebrations, he took the watch from his wrist and offered it to Boniperti: 'I'd bet that Juventus would score within the first ten minutes and set the alarm for that. It's down to you that I won the bet and Juventus the match, for which, the watch is yours. Take it!'[1]

Totocalcio: funding success

Ever since Romans charged chariots around the *Circo Massimo*, horse racing and trotting have been popular in Italy. The modern sport emerged in Padua in the early nineteenth century, but its cradle was Bologna, where Captain Giuseppe Ballerini – a Garibaldian cavalryman – formed the Italian Trotting Association, in 1885. Later becoming the Italian Trotting Union (UIU), its headquarters moved to Rome. With the majority of track revenue coming from entry fees and commercial enterprises, as hippodromes began to appear all over Italy and competition grew, Bologna introduced gambling to lure spectators and punters from neighboring regions.

A version of Lotto existed in the Genoese Republic in the mid-sixteenth century, although it is best known as an eighteenth- and nineteenth-century Neapolitan passion. Football gambling, according to Papa and Panico, was rooted in the ancient game of *Pallone*, an unimaginable fusion of tennis and volleyball with a dedicated following that loved a flutter. Reaching the height of its popularity in the 1800s, it left a tradition of betting on matches that was inherited by calcio. With wagers initially made with private bookmakers and restricted to the match in progress, the 1911 Genoa–Andrea Doria derby saw an astronomical 10,000 lire of stakes.[2]

In February 1939 *Il Calcio Illustrato* published a letter from Neapolitan student Maurizio Barendson proposing a pools-type betting system, which the FIGC president and CONI secretary General Giorgio Vaccaro rejected due to its potential to pollute the sport.[3] Almost fifteen years later sports journalist Massimo Della Pergola suggested another result-prediction scheme. Closely resembling one in Switzerland, where he spent much of the war in a concentration camp, Della Pergola presented his plan to general indifference, before his Sport Italy Society Ltd (*Sport Italia – Società a responsabilità limitata –* SISAL) was franchised to organize and manage the pools on CONI's behalf. Although Lotto already existed, it was the apparent knowledge and scientific study required that appealed to the football-obsessed nation. For non-graduates in footballology, there was still the heartfelt bet, the hunch or housewife's choice. Mixing the national passions of football and gambling, *Totocalcio* had nationwide appeal.

For an outlay of 30 lire per column Italians played their first *schedina* or coupon on 5 May 1946, during the second round of playoff matches to decide the national champion. The first to hit a 'perfect 12' was Emilio Blasetti, who collected 463,846 lire.[4] Although *Totocalcio*'s initial take-up was slow, its growing success and SISAL's refusal to reduce its commission from 18 to 13 per cent encouraged CONI to take control at the end of their agreement, in September 1948. President Einaudi then nationalized SISAL and transferred its responsibilities to *Totocalcio*, without compensation. Controlled by CONI, its profits were intended to guarantee sport's autonomy from government funding and state intervention. Raising little over seven million lire in 1946, takings grew fivefold within ten years, with 48 per cent of income allocated to prize money, 25 per cent to CONI, 23 per cent to the state, and four per cent to the agents. The first multi-million-lire winner was a Sardinian miner, Giovanni Mannu, who, on 5 February 1950, 'became the symbol of an Italy turned upside down, where the impossible had become reality'.[5] His 12 correct predictions netted him 77 million lire and 'winning a SISAL' became synonymous with a huge stroke of luck.

Following an initial lack of enthusiasm among *schedina* vendors, due to the extra demands upon their working week, *Totocalcio*'s popularity soon saw it available in bars and barbers throughout the country. By 1975, an estimated 35 per cent of Italians were said to do the pools.[6] Betting in on- and off-course bookmakers also grew, with the Tris' 1958 launch intended to attract the casual punter. Run four times per week, Monday to Saturday, the race remains an

Italian institution with bars and bookies taking easy-to-make bets on the first three horses in a specified race. As a thirst for unexpected riches grew, previous taboos about gambling were forgotten.

The economic miracle

By the mid-1950s Italy was still relatively underdeveloped, with its industrial sector concentrated primarily within the industrial triangle of Turin, Milan and Genoa. Most Italians earned their livelihoods in small factories, public administration and shops, with agriculture occupying over 40 per cent of the population. Standards of living were low, and only 7.4 per cent of households had electricity, drinking water and an inside toilet, in 1951.[7] With poverty rife, particularly among the southern rural population where there was massive underemployment and starvation, emigration was a consistent fact of life.

Italy changed dramatically between 1958 and 1963, as the economy boomed and the country rapidly modernized. Hard work, low pay, foreign loans, integration within the European economy, low taxes and generous lending rates for business, all within a golden age for international trade, saw Italy's economy grow at an incredible average of five and a half per cent per annum, from 1951 to 1958.[8] With per capita income growing faster than anywhere in Europe, the mass workforce further stimulated the boom by purchasing consumer goods,[9] 'the fetish object of society's new, lower middle class'.[10]

> Whereas in 1958 only 12 per cent of Italian families owned a television, by 1965 the number had risen to 49 per cent. In the same period the number owning fridges increased from 13 to 55 per cent, and washing machines from 3 to 23 per cent. Between 1950 and 1964 the number of private cars in Italy rose from 342,000 to 4.67 million, and motorcycles from 700,000 to 4.3 million. Eating habits changed, with more money being spent on meat and dairy products than ever before.[11]

In the meantime, entrepreneurs invested their profits, squeezed from the low labour costs of a weakly unionized workforce, into renovating their factories, which modernized dramatically.[12]

Productivity was further encouraged by the introduction of American machinery and knowledge, plus Marshall Aid. Moreover, the liberalization of Italian tariffs on over 75 per cent of products in 1951, which culminated in the 1957 Treaty of Rome and the European Common Market, was not the disaster for Italian industry that many had predicted. In fact, the end of protectionism and the stimulation of competition turned Italian brands into international household names, especially in electro-domestics. Small companies such as Candy and Zanussi began producing on a mass scale and by 1967 Italy had become the largest source of washing machines in Europe and the third biggest global manufacturer of refrigerators. Olivetti's typewriter production also increased fivefold, as Italian exports grew at over 16 per cent per annum.

Despite improvements to southern infrastructure and incentives to encourage business initiatives there, the majority of economic expansion remained in the north, which only widened the gap between the two. As the industrial and service sector boom reduced the working agricultural population by 30 per cent, the economic miracle became not just a story of wealth but yet another of mass migration. From 1958 to 1963 half a million Italians moved to Germany and Switzerland, where they often formed strong communities. Adapting to local conditions and influenced by their new environments, while many metamorphosed others developed an awareness of contemporary Italy beyond the peninsula. Besides its cuisine, Italian industrial design, architecture, painting, sculpture, fashion and film commanded international respect, and raised Italy's image enormously.

Over 900,000 southerners also moved to northern Italy, which had an even greater impact upon the development of national identity as friendships, 'inter'-marrying, mixed working environments and improving education encouraged a sharing of linguistic and cultural traditions. More negatively, totally unprepared for the influx of immigrants, housing conditions in northern cities were often terrible and landlords discriminatory. Attics, basements, buildings awaiting demolition and disused farms in city peripheries were all put to use, and overcrowding was rife.

The situation was worsened by the prioritization of export-led growth and the production of private consumer goods, over investment in schools, hospitals, public transport and low-cost housing. In the absence of such planning, the middle classes 'sought salvation in private spending and consumption: on using a car to go to work, on private medicine and on private nursery schools... The "miracle" was thus an exquisitely private affair, which reinforced the historic tendency of each family to fend for itself as best it could.'[13] Most seriously

> the lacking reforms in public housing and public assistance, in transport and distribution, aggravated the hardships and cost of living for the working classes in the big urban centres that lacked sufficient infrastructure and investment for mass immigration. This accentuated the strength of protest and social conflict that would emerge with great vigour at the end of the sixties.[14]

Figure 12: *'Cycling's champions, back on the streets':* The Radio and TV Weekly, *March 1956*

Another symbol of the boom was television, with RAI broadcasting its first programme in 1954. The 88,000 license holders that year grew to one million by 1958, over two million by 1960, passing four million in 1963.[15] A state monopoly, television was effectively controlled by RAI management and the DC, with significant influence from the Church. As Beppe Severgnini describes in his satirical look at Italian society: 'It was chaste, instructive television. It didn't tell us what we were like; it told us what we should have been like.'[16] Among the many excluded parties, the PCI was the only one really aware of TV's importance as a medium and, consequently, dedicated much time to observing its output, discussing, publicizing and sometimes opposing it.

RAI's President from 1954 to 1956, was Filiberto Guala. A member of Catholic Action, he imposed a strict code upon broadcasts that were built upon strongly anti-Communist news and current affairs, religious programmes, plus light entertainment/variety and quiz shows.

> For the young, who were to constitute the majority of the first migrants, the lure of the city was irresistible. In the evenings, in the piazzas of the southern villages, their talk was of nothing else. The television of the local bar transmitted images from the North, images of a consumer world, of Vespas, portable radios, football heroes, new fashions, nylon stockings, mass-produced dresses, houses full of electrical appliances, Sunday excursions in the family FIAT.[17]

Sport was RAI's trump card, almost from day one. The first football match broadcast was Italy versus Egypt in 1954, with commentary by Niccolò Carosio. The *Giro d'Italia*, however, was the 'metaphor of Italy's modernization... [as] the race took the products of the first Italian economic boom all over Italy: brilliantine, coffee machines, liqueurs, salami, toothpaste, refrigerators and cookers. This was the start of the *Giro* show: no longer a soap opera, but a consumerist saga.'[18] But, in becoming one of the miracle's motors, such exposure caused the race to lose some of its mystique and appeal.

> As seen on television the Giro lost the essential emotional charge transmitted by the live event on the road. By an uninterrupted repetition of images, photo finishes, slow-motion shots that scrutinized every move, revealed every secret, probed into every detail, television, first in black and white and then in colour, numbed the fancy and the imagination that had made the Giro so popular for decades.[19]

With TV initially the preserve of the rich, increased disposable income and mass production quickly changed it from a collective experience within bars, cafés and neighbours' houses to one that increasingly atomized society into close-knit family circles. A mass phenomenon by the late 1960s, it also became a powerful DC propaganda tool with unprecedented access to Italians. Even so, it perturbed the Catholic Church. While DC rule and its US alliance were strong weapons in the war on Communism, increased material prosperity and consumerism encouraged greater individualism that threatened to undermine some fundamentals of Christian democratic society. Rather than the nightmare of the Bolshevik beast, 'it was the American model of consumer society that had revealed itself as the Trojan Horse within the citadel of Catholic values'.[20]

Bracketing the economic miracle years, Pope John XXIII's papacy, from 1958 to 1963, attempted to reconcile the Church with the new consumer products and adapt American culture and lifestyle to Catholic traditions by removing all that was considered potentially dangerous. 'The Church was not only against the ethic of "the American way of life" but also to the development of consumerism for its own sake and a mass culture that wasn't rigidly organized in existing social structures.'[21] While Italy was frantically modernizing, conservative forces were trying to maintain an already outdated, traditional society.

Consuming cars

A deliberate choice by the rationalized industrial sector and the legacy of an artisanal tradition that valued aesthetics, post-war Italian goods quickly developed a recognizable style that associated the 'Made in Italy' brand with quality and innovation. One of the most emblematic sectors of Italian production was transport, in particular the creation of individual, miniature, economical means designed to appeal to working-class desires for social mobility.

In 1945, the Piaggio factory was in ruins. Seeking to diversify from aircraft production, plans were made to reproduce a small motor scooter that had either been found in an aeroplane or seen used by German or Allied parachutists.[22] Corradino D'Ascanio, who had already designed a successful helicopter, developed the first scooter that had to be able to cope with the economic and physical demands of the day. Safe, solid, affordable, practical in the city and highly economical to run, the Vespa was an immediate success, and production initially unable to match demand. With 2,000 sold in the first year and 10,000 in the second, the millionth Vespa rolled off the line in 1956.

Shrewdly marketed in daily papers and magazines and displayed in Lancia showrooms, Vespas were presented to the era's celebrities, the American military and the Pope, to arouse public interest and create a sense of lifestyle and affluence. With cars expensive and the bicycle still the prominent means of transport, the Vespa offered the prospect of travelling significantly longer distances without fatigue and with space for a passenger, tools or goods to trade. This freedom was augmented by the assurance of a network of service stations that contributed to the craze for weekend excursions to the countryside and trips even further afield to the sea or mountains. An enormous status symbol, the Vespa appealed to students and factory workers, while women, who initially rode pillion side-saddle to preserve their dignity, soon took charge themselves, two wheels once again extending their liberty.

Promoted by the astute formation of Vespa clubs that were strictly controlled by Piaggio in order to ensure the right image,[23] the company's marketing strategies targeted the aspirations of the young:

> beyond the dream, the invitation was explicit: to take up the opportunities that come your way, to not give up your desires; to enjoy your freedom and fill it to the brim; to race, on a Vespa of course, to reach the goals which your heart gives you – even if others want to stop you from reaching them.[24]

In conservative, morally and sexually repressed Italy, where those goals rarely extended beyond a regular income, marriage and a family, the Vespa's

Figure 13: *Two-wheeled, motorized pulling power*

contribution to courtship also smoothed the road to matrimony. But, while many Italians, Neapolitans in particular, learnt to balance entire families on a Vespa, the modern, urban family required an equally economical utility car that would function as efficiently as the Vespa in the increasingly crowded streets of Italy's major towns and cities.

✪ ✪ ✪ ✪

From 1955 to 1960 car sales rocketed, with production increasing fourfold in the mid-boom years. Having rebuilt its war-damaged plant and introduced American equipment and techniques, FIAT was key in the sector's amazing growth that not even the opening of European trade borders in 1956 could threaten.[25] With 400,000 of its 600 model in circulation within its first three years of production, FIAT brought 'car ownership within the means of even modest salaries... reduced the demands of unreachable dreams, while keeping them all intact',[26] thereby making the Sunday drive a possibility for many.

The 600's success encouraged the even more economical FIAT 500, the original low-cost car that heralded the era of mass motoring. Economically manufactured with a small engine, its minimal price, fuel consumption, road tax and insurance costs appealed to middle- and upper-working-class aspirations, thereby creating a new band of driver among those groups that had been decimated by the war but whose spending would drive the boom. As Emanuela Scarpellini explains:

> the motor car is the icon of the contemporaneousness of the new urban and industrial landscape; it expresses spatial and social mobility; it affirms the value of individuality; it launches new modes of work and consumption. Everything that makes the product even more desired by Italians.[27]

The FIAT 500 was sporty and compact, hinting at speed while giving the illusion of space. In addition to standard black, consumers had a choice of white, cream and blue, plus an array of optional extras, such as a fold-back roof suited to the Mediterranean climate and reclining seats that were less than appropriate in De Gasperi's sexually-repressed Italy. Freeing women and young people from social controls, the car drew suspicion and scorn from the Church, with Milan's Archbishop initially banning all religious orders from driving, as with the bicycle some 60–70 years earlier. Although arguably less dramatic than the bicycle's introduction that completely revolutionized personal, social and economic mobility, the impact of the affordable car was significant. Complementing a national transport strategy focussed upon developing Italy's motorway network to the detriment of railways, it stimulated leisure and travel. Encouraging Italians to discover their country and thereby erode centuries of regionalism,

Figure 14: The *original smart car*

the liberty provided by affordable motoring contributed to the Romagna Riviera becoming one of Europe's biggest seaside resorts,[28] as Italian tourism grew.

Car ownership and the developing motorway network also enabled football fans to travel away and watch their team. Laying the foundations of a phenomenon that was to explode in the 1960s, this dedicated fandom also reduced the mystique of distant Italian regions and their peoples on one hand, while increasing animosity between them. As former journeys of exploration became incursions into enemy territory, the positive opportunities offered by greater mobility and modern transport were undermined. That said, the impact of improved transport was enormous, with the economical family car symbolizing and inspiring change.

> In Italian society, the utility car performed the task of allowing whole social classes... to dream of the real possibility of being comfortably off. It brought a dream within reach and, indeed, immediately realisable...
>
> These are the reasons why, for better or for worse, the Italians owe much to the utility car. And certainly Italians have given much back in return: they are by far the most fanatical nation in the world when it comes to cars and car racing; they transformed a working-class vehicle into a legend.[29]

The rise of Ferrari

> The fact is that driving a car in Italy is dangerous. There don't seem to be any laws. They do U turns when they want, they drive on the left or the right, they go onto the pavement, knock down pedestrians, sound their horns like madmen, always try to overtake whatever is in front, they shout and swear at each other: yet... I've never seen an accident.[30]

Writing home from Naples, in 1960, the American author John Fante described a nation that had embraced the motor car at all costs. By the 1960s, city streets were already choked, with public transport, infrastructure and the quality of urban life sacrificed at the altar of the car. Somewhat contradicting himself two months later, in Rome, Fante continued:

> The traffic here, however, is a national disgrace. The streets simply stream with blood, while these crazy Italians kill each other in those lethal little Fiats. The motorists despise pedestrians and (without joking) love arriving unexpectedly at a crowded junction and making people run for their lives.[31]

The by-product of small, affordable vehicles was a stimulation of the luxury market, as the original car owners sought to distinguish themselves from the masses. With FIAT dominating mass production, other manufacturers focussed on exclusivity. The ultimate, expensive Italian good, Ferrari's post-war history was an alternative account of the economic miracle, luxury over utility, the sheen on the post-war grime.

> The exclusive form of the Ferrari line and the work involved seemed not to belong to the... reconstruction period. Is that why it became a myth?... Searching for the Hollywood dream instead of the Neo-Realist idea of resisting industrial speed in favour of nature and the emancipation of the poor classes? As an investment in the privileges of private property rather than the culture of public services? [32]

A small, artisan workshop, Ferrari was unsuited to mass production. Neither able nor interested in making economical utility cars, with the war over the small, highly skilled workforce began producing racing cars once again, this time with 12-cylinder engines. While the Auto Union and Mercedes teams already did this, it was Ferrari's reputation that added allure. Aware of racing's importance to publicize its commercial product, the *Scuderia Ferrari* began competing under its own name in 1947, just as the company's first sports car, the 125S, emerged from the workshop.

The car's image was embellished by the 54-year-old Tazio Nuvolari's fame, skill and unquenchable thirst to drive, despite his failing health. Overtaking 14 cars during his victory in the 18-lap *Circuito di Parma*, in which Ferrari gained its first one-two finish, Nuvolari put the winner of the Miss Parma competition (which he had adjudicated the previous evening) in the passenger seat, before conducting an impromptu lap of honour, publicity that money couldn't buy. Ferrari appealed to hedonistic, jet-set playboys and celebrities. In 1949, film director Roberto Rossellini was one of the first to visit Maranello. Having just left the Italian actress Anna Magnani, he was accompanied by Ingrid Bergmann fresh from her own scandal after leaving her Swedish husband and three children. No paragon of fidelity himself, Ferrari savoured the publicity.

Despite his almost immediate post-war success, Ferrari was reluctant to turn his back on profitable wartime industrial production to move soley into the luxury car market. He was seduced by his former driver Luigi Chinetti's tales of American prosperity where great prestige and status that were attached to the mere knowledge and appreciation of European style, were significantly augmented by ostentatious demonstrations of wealth. The heritage of the Ferrari name plus the car's growing track successes, soon made it irresistible to the international elite. Ferrari vehicles were also promoted by the working class millions that consumed its image; the only thing that they could afford.

> Investment in production and quality was therefore done with a complex strategic policy that overturned the usual equation for consumer products of low production costs and high advertising spending. Even though investments in car production were enormous, Ferrari exploited to the utmost the fantasies created not by the car user but by those who consumed the image of the name, its narration, its story.[33]

Celebrities and public figures flocked to associate themselves with the car: in 1950 the team was blessed by Pope Pius XII, while in 1953 Rossellini took the wheel of one of 28 Ferraris in that year's *Mille Miglia*, publicity coups that were maximized by television.

While this aided the international diffusion and development of brand fantasy, the glamour was dependent upon track success. Ferrari, however, was a traditional, conservative force in motor racing. With his dictatorial management-style discouraging innovation and inhibiting the car's development, the return of Mercedes Benz to Formula One threatened the prancing horse's leading role. 'In protest against what he felt was a lack of appropriate support from the state and from Italian industry', Ferrari announced that the team would only compete in major events in the 1954 season.[34] Aware of its commercial potential and national importance, FIAT bought the Lancia racing team's stock, which it used to make Ferrari competitive again.

With superstition rooted deep in Italian culture, it was no great surprise that *La Gazzetta* noted the significance of Piero Taruffi's unexpected victory at the 13th attempt, in the 1957 *Mille Miglia*, with Ferrari's new V12 engine: 'Who said thirteen brings bad luck?'[35] Considered a 'catastrophic day for Italian football', after the national team lost 6-1 to Yugoslavia, the headlines were tactless given the previous day's deaths of *Mille Miglia* contestant Alfonso de Portago, his co-driver/navigator Edmund Nelson and ten spectators – including five children – after the Spanish driver's car flew into the crowd near Mantua.[36] Reputed to value his cars more than the lives of his drivers, Ferrari was charged with manslaughter after apparently fitting the vehicle with unsuitable tyres for the conditions. Cleared four years later, the damage to his reputation was done. When Luigi Musso died at Monza in 1958, the Vatican's previous blessings became a demand for the 'severest of measures – even the abolition of such competitions, if necessary – to put a stop to this massacre of human life'.[37]

In 1963, the car manufacturing giant Ford expressed an interest in buying 90 per cent of the Ferrari business and 10 per cent of the racing sector. Intent on maintaining total control Ferrari refused the offer, but Ford's interest emboldened FIAT to satiate its longstanding takeover urge. On 18 June 1969, a meeting between Enzo Ferrari and Gianni Agnelli resulted in a partnership: FIAT bought 40 per cent of the company and would receive another 50 per cent on Enzo's death,[38] with the final 10 per cent remaining with the family. With FIAT taking over road production, Ferrari controlled the racing team. Receiving a massive injection of capital and know-how, without sacrificing the company's Italian ownership, Ferrari's subsequent successes in the 1970s earned it widespread national support for the first time. Most notable was Niki Lauda's World Driver's Championship victory in 1975, which he would probably have repeated the following season but for a horrific crash at the Nürburgring, which left him severely burnt. His return to the track, one month later, was the type of courage/recklessness that Ferrari loved. Similar in character, Lauda's replacement Gilles Villeneuve won huge popularity before dying in a crash in Belgium, in 1982.

One of Italy's most globally recognized products, Ferrari cars and their drivers exported and marketed a brand that transcended the company itself to directly represent the country. Stimulating and representing its modernization, economic growth and identity, Italian sport contributed as a whole, with its initial post-war failure and growing success reflecting the immediate post-war despair and speedy recovery.

Football failures, 1950–66

World Cup holder since 1938, Italy's performance in 1950 was the first of many post-war embarrassments. Lamed by the Superga disaster, the squad's performance was further hindered by the decision to opt for a rough, two-week sea crossing to Brazil, rather than fly. Unprepared, Italy lost the first game to a strong Swedish team and was eliminated, despite beating Paraguay in the second match. The players took a 35-hour plane journey home. Indicating the game's importance and significant number of listeners, a RAI newsflash announced the outbreak of the Korean War in the middle of the match, the bulletin also underlining Christian Democrat influence over the broadcaster's editorial line: 'War has started in the East: Communist troops have invaded the territory of the Republic of Korea. The red troops are advancing, sowing death and destruction on all fronts.'[39]

For almost the next 20 years, Italian football remained stubbornly in crisis. Besides the impact of Superga, technical and organizational problems within the FIGC hindered the emergence of new talent. With the national team run by management 'teams' and training completely separated from selection,[40] it wasn't until 1967 that the *azzurri* were returned to the custodianship of one manager. At club level, increasingly wealthy owners responded to the dearth of talent by importing expensive foreign players, first from northern Europe and then from South America. Funded by profits from the economic miracle, by 1967 the nation's dramatic economic growth was visible in a reversal of Italy's football fortunes, with *calcio* rising to fifteenth in its annual industrial turnover.[41] Some owners that had rejuvenated their clubs to become successful, high profile and marketable, began to seek a return on their investments.

✪ ✪ ✪ ✪

1950 was far from the low point for Italian football. A 3-0 defeat to Hungary in Rome, in 1953, provoked the ire of the Communist daily *L'Unità*: 'Today, the azzurri truly demonstrated the exact measure of our decadence in the field of football. Their lack of strength, their inability to resist tiredness, their submissiveness, effeminacy, and lack of virility are the fruits of years of immoral sport.'[42] The match was contested on the eve of the crucial 1953 general election, and *L'Unità*'s offence at the result was heightened by the political speculation surrounding the match:

> The fact is that an attempt to ruin this splendid day of sport was made in advance... with huge and short-sighted Christian Democrat electoral speculation... For one kilometre, between the fence and the stadium entrance, monotonous rows of banners with De Gasperi's logo accompanied us. One huge banner, 'Vote DC', hugged the immaculate white walls of a Fascist building besides the Olympic stadium.[43]

In 1954, Italy exited the World Cup in a play-off against hosts Switzerland, and failed to qualify for the 1958 tournament in Sweden after losing matches in Portugal and Northern Ireland. The defeat in Belfast was particularly painful. Scheduled for 4 December 1957, with the Hungarian referee and linesman unable to reach the stadium due to fog, Italy accepted arbitration by Northern Irish officials with the match downgraded to a friendly. The enraged crowd

> proceeded to attack the Italians after booing their national anthem. The match itself was extremely dirty, and objects were thrown at the *azzurri* as they left the pitch at half-time... After the game, a number of players were set upon before the police arrived.[44]

While there was no apparent, political/religious motive, Italy had acquired a knack of being more offensive off the field than on it. Losing the replayed match, Italy failed to qualify for the finals for the first time.

The 1962 'Battle of Santiago', was widely recalled as having been stoked by two Italian newspaper articles outlining Chilean poverty. The inferno was, however, undoubtedly fanned by the ineptitude and alleged corruption of English referee Ken Ashton, who allowed the match to degenerate into a series of punches, kung-fu kicks and mass brawls.[45] With two players sent off, Italy conceded two late goals and, once again, was eliminated from the World Cup at the first hurdle.

Chilean ire had also been stoked by the presence of four *oriundi* – first- and second-generation Italians born in South America – in the Italian squad; stolen champions that represented a professional game where money spoke. Despite their pivotal roles in Italy's 1930s triumphs, suspicions had surrounded the *oriundi* since Enrique Guaita and two colleagues tried to escape the country and avoid their military call-up, in 1936. With their national commitment already under question, they acquired an apparent responsibility for the lack of emerging talent. In the previous ten years over 130 foreign players had arrived, with the majority coming from South America. With the buck passed by all involved in the debacle of Santiago, the *oriundi* bore the brunt of the criticism. In 1964, foreigners were again banned from Italian football.

Italy's dismal performance in the 1966 World Cup, hosted and won by England, further demonstrated years of poor leadership and management, plus the growing importance of television. Whereas it had taken two days for images from Santiago to hit Italian screens, the live broadcast of the national team's demise intensified the impact of the defeat. Yet beyond the elimination from the tournament, it was the nature of it, or the opponents, to be precise, which hurt. Despite having destroyed Australia to qualify, North Korea was no force in world football. With an average height of five feet five inches, its players were not expected to trouble an Italian team with a string of impressive results behind it. Scoring the unexpected winner Pak Do Ik's name is widely recalled in both England and Italy, more fondly in the former where the North Korean underdogs were embraced by local fans in Middlesbrough, where the match had been played. As North Korea headed for a quarter-final against Portugal, Italy returned home to a barrage of tomatoes at Genoa, the plane having been diverted from Milan's airport that angry fans had invaded.

Coach Edmondo Fabbri initially shouldered the responsibility for another *calcio Caporetto*, before conducting his own inquest that revealed a number of player statements alleging negative doping with pills and injections. Although soon withdrawn, the 'allegations were incredibly serious – elements within the national staff had conspired to produce a national disaster. The "conspiracy" was apparently aimed at getting rid of FIGC president Giuseppe Pasquale. For journalist Antonio Ghirelli, Fabbri "had clearly lost his head".[46] Fabbri was sacked and banned for eleven months. While the negative doping theory warrants no re-examination, that players were talking of mysterious pills and injections was significant.

At club level, the green shoots of Italy's reconstruction and economic recovery were more evident, especially in Juventus' *Stadio Comunale* that was increasingly populated by Sicilians and southern Italians employed in the FIAT factory. Profoundly altering the social base of Juventus supporters, football mediated the tensions between the Torinese and the immigrant community.

> Among much diversity a passion for sport was one of the greatest elements of integration and dialogue, the only authentically equal relationship between the two peoples of the city that expressed itself among the youngest immigrants in support for the 'black and whites'.[47]

Owned and funded by the Agnelli family, Juventus won three league titles in four years – 1958, 1960 and 1961 – thanks to the family's considerable investment into the squad, using profits from FIAT's increased production and sales. While southern fans didn't desert their home-town teams, their presence at the *Comunale* almost never manifested itself in hostility towards the team of the hand that fed them.

Unlike the Agnelli family, Napoli FC's shipping magnate owner Achille Lauro was one of the first businessmen to openly develop populist politics through personal investment and the appropriation of the squad. Demonstrating how politicians used local football teams to establish support, Lauro appealed to local traditions while developing his own charismatic cult, as 'Napoli became a supplement to his persona and political movement'.[48] In the autumn of 1952, he led a long line of donkeys dressed in blue through the historic quarter of Naples, to publicize the 105 million lire spent on Bergamo Atalanta's Hasse Jeppson. Like the national economy, *calcio* was equally top-heavy with the majority of big clubs based within Italy's northern economic triangle. Replicated by the minimal number of southern footballers, ambitious owners began importing expensive players and managers.

With Lauro's football adventure coinciding almost entirely with his term as the city's Mayor, during the 1950s and 1960s, his catch-all slogan was: 'A great Naples for a great Naples.'[49] Intent on re-vitalizing the city and developing local tourism, he talked about 'the "taste of money, of wealth, of full wallets, of living a better life at whatever cost". He talked of cancelling images of "Neapolitan hunger", of the resignation to that total misery that marked the south, which the liberal bourgeoisie looked at little or never.'[50] Jeppson's purchase indicated Lauro's ambitions for both the team and the impending Neapolitan administrative elections, translating the south's battle against the north into an understandable language for the city's mass electorate, while simultaneously restoring hope to Napoli fans. Ignoring reason over spectacle and economic and political speculation, Napoli's failure to break the north's grip on the *scudetto* only confirmed the financial gulf between the two.

> It was necessary to wait until 1987 for an authentic 'southern' club, in the Italian sense of the word, to become champion of Italy and reach an international level, sustaining at the same time the enthusiasm of the natives and the boisterous pride of the southern population, beginning with those forced by the North–South division of labour to emigrate to the northern metropolises.[51]

Boxers and bicycle thieves

Following the end of the anti-Fascist coalition and the removal of the Communist and Socialist parties from government in 1947, both the left and right sought to establish popular bases of support. With a direct role through the CSI and UISP, sport also began to feature in Italian cinema as both poles tried to expand their control over film production, content and reception. By 1959 there were over 10,000 cinemas across the peninsula, plus smaller screens provided by local church associations and *Dopolavoro* groups. But as television ownership grew, cinema attendances began to decline, even if the Italian film industry was well compensated by increased sales to TV companies. Producing more films than Hollywood by the end of the 1960s it controlled half of the domestic market, one of the biggest in Europe, with 50 per cent of its production costs covered by international sales.[52]

In stark contrast to post-war productions intent on airbrushing Italy's image under Fascism, in a direct response to the regime's films, and in addition to a huge number of Hollywood pre-war B movies that were dumped onto Italy as soon as the 1938 Monopoly Law[53] was repealed, there were calls for a truly Italian cinema that would depict current, ordinary, everyday lives. Representing the social, economic and material conditions of the time, Italian neo-realism existed even before the war had concluded, with Roberto Rossellini's *Roma, Città Aperta* (Rome, Open City) narrating the last days of the Nazi occupation of the capital, in 1944. Neo-realism was significant, but accounted for less than one-third of Italian films made between 1945 and 1953.[54] Unable to compete with cheaper US imports, its lifespan was short. By the mid-1950s it had begun to disintegrate, not helped by the Undersecretary for Entertainment, Giulio Andreotti, who employed a 'combination of "market forces", censorship and ideological harassment to strengthen popular genre productions and cut the lifeline to neorealist films'.[55] Already suspicious of television and perceiving such films as contrary to Catholic morality, the DC government 'was hostile both to the makeshift production and methods and to the leftist ideology of most neo-realist film-makers'.[56]

Neo-realism's impact lasted well into the 1960s, however, with the early portrayals of working class hardship morphing into depictions of the new, glamorous, miraculous Italy of cars, scooters and consumer durables. Most notable was Federico Fellini's *La dolce vita*, in 1960, its glamour contrasting dramatically with Vittorio De Sica's comi-tragedy *I Ladri di Bicicletta* (The Bicycle Thieves), ten years earlier. Despite the Constitution's guarantee of the right to work, Italian unemployment had risen to 25 per cent. In this climate, De Sica narrated a father's increasingly desperate search for his stolen bicycle, the key means of working class social and economic mobility, or simply employment. Reflecting and satirizing changing Italy, it contrasted old customs with new consumerism. Ten years later, in 1960, Luchino Visconti's *Rocco e i suoi fratelli* (Rocco and his brothers) made a grittier connection between neo-realism and sport.

While there is no need to add to the wealth of existing research,[57] the genre's authenticity, neo-realism's authentic settings, plausible characters and believable stories made these movies important reflectors and manipulators of social attitudes. With neo-realism rebuked by by Andreotti for washing Italy's dirty laundry in public, the Catholic Cinematographic Centre's widely circulated movie-ratings guide declared *The Bicycle Thieves* 'a dangerous work' marred by 'excessive pessimism'.[58] If somewhat deterministic, it did provide a credible picture of immediate post-war Italy, where unemployment, alienation and poor housing were rife. From the boom years until the 1980s, Italy's major town/city centres and their peripheries changed enormously under building programmes, giving maximum freedom to private initiatives and the construction industry, sacrificing regulation in the name of growth. The biggest public initiative was Amintore Fanfani's one thousand billion lire INA-Casa (*Istituto Nazionale Abitazione*) scheme, in 1949, which produced the type of housing in which the Ricci family lived.

On getting his job as a bill poster Antonio is confronted by his lack of a bicycle, an essential tool of the trade, and is berated by his wife for having pawned his previous one. An investment made against future earnings, the bed sheets are stripped and pawned to retrieve the bike, the film's focal object that commands his attention over that of his young son Bruno.[59] Both father and son have differing appreciations of the bicycle: valuable to Antonio 'only because it promises to replace his feelings of despair and futility with a sense of purpose and meaning; for Bruno, however, the bicycle is... an end in itself'.[60] An essential means of economic survival and everyday life for Antonio, in Bruno's more innocent eyes it retained the escapist fantasy of its early appeal.

Antonio's job as a bill poster is also significant, as he replaces images of Fascist Italy with those of the new Republic and seductive apparitions of American culture and products. Pre-dating the economic miracle, the advertisements that Ricci is supposed to paste indicate the future, stimulating desire and discontent, while relating happiness and fulfilment with the consumption of material and cultural goods. Beyond the adverts, abundance is contrasted with poverty while the appetite for consumption appears to foster unhappiness, as seen in Antonio's quest/obsession to retrieve his bicycle following its theft. 'Instead of asking someone to lend him one, he falls prey to anxiety, and becomes too obsessed to be a father to his son.'[61] More than just a means of transport and employment, Ricci's bike represented pride, faith and hope in the republic, while its theft destroyed conceptions of working class solidarity and exposed the cut-throat world at the bottom of society.

The film climaxes with Antonio's failed attempt to steal a lone bike propped up against the backdrop of thousands more that have brought football fans to a match. Spotted by a member of the crowd, Ricci is chastised before being sent on his way, his failed theft apparently breaking his fixation and reuniting him with his son.

Rocco e i suoi fratelli (1960) was an even bleaker tale of the Parondi family's migration from Lucania (Basilicata) in the deep, rural south to urban, industrial Milan. Told in chapters that narrate the different experiences and destinies of the five brothers, it was a convincing portrayal of Italy during the boom, regularly contrasting the family's illusory dreams with unforgiving reality. Even if the stories of Rocco, Simone and Nadia misrepresented everyday lives within southern, emigrant families, as John Foot proposes: 'In an age when television revealed nothing about what the Communist Party called "Il prezzo del miracolo"' [the price of the miracle], once again '*Rocco e i suoi fratelli* raked through the dirty washing of Italian society.'[62]

Not always characteristic of the economic miracle, the brothers all found work. With solid relationships and jobs in construction and factories, Vincenzo and Ciro were the most stable. Their mother's favoured sons Simone and Rocco, however, shared tormented relationships with a prostitute, who Simone later murders. His desire for the miracle's trappings – glamour, glory and quick money – lead him into boxing, the established poor man's route out of the slums. Despite initial success, his supposed southern work ethic, in contrast with that, apparently, of the Milanese, ruins his dreams and pulls him into the underworld of bars and brothels. His search for *la dolce vita* via the ring brings misery and debt, which his younger brother Rocco repays through servitude to Simone's parasitic promoter.

Although boxing is not the film's principal theme, Simone and Rocco's careers say much about Italy during the economic miracle. Set in Milan, the 'moral capital', the honest toil of Vincenzo and Ciro contrasts with Simone and Rocco's experiences that show an alternative city where money is made through sex and violence. Contrary to what Visconti had intended, his representation of the Parondi family reinforced stereotypes about southern Italians that included backwardness, laziness, dirt, passion, family loyalty, violence, sexual potency, impotence, and criminality. Usually arriving on the *treno del sole* (the sun train), southern immigrants' first impressions of the northern cities

> were bewildering and often frightening. What struck them most were the wide streets full of traffic, the neon lights and advertisement boards, the way the northerners dressed. For those who arrived in the winter, the icy fog which enveloped Turin and Milan was the worst of all; these were cities which seemed not just of another country, but of another planet.[63]

Add discrimination, and Paul Ginsborg's description is more or less exactly what the Parondi family experienced on arriving in Milan.

Boxing success, however, bought acceptance and exclusion from the racism that southerners encountered. Simone and Rocco prove talented fighters, with Rocco becoming European champion. Thereafter, the discrimination that the family experienced on arrival transforms into respect: Rocco's victory is celebrated by the entire apartment block where the family live and his mother Maria is now referred to as Signora rather than Africa, as in the opening scenes. More integrated and socially accepted, the Parondis change apartments for one bearing all the hallmarks of the miracle.

Less talented or less fortunate migrants retreated into their southern communities and cultures and, just as Juventus' stadium reverberated with southern accents for the visits of Palermo and Napoli, so almost all of the spectators for Simone's first big fight were from the south. Yet despite their commonality and the implicit suggestion that southerners only mixed with their own, a fight between two rival groups, after one accuses Simone of having deserted his roots, demonstrates the identity fractures caused by and associated with such migration.

Possessing looks that stretched neo-realism's credibility, the angular features of Simone and Rocco (Alain Delon) represented the good and bad in boxing and the miracle. 'Simone, the only brother whose adult sexual state gets visualized (in the seriously ugly forms of whoring, rape, and hustling)... lose[s] his looks in the process. His face becomes drawn, his figure puffy, and – worst of all given the film's aesthetic of repose – he gets the shakes.'[64] Although despising the sport, Rocco's success is unabated, his victories saving his brother who is unable to save himself, while bettering the family. The last image of Rocco is as a cover star on a boxing magazine pinned up at a newsagent's alongside the main sporting publications of the day: *La Gazzetta dello Sport, Il Guerin Sportivo, Tuttosport, Il Calcio Illustrato* and *Lo Stadio*. Romanticized it might have been, but Rocco had made it in the year that the Olympic Games came to Rome and one young, poor, Italian boxer more or less replicated his rags-to-riches journey.

Cold War games

With the effects of the war still fresh and with many Italians yet to feel those of the miracle, few chose to take up any form of amateur sport or exercise, with any enthusiasm neutered by CONI's elite focus and the lack of facilities. Following the bombardments and their wartime military requisition, gymnasia, athletics tracks and swimming pools were the last things to be rebuilt. Football stadiums were restored to use with private money, but the remainder of Italy's sporting infrastructure had to wait until the stimulus of the 1960 Rome Olympic Games.

On 16 June 1955, the 55 members of the International Olympic Committee (IOC) chose Rome as the 1960 Olympic Games host city.[65] A high-profile opportunity to demonstrate how democratic Italy had quickly moved on from its Fascist past, this great national project within a global event also exposed changes in Italian society and identity, while revealing much about what Italy's leaders wished to show to the outside world. Wanting to be seen as an important and developed actor in the international arena, no longer reconstructing but in full and healthy economic growth, it was also hoped that the Olympics would calm right- and left-wing political extremes and that success would mask the chronic lack of investment in school and mass sport. Yet with Giulio Andreotti nominated president of the Organizing Committee, in thanks for his protection of Onesti,[66] it is unsurprising that the Games assumed a distinctly political flavour.

Muted celebrations and press enthusiasm following the victory over 15 other candidate cities was matched by a modest publicity campaign that was restricted to the months preceding the tournament. Most notable was a 20-minute promotional film that reconnected the modern city with its imperial past, while capturing Romans at play in the antique capital exuding modern tourist appeal.

Dissenting voices that accused Rome of parasitically feeding off northern profits and taxes indicated the growing north–south divide and an element of jealousy. The truth was that northern heavy industry benefited hugely from the major construction projects. One thousand, three hundred and fifty apartments were built to house athletes in the Olympic village, which became low-income accommodation after the event. The Games were split between two sites in Rome's periphery – the Foro Italico in the north and EUR in the south. They were controversial choices; not just as Rome's biggest and most easily identifiable Fascist-built zones, but also because of the distance between the two that required the construction of link roads. Stimulating development along their route, they raised building and land values significantly, most notably to the benefit of the Vatican, which held huge amounts of estate in Rome's north-western quarter.[67] As Tim Kirk argued in his architectural study of the city: 'For the same reasons that Mayor Ernesto Nathan had turned down the idea of hosting the Olympics in 1908 – encouraging real-estate speculation – Mayor Salvatore Rebecchini of the Christian Democrat party accepted.'[68]

The massive works undertaken raised serious questions about transparency, with few contracts allocated by public competition and many going to established architects that had worked prolifically under Fascism. Although costs rose dramatically, Rome gained a sporting infrastructure that included the Olympic stadium, brand new 5,000 and 16,000 seat indoor arenas, the 55,000 capacity *Stadio Flaminio*, a swimming pool and velodrome.[69] Unfortunately, some became white elephants as soon as the Olympic flame was spent, with CONI unable and apparently unwilling to build upon the huge enthusiasm for sport that the event stimulated among Italian youth.

Incorporated within the opening ceremony, the Fascist-built *Stadio dei Marmi* was also given a facelift. But for all that the Games offered a priceless opportunity to present a modern, thriving democracy to the world, former Fascist facilities required careful handling. In July, only weeks before the Games were due to begin, Fernando Tambroni's already controversial administration collapsed when its Neo-Fascist Italian Social Movement (*Movimento Sociale Italiano* – MSI) coalition partner withdrew its support after its conference, which had been provocatively planned for Genoa – a red, Resistance city that had suffered terribly during the war – was banned. While the tensions from the national issue, following violent incidents in Reggio Emilia and Rome, were eased by the appointment of Amintore Fanfani's government on 22 July, what should have been the ultimate sedative, the opening of the Games, scratched at Italy's wound that would not heal.

Some events were also held in ancient Roman structures: gymnasts performed in the Baths of the Emperor Caracalla, wrestlers grappled under the arches of Maxentius' Temple, while one marathon runner danced a jig of joy and others collapsed at the race's finish under the Arch of Constantine, close to the Coliseum and the Forum. This was a clear choice by the Organizing Committee to stress continuity between the ancient past and present, but it was unable to ignore Fascism's extensive demolition and rebuilding programme that had stamped its identity on the city. While many axes, *fasces* and insignia had been chipped away, the structures' unmistakable style was clear for all to see, and nowhere in the capital was the politicization of buildings and public space more evident than the competition's two sites – *EUR* and the *Foro Italico* – formerly *Foro Mussolini*. Contributing to a historic, impressive, and stylistically diverse range of structures, they were still political and demanded a reckoning with the past.

Most problematic and controversial were the Fascist engravings on tablets of stone in the *Via dell'Impero* (Empire way), the main thoroughfare of the Foro Italico leading from the Mussolini obelisk to the Olympic stadium, which was paved with ancient-style mosaics of Fascist sportsmen, slogans and military images. Their presence, in what was to be the first, live, global television

Figure 15: *The* Duce *would have been proud: the Stadium for 100,000 becomes the Olympic Stadium in the heart of the former* Foro Mussolini

broadcast of an Olympic Games, caused fierce parliamentary conflict and public debate, with some politicians afraid of offending athletes and visitors or giving the impression that there was still support for Mussolini in Italy; which there was. A left-wing petition to the city council demanding their removal failed, after which the Communists brought the issue into parliament, in November 1959.[70]

Propped up by the MSI until its collapse in July 1960, Tambroni's government avoided the issue. His successor Amintore Fanfani was, however, was unable to ignore renewed attempts to erase the unpleasant past so close to the Games. No Fascist sympathizer, his order that the tablets be covered and some mosaics removed met with neo-Fascist anger. As the left continued to protest, contrary to the government's desire to show a new Italy, the issue attracted international attention and comment; not so much for the Fascist symbols but more for the PCI's activity that some of the American press interpreted as Soviet trouble-making by proxy.[71] What was essentially the residue of Italy's liberation and post-war division, expressed in a domestic argument over representations of the Republic, became a Cold War political football. With Italy a critical border in the west's battle against Communist expansion, the conflict in the Italian parliament indicated how the Games had become a pawn in international politics.

1960 was already a tense year in east–west relations: Gary Powers' U2 spy plane was shot down over Soviet airspace in May; the Soviet premier Nikita Khrushchev walked out of a four-powers summit meeting in Paris; US President Eisenhower cancelled a planned visit to the Soviet Union; the USSR promised to defend Cuba with missiles if necessary; and, on the eve of the Games, Powers was publicly tried for espionage, in Moscow. It was hardly surprising that Rome 1960 was far from apolitical.

Indicative of the tensions and contradictions within the Olympic movement was the 'united' German squad. More or less single-handedly forced to compete as one team by the American IOC President Avery Brundage, the East and West German Olympic delegations only reached an agreement two weeks prior to the event, when confronted with the choice of competing as one or not at all. There were also no representatives from the People's Republic of China, which had officially withdrawn from the Olympic movement two years earlier in protest at the IOC's recognition of Taiwan. Protesting itself at being considered part of Chinese territory, the Taiwanese delegation entered the opening ceremony carrying a small sign declaring: 'Under Protest'. American athletes were also pressed into action by the CIA, in an attempt to encourage their Soviet rivals to defect. Some, such as the sprinter Dave Sime, were given specific targets, while on boarding their flights all squad members were armed with a Berlitz Italian phrasebook, plus copies of the US Declaration of Independence and a booklet on the virtues of the American lifestyle. All printed in Russian, athletes were told 'they should pass on their copies to members of the Soviet team at the Olympic village in Rome'.[72] Catholic, anti-Communist propaganda was also printed in multiple languages to be distributed among athletes and tourists.[73]

Despite its heavy overtones, Rome 1960 was a political and diplomatic success and a triumph of sport and spectacle that saw the Olympic Games transform into a truly global event. Deemed the first 'non-amateur' or professional Games, athlete numbers nearly doubled from Melbourne four years earlier, while the sale of almost one-and-a-half million tickets reflected the booming economy and a rediscovered confidence and pride among Italians. Key in this projection of Italy's new or desired identity and the new style of Olympics was its television coverage. Run by the Italian Organizing Committee and not the IOC, the Rome Games was the first Olympic tournament to commercially sell its television rights. Replicating Fascism's seizure of the commercial rights to official postage stamps for the 1934 World Cup, the Organizing Committee was quick to realize the profits to be made from TV and claimed sole right to establish broadcasting contracts. Supported by technological developments, plus the global economic and consumer boom, Rome 1960 was the first Games to be broadcast live on television, reaching 18 European countries instantaneously and the USA, Canada and Japan with only a few hours delay. Indicative of the quality of the Italian transmission was the US cyclist Jack Simes' diary entry. 'I'm surprised that the European TV is clear, too. Hartman [Jack Hartman, his cycling teammate] once said it's because they have more lines on the screen than we do. I thought everything was supposed to be better in America and we invented TV.'[74]

The event was recorded in a feature-length documentary scheduled to appear no more than three months after its conclusion. Planned by a committee of directors, technicians and journalists who studied the most important sports films to date, CONI awarded its production to the Italian National Film Institute (LUCE) to be directed by Romolo Marcellini, a documentary-maker trained under Fascism and renowned for his epic style.[75] With television having swollen viewing figures to unprecedented levels, 'tens of millions of spectators, even more attentive and critical, gathered in cinema [sic] to follow in the brief space of two hours the coloured re-evocation of the Rome Olympic Games'. Aware that 'the eye of television and cinema lenses were thus spectator number one'[76] and that it was primarily through this eye that the new Italy would be seen, the Olympic Organizing Committee planned the events to help the directors and avoid schedules clashing.

The film's coverage was divided into chapters for each event and accompanied by a musical score bearing all the hallmarks of the era. Creating an atmosphere somewhere between a 1960s heist movie and Carry On up the Capitol, it perfectly encapsulated the newly democratic, relaxed, sun and fun-filled nation. The result was a distinctive, beautifully shot, evocative record of Italy, Rome and the 1960 Games that received an Oscar nomination for the best documentary, in 1962.

In spite of Rome's previous appropriation by Fascism, democratic Italy also exploited the ancient city in its publicity and self-legitimization, most notably during the Olympic flame's passage from Greece to the capital. For this reason, an itinerary was established that 'coincided with and bore reference to the two apexes of classical civilization, Athens and Rome, and which would pass through the sites of Magna Grecia'.[77] Rather than cross the Balkans or follow the less evocative route from Brindisi to Rome, the torch left Athens, via the ancient Olympic Panathinaikos stadium, before being dispatched to Siracuse, Sicily, on an Italian naval training ship. From there, it was carried by local athletes from each of the provinces it passed. After crossing the Straits of Messina onto the Italian mainland, it hugged Italy's southwestern coast to Taranto before turning back east and passing the ancient sites of Pompei, Herculaneum, Naples, Cuma, Terracina, the papal residency of Castel Gandolfo, before reaching the Appian Way, the Capitol Hill and the Olympic stadium. Enthusing crowds across southern Italy, peasants, tourists and locals in traditional dress celebrated the torch's passage through towns and villages decked in red, white and green. With further spectacle added by the Italian passion for unrestrained pyrotechnics, special attention was given to 'the floodlighting of points of attraction particularly along the Amalfi coast road where bonfires were to be lit on the heights above Sorrento and Villa Ioni on Cape Tiberius at Capri'.[78]

The documentary opened with an aerial tour over the principal attractions of the city before swooping in and out of the packed stadium and across the Milvian Bridge,[79] where the athletes were marching from the Olympic village to the opening ceremony. After a speech by the President of the Organizing Committee, Giulio Andreotti, the President of the Republic, Giovanni Gronchi, declared the XVII Olympic Games officially open.

Benvenuti, Berruti, Bikila

LUCE's spectacular was assisted by the presence of international sports and show-biz stars in the Eternal City, who added glitz and glamour to the rejuvenated nation in the throws of the *dolce vita*. Courtesy of Onesti's investment in the elite, Italy's third-place finish, behind the USSR and USA, made the Italian nation appear to be riding the crest of an athletic wave.

Further popularizing sport across the peninsula, the Olympic success and unprecedented economic prosperity launched a new era in which sport became a consumer commodity as much as a leisure-time activity.

Italian athletes at the Rome Games indicated society's dramatic change. No longer just an escape from hunger, poverty and misery or a preserve of the wealthy elite, sport had become a middle-class leisure activity and a working-class means of social mobility. With an increase in female competitors too, the varied backgrounds of the athletes showed sport as both an indicator and facilitator of social change. Contributing to the growing tension between the amateur and professional, the clash exposed Avery Brundage's contradictory attempt to maximize profit while championing amateurism.

Italy's team consisted of 249 athletes, of which 34 were women. Among these 'we remember the names of Leoni, Paternoster, Saini, della Ragno, della Soprani, names that launched the rebirth of women's sport in post-war Italy, thus as equally important... as Berruti, d'Inzeo, Menichelli, Benvenuti'.[80] Italy's sexual paranoia was reflected however in the barracking of female athletes behind a two-and-a-half metre fence in the Olympic village, beyond which men were strictly forbidden to go. Nonetheless, the rapidly modernizing Games began to spread a new female image; that of the honed athlete.

Thirty-six medals equalled those of 'Mussolini's boys' at Los Angeles in 1932, with the added weight of one extra gold making it Italy's best ever Olympic haul. The nation's traditional strengths came to the fore: five cycling medals in the new velodrome, plus six in fencing and three in boxing. In a tournament in which Mohammed Ali (Cassius Clay) also won gold, Giovanni 'Nino' Benvenuti became welter-weight champion, and Livio Berruti won the 200 metres gold and the nation's hearts. From completely different backgrounds, they showed just how Italy was changing.

By the time of the 200 metres final, the 21-year-old Berruti had already equalled the world record. Most unusually, however, while his adversaries kept warm between the semi-final and final, Berruti focussed upon his university text books in preparation for an imminent exam. Seen as arrogant by his rivals, in fact, so charged was he by his semi-final time that he claimed to be seeking to retain composure while conserving energy. Any concerns that he harboured were unfounded, as the rank outsider repeated his record-equalling time to win gold. As Giulio Onesti later stated: 'This is naturally one of those epoch-making victories, and I don't know how to describe what I felt that day when Berruti, our pallid student, beat the American aces. It was that victory, above all, that enthralled the crowd.'[81]

But the crowd's unconditional joy soon became controlled admiration for the reserved chemistry student from a well-off Turin family. Unlike previous Italian champions whose social and geographic origins were evident in a variety of unrefined local dialects, Berruti's command of Italian equalled that of his interviewers. A product of free time and the need to fill it, he also contrasted with his predecessors that were toughened by physical labour and motivated by hunger.

> The beauty of the other champions was, nonetheless, filtered through a symbolic mediation. Coppi had superb leg muscles and a perfect position in the saddle but always a hooked nose, the hereditary leanness of hunger and a chest like a bird. In Berruti, every contradiction, even internal, was resolved. His was not a poem of strength but of smooth agility; his poem was not a fight with nature but rather a harmony with it. In the eyes of the Italians he seemed emblematic of the economic transformation.[82]

A victory for his class as much as the nation, Berruti showed not only how sport connected with social and economic change, but also how Italians continued to idolize those who achieved their goals, or not, with the minimum effort necessary.

Another of Italy's gold medal winners, Nino Benvenuti also demonstrated social change, but in almost total contrast to Berruti. This son of a fisherman who practised one of the most hunger-driven sports – boxing – rejected his humble origins. Declaring himself a representative of the bourgeoisie, he strove to demonstrate intelligence over strength, and style above aggression. An unquestionably intelligent boxer, according to Bassetti, 'he exaggerated in showing his self-taught acculturation: he made it known that he read Hemmingway [*sic*], owned a Picasso, studied Voltaire and prepared for fights by relaxing to Beethoven's violin concertos'.[83] Harsh as it is, the temptation to compare him to the British boxer Chris Eubank is great. Evidence of his public appeal that continued well beyond the Rome Olympics was his conquest of the world middleweight title at Madison Square Garden in 1967, which provoked the first sleepless night in the nation's sporting history, as 18 million Italians tuned in to RAI2's commentary at 4 a.m.

The last event of the Games was the crowning chapter in LUCE's documentary; no leisurely stroll but an exhausting, spectacular tour of ancient Rome. Small, lean and barefooted, in bright red shorts and green vest, the Ethiopian Abebe Bikila, a private in Haile Selassie's Imperial Army, contrasted starkly with the concept of the modern athlete, at the start of the marathon. None of his competitors took his challenge seriously, with his unofficial personal best for the

Figure 16: *Rome 1960 – A knockout for new Italy*

42.2 kilometres chauvinistically dismissed as impossible. Bikila had brought running shoes to Rome, but training in the month prior to the Games had ruined them. With new shoes causing his feet to blister he chose to run barefoot, having already toughened them with miles of shoeless training in Ethiopia. His bare feet raised eyebrows and interest in the endurance event which, in order to create further spectacle, broke with tradition by not concluding in the Olympic stadium. But as much as the ease with which he consumed the capital's kilometres it was its significance that fascinated, coming less than 25 years after Mussolini's forces had conquered Addis Ababa at the end of a cruel colonial war.

Starting from the Campidoglio, Rome's civic centre above the Forum, the athletes set off along Mussolini's triumphant thoroughfare, the *Via dei Imperiali*, past the Coliseum, the Palatine hill and the Circus Maximus. Here, at the back of the leading pack, Bikila passed the second-to-fourth-century Axum obelisk that Fascist forces had plundered from Abyssinia in 1937.[84] Continuing southwards out of Rome along the *Via Cristoforo Colombo*, the marathon passed through EUR before exiting the city and entering the countryside. Turning back at Acilia and bizarrely following a section of the *Grande Raccordo Annulare* – Rome's outer ringroad/motorway – at the 32nd kilometre mark runners turned onto the Appian Way, which had connected ancient Rome with Brindisi on Italy's south-east coast.

Breaking with the tradition of Olympic marathons being held in daylight, the early evening start saw the athletes run eight kilometres of the cypress-tree-lined Appia in darkness. To the rhythm of Bikila's bare feet kissing the uneven stones, the half moonlight, the illumination of ancient Roman monuments, plus hundreds of torch-bearing soldiers intensified the atmosphere and drama. As Alberto Cavallari wrote in his race report: 'It wasn't a marathon it was "Aida", with the roadside Romans making up the chorus.'[85] Re-entering the city at the *Porta* (Gate) *San Sebastiano*, with impeccable timing Bikila left his sole pursuer as the race re-passed the Axum obelisk. Sealing victory under the Arch of Constantine, in two hours, 15 minutes and 16 seconds, he set a world best and shattered the Olympic record.

Seventeen days earlier Bikila and the small Ethiopian team had marched into the Olympic stadium alongside Fascism's *Via dell'Impero*, past the huge, controversial tablets of stone commemorating the regime's 'achievements', one of which was dedicated to the conquest of Abyssinia. That another African athlete finished only 25 seconds behind him was significant in signalling the future of distance running. But in the days before the rise and dominance of East African athletes; in the context of Italy's two invasions of Ethiopia and its colonization after 1936; following the decolonization of many African states in 1960; in the presence of the all-white South African team that the IOC chose to ignore; and against superiorly funded and equipped Soviet, US and European athletes, Bikila's marathon victory made an enormous impression upon the Games and left a huge mark on the sport that transcended his, admittedly incredible, lack of shoes for which he is most fondly remembered.[86]

His win was also a triumph for Rome and the Games, dramatically closing the event under the lights and arch of a long departed Emperor who, along with his predecessors and successors, continued to inspire the modern city under whatever regime ruled it. For all of the debates in parliament and the Fascist graffiti, there was no better, more apt or significant indication of the break from the past than the comparison of mass, Fascist sport with the celebration of the glorious solo victory of an ex-colonial subject. As the editor of the British Olympic Committee's magazine *World Sports* arrogantly concurred in his report:

> It is a scene to remember – a moment of theatrical drama; a moment so unusual in modern world athletics when a virtual unknown from an insignificant country crosses the seas and conquers the heroes. It is a fine, unsophisticated, illogical victory...
>
> This... was an historic Olympic marathon both in terms of performance and backcloth. Thankfully it offered little in the way of grotesque contortion by men near collapse; its drama was in its setting, presentation and outcome.[87]

Having railed against sport's distraction from the class struggle and the battle against Fascism, in 1934, Carlo Levi's words in 1960, exposed the dramatic change in the new Italy.

> And so, the Olympics were over, and even Rome returned to its daily life like all the cities, villages and countryside untouched by them, where there were no holidays from work or need. The Games were a beautiful spectacle from every perspective: colours of peace, flags, strength, youth and the fascinating test of the limits of man's strength. They were a spectacle so beautiful that even the old impenetrable Romans, these body-armoured tortoises, these lizards on their walls encrusted by time, ended up taking an interest.[88]

By the end of the Games, sport had become 'the new status symbol for the average Italian'.[89] Both Benvenuti and Berruti had shown the impact of the expanding middle class upon sport, which continued to grow. In 1962, the Italian water polo team withdrew from an international tournament in

Belgrade, claiming the pool water was too cold. Meanwhile the Hungarian, Yugoslav and Russian athletes, toughened by their harsher domestic conditions, played on. There was also a growth in traditionally non-working-class sports, such as tennis. Born in Tunisia into a rich family that lost its fortune during the war, Nicola Pietrangeli was a strong baseline player suited to clay-court endurance battles. Winning the French Open in 1959 and 1960, he missed out on a third consecutive title by a whisker, and led the Italian team to two consecutive Davis Cup finals against Australia, in 1960 and 1961. An off-court fashion-following admirer of high-society, Pietrangeli mixed with princes and actors, truly living *la dolce vita*. 'Between the champions and the masses the abyss had now been dug.'[90]

Terrorists, trade unionists and televisions

Phoenix from the flames

One of Italy's strongest clubs since its formation by the industrialist Piero Pirelli in 1908, FC Internazionale's golden era ran from 1963 to 1966. Under the tempestuous leadership of its oil-baron president Angelo Moratti and coach Helenio Herrera, the 'Great Inter' won three championships, two European and two Inter-Continental Cups in four years, revolutionizing Italian football in the process. Within two years of his arrival Herrera had constructed a side that finally ended Real Madrid's European hegemony. Claiming three Italian titles in four years, it was Inter's first European Cup victory in 1964 that won it international acclaim. Its defence of the trophy polished the sheen, with the unprecedented era of success attributed to Herrera's defensive counterattacking, or *catenaccio*.

Built upon defensive frugality with an often unrecognized element of flair, *catenaccio* and Inter's success reflected Italy's post-war recovery. Supported by an influx of immigrants, like Milan's factory floors, Inter's ability to create and exploit space on the field mirrored Italy's skilful penetration of European markets. As Inter developed an international fan base and a cynical reputation, the 'Made in Italy' brand assured style and product quality. In fact, as John Foot notes, Inter's double collapse in 1967 and the departure of Herrera 'were sure signs that the miracle was over'.[1]

Attracted by the investments of club owners enriched by the boom, Serie A spectators increased by 30 per cent from 1953 to 1963 and one of Herrera's most astute moves reflected his awareness of the crowd's importance. Based upon his experience in Spain, he persuaded Moratti to establish and subsidise a group of passionate fans (*ultras*) – the Inter Club *Moschettieri* – who would travel and support the team wherever.

A progressive idea, it was only the liberation of the 'miracle' that made it conceivable, let alone practical. Although often credited with inventing the *ultrà*, these official supporters' clubs that were replicated by Juventus and AC Milan, were very different and soon became influential mediators between club directors and supporters.[2] As Dal Lago and De Biasi note:

> Organized fans can influence the policies of the club, through official interventions or demonstrations inside the stadium. They arrange meetings and parties with the players. But above all they find in their... club activities the opportunity to create social relations... In sum, official football clubs represent, in the sporting realm, the general trend towards a politics of exchange, widely prevalent in Italian society.[3]

While this appeared a positive, empowering role, for the first generation to live football almost as a religion, the cost of blind loyalty was potential exploitation by unscrupulous and ambitious club owners. As one Neapolitan worker convincingly proposed: 'I don't see sport as anything other than a weapon in the hands of the bourgeoisie. I've never seen a worker who's president of a football club.'[4]

Thirty thousand *Interisti* did see their club win the 1964 European Cup Final, in Vienna. The miracle in action, millions watched the game at home on television and thousands more took their cars to Milan's Linate airport to greet the team on its return before forming a cavalcade into the city. One year after AC Milan's victory in the same tournament, it confirmed *calcio*'s resurgence and a flourishing new generation that would claim the European Nations Cup in 1968 and rubber-stamp Italy's emergence from its post-Superga depression. Milan's Gianni Rivera embodied rejuvenated Italy, along with a young Inter midfielder whose two goals in the 1964 European Cup Final encapsulated the country's rise from the ashes of Fascism, war and Superga: Sandro Mazzola, son of the legendary Valentino who died in the 1949 disaster. As Maurizio Mosca described:

> After years of struggle it was finally won. And what of the players? Let's not make out that the name of one, Mazzola, wasn't the most applauded, demanded and surrounded with love, and we can't tell if this love was more for him or the memory of his father.[5]

1968

By the late 1960s Italy's succession of Christian Democrat administrations had failed to address the problems arising from the country's dramatic post-war changes. Desperately needed and frequently promised reforms made no progress in a political system that guaranteed only stagnation. While the PCI had grown in strength, it remained unable to convince the electorate that its embrace of democracy was anything more than a Trojan horse to establish a Soviet-style dictatorship. With the left incapable of uniting, the DC's position in government remained unchallenged. Comfortably maintaining power with less than 40 per cent of the vote resulted in a blocked political system riddled with clientelistic loyalty and outright corruption. Stunting Italy's growth, it stimulated a movement from below intent on forcing change. Although less dramatic than that in France, Italy's 1968 protest movement was Europe's most enduring.

Its roots were in the early 1960s reforms that introduced mass education beyond primary school, for the first time. Although limited in scope, they enabled many middle-class students to finally reach university. While the undergraduate population grew by almost 200,000 to approaching half a million between 1960 and 1968, this 'opening-up' of universities was severely limited by a lack of grants. With the poorest students forced to work while studying, failure/drop-out rates increased among the expanding urban middle classes. Those who somehow managed to navigate 'the obstacle course of formidable dimensions... [and]... emerge from the long and distinctly dark tunnel of Italian education' with a degree, were then confronted by worsening employment opportunities.[6] The result was a demand to modernize education and address the needs of students and universities, with the aim of increasing the number of graduates.[7]

The authorities had already been forewarned of the disaffection by PE students within the Higher Institute for Physical Education (*Istituto Superiore Educazione Fisica* – ISEF), at the *Foro Italico* (formerly *Farnesina/Foro Mussolini*). Opened in 1952, the Institute trained PE teachers initially for secondary and then primary schools. But while the 1958 Moro law declared physical education an integral part of the school system and opened further ISEF campuses, PE students remained second-class citizens, which fuelled resentments and the occupation of the Italian Youth Movement's offices, in 1967.

Officially in exasperation at poor teaching and sports facilities, their protest was rooted in the lack of respect for their profession: for three years of university study they received a diploma, the equivalent of two years' study at a lower level. With four years required to graduate with any degree, PE teachers remained subservient to traditional disciplines, which stimulated demands to re-evaluate their profession and ISEF's transfer into the university sector.[8] In the hot summer of 1968, ISEF attendees were not at the vanguard of student activities, however, and neither was sport. It 'was nothing to be proud about', according to UISP's monthly *Il Discobolo*:

> It is an indication of disinterest, a sad result of politics that has not made sport a primary requirement in the life of our country. The only reality that needs to be taken account of, is that millions of young Italians either take no interest in sport or do so in the wrong way.[9]

The revolt within Italian universities ran from the autumn of 1967 until the spring of 1968. Launched with a number of sit-ins and occupations in the Catholic University of Trento, the insurrection spread to Milan's Catholic University and then Turin. Fanning out across the country, its height came after police ended the occupation of Rome's '*La Sapienza*'. Having regrouped, the students embarked on recapturing the Faculty of Architecture, isolated on the edge of the Villa Borghese. In the 'battle of Valle Giulia', cars and vans were set ablaze, students injured by police baton charges and 46 officers hospitalized. A radicalizing moment, it brought the previously pacifist movement onto the national front pages and established mutual loathing.

While the movement began to decline having achieved little, protests continued and ISEF students demanded the restriction of PE teaching to qualified staff. When, in September 1969, the Communist parliamentary deputy Liberato Bronzuto introduced a law awarding permanent positions to existing PE teachers without formal qualifications, the ISEF campaign intensified to include the temporary abduction of professional sportsmen: the Ternana footballer Franco Liguori was followed by national basketball team member Paolo Bergonzoni, and the footballers Giacomo Bulgarelli and Luciano Mujesan, who all had ISEF connections. By 1973, ISEF students had mellowed and become part of the wider university struggle, but however brief and unthreatening the abductions were, they indicated a potentially violent strategy.

While the student movement was a libertarian revolt against Italy's post-war capitalist development, middle class and non-revolutionary, its radicalization required the export of its aims and ideas to the factories. Besides their tough working environments, the bitterness felt by many southern workers who had needed to migrate in order to survive was intensified by the inhospitable conditions they encountered on arrival. Moreover, despite the boom, the shortage of unskilled jobs and semi-skilled labour was aggravated by the expansion of education that enabled more young people than ever to avoid the factory floor. At the same time, increasing literacy ensured that those entering the factories were more capable of formulating and expressing opinions.

Demanding higher pensions, in March 1968, industrial protestors were joined by radical students and new-left revolutionary groups. Undermining trade unions, revolutionary committees began agitating on factory floors, where violence and intimidation replaced traditional walk-outs and mass picketing, and demonstrations often led directly to the managing director's office who, on occasion, would be temporarily kidnapped. With factory agitations increasingly violent, and managers, foremen and strike-breakers all seen as legitimate targets, by the end of 1973 it was clear that anti-authoritarian forces had not been confined to 1968.

✪ ✪ ✪ ✪

Going beyond a simple protest against poor conditions and injustice, the 1968 student demonstrations challenged the fundamental sectors of Italian society: the workplace, the family and the Church. Many young Italians began rejecting the miracle's consumerism in favour of rock music, radical literature, demands for social justice and the enjoyment of guilt-free sex, all of which increased their alienation from mainstream society. Their challenge, however, drew a response from dark, right-wing counter forces. In 1969, a bomb placed outside a bank in Milan's *Piazza Fontana* killed 16 people and wounded 88. Two similar devices were detonated that day in Rome, wounding 16 more. Hastily blamed upon anarchists, one of those quickly arrested, Giuseppe Pinelli, died in police custody and his death registered as suicide. Six years later he was cleared of any involvement; the truth remains unknown.

Responsibility for the bomb was eventually traced to a neo-Fascist group, based in Italy's north-eastern Veneto region, which had strong connections with the Italian secret services. However, the *Piazza Fontana* investigation was blocked by fabricated evidence and a series of condemnations and acquittals on appeal that lasted 20 years. The attack was part of the 'strategy of tension', whereby a series of bombs were intended to create panic and uncertainty that would lead to an authoritarian crackdown. News of a planned military coup further confirmed the right's institutional links. The threat was vague, but a parliamentary inquiry revealed the existence of a potentially dangerous conspiracy in the summer of 1964, led by former secret services head and then commander of the military *carabinieri* police force, General Giovanni De Lorenzo. The unease was intensified by a further revelation. Since 1948, unknown even to some prime ministers, a NATO/US-funded armed force had been established to resist any possible Communist insurrection or electoral victory.

As Italian politics polarized, General Pinochet's coup in Chile, in 1973, underlined the real potential for an authoritarian takeover in Italy. Reacting to this threat and the prospect of the PCI becoming a completely ineffective opposition with no realistic hope of governing the country, the Communist Party leader Enrico Berlinguer sought to defend the state.

> The gravity of the country's problems, the persistent threats of reactionary adventurers and the need to finally open the nation to a secure means of economic development, social renewal and democratic progress makes... what can be defined as a new, great 'historic compromise' between the forces that hold and represent the majority of the Italian people, increasingly urgent.[10]

A primarily defensive measure, the 'historic compromise' was 'a grand strategy in which Communists and Catholics would find a shared moral and ethical code on which to base the political and social salvation of Italy'.[11] The major political initiative in the crisis years, the former DC prime minister Aldo Moro appreciated the merits of an association with the left, if Italy was to resist unconstitutional forces and break the political deadlock. But Moro's vision was different, and included 'the full legitimation of a reduced Communist Party at last capable of competing with a reformed Christian Democratic Party, though never able to defeat and replace it'.[12] Despite trying to stifle the PCI, for his openness to change Moro would pay with his life.[13]

Armed sport

Conscription and incentives for language learning made the army a major force in the creation of Italian national identity in Liberal Italy. It was also important in the physical education of Italian youth, striving to create the citizen-soldier who would theoretically emerge from the fusion of sport and the military, mentally and physically equipped for battle. There was little appreciable difference between this idealized troop and that described by Lando Ferretti, in 1938: 'Citizen, soldier, it's the same... soldier in every sense of the word: in the healthy and hardened body, in the spirit ready for the ultimate sacrifice, in the regularly updated technical preparation, in a disciplined atmosphere that makes enthusiasm the decisive weapon of all victories.'[14] Fascism sought to militarize Italian society through metaphorical and very real conflicts, but the army failed to win the nation's favour due to its continued failings and often repressive domestic actions.

The shock of the armistice and the military's dissolution in 1943, plus its loss of identity and leadership, made the rebuilding of Italy's reunited armed forces an enormous challenge. Limited by Allied desires and economic weakness, the post-war Italian military returned to its pre-Fascist state; that being primarily defensive. Not required to fight again until 1990, its energies were directed towards domestic affairs. Effectively redundant, the armed forces remained large, with nearly 400,000 on the payroll by the end of the 1960s, excluding the military *carabiniere* police force that added another 80,000.[15]

Considering the best means of training Italian troops in 1946, Guido Vianello, technical director of the Cesano Military School of Physical Education, established an explicit set of objectives: 'the harmonic strengthening of the body; specific exercises to technically train the soldier; recreation and propaganda'.[16] Sessions were built around gymnastics, dexterity exercises, obstacle climbing, courage development, self-defence, marching, running, jumping, throwing, resistance training, plus team games, such as volleyball and football. Consistent with established military training, Vianello's programme was a pillar in the production of the military athletes and sportsmen that were integral in Italy's post-war success. As Ferretti argued, in 1950:

> As with opportune courses that seek to rectify illiteracy among conscripts who don't know how to read or write, it is necessary to start from the beginning to provide today's young men, who make no methodical physical effort and lack any combative spirit, with bodies and characters (with appropriate gym and sporting activities) fit for military demands and warlike missions.[17]

The development of military physical exercise, training and sport was further encouraged by the International Military Sports Council (CISM). Formed in 1948, just prior to Europe's division into ideologically competing blocs, CISM's aims were: to develop friendly relations between the armed forces of member nations; promote physical education and sports activities; provide mutual technical assistance; contribute to the development of military personnel; and promote friendship through sport. Although not among the founding members, the Italian military quickly became one of CISM's leading organizers, hosting more international championships than any other country between 1949 and 1995.

Italy's commitment to hosting such events not only extolled the values of military sport but also reflected the role of military and civilian bodies, such as CONI, in the construction of a national sporting network that maximized Italian performance. The military and CONI's relationship became closer following the award of the 1960 Olympic Games to Rome, with both bodies keen for Italian athletes to impress. Among their many achievements in the Games, one of the most high profile successes was that of the sprinter Livio Berruti. A member of the *carabiniere*'s *Fiamme d'Oro* (Gold Flame) squad, it 'was an extraordinary result... for which the armed forces never claimed their true role'.[18]

In the same year, the alliance between the military and CONI was sealed by the formation of the *Centro Sportivo Esercito* (Army Sports Centre – CSE), within which Companies were given responsibility for specific sporting disciplines. The First Company focussed on athletics, the Second on sailing, canoeing, rowing, cycling, tennis, volleyball and rugby, with the Third Special Company containing footballers of clear international potential. By agreeing to remain for 60 days after their discharge, during their military service footballers were allowed to train each morning under the supervision of CONI/FIGC coaches and released at the weekend to represent their clubs. As AC Milan's third choice goalkeeper Luciano Alfieri found out, in 1958, their release remained a privilege to be requested and granted. Called into the first team at short notice, on his return to barracks Alfieri was punished with five days in solitary confinement for not having obtained the correct permission.[19]

In general, however, Third Company players barracked in Bologna had their talents recognized and careers advanced during what could only loosely be described as military service. A highly practical means of ensuring that national service applied to all Italian males without exception, Italy's eight CISM world titles, from 1950 to 1991, made it military sport's most successful football nation. Determining the Third Company's all-time strongest eleven would be no easy task but including the likes of Giovani Trapattoni, Giacinto Facchetti, Gigi Riva, Paolo Rossi, Giuseppe Bergomi and Paolo Maldini, it would be formidable.

Other sports were catered for in different areas of the country, with show jumpers and modern pentathletes attending the Military Riding School at Montelibretti, just outside Rome, and winter sportsmen based in northern alpine regions of Bolzano and the 'Perenni' barracks in Courmayeur, where the pre-war ski patrol group was re-launched. Integrated within the CSE in 1960, this Special Nucleus of Skiers produced a huge number of national, international and Olympic champions whose successes encouraged alpine tourism.

While footballers' military obligations were hardly strenuous, especially from the 1980s onwards once their rising salaries and status made their duties little more than a curious anachronism, less renowned and remunerated athletes pursued regular military careers. One highly controversial example was the show-jumper Raimondo D'Inzeo, who won the Olympic individual event in Rome, 1960. A member of the *carabiniere* mounted police, he was strongly condemned by the left for his role in controlling the Roman protest demanding the resignation of Tambroni's administration, after its refusal to outlaw the MSI conference in Genoa. While military sport might have been based upon ideals of physical and spiritual training, fraternity and peace, there was, on occasion, no escaping the fact that athletes were military members, first and foremost.

Following the establishment of the CSE, military sport's structure remained more or less the same until 1998, when all individual groups were brought under the umbrella of the Army's Sporting-Gymnastic Training Centre at Cecchignola, Rome, which lasted until the abolition of national service, in 2005. By then, over 11 million men had served in the army, guaranteeing an enormous pool from which Italian sportsmen could be discovered and supported.

The sport business

The left's sporting mobilization drew an almost immediate response from business with *Confindustria*, the Italian equivalent of the Confederation of British Industry, organizing a 'Sport and Industry Conference' in Rome, in 1968. Led by Giulio Andreotti and attended by CONI chief Giulio Onesti, plus the directors of Italy's four sport dailies, the event discussed sport's role in the workplace. Focussing upon its contribution to maintaining industrial peace and minimizing sick leave, its vision of sport and PE[20] affirmed the left's century-long critique. 'The bosses have spoke clearly and shamelessly: sport must be put at the service of productivity as it increases the capacity for work and can become... a free zone where the aggression of the young and workers can be released.'[21]

Applying itself to the education system it also instigated the Youth Games (*Giochi di Gioventù* – GdG), a collaboration between CONI, the Federations, industrial sporting bodies and school groups. First held in 1969, over 5,700 communes and 600,000 ten- to sixteen-year-old boys and girls participated, prior to the finals in Rome. Questioning young people's rebelliousness, an open letter to an imaginary contestant in the daily *Il Giornale d'Italia* targeted the Games' inspiration as a classic way of allowing youth to let off steam.[22]

An effective means for the centre-right to undermine the left's organization of mass sport too, the Youth Games undoubtedly limited UISP's penetration of mass society. Within business sectors, however, technological advances and the boom in sport's commercialization, since the 1960 Olympics, revealed a growing economic force seeking new opportunities, as company heads began to appreciate the potential profits in sport.

A supremely effective means of promoting industrial products in Fascist newspapers and magazines, sport and advertising's relationship took off in the post-war boom. As television and the lust for consumer goods grew, even football, which had long been considered of little profit, began to exploit the new opportunities with ruthlessness and ingenuity. Circumventing the ban on tobacco advertising, in 1967 an Italian cigarette brand rented pitch-side advertising boards during an international football match in Romania, which RAI cameras could not avoid. By the mid 1970s, football's ever-growing television exposure had resulted in widespread shirt sponsors, only a few years after the word entered the Italian dictionary.

As the clamour for sponsorship opportunities grew along with the sums demanded for prime slots, the left's critique of money's stimulation of athletic performance appeared increasingly salient. Worse still, both sponsors and the sponsored soon realized that sport, unlike other areas, could not always guarantee prime coverage, even if it had been paid for. The human element and the increasingly small margins between success and failure, the variables that made sport so attractive in the first place, made it equally impossible to guarantee product placement. While many turned to sponsoring events rather than individuals, some sought alternative means of guaranteeing success.

As the first truly commercial Games UISP's analysis of the Rome 1960 Olympics focussed upon the relationship between sport and money. Pragmatic enough to support the event and the Italian squad, UISP was rewarded with the final leg of the Olympic flame's journey to Rome being assigned to its middle-distance runner Giancarlo Peris. Yet, by playing a prominent, national role in the tournament's success, UISP's implicit, passive support for the Italian sporting structure indicated the left's uncertainty as to whether it should oppose or defend it. Unwittingly, UISP contributed to sealing the relationship between the political and sporting powers of CONI and the Christian Democrats – Onesti and Andreotti – while the Italian Olympic team's success appeared to justify CONI's focus upon the elite and the competitive system to which UISP objected. As its President Arrigo Morandi explained, in 1968:

> The discussion about Italian sport is another thing. It relates to the old and new injustices of a society that wasn't built for men but, first of all, for how they must serve the dominant economic and social interests... you can put it this way: why can't the majority of the population practise sport for their health and pleasure?[23]

In 1960, a survey revealed that only 2.5 per cent of Italians actively participated in sport, of which only 0.5 per cent were women. While the left was increasingly open to sport's merits, a persistent ambiguity and confusion continued to hinder its courtship. Sport for sport's sake simply wasn't enough; there had to be something extra. Needing to directly relate to the world in which it functioned, mass sport with a social angle or conscience became UISP's goal and a reason for its membership growth, well into the 1970s.

Nonetheless, the left continued to underestimate sport's popular appeal and propaganda potential. According to the PCI model, mass sport needed the legitimization of bodies like UISP, the CSI and even smaller local groups, while overcoming CONI's centralized, dominant bureaucracy. This critique focussed upon the Olympic movement and its emphasis upon medals as markers of success that were deemed to reflect and reproduce the capitalist system. By nature the Games were classist, selective and based upon results that corresponded to the availability of facilities and opportunities, which favoured northern Italians over southerners, rich over poor and valued victories and results above personal growth.

> The principal victims of this machine are the athletes who are integrated into the mechanism that they don't control, who provide unconscious and free publicity for sporting commerce, whose physical strength is exploited until exhaustion. And there is always a country to save, a flag to defend for which they are called to guarantee their presence... and thus publicize the event. [24]

Continuing the theme in 1972, *Il Discobolo* protested at how the 'dominant trend has turned sport into a commodity, the source of direct and indirect products in which money is the determining factor, which has brought the sport show into excess, which survives on a mass of spectators, passive consumers of the activities of others'.[25] Once again, the left was paralysed between embracing and rejecting what had become *the* medium to the masses.

The match of the century

By the late 1960s, sport was increasingly featuring in political protests. On 14 December 1968, one week after students had protested against demonstrations of wealth outside Milan's La Scala opera house, they did the same at the San Remo theatre prior to the world middleweight boxing title fight between the American Don Fullmer and Nino Benvenuti, a *Movimento Sociale Italiano* (MSI) party sympathizer. Fans gathered outside the theatre were pelted with rotten eggs and the local council attacked for having spent money on a boxing match rather than investing in community projects.

There was even change in the conservative institution of football. Attempts to form a players union dated back to 1917, with the formation of the Free Italian Football Union (*Unione Libera Italiana del Calcio* – ULIC). Effectively running its own national league and theoretically representing the working class, it was swallowed by the FIGC in 1926.[26] With another attempt in 1945 quickly disappearing,[27] players had to wait until 1968 for a true representative body.

Led by civil lawyer and former Vicenza and Bologna winger Sergio Campana, and fronted by Sandro Mazzola and Gianni Rivera, the Italian Footballers Association (*Associazione Italiana Calciatori* – AIC), challenged how players had effectively become the property of their clubs, unable to refuse transfers and forced to accept contracts in which they had no say. Although the majority of its early members were well-off and protected by pension plans, insurance and personal injury schemes, the union demanded that footballers be treated like any ordinary employee. While strike action was impractical and would have alienated fans, its mere threat was enough to exert pressure, especially once the mass of poorer players began signing up.

A 1974 protest against their 'slavery' saw all Serie A teams come onto the field ten minutes late. Soon after, all players' contracts were modernized to include pension rights and insurance schemes, while individuals were freed to decide where they wanted to play. Reinforcing the stereotype of footballers who cared for little other than their own private worlds, however, the AIA failed to engage with Italy's wider problems. When Perugia's midfielder Paolo Sollier suggested the union take interest in the world of labour and the nation's lack of development, the AIA merely affirmed the individual's right to undertake personal initiatives.

An extreme-left sympathizer, Sollier's proposal connected with the changing face of football supporters. As *Il Calcio* magazine's 1968 survey of social class revealed, 57 per cent of fans now came from the lower middle class and below. According to Sergio Giuntini, the responses

> testified how... the usual customer of the stadiums in 1968 was now more likely the southern Neapolitan than the Milanese or Torinese of the rich, northern cities and clubs. That working-class mass (generally young, immigrant into the industrial north, with low professional skills) that w[ould] be the major protagonist of the class struggle from 1969–71.[28]

The mentality of fans also changed. The mass crowds that celebrated in the streets after Italy's 1968 European Championship victory demonstrated little sense of nationalism. Following Italy's 4–3 extra time defeat of Germany in the 1970 World Cup semi-final, the reaction was entirely different. The final whistle

> sparked an unforeseeable explosion of joy throughout the streets and piazzas of the peninsula. The rowdy scenes of celebration after the 1968 European Championship victory were repeated, but with a greater intensity and extent, in a climate of excitement in which public spaces became the houses of all and in which carnival-like intoxication suspended the rules of daily life. For many older Italians it brought back memories of the days at the end of the war.[29]

Broadcast live from Mexico City, in Europe's early hours, over 28 million Italians watched the game: 'men, women, children, pensioners, the sick, prisoners, fans and the uninterested, intellectuals and illiterates, communists and fascists'.[30] The first 90 minutes were dull; Italy took an early lead and characteristically looked to defend it at all costs with a combination of *catenaccio* and time wasting. Germany's equalizer, with less than a minute remaining, took the match into extra time, the bitter pill made harder to swallow by the goal scorer: AC Milan's Karl-Heinz Schnellinger, who had never scored in any of his 222 appearances for the club, from 1965 to 1974. 'Hitchcock couldn't have done better', according to *Il Giorno*.[31]

Extra-time proved completely different, the game swaying from one side to the other as Italy attacked in an unrecognizable, free-flowing, carefree style. In shaking off its regimented, disciplined, often cynical game plan, Nando Dalla Chiesa detected the promise of a better society in his novel based on the match: 'In the half hour [of extra time] there were no more tactics, there were no longer strict positions on the field, there was no longer cynical wisdom. Suddenly, the rules of the past lost all of their power.'[32]

With Italy leading 3-2, golden-boy Gianni Rivera made a defensive error that gifted the Germans parity, the ball passing between him and the post he was supposed to be defending. Straight from the restart, before any German player could touch the ball, Italy attacked and Rivera slotted home the winning goal. Reaching the final against Brazil or, more specifically, defeating Germany, was a cathartic moment.

> [During] that night, more precisely in the thirty-two to thirty-three minutes between the goal of... Schnellinger and the end of the second half of extra time, Italians discovered the nation. Behind the blue of Valcareggi's boys they saw... the flag. They united in a spontaneous leap... Where was the conflict between fathers and sons, between friends and friends, colleagues and colleagues, the middle class and workers? For sure it would be back... But later. That night it was as if history had taken a break, returning to the Italians what they were burning on their altars.[33]

Despite Italy's growing political violence, joyful millions poured onto the streets across the peninsula. An unexpected and unprecedented moment of unity, the spontaneous festivities transcended the result to celebrate Italy's progress in the 25 years since the end of the war that had split the nation. As Arrigo Benedetti argued:

> There was another motive for the nocturnal rejoicing: in the end it seemed Italians felt authorized to not be sorry for, or even to not be ashamed of being born in this country... Finally, it seemed possible to turn the page and move on.[34]

Having lacked a guilt-free pretext, Italians threw the party they had wanted for years.

> Tricolours, club flags, sheets, shirts, banners... fluttered from balconies and corteges of cars proceeded with their horns blaring, while other lines marched towards the monuments and the fountains, decorating them with Italian flags... [where]... some stripped off and took night-time swims worthy of Fellini.[35]
>
> In Milan, the capital of protest, target of the strategy of tension in the Piazza Fontana, the streets filled with an absolutely new type of demonstrator that launched an extraordinary and unforgettable night.[36]

Arguably it was the defeat of Italy's wartime occupier that made it so particular. The peaceful revenge and collective joy extended into Germany, where the major cities were overtaken by those Italians who, less than 20 years earlier, had emigrated in humility and poverty. The *azzurri* also embodied Italy's changes, with the previous domination of players from northern teams slowly eroded by the growing strength of clubs south of Bologna. More incredible than Fiorentina's league title win, in 1969, was that of Cagliari in 1970. A *calcio* outpost that provided four players for that year's World Cup squad, the presence of names from across the country encouraged the concept of true national representation. Sharing their knowledge of previous hardships, in a golden period of economic growth, employment, consumption, democracy, peace and hope, Italians united in a sporadic outburst of national joy.

> Behind the azzurri there wasn't this or that section of society, as in other sports... There wasn't only well-off Italy, as in fencing, sailing or horse riding, nor that of the outcasts like boxing. There was Italy as it had grown in the previous decades, with all of its transformations, its passions, its structures.
>
> And this, because of the simple fact that all of Italy had played football in those decades. The easiest sport, the least expensive. Rags held together with a piece of string were enough to make a ball. Or newspapers soaked and crushed in the houses where papers were read. The street was as good as a field... even in the big cities...
>
> Thus, all of Italy had played football and its champions that night represented it in its entirety... [and]... in its recent history.[37]

With the Italian flag divested of its Fascist connotations, the celebration of a national success was permissible without offending the memory of the Resistance.

The first time since the demise of Fascism that Italy had witnessed nationalistic patriotism, some commentators were disturbed by what they saw. Writing in the weekly *L'Espresso*, Ennio Flaiano likened the mass celebrations to those following the conquest of Ethiopia under Fascism,[38] while veteran journalist Indro Montanelli made a similar connection with the past:

> As a child I remember seeing with my own eyes those half-naked yobs that caused chaos in the cities with their noise, turning over cars and breaking windows: they were the *squadristi* of '19 and '20. The same faces. The same expressions. The same people.[39]

Contrary to appearances, the final exposed this newfound unity and identity as shallow and short-lived, which *Il Mondo*'s editorial deemed indicative of the country's plight. 'The Italians – we could conclude – are tired of frustrations to the extent that a sporting exploit is enough to re-ignite any hope. For sure they are looking for something to believe in: football this time; tomorrow, who knows.'[40] More graphically, Flannio described one psychologist's take on the celebrations: a 'preventative masturbation in the certain knowledge of coitus that would never happen'.[41] Reverting to more traditional, defensive, tactics, Italy hung on for an hour before Brazil finally made its superiority count in one of the great World Cup displays. Despite Rivera's decisive semi-final goal, coach Valcareggi's decision to keep Mazzola in the starting eleven reopened the divisive national debate over the two.

The son of Valentino, Sandro Mazzola had special significance for the generation that had lived through Fascism, the war and Superga, his mere presence creating an almost genetic bond between the 1970 squad, the nation and its past. By contrast, Rivera's place in the team was never secure, rarely considered to have been earned, and always seen to have come at somebody else's expense. Heavily criticized for his style of play, character, timidity, and perceived conceit, having been central in the 1966 World Cup debacle, the national debate surrounding him was well stoked by 1970. Rivera and Mazzola were, according to Antonio Ghirelli: "the heroes of Christian Democrat, refined Italy, full of talent but of very very moderate effort".[42]

As if unable to resolve the issue but more likely in response to the demands of playing at high altitude, Valcareggi opted for a rotation system in which Mazzola played the first half before being replaced by Rivera. Having reached the final and avoided recriminations from the supporters of both, the inevitable argument exploded after the coach decided to introduce Rivera with only six minutes remaining, when all was lost. The most famous six minutes in

Italian football, some declared the decision a public insult of the then world player of the year while others, such as Italy's greatest football critic Gianni Brera, attacked the Milan midfielder.

> Finally the coaches understood that Rivera's contribution wasn't enough, as and even more so than before. He played the passes that others... had won: adorning them with dull moves that delayed play so much as to render in vain his attacking colleagues' pursuit of space.[43]

Demonstrating the ease with which sport could divide the nation,[44] after the collective celebration following the victory over Germany, reaction to the defeat by Brazil indicated the unresolved issues and differences between two extreme camps in Italian society that were dragging the country into one of the darkest periods in its history. In fact, the celebrations were little more than a parenthesis, a pause, a lull in political and social combat prior to the even greater violence to come.

Despite Italy's second place finish – the best since 1938 – on arriving at Rome's Fiumicino airport the team again failed to avoid the tomatoes, as Brera recalled:

> Instead of coming to celebrate... a sensational success, the azzurri and their leaders had to hide in an aircraft hanger to save themselves from lynching. Grotesque banners of disapproval were held up by those more used to publicly saying what they thought.[45]

✪ ✪ ✪ ✪

While the left had temporarily suspended its opposition to sport and celebrated the semi-final victory, its deep-rooted suspicions remained:

> The fact that all the tricolour flags available have been pulled out and millions more have been made in a rush must not, however, delude whoever might like to speculate about a return to a certain rhetorical patriotism that has no sense today... Instead, it is important to understand the Italian enthusiasm for the World Cup. An enthusiasm which is, at the same time, a protest and a demand that sport might find its right place in the modern society that we are trying to create.[46]

According to Paolo Sollier:

> The left's relationship with the world of football was quite hypocritical. Many members were passionate about it, but they were ashamed of

themselves. Having an interest in such a futile and lightweight thing as a match was seen as a sin, an acceptance of middle-class values, a betrayal of class spirit.[47]

Chile 1976–Moscow 1978

Six years after Mexico, another South American country exposed the difficult relationship between Italian sport and politics, after the national tennis team, including flamboyant entertainers Adriano Panatta, Corrado Barazzuti and Paolo Bertolucci, qualified for its third Davis Cup Final. Scheduled to meet the winner of the USSR–Chile semi-final, the Soviet team refused to play against General Pinochet's representatives and withdrew. The second time the USSR had forfeited a sporting tie in protest at the military dictatorship, in September 1973 its football team had withdrawn from the second leg of a World Cup qualifying play-off. Despite having already been awarded the match by default, Pinochet filled the stadium with soldiers and bribed 'fans', before ordering the team onto the field. On the referee's whistle, Chilean captain Francisco Valdes scored against non-existent opponents, in one of political sport's most farcical moments.

The USSR's protest was focussed upon the match venue, Santiago's National Stadium, where many of the regime's political opponents had been interrogated, tortured and executed during the military coup. When the Italian Tennis Federation (FIT) and the players rejected the suggestion that they also withdraw, a campaign began to discourage their participation on the basis that it would legitimize Pinochet's regime. At the vanguard was the Communist '*Lotta Continua*' (Unceasing Struggle), one of a vast number of revolutionary groups that emerged from 1968 to form the largest new left in Europe. Despite its aim of creating an anti-Capitalist, revolutionary consciousness among the working class, its opposition to the Davis Cup attracted a broad cross-section of individuals and groups from outside the revolutionary left.

On 2 October 1976, the 'Committee for the Boycott of the Chile–Italy Match' – a mixture of the Italy–Chile Association, UISP, the CSI and Italian Association for Culture and Sport (*Associazione Italiana Cultura e Sport* – AICS) – launched a protest. It was supported by the CGIL trade union, the national newspapers *Tuttosport*, *La Gazzetta dello Sport*, *Il Messaggero*, *L'Unità* and *Avanti!*,[48] plus leading cultural figures such as Giuseppe Fiori, the future vice-director of TG2 news, and film director Gillo Pontecorvo. Grappling with the old dilemma, *La Gazzetta*'s new director, Gino Palumbo, took a refreshingly honest line: 'My opinion is that sport cannot and must not feel above or indifferent to politics: sport is an active element not a foreign body in the nation's life.'[49]

While the libertarian Panatta proposed playing in order to expose the situation, and his teammate Bertolucci asked why the dictatorships of East Germany and the Soviet Union were not treated the same, manager Nicola Pietrangeli argued that his team were competing against Chilean tennis, not Pinochet.[50] The DC took a similarly neutral position, while journalists Gianni Clerici, Indro Montanelli and the Roman *Corriere dello Sport* openly supported Italy's participation.[51]

The PCI's position was complicated by its involvement in the 'historic compromise'. Requiring skilful management of the various opinions if inter-party cooperation was to be maintained, the PCI's difficulty was captured within the ideological gymnastics of its plenipotentiary for sport, Ignazio Pirastu, during a TV debate with Nicola Pietrangeli: 'If I were in your shoes I would fight to go to Santiago. It would be advisable not to go, but if the Federation decides to go [then] we will support Italy.'[52] With CONI equally unsure, Giulio Onesti passed the buck directly onto the government and the Tennis Federation in whose affairs he was no doubt relieved to declare CONI had no legal right to interfere.

The PCI's lack of opposition was fundamental in Italy's eventual participation, which was supported by Chilean Communists who feared the boycott would strengthen nationalist resolve around the dictatorship.[53] Undeterred by the PCI's pragmatism, the revolutionary 'new left' continued to resist what it later declared as yet another DC victory over Communism.

> Once again, and certainly not over a marginal issue, the DC succeeds in wearing out the PCI's political heritage.
> The Davis salad bowl is perhaps the new symbol of that 'national harmony', in the name of which Andreotti is allowed to survive and perform his nefarious deeds, one after another.[54]

The ultimate decision rested with Andreotti's government, which predictably followed CONI's lead: In a 'country as divided and differentiated as Italy it is essential that sport is kept out of politics'.[55] Game, set, and match. The team left for Santiago and, on 19 December 1976, claimed a 4-1 victory that put the Davis Cup in the Italian trophy cabinet and gave Pinochet a moral victory. Rhetorically questioning: 'Who really won the Davis Cup? Pinochet beats Italy five-nil', *Lotta Continua* laid out the five sets in which CONI, the players and politicians were defeated by the Chilean regime.[56] Having experienced the conditions within the post-coup national stadium/concentration camp, the paper's young correspondent Paolo Hutter argued that the match had been 'another step towards the "legitimization" of Pinochet on the international stage. A new attempt to pass-off the Santiago stadium as a "normal" sports stadium.'[57] As an earlier editorial had underlined:

The Davis Cup Italy–Chile match is a real provocation to democratic Italians and Chileans.

CONI, the Italian Tennis Federation and all of the politically apathetic and reactionary groups try, with all means, to present a match between professionals, who earn hundreds of millions a year, as a sporting success for our country which, instead, remains among the weakest in terms of mass participation and facilities.

Hidden once more behind the false concepts of neutral and apolitical sport is the hypocrisy of the sporting leaders and governors of our country who are always at the front of the queue to support Fascist regimes throughout the world.

Right now, accepting to go to Chile supports the hangman Pinochet [and] contributes to bringing the junta out of the isolation to which the world's workers and democrats had condemned it.[58]

A defeat for the left, the affair had clearly demonstrated sport's powerful potential to express democratic protest, which re-emerged once again before the 1980 Moscow Olympic Games.

✪ ✪ ✪ ✪

The USSR interpreted the IOC decision to award the Games to Moscow as 'clear evidence of the effectiveness of the Soviet government's policy of developing international links, broadening participation, relaxing tension and promoting peace'.[59] By the end of 1979, preparations for the first Games to be held on Socialist soil and its accompanying propaganda programme appeared to support this claim.

On 27 December 1979, Soviet army units crossed the Afghan border, overthrew Hafizollah Amin's government and imposed a new administration under Babrak Karmal. The US response was immediate. On 4 January 1980, President Carter raised the possibility of US non-participation at the Moscow Games, if USSR troops did not withdraw. By the end of the month resolutions backing the proposed 'boycott' – the term was actually never used – had been passed in both the US Senate and House of Representatives. Contravening the IOC's charter protecting the independence of national sport, extreme pressure from the Carter administration saw the US Olympic Committee withdraw its team in April. Forty-six countries followed suit. Within Europe there was strong opposition to the boycott from France, which had traditionally opposed US foreign policy; Ireland, which was neutral; Greece, which had designs on hosting the Games itself; and Finland, whose close proximity to the USSR was an understandable motive for maintaining peaceful relations with its neighbour. As Coakley and Dunning explain: 'States used the episode to demonstrate independence and/or solidarity, to build stronger links with particular states or groups of states or to loosen ties with particular power blocks, and to demonstrate commitment to causes.'[60]

Using tortuous double-speak worthy of the PCI, Francesco Cossiga's DC-led government inched towards non-participation, so long as *it* did not have to take that decision. On 19 May, the government announced that CONI was entirely free to make an independent choice, so long as it reflected national interests. Having been cleanly passed the baton of responsibility, CONI announced the entry of its 'athletes into the Games... in the hope that their free will to participate might be respected without difference'.[61]

Following the Davis Cup debate, it is hardly surprising that there was little consensus of opinion, with *Lotta Continua*'s position evident in its headline: 'This year the Yankee doesn't run.' It was placed beneath a photo of President Carter jogging alongside a security guard wearing a Diet Pepsi t-shirt with the slogan 'Run America Run'.[62] But with the left and centre/right divided over sport and its connection with Italian foreign relations, old arguments resurfaced about its separation from politics. The only difference was their reversal of positions. With each having now hidden behind the argument of apolitical sport, this only confirmed the overtly political nature of their decisions.

The presence of Italian military athletes was a particular thorn of contention with the Minster for Defence, Attilio Ruffini, proposing that Italy go without them, as early as February. Following confirmation of CONI's participation, in a clear attempt to placate the US the selection of Italian military athletes was vetoed. Given the number within its military system, it was a huge blow to Italy's and individual Olympic ambitions, as *Atletica Leggera* sourly noted:

> For many, the Olympics bought only bitterness. Let's talk about the military athletes who, only because they wear the vest of a military sports club, were unable to participate in the Moscow Games because of the emotional insensitivity of some politician who, for the first time in his life, fatefully busied himself in the phenomenon of sport.[63]

Furthermore, those athletes that did attend competed under the name of CONI rather than Italy, and did not carry the national flag or use the national anthem, which saved the independence of Italian sport while making some sort of a statement to the Soviet Union and the USA. As the government announced:

> Not believing that the Olympic Games can be seen as isolated from world events, if the Soviet military occupation of Afghanistan has not ended by the beginning of the Games, the Italian government and its representatives will

not be present at the respective ceremonies and believes... the use of the Italian flag and national anthem to be incompatible with this position.[64]

Italy's, or CONI's, participation was a compromise measure that suited nobody. Backing neither America nor the Soviet Union, it alienated the many military athletes forced to remain at home while appearing to contradict its own assertion that, as 'athletes have the right to full recognition of their long-term sacrifices... in preparation for the Olympic Games, it would be unjust to take away an opportunity for which they have subordinated important life choices'.[65] The offence was worsened by President Pertini's official reception of medal-winners who had effectively participated against the will of the state. As the sprinter for the police's *Fiamme d'Oro* team, Luciano Caravani later lamented:

> It's perhaps worse now than at the moment of the government's no. Nobody remembers us. At the summer meetings they don't watch you. And why is this? Because we are not 'Olympians'. But is it our fault? Everybody forgets that only we... paid for a decision taken outside of sport. Even the Minister of Defence, Lagorio, let us know that he would see us to explain the reasons for the government veto. We're still waiting for the meeting.[66]

Football's left and right wingers

Sport's increasing commercialization contributed to it assuming secular, quasi-religious characteristics as elements of the national obsession began to assume their own rituals, festivals and rites. In the tense political atmosphere of the late 1960s and early 1970s, spectating also took on a distinctly political bent as the protest movement spread from students to even blue-collar workers. Radicalizing large sectors of society, the 1968 'long May' of protest left a tradition of small, politicized groups of young people.

From this mixture of new subcultures and extremist politics emerged the *ultrà* football fan groups. Named and organized after hard-line political bodies, they took the extreme-left-wing culture of grass-roots activism into the stadiums. While Milan's left-wing *Fossa dei Leoni* (Lion's Den) was probably the first modern *ultrà* group, in 1968, and AS Roma fans were closely associated with the extreme left from the early 1970s,[67] *ultras* were not the preserve of any particular brand of politics, with fans of Milan's city rivals Inter forming the uncompromisingly named Inter Boys SAN (Armed Black-and-Blue Squad).[68]

Strongly identifying with the stadium and the club, *ultras* were inspired by the militant and often thuggish occupation of city areas by extremist political groups, mimicking their style, structures and countercultural features.[69] While their strength and organization has been attributed to their experiences of extra-parliamentary political activity,[70] an equally plausible counter-proposal identifies their objection to all forms of organization and control, even within their own ranks.[71] Either way, the insurrectionary experience of 1968 certainly contributed to this new fandom that reflected the different approaches to the post-1969, anti-state, armed struggle of 'new left' organizations, such as 'Autonomia Operaia' (Workers' Vanguard) and the 'Brigate Rosse' (Red Brigades). As a letter to Lotta Continua observed, in 1976:

> The way in which sports fans express themselves is increasingly taken from the language of politics: the old tradition of the proletarian Roma fans and the bourgeois Lazio supporters, the corteges of fans with a real security force, graffiti on the walls, the names of some clubs, slogans and songs, very similar to those of our rallies, are only part of the phenomenon.[72]

✪ ✪ ✪ ✪

While violence and militancy were commonplace on football terraces by the mid-1970s, the game, its administrators and players remained bastions of conservatism. Yet even within this castle of conformity there was evidence of society's post-1968 radicalization, with some managers, players and even teams declaring political allegiances.

In 1974, Lazio won its first league title with an eclectic mix of eccentric players that would have made Wimbledon FC's 1980s 'Crazy Gang' seem somewhat mainstream. Renowned for their passion for firearms, prior to flying to away matches the team captain collected the guns before leaving them with the pilot. The squad was also viciously divided, so much so that many players wore shin pads for training, only to relinquish them for Serie A matches when the fractious unit solidly came together. The group's commanding figure, Giorgio Chinaglia, was the embodiment of Lazio's national hatred, much of which derived from the team's extreme-right-wing politics and Chinaglia's forthright support for neo-Fascism.

Loving guns, militarism, violence and the MSI, SS Lazio equalled Fascism for many, with even those who said they knew nothing about politics easily labelled. Midfielder Luciano Re Cecconi claimed to be just that. He was also a keen parachutist and practical joker for which he paid with his life, in 1977. Holding up a Roman jewellery shop for a prank, the owner shot Re Cecconi, who died soon after at the age of 28. Initially charged with the excessive use of self-defence, the shopkeeper was acquitted 18 days later. As John Foot explains:

> The concept of self-defence – outlined in Article 52 in the Italian penal code – was a controversial one. But the 1970s were the 'Years of Lead', when

right- and left-wing terrorists... used armed robbery to finance their political activities. Murders were common, and shopkeepers and bank tellers very jumpy.[73]

High on Lazio's wanted list was the long-haired, bearded Perugia midfielder Paolo Sollier, who suffered accordingly on his visits to the *Stadio Olimpico*:

> It was evident that the Fascists didn't like me, but I was never attacked...
> I received anonymous, threatening phone calls but they never had any great
> effect on me... Then, within the stadiums I took an infinite amount of insults
> and read some banners like, 'Sollier to the gallows', on the Lazio terraces.[74]

An ex-FIAT worker in the Cossato factory, north of Turin, Sollier was an active member of *Avanguardie Operaie* (Workers' Vanguard), one of the most important far-left revolutionary groups to emerge from 1968. He also made regular political donations and was said to have a clause in his contract giving two free season tickets to the *Quotidiano dei Lavoratori* (Daily Worker) newspaper for every goal that he scored.[75] A heretic in the world of football, he lived in a communal open house, refused to wear the club suit, would not attend the pre-match *ritiro* (retreat) and was generally outspoken, all of which probably shortened his career.

His biography, *Kicks and Spits and Headers: The Autobiographical Reflections of an Accidental Footballer*, the cover of which depicted the bearded Sollier with his customary raised clenched fist, exposed the contradictory life of the revolutionary footballer who frequently moved from free-thinking political meetings to the intellectual confinement of the professional football prison camp. Exposing the banal lives and worlds of sex-obsessed footballers, he reserved particular ire for their union and its isolation from the struggle of the major trade unions (CGIL, CISL and UIL) for reform and jobs. Questioning why it didn't collaborate in developing mass sport, Sollier defined the organization as 'a trade union "without colour", a mish-mash of all political ideas' and, thus, 'a faithful reflection of the average footballer: he defends his corporate interests and absolutely doesn't give a damn for anything else'.[76]

Sollier also attacked his fellow comrades, drawing attention to the difference between the theory and practice of UISP's mass sport campaign and the PCI's role in its failure. Reflecting upon the importance of mass popular culture in the left's campaign, his observations were sharp:

> Why in the *Quotidiano*, but also in the *Manifesto* or *Lotta Continua*, does
> every statement about sport double you up laughing? I think it is because
> beyond the generic 'let's get hold of sport', the comrades don't have a clue

about it. They have never been interested in it. Instead, among those who practise it (too few), who support (too many) and suffer it, sport involves everybody.

Thus, it has to be said that it belongs to everybody and that facilities to sweat, improve health and enjoy oneself must be provided everywhere; but it's also necessary to start thinking about how to do this, how to jump off the rhetoric wagon, how, in practice, to take control of this damned sport.

UISP says something, but in between the doing and saying there is the... PCI. On one hand are the good suggestions, on the other are the red committees that follow the previous line: money and facilities for the important sports, which are professional; crumbs for alternative sport. And it should be exactly the opposite.[77]

Attacking the left's inability to embrace sport, let alone make political capital from it, Sollier drew attention to its failure to serve mass society that contributed to the time-bomb of frustration among Italy's discontented youth, which was visible in weekly violence upon the nation's terraces:

Berlinguer has a lovely saying that the stadium is no longer a drug and that the mechanism of fandom as a release has been broken. I don't know if he goes to watch matches or if this is yet another piece from the compromised bastard, but it's not true. I've seen stadiums from every angle – the field, the terraces, the main stand – and fandom as a social illness has been anything but defeated... This year's facts show it, the air of tension in the stadiums shows it, the scent of war that you breathe.

Who isn't politicized and submits each week to the torture of work, of prices, of not counting for anything, becomes a potential human bomb. He has been charged by the press and has charged himself arguing, betting, selling his arse to the pools coupon, paying extortionate prices to enter the stadium. If his team then loses, plays badly, or the referee invents something, the fan becomes violent and dangerous.

Because of political immaturity and because he isn't sporting. And he isn't sporting because he's never played sport. And he's never done it because they never allowed him to, because they never built him any facilities, because he's not a champion. Because mass sport does not exist. Let's look around: children must play in between cars; to swim they need to drown in the canals. And let's not talk of the adults: those few that want to, have to reduce themselves to running along the streets at night breathing fumes and taking risks.

Thus, practising sport, sweating because afterwards you feel better, the satisfaction of feeling fit are still confined to the rich.[78]

But however politicized stadiums had become, the primacy of football remained. As Umberto Eco questioned, in 1978: 'Is the armed struggle possible on World Cup Sunday?... Is it possible to have a revolution on a football Sunday?'[79]

Terrorism

Theoretically protecting democratic Italy against unconstitutional forces, the 'historic compromise', from 1976 to 1979, was strongly opposed by both left- and right-wing extremes intent on undermining social stability and conciliation. In this period Giulio Andreotti led two Christian-Democrat governments of 'National Solidarity' in which the PCI had a greater consultative role and some minor positions in government. Without controlling any ministries, it was drawn into the system whereby jobs and zones of influence were distributed according to party membership and strength, which would be dramatically exposed in the early 1990s.

Among more radical members of the extreme left the 'historic compromise' contributed to a growing sense that civil society and mass politics were not the means by which Italy would be transformed. From 1972 onwards, right-wing trade unionists, foremen and factory managers in Turin and Milan became regular victims of red terrorist activities, which varied from vandalizing cars and beatings to brief kidnappings. This strategy escalated in April 1974 with the Red Brigades' (BR) kidnap of Genoese judge Mario Sossi, who was released unharmed after 35 days. The BR achieved national notoriety, even if their demands for a prisoner exchange were rejected.

Sossi's kidnap stimulated police infiltration of the Brigades, which reduced its active membership but could not stop the escalation of its activities into direct action against members of the professions, journalists and servants of the state. In May 1976, the Genoese judge Francesco Coco, who had refused to negotiate during Sossi's kidnapping, and his two police escorts were ambushed and killed. On 16 March 1978, having already received a number of death threats, Aldo Moro, the former five-times prime minister, was seized in a busy Roman street and his five bodyguards and driver killed. For 54 days the Red Brigades held Moro, who was allowed to release a number of anguished letters to his family and colleagues, who he implored to negotiate his release. Defending the integrity of the state, Andreotti's government, supported by the PCI, refused to negotiate with terrorists, effectively leaving Moro to his fate. As *La Repubblica*'s editor Eugenio Scalfari coldly determined: 'The decision to be taken is terrible, because you are talking about sacrificing the life of a man or losing the Republic. Unfortunately, for democrats, there are no doubts.'[80] On 9 May, Moro was assassinated and his body left in the boot of a car in central Rome, symbolically equidistant between the DC and PCI central offices.

Figure 17: *Get by with a little help from my friends? Aldo Moro pleads for his life in vain*

Combined with an intensification of the Cold War after the Soviet invasion of Afghanistan and a sharp drop in PCI fortunes, Moro's murder effectively ended the DC–PCI coalition but not the violence, with dozens killed and hundreds wounded from 1978 to 1980. Yet, while many feared for democracy and the Republic, life carried on much as it had done before, with some arguing that the Italian state had been strengthened by the revulsion at Moro's murder. The Brigades' power was ultimately neutered by General Carlo Alberto Dalla Chiesa who, with new legislation that promised lighter prison sentences in return for cooperation, began to persuade disillusioned terrorists to become super-grasses. His effective work won Dalla Chiesa the dubious honour of being sent to Sicily to combat organized crime, which replaced extremist political groups in bringing fear to Italy.

On the mainland, the investigation into the suspicious deaths of two Italian bankers with Mafia links, Michele Sindona and Roberto Calvi (Calvi was found hanging under Blackfriars Bridge in London in 1982), led to the revelation of an enormous, secret Masonic lodge. With secret societies constitutionally forbidden, the list of Propaganda 2 (P2) members included bankers, 44 parliamentary deputies, three ministers, ex-ministers, judges, civil servants, newspaper editors, plus members of the police, armed forces and secret services. Another was Silvio Berlusconi, who declared in court that he had just joined P2 and had never paid his membership fee. Both statements were untrue and, in 1990, the Venetian Court of Appeal found him guilty of false testimony, the only definitive conviction that he has suffered.[81]

The government investigation revealed a powerful elite with conspiratorial and anti-Communist aims. However, the thwarting of investigating magistrates inquiries delayed the uncovering of highly dubious party funding, such as Calvi's deposit of seven million dollars into a secret Swiss bank account of Bettino Craxi, the secretary of the Socialist Party. Thirteen years after the original investigation the Court of Cassation, the highest in Italy, declared that P2 was not a conspiracy but a 'business committee'. Nonetheless, the body's mere existence was indicative of dark forces at work within a variety of national institutions.

The road to modernity: civil marriages, divorce, abortion

If student and worker agitation didn't bring about revolution, it did force the government to make concessions to what was a rapidly changing society. Responding to protestors' demands, reforms – albeit patchy and uncoordinated – suddenly increased. Among these, the autonomy that had been promised within the constitution was finally realized in the establishment of five regional governments in 1970. Health, education, transport and housing legislation was also introduced, all of which had limited success.

From 1965 onwards, the Italian birth rate began to decline, as did the size of the average family. While the number of extended families decreased very slowly, all were becoming increasingly isolated by the impact of urbanization and the loss of collective lifestyles. Traditional authority within families was also often challenged by the younger generation that was liberated by new jobs and financial freedom. Italian women, however, still contributed one of the lowest European percentages of the workforce. With many becoming full-time housewives in the post-war period, this was reflected in the increase in images of domestic goddesses in the burgeoning numbers of magazines and advertisements targeted at women. While the move into large urban environments offered greater freedom from traditional family ties for many, the 'idealised confinement of women to the home in the 1960s served to enclose them in a purely private dimension, and to remove them even more than previously from the political and public life of the nation'.[82]

The release of Pietro Germi's film *Divorzio all'italiana*, in 1961, contributed to an already shifting public opinion. Highlighting how the only way to get a divorce in Italy was through the death of a spouse, the film supported the growing pro-divorce movement that finally saw a bill introduced into parliament in 1965. In December 1970, after 100 hours of parliamentary debate, divorce was finally legalized after some Catholic MPs rejected a Vatican ruling and joined the opposition. In 1974, the DC employed a previously unused constitutional article that enabled the abrogation of legislation by popular referendum. Indicative of a political hierarchy that was completely out of touch with the average Italian, the DC secretary, Amintore Fanfani, thought his party could gain votes on the right, while the PCI's Enrico Berlinguer opposed the referendum through fear of being accused of destroying the Italian family[83] and undermining the consensus that he was seeking with the DC. Of the 88 per cent turn-out, over 59 per cent voted in favour of maintaining divorce.

Far from a victory for laicism, progress or democracy, the writer, film-director and non-conformist Pier Paolo Pasolini argued it represented a defeat for the PCI as well as the DC, indicating how both leaderships had failed to understand the recent changes in the middle-class that chose 'the hedonistic ideology of consumerism' over the restrictive values of the Church.[84] The decision certainly indicated an increasingly secular society in which sex was causing some concern, even if Italian sex lives were changing slower than anything else in the country. But since the early 1960s there had been some signs of a more open approach, with timid discussions of pre-marital sex appearing in some women's magazines.

Most worrying was the falling birth rate and reported figures of live births being matched by illegal abortions. Combined with the emergence of feminist groups, the demand for women's autonomy was closely related to control over their reproductive systems through contraception and abortion. With the crime of abortion still punishable by up to five years imprisonment in the early 1970s, tens of thousands of illegal, back-street terminations were conducted every year, while the wealthy flew to clinics abroad. In 1975, over 800,000 signed a petition demanding a referendum on the issue, which deeply divided Italy again. In an effort to stave off an abortion law following a demonstration of 50,000 women, in April 1976, parties tried to agree to amend existing legislation. They failed, and after a long struggle abortion was legalized in 1978.

Although flawed, the abortion law was another leap in Italy's modernization and secularization. The first kicks against the '*partitocrazia*' (partyocracy) that had governed Italy since the war, demands followed to end the Savoy laws on public order and to vote against the public financing of political parties, after the exposure of a bribery scandal involving government parties and the Italian Oil Union. With the family apparently under threat following the introduction of civil marriages, divorce and abortion, all of which had drastically undermined the power of the Church, only one institution remained that was capable of holding the fundamental Italian unit together: television.

Political footballs
in Berlusconia

TV winners

Following the introduction of colour broadcasting in 1974 and commercial channels soon after, TV became a pillar of Italian life. The 'only "cultural" activity that the great majority of Italians indulged in on a daily basis', some critics were severe while others recognized its capacity to unite, provide escape, comfort and education.[1] Either way, television's negative and positive aspects depended upon its control, content and consumption.

The 1970s also witnessed a growth in alternative information, with the emergence of a number of hard-left, radical periodicals and dailies, such as *Il Manifesto* and *Lotta Continua*. Responding to coverage of terrorism and the 'editing' of stories in accordance with official versions of events, increasingly politicized journalists challenged traditional views, opinions and news. Also, in April 1975, state broadcasting was liberated from DC clutches. Reconfirmed as a public service and state monopoly, RAI's control was transferred from the government to a Parliamentary Commission and its channels divided between the major political parties (DC – RAI 1, PSI – RAI 2, PCI – RAI 3). A Constitutional Court ruling the following year confirmed RAI's monopoly, but only at national level. Permitting private, local broadcasting, by 1980 there were over 400 TV stations across Italy. Requiring urgent regulation, parliament dragged its feet and allowed private television's unchecked growth. Yet, in the construction of a media monster, this was only the groundwork, as Beppe Severgnini notes:

In the 1980s it was the socialists, the most modern and least scrupulous of the period's powerful, who helped Silvio Berlusconi transform this slightly overblown – and therefore very Italian – carnival into an aspiring American-style big business. He didn't invent its taste or its audience. He guessed the former, and pandered to the latter. Did he know that one day the audience would become the hardcore of his electorate, doubly precious because it was lifted from the Left? I don't think so. If in 1980, the year Canale 5 was born, Berlusconi had been able to foresee the anticorruption campaign that would sweep away his political protectors, and his own entry into the electoral fray with the big guns of television behind him, he would have been gifted with second sight. Which he isn't. He is a spinner of dreams, skilled at turning reality into entertainment. Without realizing it, Berlusconi took Norman Rockwell's America of lavish dinner tables, smiling old people and shapely girls, and then imported it, adopted it, adapted it, undressed it, and pretended it was real. Embarrassingly, we fell for it.[2]

After completing a prize-winning law degree at the State University of Milan and becoming Mediterranean cruise ship compère, Silvio Berlusconi turned to construction. Successfully completing four modest blocks of flats in 1962, he undertook a larger project to build 1,000 apartments on the edge of the city. By 1969 all were sold and Milano 2 was in the pipeline. Containing houses rather than high-rise blocks, green spaces, shops, a church, theatre, sports facilities and six schools, the complex was effectively a small town. Most significantly, it had its own six-channel, cable television network, the last of which, TeleMilano, became Canale 5, the keystone of his empire.

Courtesy of his TV network, Berlusconi transformed from a very successful, provincial builder into a nationally recognized figure, in the 1980s. With clients desperate to exploit the medium, working directly with his advertising company Publitalia, and a toothless regulatory body, his television network broadcast more advertisements per day than all of Europe together. His success 'had little to do with any media skills' and 'everything to do with his ability to nose out potential advertising markets and to sell advertising space'.[3]

Despite the Constitutional Court's outlawing of private *national* broadcasting, with no legislation preventing local stations from transmitting the same programme at the same time, *de facto* national channels arose. Unconcerned by anticipated competition law to stop this, Berlusconi bought Rete 4 and Italia 1. Exploiting the legal loophole his three stations, which were not subject to political, advertising or content controls, reached 70 per cent of Italy. Focussed upon ratings, TV Berlusconi offered films, serials, soap operas, quiz and variety shows, cartoons, sport and advertisements, all decorated with scantily clad Italian beauty. Rather than provide an alternative, RAI mimicked it.

In October 1984 magistrates in Turin, Rome and Pescara blacked-out Canale 5, Italia 1 and Rete 4. Deprived of *The Simpsons, The Smurfs, Dallas* and *Dynasty*, the consequent protests reflected RAI's awful schedule more than the quality of Berlusconi's programming. In total contrast with the stagnation of post-war Italy the 'Berlusconi decree', introduced that December by his old friend Prime Minister Bettino Craxi, overruled the decision and national transmissions resumed. Craxi was the Republic's first Socialist prime minister, and his two governments, from 1983 to 1987, made a huge impact.

> Craxi reaffirmed in a modern form certain perennial values of Italian politics, according to which the strongest and the most cunning must perforce prevail. The Craxi years, in fact, saw a radical divorce between politics on the one hand, and morality and the law on the other....
>
> Under Craxi's leadership, politics were to be personalized and simplified, they were to have a strong showbiz element, their principal medium was to be the television.[4]

With Craxi intent on making the PSI a dominant force, the unfettered rise of Berlusconi's media empire was a perfect opportunity for two highly ambitious men to scratch very itchy backs. Moreover, from the 1980s onwards football began to dominate Italian sport, its relationship with television cemented by the mutual desire to satisfy advertisers on a weekly basis, for almost three quarters of the year.

Winter games

The 1956 Winter Olympic Games in Cortina d'Ampezzo stimulated the Dolomite alpine region and Italian winter sport. As the tournament's Official Report noted:

> although every winter brings an abundance of snow to both mountain and valley, winter sports were little known or practiced in our country. In a land where lemons flourish, and where the sun, sea and flowers delight the senses, the snow and ice represented something unwelcome that did not appeal to the majority of Italians.[5]

Designed to protect Italy's alpine border, Fascism's training of skilled mountaineers and skiers had already encouraged winter sports and modest tourism.[6] The National Association of Alpine troops was formed in 1924 and the Central Military School of mountaineering in Aosta, ten years later. Schooling troops in summer and winter conditions, it also selected and prepared athletes for international competition, with its Duca degli Abruzzi division containing Zeno Colò, one of the best downhill and slalom skiers of his era. Interned in Switzerland, in 1945, he continued to race under the pseudonym of 'Blitz' before winning world titles in Aspen, in 1950, and another in Oslo.

An accomplished winter sportsman and brief head of CONI, Count Alberto Bonacossa encouraged Cortina d'Ampezzo's town council to bid for the 1944 Winter Olympic Games. Awarded the event in 1939, preparations were halted by the outbreak of war. After its bid to host the 1952 tournament failed, Cortina's hour finally came in 1956. Closely followed by the economic miracle, the two events began to loosen the bourgeoisie's grip on winter sports. With the growth in disposable income enabling Italians to consider such pursuits, by 1970 the Sauze d'Oulx resort held over 25 ski runs, with nearby Val Gardena becoming the model for Alpine tourism.

Winter sports also enabled the expression of identity in the South Tyrol that Italy had annexed from Austria, in 1919. While there were approximately only 15,000 Italians to 215,000 Austrians in the region, its demographics changed dramatically after Fascism moved in thousands of Italians, banned the use of German outside the family home, and conducted all education in Italian. Maintaining control of the region after 1945, Italy granted autonomy to the German-speaking minority and restored German-language education. However, the South Tyrol's inclusion within the new Trentino–Alto Adige region resulted in an overall Italian majority. With administrative autonomy watered down and proposed devolution delayed, a German national movement developed.

A new agreement in 1972 divided the region. Transferring autonomous powers to the German-speaking province of Bolzano, the local authority set about restoring balance by prioritizing funds for schools, where only one in five pupils was Italian, and local facilities that were run and attended primarily by German speakers. Italian identity in the Bolzano province continued to weaken under pressure from a declining birth rate, emigration and the inter-marrying of Italians and ethnic Germans.

A means of developing pride among the German-speaking minority, sport was naturally high profile in the region's ethnic politics. However, with its athletes also representing Italy in international competition, it also had the potential to undermine it. One of the best examples was Klaus Dibiasi, who competed in four consecutive Olympic Games, from 1968 to 1976, and dominated international diving. After winning two silver medals in Tokyo, he became the only diver to win three consecutive Olympic golds, in the 10 metre platform event. Renowned for his corkscrew twists and knife-like entry with minimal splash, Dibiasi was almost unbeatable, winning the World and European championships in the same period. Defeated only by his Torinese compatriot Giorgio Cagnotto in the 3 metre springboard, Italy ruled international diving with only two competitors.

Born to Italian parents in a village near Innsbruck, Austria, Dibiasi lived in the South Tyrol/Alto Adige. With German the mother-tongue of the majority, even though Dibiasi's command of Italian was less than perfect his success as an Italian representative was not welcomed by all in the region. With local custom frowning upon 'mixed' marriages with 'outsiders', especially when the groom was a mother-tongue German speaker, sympathies were further reduced by his decision to marry a Roman and move to the capital.

Another particular case was Gerda Weissensteiner, who, after winning Olympic gold in the luge, in 1994, gave an interview in which she affirmed that the only foreign language she knew was Italian. Later retracting the comment, she was filmed with the tricolour painted on her face. On her return Weissensteiner and her coach received a number of threatening phone calls before her Olympic medals were stolen in a burglary, as she attended her brother's funeral. While police rejected any ethnic motive for the crime, suspicion remained that Italy's gold had been specifically targeted. As Bassetti notes: 'Feelings towards Italians are tolerance at best, but their extraneousness is brutally exposed if Italy does well thanks to Alto-Adige citizens, which is experienced as usurpation.'[7]

Winter athletes from the region naturally won numerous medals for Italy, most often in skiing, one of the great national success stories. While a number of female cross-country, downhill and slalom skiers won at international level, it was the Alto Adige's men that dominated. Slalom and giant slalom specialist Gustav Thoeni was pivotal, winning the World Cup[8] four years out of five, from 1971 to 1975, with only his team-mate Piero Gross preventing a clean sweep, in 1974. Winning gold and silver medals at the 1972 Sapporo Winter Olympics, Thoeni was an a national skiing legend..

Renowned for his monosyllabic interviews in Italian, which reflected his preference for German and those journalists who practised it, a formidable group of Alto Atesini skiers formed around him. Separating themselves in the national training camp, they spoke German, ate together and formed a German team during football or volleyball matches with Italian colleagues. On 7 January 1974, 'Thoeni's team' claimed the first five places in the World Ski Championship individual giant slalom. Thoeni, nonetheless, never supported separatism, embodying instead the contradictory split identity of the region and its citizens: 'He was registered Italian at birth and for him that was enough. Thus, he was German in his way of being honestly Italian.'[9]

Following the 1970s devolution, local investment in sport began to increase and finally address CONI's almost complete lack of interest in grass roots, mass activity. The impact upon Italian skiing was huge, with the construction of tourist facilities across the Alps finally opening the formerly bourgeois activity to all. Unfortunately, this development appeared to focus more upon the money to be made than the glory to be won, with the previous production line of skiers drying up. Only Alberto Tomba continued to raise the flag, becoming another Italian cult figure.

Born in Bologna, close to the Apennines, he was the only Italian skier to come from a city. Winning the World Cup slalom and giant slalom titles in 1987, he lost out in the overall classification to Swiss legend Pirmin Zurbriggin, before repeating the feat in 1992. He also won three Olympic gold medals and two silver medals, from 1988 to 1994. Reviving Italian skiing after almost 20 years of gloom, Tomba appeared to have invented a new, elegant style, while his appearances were often backed by a loyal band of noisy supporters. Finally winning the World Cup in 1995, one of Tomba's most endearing characteristics was his fallibility, a feature of some of Italy's most popular champions. More than his ability to win, it was his apparent capacity to do so more or less when he wanted which appealed. Despite the intense years of training and preparation, skiing seemed to come easy to him, which was reflected in his occasionally too relaxed, easygoing approach. A good-looking, Ferrari-owning, lover of the *dolce vita*, his relationship with Miss Italy 1999, Martina Colombari, was one of many that embellished his off-piste reputation. One of the last great aspirational figures for Italian men, he reinforced the national stereotype of the all-conquering male, brimming with talent who barely broke sweat.

Totonero

Following *Totocalcio*'s introduction in 1946, Italians cast aside their inherent suspicions to dream of a perfect 13 that would change their lives. By the mid-1970s some 50,000 had become lire millionaires, with 500 more having won over 200,000 million lire each. But as the prize money grew so did temptation, with gambling soon accompanied by its side-kick, corruption. Before the state's deregulation of gambling in the mid-1990s, individual bookmakers did not exist and betting on single matches was illegal, which inevitably resulted in a flourishing black market.

The *totonero* scandal was instigated by two Romans, the fruit and vegetable seller Massimo Cruciani and restaurant owner Alvaro Trinca. Friendly with a number of Lazio players who dined at Trinca's, a scam was forged whereby certain footballers across the country would receive money for fixing games that Cruciani and Trinca would bet on during the 1979–80 season. After early matches failed to come up trumps, even when it appeared the players were doing their best, or worst, their 'alternative' *schedina* seemed jinxed. Their first win raised the stakes, but the hit and miss nature of subsequent flutters increased their suspicions that they were being duped.

After the Roman dailies *Il Messaggero* and *Paese Sera* launched vague accusations against unspecified footballers, a sporting inquiry failed to make any significant breakthrough, despite establishing a strong gambling culture. When the magazine *L'Europeo* published a bookmaker's testimony listing the number of players who bet against their own teams to insure against losing their win bonus in the event of a defeat, the investigating magistrate Corrado De Biase redoubled his efforts.

Having lost serious money, Trinca and Cruciani began gambling on credit that their lenders were eager to see repaid with interest. Fearing for their safety, they went directly to the FIGC president Artemio Franchi to try and resolve the problem without involving the police. With no deal forthcoming, Trinca and Cruciani somewhat incredibly denounced the players for fraud to the Rome Prosecutor's Office, thereby exposing an illegal gambling system involving tens of billions of lire and huge tax evasion, which rivalled that of the state and totally undermined *calcio*'s integrity. Confessing to having received significant sums of money in return for fixing matches, the players claimed to have reneged upon the deal.

The rumours that had long circulated were finally confirmed by Lazio's Maurizio Montesi, on 4 March 1980, who expanded upon football's systematic corruption.[10] Politically left wing, Montesi was already a black sheep within the football family and the ranks of Lazio's neo-Fascists, from whom he was isolated having wanted no part in the scandal. As Foot notes, there were considerable question marks over 'Montesi's absence from a particularly "suspicious" game with Milan when he had "been injured in the warm up".[11] Predicting that nobody would take such damaging accusations seriously and, even if so, a couple of scapegoats would be found and *calcio* would soon return to normal, Montesi was dismissed an extremist.

After Trinca was arrested on 7 March and Cruciani surrendered five days later, both provided full details of the con.[12] On Sunday 23 March, one of the most dramatic days in *calcio*'s history, the AC Milan President Felice Colombo was arrested and charged with aggravated and continued fraud, along with the club's goalkeeper Enrico Albertosi, Lazio players Bruno Giordano and Pino Wilson and, most sensationally, the Vicenza and Italy striker Paolo Rossi. Seized by the Finance police and *carabinieri* in well-coordinated, spectacular, public raids, most were sent to Rome's ancient Regina Coeli prison, where they remained for eleven days.

Almost one month later, 33 players were among the 38 charged by the Rome Prosecutor, while sporting justice, led by Di Biase, charged 21 with sporting crimes. Relegating Milan and Lazio to Serie B, the sporting court gave points deductions to other clubs, imposed a life ban upon Milan's president, and issued bans of two to six years to the players involved. The state trial ran from June until December, when all of the accused were acquitted, including Trinca and Cruciani. To Italian law, which did not encompass 'sporting fraud', it appeared that no crime had been committed.

With everybody innocent according to state law many of the players' bans were shortened or rescinded on appeal, with Paolo Rossi's suspension reduced just in time to make the 1982 World Cup. Italy won it, and Rossi was the tournament's top scorer. Storing up trouble for the future, there was an understandable sense that crimes had not been paid for. Another scandal in 1986, involving Bologna and Juventus, only added to the doubt that nothing had changed, as Montesi had predicted.

Pertini's World Cup

If the 1974 'Match of the Century' liberated the Italian flag from its Fascist connotations, the regime's final metaphorical shackle was removed by Italy's 1982 World Cup win, its first outside of the Fascist period. The unexpected success provoked a national celebration that was exploited by politicians now adept at identifying and squeezing every drop of political capital from the game. Now, according to Aurelio Lepre, 'in Football Italy almost every Italian recognized himself'.[13]

Following a series of defeats and poor performances prior to the tournament, Italy somehow managed to qualify from a desperate group stage with only three draws. The eventual victory was a classic Italian miracle and a cathartic moment for the nation, with Marco Tardelli's primal, Munch-like scream, following his goal in the final, becoming an iconic moment in the tournament's history. Symbolizing the release of the nation's stresses and pain accumulated during the 'Years of Lead', it was the 'efficiency of football's message that encouraged official politics to no longer sit at the tables of the official party courts but rather at that of bar sport'.[14]

During the quarter-final against tournament favourites Brazil, with the score at 2-2, the lower house of parliament was suspended by Prime Minister Giovanni Spadolini. After one of the most dramatic victories in Italian football history, Spadolini walked the streets of Rome, wrapped in the tricolour, where he was photographed embracing celebrating fans.[15] Having earlier confessed to not being a football lover, the *azzurri*'s success, in a period in which his administration was in serious trouble, was political gold. 'A team game, without individuals: this is what the government needs to confront the second phase of this troubled legislature', he declared.[16]

Equally aware of the potential to commune with the Italian nation was the 86-year-old Italian President, Sandro Pertini, who some 24 years later was recalled by one scribe as having 'become everybody's granddad' in Madrid.[17] Declaring himself the representative of all Italians back home, he turned to captain Dino Zoff: 'You are an example of serious Italy... of an Italy that believes in itself.'[18] Congratulating Paolo Rossi on his goals that had brought Italy this far, he focussed on the team's role and indulged in populist national stereotyping:

> Well done, very well done for your goals, but remember they are the product of everybody's work. So well done everybody. And remember, shoot tonight, shoot! And watch your legs. As soon as the referee turns his back the 'chopping' Germans will hit you. Keep one eye on the ball and one eye on your legs.[19]

The most popular president in the Republic's history, the tiny, frail, former Resistance leader reinvigorated the role after his election in 1978. 'His outspoken advocacy of democratic values, his constant re-evocation of his anti-Fascist youth, his invitation every year to thousands of schoolchildren to come and meet him in the Quirinale palace, left an indelible impression on Italian public opinion.'[20] Bolstering Italian democracy when it was seriously under threat, Pertini revived respect for institutions and encouraged popular reaction against terror and corruption. Courting local support by demanding Spain's admission to the European Community,[21] his last-minute decision to accept King Juan Carlos' invitation to attend the Final in Madrid indicated his close relationship with Italians, according to *La Gazzetta*:

> we think Pertini's journey was inspired by one of the blessings that make this individual so loved and popular: the ability to be on the same wavelength as the people. Pertini had no intention of going to Madrid... 'If the squad then loses with me in the stand it will be said that I brought bad luck.' It was the same sense of fear, hope and sorcery that the people were feeling about the azzurri's exploits at that moment. The fear of opening your eyes only to realize that it was a dream... Pertini – the Italian among the Italians – got onto the same wavelength of the people.[22]

Representing the nation, Pertini was an unusually animated dignitary. Sat next to the King Juan Carlos of Spain and the German Chancellor, Helmut Schmidt, he broke every 'law as he jumped from his seat and failed to stay still, just like all of us', his history, personality and behaviour in the stadium making him 'a living incarnation of a national cohesion founded upon the memory of the resistance to Fascism'.[23] Having watched the match in Milan, Spadolini described the victory as representing 'the cement of the country, a spirit of national unity in the explosion of the tricolour'.[24] Although far from Fascism's ideological appropriation of sporting success, Pertini and Spadolini demonstrated the continuing power of football and the media to commune with the masses, irrespective of the political system. Pertini invited the squad to return on his presidential plane, and Italy's triumph was encapsulated in a photo of the President playing *scopone* – a nationally popular card game – with Dino Zoff, Franco Causio and team coach Enzo Bearzot, the World Cup apparently ignored on the table in front of them.[25]

An unprecedented 37 million Italians watched the final, with 40,000 fans meeting the players at Ciampino airport, and another one million lining the streets to the Quirinale Palace, where Pertini had invited them to lunch. 'I don't know when you'll get there because there will be a lot of people but don't worry, I'll wait for you and get the pasta ready.'[26]

The success was also a golden opportunity to underline the importance of unity. After Pertini implored Italians to 'follow the example of the national

Figure 18: *Mission accomplished, Dino Zoff, Franco Causio, Enzo Bearzot and President Sandro Pertini concentrate on the cards in hand*

team that knew how to overcome enormous difficulties, against every prediction',[27] Spadolini ensured sport's entry into the political vocabulary:

> The hopes of the Palazzo Chigi worked. You left here on 1 June and you've returned world champions. Now let's hope they also work for me... [It is] an example for all Italians that all difficulties can be overcome with unity, with imagination... In these days millions of Italians have followed... a sporting event in which the most interesting thing... was the exact capability of a group of Italian athletes to suddenly rediscover a collective understanding and game that seemed to have been irretrievably lost. As the captain of the football team called government, which in these forty days has had its own difficult rounds to get through and still has many tough matches to play, I also see in this... a good omen for my squad.[28]

Among the renewed, patriotic fervour there were, as always, dissenting voices. Journalist Alberto Ronchey observed 'an escape from problems... and the prolonged frustrations of a shelled, often disorganized and disturbed, rather unhappy society'.[29] Also arguing that the euphoria indicated society's unease, the psychologist Emilio Servadio suggested 'the popular joy at the sporting victory had a therapeutic value; in a difficult social and economic position like Italy's, turning aggression towards another direction might have been healthy'.[30] With the celebrations papering over cracks in Italian society, Umberto Eco's 1969 analysis of the negative political impact of idle talk and sports chatter is interesting:

> In fact, the chatter about sports chatter has all the characteristics of a political debate. They say what the leaders should have done, what they did do, what we would have liked them to do, what happened, and what will happen...
> Afterwards, there's no more room – because the person who chatters about sport, if he didn't do this, would at least realise he has possibilities of judgement, verbal aggressiveness, and political competitiveness to employ somehow. But sports chatter convinces him that this energy is expended to conclude something. Having allayed his doubt, sport fulfils its role of fake conscience.[31]

Ultras and Maradonapoli

While the 1982 victory created some temporary commonality among Italians the cracks were still there, evident in violence among increasingly extreme football fans. As Winston Churchill apparently quipped: 'Italians lose wars as if they were football matches and play football matches as if they were wars.'[32]

Inter-fan rivalries pre-dated Fascism's take-over of the game and continued after the war, with a notorious match between Napoli and Bologna, in 1955, involving a pitch invasion and an exchange of shots between fans and police.[33] Rarely premeditated however, crowd disorder was usually an impetuous, unplanned reaction to on-the-field events. This changed in the 1960s, with pitch invasions, violence and confrontations with the police reflecting and releasing society's accumulated tensions. 'In a highly politicized context, the advent of young rebels in the second half of the 1960s and the consequent birth of the *ultrà* groups are not only the expression of a social and cultural form of behaviour, but they are also deeply related to the political situation.'[34]

The *ultras'* arrival was most evident in the *coreografia* (choreography) of flags, clouds of coloured smoke that covered the *curva* (home end), drums and loud hailers that incited the fans, plus banners that took political murals into the stadiums.[35] Another legacy of the protest movement and its increasingly tough policing was an escalation in violence and the use of weapons, knives in particular.

> Political riots brought an increased potency in the equipment and techniques of repression used by police and *carabinieri*. In turn, the intensification of police control inside and outside the stadia led the *ultras* to adopt a mode of military organization and a warlike attitude against the police. As a result, football hooliganism *qua* social problem has to be regarded as the legacy of such policing.[36]

Equally serious for a country in which kinship and family ties had provided social order and education, *ultrà* groups began to make obsolete the traditional role of the family in the stadium; that of the father who introduced his son not only to the venue, but also to a more pacifist tradition of support. Thus, stadiums provided an escape from the constraints of the family within the 'security' of a more lawless, often politically extreme and certainly more exciting community.

Between the 1970s and 1990s, the *ultrà* phenomenon mutated further, with the fragmentation of groups and the emergence of more violent unofficial ones outside of previously recognized leaderships, leaving almost every club, down to small semi-professional teams, with its own section.[37] Not all were necessarily political or aggressive, although some were mobilized by extreme right political groups, such as *Forza Nuova*.[38]

Increasing tensions by heightening territorial awareness while conveniently identifying and collecting the enemy ready for attack, the rigid separation of fans in stadiums also forced the violence outside. But even this wasn't indiscriminate, as the development of alliances or 'twinning' between fans of different clubs meant that violence only erupted against specific, enemy *ultras*. When incidents did occur they were usually well away from the stadium, often in motorway service stations following chance meetings between travelling fans with no previous animosity, on the simple basis that 'the friends of my enemies automatically become my enemies'.[39] Often inspired by English hooligans, *ultras* established their own ritualistic culture of songs, clothes and lifestyle within which individuals found a faith, identity and strong collective voice.

They also formed relationships with club owners who knew no limits in the pursuit of success, as former national team coach Arrigo Sacchi expanded upon, in 2007:

> Some directors began using... all possible means to win at all costs. Allowed or otherwise. They made a pact with the devil, with the most vulgar and violent groups, to intimidate the adversary, referee and sometimes their own players. These groups organized themselves in this way and, in some cases, began to ask (and get) economic advantages. At the beginning they had away travel paid for and free tickets they could re-sell. Some managed to earn a salary and others even managed to open commercial enterprises... They have become so powerful as to get almost everything they ask for from the clubs.[40]

While the average fan was searched and prevented from entering the stadium with a plastic bottle of water complete with its top, which would make it a potentially offensive weapon, somehow *ultras* made it in with huge flags, banners, drums, megaphones, flares, fireworks and distress rockets. They were also traditionally self-financed through membership fees and the sale of merchandise, which in the case of Lazio's *Irriducibili* extended to the club's official products. After taking control in 2004, Lazio president Claudio Lotito fought a long battle to reclaim this significant source of income.

One major difference between Italian *ultras* and British fans was the former's complete lack of interest in the national team. With greater importance given to the sense of local belonging, aggression was directed towards internal rather than external enemies. While saving Italy from the embarrassment of fans rampaging across Europe, it further indicated the continuing strength of local identities. As Triani suggests:

> the Sunday warriors, the supporter extremists, seem to demonstrate a deep regret for the lost local identity. The image of a mythic time in which the individual had roots, a personal history, a family, a sense of belonging to

a place and a community that guaranteed them support, solidarity and defence from the ugly reality.[41]

And nowhere was this local identity, which occasionally turned directly against the nation, demonstrated more clearly than in Maradonapoli: Naples during the reign of Diego Armando Maradona.

Napoli's emergence as a football force in the late 1980s came more or less at the same time as that of AC Milan, which we will come to in due course. Breaking the domination of Juventus, Napoli led another divisive battle between Italy's north and south, its rich and poor. Owned by businessman Corrado Ferlaino, who succeeded Achille Lauro, a mixture of talented Italians and established international stars, such as the Brazilian Careca, formed a squad capable of rivalling Milan. Napoli's talisman was Maradona, who flew into the San Paolo stadium from Barcelona in a helicopter, in 1984, to a reception of 70,000-plus delirious, paying fans.

Their relationship with the Argentinian was intense. Besides his unquestionable status as the greatest player of the period and potentially of all time, Maradona and Napoli had much in common. Full of defects that made them infuriating, especially in relation to rules, their passion, spontaneity and capacity to amaze made them equally irresistible. The city's intellectuals were less impressed, with over one hundred signing a petition in protest at the immorality of such expense in a town that lacked essential structures and drains. No doubt with one eye on the potential threat to its football hegemony, the Neapolitan 'recklessness' was equally frowned upon by many in the north. While the demands for economic sense could not logically be refuted, with Italian football becoming highly profligate the calls for prudence appeared to be directed at those clubs that threatened the equally spendthrift elite.

After 60 years of waiting, Napoli's 1987 *scudetto* victory launched one of the biggest parties in the peninsula's history. Celebrated across Italy and the world by Neapolitans and anti-Milan fans, sales in curly black wigs rocketed in the city along with the registration of babies called Diego(a). Suspicion still surrounds the team's collapse at the end of the following season, which saw it go from champions-elect to runners up in the last four matches, when it accrued a single point. Despite Napoli winning the UEFA Cup and claiming another title in 1990, 1988 was the end of Maradona's honeymoon in the city. Thereafter, being photographed in jacuzzis with Camorra bosses, hard partying, tax evasion, a contested illegitimate son, pimping and cocaine abuse were among the scandals that plagued him. The latter finally earned him a 15-month ban from football in 1991, which ended his Italian adventure.[42]

For all of his faults, as Napoli's leader Maradona still restored pride to the downtrodden south at a time when the rise of northern regionalist sentiment was intensifying existing regionalism and prejudices that had seen extreme anti-Neapolitan banners on northern terraces: 'Welcome to Italy'; *'Forza Vesuvio'*; 'No to vivisection, use a Neapolitan'; with the unveiling of 'Neapolitan, help the environment, wash yourself', often followed by a barrage of soap bars. Unsurprisingly, the north reserved particular ire for Maradona. Not only because he threatened its hegemony and represented resistance to Milan, the club and city, and neither because he appeared to embody all of the customary, negative stereotypes of the *Mezzogiorno* (south) but, above all, for the way in which he became a footballing freedom-fighter for downtrodden, rebellious Neapolitans.

These fissures were further exposed during the 1990 World Cup where, having just led Napoli to a second *scudetto* after a long and bitter battle with Milan, Maradona played the bad guy to Italy's unexpected hero, Totò Schillacci.

> At the end of a... [league]... championship that was everything but serene due to the polemics between the Neapolitan club and Milan, the Argentine champion who had led Napoli to its second scudetto, in 1990, was the subject of protests that projected the resentments and rivalries between the club teams onto the colours of the nation.[43]

As holders, Argentina opened the tournament against Cameroon, in Milan, where Pete Davies recalled its anthem being 'roundly and universally jeered and whistled', with 'the booing and shrieking redoubled in ferocity' as Maradona's name was read out. 'The Cameroon anthem... was an altogether jollier affair... and each of their players were mightily applauded.'[44] Suggesting the tournament had been fixed in Italy's favour, Maradona had hardly offered the olive branch, which only sweetened the taste of Argentina's 1-0 defeat.

His revenge came in Naples, in the semi-final against Italy. Unsure of which way the locals would side, political leaders and sportsmen implored Neapolitans to support the national team, while Maradona counter-attacked by declaring his love for the people of the 'capital' of the south. Underlining their status as national outcasts, he questioned if it was really worth supporting Italy? Nobody knows how many fans inside the San Paolo did, or did not, support the *azzurri* that night, but a significant minority seemed to ditch them in favour of their leader. When Maradona's decisive penalty hit the back of net, the silence was far from golden. The final in Rome was no spectacle, one of the worst in World Cup history with Germany winning a battle of negativity. As Roman fans this time hissed and whistled the Argentine national anthem, the camera focused on Maradona, whose quivering lips muttered *'hijos di puta'* (sons of bitches) for the world to see.

Dirty deals and clean hands

In 2003, the former *Corriere dello Sport* editor Mario Sconcerti argued that 'football's problem has slowly become that which, ten years ago, Tangentopoli showed to be the problem of all Italian society: not only and not so much the great corruption, but the habitual minor corruption, considering it almost as an inevitable way of being'.[45] While Sconcerti had a point, the everydayness of *calcio* corruption was hardly new.

Preparations for the 1990 World Cup included the redevelopment and building of new stadiums and an accompanying programme of infrastructure development. From the original estimates, costs rose astronomically in order to 'satisfy the hunger for bribes that regulated the relationship between big business and the political class'.[46] Providing a snapshot of the type of corruption that had developed since the 1960s, the irregular, direct transfer of state funds to families and businesses, plus the creation of a massive tax avoidance system, made Italia 90 a huge opportunity to move money.

In Bari, internationally renowned architect Renzo Piano created a futuristic stadium of considerable beauty. With a capacity of 60,000 that far exceeded the needs of a team rarely in Serie A, it reflected the ambition and desire of the

Figure 19: *Matarrese's monolithic memorial: the San Niccola struggling to contain the Bari faithful*

FIGC president and DC deputy Antonio Matarrese, whose home town and club was his political power base. To connect the stadium to the outside world, 10.5 billion lire were spent on its by-pass and another six billion on the airport. Nonetheless, the Cameroon team's flight for a group game was diverted due to the radar system being unfinished, while nobody had thought about the stairs to disembark passengers anyway.

But this wasn't just a hackneyed tale of southern corruption, for at the other end of the country in Turin, spiralling costs didn't deter Primo Nebiolo, president of the International Amateur Athletics Foundation (IAAF), from imposing a running track upon the new *Stadio delle Alpi*. A compromise measure, the stadium was hated by all. Stuck out in Turin's often fog-bound periphery, the view was awful from virtually every seat in the ground which, almost 20 years later, finally underwent a complete overhaul. Late starts and eternal delays left some stadiums unfit for use so close to the tournament that a special decree was required. 'In Naples', explained the city's Mayor, 'punctuality isn't a rule,'[47] while in Rome the Vigna Clara station, intended to alleviate public transport pressure in the city's north, closed one day after the final. Elsewhere state money funded projects in cities where no matches would be held, such as the Aosta and Catania by-passes and Padua's stadium.

Most seriously, building accidents, many of which were the consequence of dangerous and unregulated working conditions, occurred 15-times more than the national average. When the football festival began, 24 construction workers had lost their lives, with 678 injured.[48]

> Rumour spoke darkly of the work being delayed by sabotage bombings, Byzantine strife among unions and management and architects and government, while the unions (and many others) expressed outrage at the death toll... At a union meeting, a placard listed the lost names under a headline, 'This squad will not play at Italia '90'.[49]

Such revelations and a number of arrests related to Italia 90, between 1992 and 1993, indicated the widespread state corruption that would delegitimize almost the entire political class and collapse the system in 1994.[50]

The 'Clean Hands' investigation into the *tangentopoli* (Bribesville) scandal, launched by Milan's chief prosecutor Francesco Saverio Borrelli, exposed an enormous web of corruption. Principally involving the PSI and DC, it ended the Christian Democratic Party's post-war domination of Italian politics, left the Church reviewing its relationship with politics and, most significantly, created a vacuum for Berlusconi's new, Catholic, right-wing, media-savvy party.

In July 1989, Giulio Andreotti formed his sixth government. Lasting until the cataclysmic general elections of 1992, it was an uncharacteristic period of reforming zeal, as if politicians realized they were pressed for time. Among the legislation processed, the 1990 Mammì Telecommunications law finally addressed the media issue. More or less sanctioning Berlusconi's monopoly, it removed any need for him to enter politics, were he even considering it. Allowing his channels to transmit live and broadcast news, he was able to interfere from the outside and reciprocate support received from sympathetic politicians. Having failed to introduce desperately needed changes, the major parties haemorrhaged support at the 1992 'Earthquake elections', much of which went to the Northern League's anti-Roman rebellion that claimed 8.7 per cent of the national vote.

With faith in government and the state plummeting, a number of strong and courageous figures began campaigning against corruption and illegality. Former Palermo Mayor Leoluca Orlando's 'La Rete' (The Network) party gave focus to a growing sense of civil society and anti-Mafia sentiment in Sicily. This became peninsula-wide revulsion following the assassination of magistrate Giovanni Falcone, on 23 May 1992. The Mafia's response to the failure of its political protectors to undermine the Palermo 'maxitrial' that sentenced a number of leading bosses to life imprisonment, a reportedly ashen-faced Andreotti attended the funerals of Falcone, his wife and three bodyguards. Further demonstrating the Mafia's apparent invincibility and the end awaiting any public official that stood in its way, on 19 July a bomb exploded as Falcone's replacement, Paolo Borsellino, rang his mother's doorbell.

Similarly dedicated to public service and restoring the rule of law to Italy, Francesco Borrelli's investigation of corrupt politicians and their business friends saw the old order attacked from all sides. With extraordinary haste, the 'Clean Hands' investigation went from the Milanese politician Mario Chiesa – arrested trying to flush 30 million lire down the toilet – to the height of government. During Giuliano Amato's short-lived administration, from June 1992 to April 1993, seven ministers resigned after being placed under investigation. In December 1992, the spotlight turned on Bettino Craxi for the corrupt funding of political parties. Declaring it a political plot, he fled to his Tunisian villa in May 1994, where he died six years later. On 28 March 1993, Andreotti was placed under investigation for Mafia association, by Palermo's Chief Prosecutor.

Initially well supported, 'public opinion became more tepid, alarmed that the inquiry might delve too deeply into Italian life. "Accommodations" and illegalities were too much part of daily life for Italians to feel comfortable with an overzealous judiciary.'[51] Many of the investigations focussed upon corruption or financial kickbacks paid by local firms to politicians, to ensure they were included on local government tender lists, made privy to 'confidential' information, or simply paid on time. This money went either directly into party coffers, to the leaders of party factions, into individual pockets, or towards securing support in a local area. With the costs of politics raised by mass communication and electioneering, the unholy DC and PSI alliance was the principle beneficiary of a systematic fraud that was so widespread it was considered almost normal.

In April 1993 a huge majority of Italians voted in favour of electoral reform after Operation Clean Hands left the ruling DC and PSI parties powerless to defend the system that had sustained their rule. It was a fundamental moment in modern Italy's development: 'the referendums and the subsequent laws destroyed the old style of conducting politics in Italy, almost completely burying all the dominant parties of the First Republic'.[52] Confronting the issue of electoral reform, parliament's response was a complex compromise in which 75 per cent of the lower and upper houses would be decided by a UK-style first-past-the-post system, with the remaining 25 per cent by proportional representation. Keeping medium-sized parties in parliament, it required pre- rather than post-electoral pacts.

While this was ably exploited by Berlusconi with the help of his immense media empire, his rise was also facilitated and enforced by the demise of the old political order. Furthermore, following the collapse of the Berlin Wall and the disintegration of the Soviet dictatorships in Eastern Europe, the fear of Communism, upon which the DC and the right had traded since 1945, was gone. With the left now theoretically capable of winning a majority of single-member constituencies with little more than 30 per cent of the vote, plus a huge vacuum on the political right that none of the remaining parties could fill, there was a tailor-made opportunity and incentive for a new, national party like *Forza Italia!* Offering more than a change of packaging, it proposed a simple, conservative, populist programme of Christian Democracy in new clothes: 'God, the market and family',[53] spiced up with a healthy dose of anti-Communism.

The rise of Berlusconi

'Footballization'. The term is ugly and also sounds bad. However, it perfectly conveys the idea of a curious and worrying phenomenon... that sees football not only surpass and engulf all other sports but also infiltrate all areas of daily life, imposing its fiction on everyday reality, literally seizing the language and form of communication.[54]

With his patron Craxi gone, Berlusconi's position was no longer quite so comfortable. Adding to his ill ease were growing debts from his retailing and publishing businesses, a downturn among his media outlets, plus the prospect of a left-wing victory in the spring 1994 elections, which potentially threatened his media monopoly. Most alarmingly, 'Clean Hands' was coming closer, with a number of his Milanese business associates under investigation.

On 5 November 1993, the National Association of *'Forza Italia'* was launched and supporters' clubs soon appeared across the country. Two months later Berlusconi finally announced his entry into politics or, more revealingly, his entry onto the field of play – his *discesa in campo*. His choice of language and party name 'was an astute appropriation', according to Gianni Mura, 'another contribution to the footballization of Italian life and politics'.[55] Rooted in the metaphor of football, it was not coincidental: 'The political movement that I am proposing to you is not by chance, called Forza Italia,' Berlusconi confessed.[56]

A terrace chant and *La Gazzetta*'s headline on the morning of the 1982 World Cup Final,[57] *Forza Italia!* was instantly recognizable by all. As the philosopher Norberto Bobbio bitterly noted, its

> greatest criterion as Italian [wa]s its identification in sport, in football...
> They don't identify themselves in the Italy of culture, but in that of Milan or
> Juventus... For the majority of people it doesn't matter that Italy took the lead
> in the world for having given birth to a Dante, a Verdi. Many Italians feel so
> much more for Fausto Coppi than Eugenio Montale.[58]

Accelerating his political appropriation of football, Berlusconi named his 1994 election team the *azzurri* (the blues), after the Italian squad, with local *Forza Italia!* branches emerging from the nationwide network of AC Milan supporters' clubs that had incubated his political movement.[59] Presenting his list of election candidates as a 'purchasing campaign',[60] he took the idea to the extreme by running Mariella Scirea, the widow of former Juventus player and 1982 World Cup winner Gaetano Scirea, as a candidate, plus his team-mate Ciccio Graziani.[61] Unlike traditional parties *Forza Italia!* had no mass membership, and there was no internal democracy and no conventions, until 1998. Votes were won using modern, mass communication and the charisma of Berlusconi, who was its undisputed leader.

Rumoured to have supported city rivals Inter, Berlusconi bought the financially stricken AC Milan in 1986. In a country well accustomed to division, especially over sport, his hesitation over its potential to create a solid bank of enemies, as well as supporters, was valid. But possessing huge control of the Italian media and the ability to manipulate his coverage, and with football

Figure 20: *The media master working his audience*

attendances and TV viewing figures rising since 1982, the proposition was too tempting. Using wealth accrued from his media empire he bankrolled the club to world primacy in the 1990s, blending the Dutch/European elite with young and outstanding Italian talent.

Not the first high-profile businessman to enter football, his purchase of Milan brought a completely new dimension to its relationship with business. Originating with the Agnellis' ownership of FIAT and Juventus, this well-known aristocratic family had no need for cheap publicity and propaganda stunts. Juventus was an end in itself and not a conduit to arriving elsewhere. With huge numbers of FIAT workers Juventus fans, success was naturally important, especially if football was to act as the soporific that many thought it was. But it was equally important that Juventus was prudently managed, thereby providing a reassuring demonstration of FIAT's solid, paternalistic business philosophy. When hard times hit the motor industry, Juventus moderated its spending out of sensitivity to the workforce.

Berlusconi's relationship with Milan was completely different. With his fortune made in television and marketing, his purchase of the club was an investment that could only be repaid with success. While confirming the transfer of his business techniques and strategies to the world of football, which 'he saw as a corporation needing restructuring',[62] Milan's string of achievements would enable him to increase the price of advertising space sold on his television stations during matches.

Possessing a high-profile, successful football club and a national television network, Berlusconi had two special advantages that no businessmen or politician could match. With one feeding the other he engaged in politics as spectacle, often leaving the 1994 campaign trail to head to the San Siro stadium. Clinching a third consecutive league title and the European Cup, only three weeks after winning the elections, Berlusconi promised to make Italy like Milan. 'Ours is a winning philosophy that has achieved good sporting results in good time.' Further evolving the language of politics, he echoed Spadolini in 1982: 'The country will take an example from the red and blacks [Milan].'[63]

As an aspiring politician, his manipulation and control of the Italian media were unique in Western Europe. While his Publitalia marketing networks fully exploit AC Milan's political potential, as club president he enters directly into Italian homes to self-publicize and talk about football, where other politicians talk of less interesting things, like politics. In this way, his roles as *primo Milanista* (No.1 Milan fan) and *Primo Ministro* (Prime Minister) became increasingly blurred, the former offering him sporting airspace that he exploited in an overtly political way.

Slightly more covert was the integrated use of AC Milan to promote the Berlusconi brand and philosophy in a variety of spectacular and theatrical gestures. 'Forza Italia from this point of view was an incitement and a promise. A lot more than a political programme. A miracle. Like club presidents and coaches promise the fans at the start every season.'[64] In July 1986, Milan's new owners and directors presented themselves, alongside their first signings, in the Milan Arena. Broadcast on all three of his television channels, they arrived in helicopters to Wagner's *Ride of the Valkyries*. A record number of season tickets were sold. Following the Championship win in 1988, the theatrics continued in a choreographed display at the San Siro during a party for 80,000 fans while, in 1989, a trip to Barcelona for the European Cup Final was organized for another 70,000. It was, as Alessandro Dal Lago explained, 'the era in which Berlusconi appropriated the efforts of the Milan players and attributed to himself the merit of their successes, an era that culminated in the spring of 1992 when he defined Milan's second title victory as a result of his business strategy'.[65]

Having sufficiently expanded his public profile to forge a political career, Berlusconi used his television network and AC Milan to completely footballize the language of politics. Expressed more than a decade earlier, Umberto Eco's 'malevolent' thoughts on football and its absurdities had come disturbingly true.

> In fact... sport debate (I mean the sports shows, the talk about it, the talk
> about the journalists who talk about it) is the easiest substitute for political
> debate. Instead of judging the job done by the minister of finance (for which

you have to know about economics, among other things), you discuss the job done by the coach; instead of criticising the record of Parliament you criticise the record of the athletes; instead of asking (a difficult and obscure question) if such-and-such minister signed some shady agreements with such-and-such a foreign power, you ask if the final or decisive game will be decided by chance, by athletic prowess or by diplomatic alchemy.[66]

A drugged old lady, a doped pirate and dirty feet

The cycling prime minister

Within the Pole of Liberty alliance, *Forza Italia!* was joined by *Alleanza Nazionale*, which included the neo-Fascist MSI,[1] and the Northern League. Using Berlusconi's huge media resources, the 1994 election campaign was one-sided. The left coalition's expectation of victory indicated a lack of self-awareness and its inability to comprehend let alone combat this new force. With *Forza Italia!* the leading party in the coalition that claimed over 42 per cent of the vote, Berlusconi became prime minister.

On 19 May 1994 parliament held a confidence vote on the new administration, as Milan destroyed Barcelona 4-0 in the European Cup Final. Conveying the drama on its front page, *Il Corriere dello Sport* reported: 'Confidence vote while score 2-0'.[2] With Berlusconi's parliamentary victory announced contemporaneously with that of his team, *La Gazzetta* had difficulty discerning the more important event. 'An incredible evening for the president of Milan: almost at the same time came the confidence vote in the government and the cup.'[3] Distracting from the administration's severe instability, both events briefly bolstered Berlusconi's premiership.

Milan's win was almost certainly the high point of his crisis-ridden first-term, as he uncertainly struggled to introduce his business strategies and practices into the political arena. While his relationship with the Alleanza Nazionale leader Ginfranco Fini went well, despite Europe-wide concerns about the MSI's presence, the Northern League's Umberto Bossi proved more difficult. Neo-fascists accepted ministerial positions and, in a blatant attempt to limit the Clean Hands investigation, the Interior Ministry was offered to one of the leading prosecuting magistrates, Antonio Di Pietro, who refused it. The attempt to quietly pass a decree law in midsummer, which would have effectively concluded the inquiry early, caused public outcry. One of many embarrassing retreats, Clean Hands ultimately brought Berlusconi down when, in the following November, he too was placed under investigation for bribery of the Finance Police in return for ignoring false tax declarations. Although he denied the serious allegations, Bossi lost faith and the Northern League withdrew its support, after less than six months in power.

For more than a year Italy was governed by an interim administration and a cabinet of technocrats led by the former finance minister Lamberto Dini. Failing to rebuild the centre-right coalition, Berlusconi's majority in the April 1996 election was undermined by the Northern League staying out of the coalition and polling ten per cent of the vote. Unable to form a government, the left's Olive Tree coalition, with the support of the ex-PCI Rifondazione Comunista,[4] formed a highly fragmented alliance under the leadership of Romano Prodi.

An economics professor from Bologna, he was also a keen amateur cyclist upon which he traded heavily in the new political world where sporting connections counted. Rather than focus upon his depth of knowledge and connections within Italy's financial system, Prodi drew attention to his friendship and excursions with cyclist Gianni Bugno. On making his own *discesa in campo* Prodi described himself as a middle-distance runner who'd never lost a race in his life.[5] Furthermore, with his fellow coalition leader, the deputy prime minister Walter Veltroni, he used that year's European Championships to combat the separatist Northern League by rallying the nation around the Italian flag. Veltroni's statement as the players departed was familiar: 'Apart from 1968 we've never won the European Championship... so the time has come to break the trend. Everybody is watching you, and among the country's many difficulties you represent the heights of a diffuse sporting culture... as Matarrese said, football unites Italy.'[6]

Committed to implementing institutional reform and restoring Italy's economic health in order to join the European Union, Prodi's fragile coalition was hindered in its capacity to take great policy decisions, most crucially in the production of a new telecommunications law or one governing conflict of interests. Preferring to let sleeping dogs lie, the left chose to not risk upsetting the electorate with unpopular media controls, which was compounded by the failure to drive on the Clean Hands investigation.

When *Rifondazione Comunista* opposed the budget law in October 1998, Prodi's government collapsed. The unity that had been maintained to ensure that Italy was among the first group of nations to join the common European currency was shattered by a confidence motion that the government lost by one vote. Although the centre-left assembled two further coalitions, which saw Italy through to the 2001 general election, these 'offered no coherent vision or systematic programme for implementing reforms... and they accordingly failed to inspire much enthusiasm in the country'.[7]

Separatism and the Northern League

One of the early indications of the impending political crisis was the rise of the Northern League. Led by the non-conformist, charismatic and authoritarian Umberto Bossi, the League threatened to dramatically change Italian politics. A northern coalition of like-minded groups, its early secessionist demands were moderated into a broad ambition to reorganize the country into highly autonomous macro regions, one of which included the entire north of the peninsula. An ethno-nationalist movement focussed upon 'territory', from 1987 to 1992 the League won strong support in the formerly Christian Democrat northern heartland of Lombardy across to the Veneto. Forging an anti-identity that reflected a loss of confidence in traditional politics, it

> promised revolt against the Roman politicians and parties, their inefficient bureaucracy and increasingly vexatious taxes. It promised 'freedom' in the sense of autonomy, of liberation from centralised oppression and corruption... The values of the North, entrepreneurship, efficiency, the capacity to work hard and to save, were contrasted with those of a lazy and parasitic South, which most certainly included Rome.[8]

Building its base of support through traditional fly-posting, leafleting, meetings and door-to-door canvassing, the League's provincial, male culture made sport a highly effective means of communication.

> Like the threats that the *ultras* exchange on the terraces, like the arguments in bar sport. Places in which everything is easy and understandable: you support your cause or town you win or lose without coming to blows too much, everybody is a coach... It is in such a context, and only in this context that it can be understood how the language of politics, usually prudent and measured, becomes irreverent and proud of the *ultras* verbal fights and the teasing of bar sport.[9]

As the *ultrà* movement reached the stadiums and teams of smaller towns where its distinctly regional and local identities were defended on the terraces,

Italy also experienced a wave of mass immigration. With the political right attempting to transform terrace youth into a united front against national fragmentation and multiracial society, this further aided the Northern League's xenophobia that was as opposed to southern Italians as African immigrants.

When the national anthem played prior to the second leg of the *Coppa Italia* Final between Vicenza and Napoli, on 29 May 1997, half of the stadium reportedly remained 'provocatively seated' while the red and white crossed flag of 'Padania' and that of the League flew inside and outside the ground.[10] As the Northern League's mouthpiece *La Padania* argued, it was the 'regime's disgracefully patriotic and anti-League use' of the national football team that gave a political, irredentist significance to 'a joyful and sporting show'.[11] Opposed to the exploitation of Italian footballers by national television and journalists, in 1998 an Alassio councillor formed an 'Anti-azzurri association' – '*Teniamo per gli altri*', Let's root for the others. The initiative, he explained

> was born from the nausea of seeing every sporting event involving Italian athletes being used by the regime, through the media, for nationalistic purposes, for political speculation, in defence of the so-called motherland... In Rome they have understood that sport is the last glue that can still hold together some pieces of a state in disorder.[12]

To combat the publicity around the national team that had achieved little since 1982, the League began campaigning in bars, piazzas and sports grounds of the north, against what it considered a fundamental part of a patriotic 'propaganda machine' directed against 'the autonomist yearnings of the North'.[13] As *La Padania* claimed, the campaign had already forced the national team to play further away from the north if it was to maintain the appearance of national representation.

> Since the proclamation of Padania on 15 September 1996, the Football Federation has respected the boundaries and chosen central-southern cities as usual, with the only digression being Trieste in the name of the Maldini clan and in the knowledge that the halberd centre is a sort of free port that sells nostalgia and patriotism in industrial quantities.[14]

Contrasting previous attempts to use football to create some sense of national community, the Northern League now used it to promote its anti-national agenda and 'Padanian' identity. Inspired by the examples of Catalonia and ex-Yugoslavia, 'Padania' formed its own 'national' team in 1998.[15] VIVA World Cup champions in 2008,[16] it hosted the tournament the following year. Broadcast on national TV and Berlusconi's network, 'Padania' retained the trophy, defeating

Kurdistan 2-0 in the final. But while stadiums contained a receptive audience for the League's ideas, secession/autonomy were strange policies with which to combat Italy's perceived collapse. In fact, outside of its stronghold, the League's regionalism contributed to a rediscovery of Italian identity. It was

> a choice born in response to the growth in northern stadiums... of a strong Lega trend – in the sense of extremist, secessionis[m]... To those that raised red and white crossed flags and greeted those who came to the north with cries of 'Africans, Africans' or 'soap and water, you need some soap and water', the response was the tricolour and the national anthem together with an outstretched arm.[17]

Thus, the League's campaign against the national team exposed its fundamental weakness. Following considerable early success, from 1994 onwards its electoral appeal was squeezed by *Forza Italia!*, which was tied to no geographical agenda.[18] As Patrick McCarthy observed: 'Bossi had voiced the protest of northern Italian small business people; Berlusconi would bring them to power'.[19]

Berlusconi and *calcio* crises

In the run-up to the 2001 general election, *The Economist* cited one of ten court cases among the reasons why Berlusconi was unfit to govern.[20] Found guilty of corruption in 1998, he was sentenced to two years and nine months imprisonment. Upheld in 2000, this could only be enforced once all levels of appeal were exhausted. Confronted by this possibility, he fought the election campaign with every resource available. In addition to huge, national advertising hoardings featuring only the *Forza Italia!* leader, voters were bombarded with his photo and thoughts. They were no safer in their own homes, due to his media monopoly and election magazine *Una Storia Italiana*. Dropping through 18 million letterboxes across the country, the glossy brochure put a sepia sheen on his life, focussing on his political, business and sporting achievements.

When asked to lift the World Cup at a press conference in 1982, President Pertini refused. Not averse to a photo opportunity, even Mussolini had done the same. In *Una Storia Italiana*'s chapter devoted to Berlusconi's football success, seven of the nine photos capture him either with Milan players or lifting a major trophy.[21] Following Milan's 2007 Champions League victory he took to the field in a lounge suit, before being hoisted aloft by the players with the trophy in his hands. The following day Carlo Verdelli trumpeted: 'this Milan has completed a masterpiece that few (nobody?) could have believed in: notwithstanding the trophy cabinet, notwithstanding Ancelotti's wisdom, notwithstanding a president like Berlusconi, the most capable at motivating his squad, all of his squads'.[22]

Forza Italia!'s association with success was shrewd, 'because many Italians, while prone to *gattopardismo* (appearing to favour changing everything while in reality seeking to preserve positions of privilege) when discussing political change, believe in the post-war transformation which they experienced directly.'[23] For those unaware or unconvinced of Berlusconi's business acumen, AC Milan provided compelling evidence while evoking memories of *calcio*'s resurrection in the 1960s boom. As Berlusconi stated:

> I dreamed of winning the European Cup... but I also imagined how, in what style... Our victory hasn't only been that of the football team, it has been the victory of those values in which we have all believed so strongly.[24]

Although Berlusconi was the only face of *Forza Italia!*, his campaign brochure still paid lip-service to the important role of others in his success, even if only to confirm his capacity to assemble a winning team. 'The adventure of Berlusconi's Milan is also a story of formidable coaches. Bench strategists chosen by the president, not only for their technical qualities but also... for their capacity to adhere to the "Milan-philosophy".'[25] Those who didn't adhere became political fodder, whether Milan coaches or not.

After Italy's narrow failure to win Euro 2000, the blame fell squarely on coach Dino Zoff: 'Berlusconi slaps Zoff. "Zidane was left too free. A shameful decision by amateurs".'[26] It was a personal and very public attack, even if he claimed to speak as AC Milan president rather than leader of the opposition. Refusing to 'take lessons of dignity from Signor Berlusconi', Zoff left the job in disgust.[27] The first campaign victim one year prior to the election, Alberto Zaccheroni went next, more or less sacked live on air after Milan's shock Champions League exit, in March 2001. Their relationship had never been good, and Zaccheroni's assertions that he was nobody's property made divorce inevitable. It was *Berlusconismo* in action, according to *Il Manifesto*:

> Today him, tomorrow us. Zaccheroni sacked on the spot by Berlusconi who is occupied by the 13 May elections. This is how *Il Cavaliere*'s Italy will be: who loses pays, who makes a mistake is out, who is weak is eliminated. But, above all, the winner takes it all.[28]

The new electoral system and distribution of seats converted the House of Liberties' (*Casa della Libertà*) narrow victory into a significant parliamentary majority. Leading a reunited coalition, Berlusconi's return to power confirmed that his first win had been no 'freak of post-modern politics, but had deep roots

Figure 21: *Berlusconi 'scende in campo'*

in Italian life'.[29] It also demonstrated his unquestionable tenacity, political skill and continuing need to stay in power if he was to protect himself from Milan's magistrates, who had extended their charges to include the illegal financing of political parties, tax evasion, false accounting and the corruption of judges.

On 19 October 2001, the Court of Cassation, the highest court in Italy, found the Prime Minister not guilty of the bribery charge that had dogged him for almost a decade. In June 2003 his government passed legislation protecting the five highest officers of the Italian state from prosecution, for the duration of their office. With one of Berlusconi's cases reaching the summing up stage, 'at the very last moment, the Prime Minister was granted immunity by his own government and parliamentary majority, and by the President of the Republic'.[30]

On achieving office for the second time Berlusconi withdrew from football almost immediately and restricted his spending on AC Milan, the relative failure that followed apparently confirming his crucial role. His savings were repeated in Italy, where the economy slumped in the early years of the new millennium. But while local government budgets were slashed and services cut, taxes were also reduced and various amnesties introduced, to the greatest benefit of ailing football clubs burdened by years of overspending. Following its 1990s boom, *calcio*'s crisis in the early years of the twenty-first century was a portent of the national economic storm to come. The bankruptcy of Fiorentina – owned by film director Mario Cecchi Gori – the collapse of Calisto Tanzi's giant Parmalat dairy company that had bankrolled Parma, plus the near-death experience of Lazio following the crisis of club president Sergio Cragnotti's Cirio food corporation, all indicated Italy's perilous economic state. With both Tanzi and Cragnotti in jail and Cecchi Gori under arrest, they also evidenced the game's endemic corruption. At a time when unprecedented television revenue should have been increasing wealth, clubs like Palermo, Ternana and Livorno were declared bankrupt, which was often a blessing. Purged of their debts, many reformed and quickly returned to the top flight. 'Football was sick', as John Foot noted, 'but it was only part of a warped financial-industrial system, built on power, corruption and evasion.'[31]

Each new season witnessed almost all Serie A clubs thrusting hands down the back of luxury leather sofas in search of the huge sums required to pay the league's taxes and insurance premiums. The 1995 European Union ruling on the Jean-Marc Bosman case, which freed players at the end of their contracts, also escalated salaries astronomically. One response was the creative *plus-valenze* accounting system[32] that almost brought *calcio* to its knees. So desperate had club finances become that many turned to law when faced with relegation and exclusion from the trough.

Having played while suspended, in Siena's Serie B 1-1 draw with Catania, on 12 April 2003, Luigi Martinelli's presence caused the Sicilian side to contest its eventual relegation by one point. Catania's drawn-out appeal over the summer of 2003 saw the club bounced between Serie B and C1 following interventions from the local court and the FIGC. With the game in crisis after a two-week Serie B strike that saw referees and officials farcically arriving at stadiums – for Coppa Italia matches – that they knew would be devoid of teams and fans, FIGC President Franco Carraro's head was on the block. It was a strange moment for Prime Minister Berlusconi, of all people, to demand the separation of politics and sport.

> Politics should stay out of sport. I don't see how or why politics might involve itself in sport. We criticized the Left that wanted to put its hands on sport, but we will not do it. The world of sport has its own judges and juries.[33]

The imposition of 24-team Serie B, which included Catania, resolved the issue to nobody's satisfaction, as ever.

With the potential for further chaos stored within the crumbling edifice of football finances, the government introduced the *Decreto salva-calcio* (save-football decree), on 19 August 2003. Alternatively known as the debt-spreading decree, the emergency measure allowed clubs to pay off their enormous deficits over a number of years. Juventus took the moral high ground, declaring the offer 'administrative doping'. Later investigations suggested the club preferred the real thing. Unabashed, Inter saved €319 million and Milan a modest €242 million. In return, the government reserved the right to intervene in any football dispute deemed relevant to the Republic, which the Northern League Senator Roberto Calderoli thought a return 'to the times of the Duce'.[34] Not only had the government removed *calcio*'s autonomy again, it had done so in order to support the illusion that in Berlusconi's Italy, football ran on time.

The drugs might work?

In the late 1980s, some Italian athletes suddenly lost the ability to raise an arm, others lost their libido, while the really unfortunate found cancerous growths. A doping scandal from 1985 to 1988 exposed how the Italian Athletics Federation didn't only 'tolerate individual athletes' personal initiatives but also directly promoted the taking of anabolic steroids (in frighteningly high quantities) making the athletes... sign a disclaimer declaring their full awareness of the connected risks'.[35] Earlier in the decade, a technique was developed whereby blood was extracted and frozen, before being put back into the athlete once their red blood cells had naturally replenished to normal levels. Increasing the number of red blood cells in the system, their capacity to transport oxygen during competition was significantly boosted. Widely considered to have been pioneered by the sports medicine professor Francesco Conconi, during the doping inquiry led by the public prosecutor of Ferrara, Sandro Donati testified:

> I had just become manager of the Italian men's middle distance (800 and 1500) running team and Conconi asked if I would let him treat the athletes with a haemo-transfusion, which we can call doping according to CONI's terminology. Conconi asked... to treat the athletes that I had selected as the most likely to win medals in the big tournaments...
>
> Haemo-transfusion brings enormous advantages in the performance of athletes, which he clearly quantified. It completely changed the order of merit among athletes: an average one became strong and strong became unbeatable.[36]

It was a classic demonstration of the conflict of interests in international bodies demanding sensational performances from the athletes they trained and tested.[37] Success, according to Barry Houlihan's analysis of doping and sport, was generally a

> convenient and relatively cheap way of enhancing the country's prestige and as a means of expanding the repertoire of diplomatic tools available to government. It is in relation to these two overlapping motives that the temptation is strongest among governments... to sanction the use of drugs or, at best, to turn a blind eye to their use.[38]

Up until 1998 CONI was proud of its testing programme. Comprising ten per cent of worldwide controls, only 0.35 per cent were positive. However, of the 10,000 tests conducted only 117 were random and unannounced, among which the positive results rose to 8 per cent.[39] On a number of levels, Italy had a problem. When parliament addressed the issue on 12 January 1988, six out of 630 deputies managed to attend.

Performance-enhancing drugs are far from a modern evil, with ancient Greek athletes said to have used various mushrooms and herbal drinks and Roman gladiators using supplements to increase their strength. In the early twentieth century Olympic marathon runners dabbled with strychnine, with occasionally deadly consequences. After Second World War military experiments with steroids and amphetamines increased knowledge of drug properties, their use in sport and the number of fatalities began to increase.[40] It was especially true among cyclists, such as the Danish rider Knud Jensen, who died during the 1960 Rome Olympics 175 kilometre team time trial, and his two team mates, who were hospitalized after suffering the combined effects of extreme heat and amphetamines. The latter also contributed to the death of the British cyclist Tom Simpson, during the 1967 *Tour de France*.

History suggests that since the beginning of competitive sport athletes have explored alternative methods of gaining an advantage over their rivals, be it for the social and economic benefits of victory, or in response to the demands of unscrupulous political leaders or extreme events that cannot reasonably be expected to be completed without some form of help. Cycling, as one of the most seriously affected sports, qualifies in both the first and final categories. As Matt Rendell argues in his biography of Italian cyclist Marco Pantani:

> The idea of sport that Marco embodied wasn't one that encouraged athletes to face the truth about their existences. It conceived of sport as media content (especially television content), of athletes and events as advertising

billboards, and of physical movement as applied *medical* science. To be talented meant not only to have prodigious physical capabilities but also to be responsive to doping products and to be ready to play an almost literally blood-curdling game of Russian roulette using hormones, blood transfusions and steroids.[41]

On 8 July 1998, three days before the start of the *Tour de France*, French customs officers found vials of human growth hormone and 234 doses of r-EPO, among a cache of pharmaceuticals in a vehicle belonging to the Festina team. The initial lack of concern grew when police began raiding hotels and questioning doctors. The premier team in the world with three serious *Tour* contenders, Festina was excluded from the race after its director and doctor confessed to supplying their riders with doping products. Another team followed and five more withdrew in protest. Less than half the original riders completed the race.

Investigations into Festina, plus the testimony of rider Richard Virenque, exposed the widespread use of EPO, a man-made drug that replicates blood doping by stimulating bone marrow to produce red blood cells. Thickening the blood as a consequence, EPO was thought to have resulted in the deaths of numerous cyclists from cardiac failure. Such was the threat that many slept next to exercise bikes, wired-up to heart rate monitor alarms should their pulse drop too low.

✪ ✪ ✪ ✪

The diminutive Italian Marco Pantani, one of cycling's most charismatic figures, emerged from the chaos and recriminations to claim his first *Tour de France* victory, only weeks after his *Giro d'Italia* win had made him a national hero. His domination of the sport over the next 18 months was a golden moment for Italian cycling. But his time at the top ended suddenly following his exclusion from the 1999 *Giro d'Italia*, on the eve of a second consecutive victory, after blood tests revealed abnormally high haematocrit – red blood cell – levels. Quite simply, he had failed a dope test. It was a hammer blow to the sport and signalled the beginning of the end of his tragically short life.

Pantani entered the national consciousness on 4 June 1994 when the 24-year-old broke from the peleton to win his first *Giro d'Italia* stage, from Lienz-Merano. The following day from Merano-Aprica, the *Giro*'s toughest stage with 195 kilometres of mountains, he claimed another win before securing second place overall. Relieved to have finally broken through, he was a breath of fresh air for cycling. Renowned for his breathtaking accelerations on steep mountain ascents, Pantani descended like a downhill skier, the saddle uniquely tucked into his stomach with his lower half resting millimetres from

Figure 22: *The rebranded Pirate attacking the Alpe d'Huez in 1997*

the back wheel turning at eye-watering speed. Following his impressive *Giro*, a third-place finish in the *Tour de France* made Marco the face of Italian cycling.

A horrific collision with a police car in Turin, in 1996, shattered his leg and threatened his career. After six months of physiotherapy he returned to lead the new Mercatone Uno team, rebranded as the pirate (*il pirata*).

Fully recovered and with much to prove, 1998 was his greatest season. After winning the *Giro d'Italia*, his *Tour de France* victory immortalized him. During the last mountain stage, on the *col du Galibier* climb, his extraordinary attack turned a seven-and-a-half-minute deficit into almost six-minute's advantage over race leader Jan Ulrich. More significantly, Pantani's agonized finish with arms outstretched in cruciform made him a sporting icon.

Evoking memories of Fausto Coppi,[42] Pantani 'became the toast of press and media celebrating almost the rediscovery of a sport which in the popular mind evokes exertion, sweat, and provincial life: the Giro d'Italia was once again proposed as a quest for time lost'.[43] One of the keenest to associate with the triumph was Prime Minister Romano Prodi. Pantani's home town Cesenatico declared 13 August 1998 'Pantani day', and an estimated 50,000 fans swarmed into the Adriatic coastal resort, where Prodi shared a platform with their hero:

> This year will be remembered for Pantani, not doping... There is no relationship between his success and the negative events that have recently concerned the sport. His victory was so clear that I have no doubt he's clean. He gave a show of courage that will be remembered in time, we are here to celebrate this.[44]

As Matt Rendell observed, 'where Berlusconi had AC Milan, Prodi had Pantani, who was medically assisted by the prime minister's close friend Francesco Conconi'.[45] Head of the University of Ferrara's Centre for Biomedical Studies, Conconi had recommended 54 per cent haematocrit thresholds rather than the 50 per cent established by the sport's international governing body (*Union Cycliste Internationale* – UCI), which Pantani's team mate Riccardo Forconi had already exceeded in that year's Giro. His subsequent suspension raised few concerns.

During the 1999 race, however, the issue was unavoidable. Pantani's domination of the mountain stages commanded national attention, with as many as five million viewers tuned into the afternoon finishes. On the morning of 5 June, *La Gazzetta dello Sport*'s headline, 'Insatiable', was unintentionally apt. Prior to that day's final mountain stage and with the *Giro* apparently secure, Pantani was excluded to protect him from the risks associated with an elevated haematocrit level.

Two weeks later, Turin magistrate Rafaelle Guariniello launched an investigation into pre-operative tests, following his 1995 crash in Turin, which showed his haematocrit level to have been extraordinarily high. It was apparently three days later that Pantani turned to cocaine, unable to cope with the public shaming.[46] Found guilty of artificially enhancing his performance, on 11 December 2000, he received a three-month suspended prison sentence and a fine of € 6,000. His conscience was apparently clear, eased by the all-too-familiar excuse of having been singled out in a less than clean sport.

Pantani's suspension from the *Giro* had little impact upon his brand and commercial appeal, however. With Citroën's Italian sales having increased by 25 per cent during the period of his endorsement, the French manufacturer was keen to renew the contract.[47] Equally, when *La Gazzetta* wanted to start the 2000 race from the Vatican, the deal for the Jubilee *Giro* was sealed by a Marco-signed pink jersey being given to Monsignor Crescenzio Sepe, the Vatican's General Secretary.[48] Pantani's poor performance, especially in the mountains, was fodder for those who questioned his previous domination. Appearing to have returned to form with a stage win in the *Tour de France*, his retirement from the race days later, after a suicidal attack, fuelled 'a series of malicious accusations', according to his physiotherapist Fabrizio Borra, that he had done so 'because the following day there would have been [doping] controls. There was also this will in a part of the mass media that looked for a negative motive.'[49] True or otherwise, it indicated a paranoid mood within his team that did not help Pantani confront the growing case against him, if indeed he was an innocent victim. On 29 May 2002, a preliminary investigation into his 1999 *Giro* blood tests recommended his trial for sporting fraud. Refused entry into that year's *Giro* and the subsequent *Tour de France*, formerly friendly race directors nailed down the coffin on his career.

On 14 February 2004, Marco Pantani was found dead in his room in the Hotel Residence Le Rose, Rimini. Staff reported his extreme paranoia in the preceding days and forensic analysis of the completely destroyed room found cocaine on almost every horizontal surface. Bone marrow samples indicated his huge, long-term consumption of the drug. With not a gram remaining of the € 20,000 consignment purchased in the last month of his life, the autopsy declared cocaine poisoning the cause of death.

No analysis or narration of Italy's sporting history could possibly ignore Pantani's career, but equally this is not intended to pass judgement upon any aspect of his life or death. There is not the time and neither is this the place to re-examine his enormously complicated life, in what would probably be a vain attempt to better Matt Rendell's excellent account, in addition to the differing versions of Pantani's team manager and family.[50] While historians strive for impartiality and balance in unpicking the past, I freely admit to bias on this occasion. Good or bad, doped or otherwise, flawed for sure, I care not. Pantani was awesome.

A victim of his own psychological weaknesses and cocaine use, he also competed in a sport that used doping to exceptional levels, in a country that was equally lax in confronting the problem. Cycling was certainly not the only sport to dope and Italy far from the worst offender in an era of international drug abuse, but even if it is 'clear that everything Marco had achieved between May 1994 and August 1995 had been chemically assisted',[51] with the obvious implications for his most successful years that followed, the commercial pressures upon cyclists and team managers eager to serve sponsors must be considered.

Most interestingly, for all of his defects and weaknesses, Pantani remains an Italian sporting hero who engendered enormous national pride with few dissenters. In memory, he remains the athlete who dominated cycling for the best part of two, probably drug-fuelled years. Celebrating what would have been his 40th birthday, on 13 January 2010, the Marco Pantani Foundation[52] awarded its first Pantani Prize to AC Milan footballer Gennaro Gattuso, 'who best demonstrates the great cycling champion's determination and capacity for suffering'.[53] Presented with a bicycle by Pantani's parents, Gattuso's memory of the pirate must have resonated across the peninsula.

> Me and my dad in front of the TV... my dad even crazier than me... I never had those emotions again that Pantani gave me, like when he attacked on the Galibier and then left Ullrich behind to win on Les Deux Alps. He was a great, not only of cycling but of Italian sport... But what I like to remember about him was his smile. For me, Pantani was an example.[54]

The ripples of cycling's 1998 crisis were felt elsewhere after AS Roma's coach Zdenek Zeman was asked if football was really any different?[55] So broke 'the case of the swollen legs'. Containing drugs, deaths, super-personalities and lawyers, it might easily have been a classic, Italian *giallo* (detective novel). But the legs belonged to footballers Gianluca Vialli[56] and Alessandro Del Piero, Juventus players who appeared to have experienced growth spurts in their mid-20s. Neither was Zeman's comment marketing hype. It was a direct attack on Juventus that brought *calcio* into the dock. The arguments were familiar. Besides questioning testing techniques, there was the need to serve vested interests. As more advertising and television money entered the game, more matches needed to be played, and footballers required more help to fulfil their increasingly demanding programme. The players had their own responsibilities too, as the former Genoa, Torino, Milan, Roma and Bologna striker Carlo Petrini delightfully explained in his exposé of *calcio*'s longstanding drug problem:

> We doped ourselves for three reasons: because the club asked us to when it was absolutely necessary to win; because as players we wanted to be even better and thus worth more on the transfer market; and because we suspected that our adversaries were doing the same and we wanted to be even bigger assholes.[57]

Banned for three years for his involvement in *totonero* and having written at length about his experiences of doping and drug-taking within football, Petrini's comments won him few friends.[58] Neither did Zeman's questioning of the Serie A system.

In one respect Zeman's accusations were hardly newsworthy, with so many players having tested positive since controls began in the 1960s. As Petrini described, dope testing was scrupulous and easily overcome 'with an enema syringe, containing "clean" urine from a teammate on the bench, hidden in an inside pocket of a dressing gown'.[59] Hardly rocket science, along with incompetent testing centres that lost hundreds of records and samples that were regularly/easily tampered with, it was one of the principal ways that Maradona evaded detection at Napoli until 1990. Zeman's remarks could not be ignored, however, and Torinese magistrate Raffaele Guariniello began investigating football and the many suspicious deaths of ex-players.

At the time, over 70 ex-footballers from the 1970s and 1980s had either died prematurely, or were suffering from leukaemia, cancers of the liver, colon, pancreas and other rare illnesses. The figures would have been significantly higher had the inquiry included players from the 1960s. Most renowned were cases of the neurological wasting disorder Lou Gherig syndrome that affects footballers six and a half times more than the national average. While there is no concrete evidence as to what causes this or the collection of rare illnesses that appear to afflict footballers in particular, suspicion surrounds performance-enhancing drugs.[60] Grossly premature but perfectly timed to underline the reality of the issues at stake, the former Parma, Genoa and Roma player Gianluca Signorini died mid-inquiry, in 2002. He was 42 and had been paralysed since 1999. At the time, two more ex-players were fighting a similar battle in addition to the eleven already lost. [61]

In the course of the two-year investigation, CONI's president Mario Pescante resigned along with the president of the sports-medicine federation. Rome's testing centre was suspended[62] and sample counter-analyses sent to Barcelona, Lausanne and Cologne, where positive tests increased. A growing number of high-profile players also began to test non-negative, the definition itself indicating the problem. The not-innocent received correspondingly weak fines and bans that were soon reduced. There was, however, enough evidence to put Juventus on trial for sporting fraud and the illegal use of medicines.

Running from 31 January 2002 until the end of 2005, the trial heard a procession of current and ex-players support Juventus and its doctor. French international Zinedine Zidane admitted to using the energy booster creatine, a supplement for high-intensity training and explosive sports, such as football. Legal up to a maximum dose of six milligrams per day, it was suggested that Juventus players had been using up to 30 milligrams.[63] The club argued that the drugs were legal, it had informed the Federation of everything and, above all, that Guariniello was once again persecuting an Agnelli asset.[64]

Protecting its doctor, Juventus' defence rested on everybody being at it. *'Così fan tutti'*, just as Bettino Craxi had argued during the *Tangentopoli* inquiry:

'If a great part of this subject is to be considered purely criminal... then the majority of the system should be criminal.'[65] Thus, if the system was corrupt, why was the individual prosecuted? Juventus had a potential case, given that no other clubs were subjected to such scrutiny when it was implausible that it was the only culprit. However, can a corrupt system really exclude individuals from responsibility? Moreover, when the Juventus medicine cupboards were thrown open, the inquiry found 249 different types of drug, while the haematocrit levels of Antonio Conte and Alessio Tacchinardi suggested use of the cyclist's favourite, EPO.[66]

On 26 November 2004 the Juventus doctor, Riccardo Agricola, was given a one year and ten months suspended sentence for sporting fraud and supplying drugs that endangered the health of the club's players. The club went unpunished as the court was unable to prove that it had ordered the doping. Some demanded the head of the former Juventus and current national team coach Marcello Lippi, while others wanted the *bianconeri* stripped of all titles won between 1994 and 1998, including the Champions League. Absurdly, Juventus General Manager Antonio Giraudo was absolved of any responsibility. Only in Italy could the manager of a club whose doctor had just been found guilty of doping its players, unashamedly state that: 'Juve can walk with its head held high... [Agricola] too, who was, is and will remain the club's doctor... This is only a matter of procedure... We're sure he will be cleared on appeal.'[67] As the club's lawyer Luigi Chiappero added, in classic Berlusconian terminology: 'We've drawn 1-1 away from home. But this was only the first half.'[68] It was a reasonable assessment given the Italian legal system allows a second and third chance before implementing guilty verdicts and sentences.

In December 2005, the appeal verdict found everybody at Juventus innocent of sporting fraud. What had happened was no longer illegal in the eyes of the law, and EPO had not been used. Giraudo and the Juventus management were safe for now but, as Foot notes, they had been seriously rattled by somebody from outside of football.[69]

Scandalized... again

Franco Carraro was a European and World water ski champion in the 1950s. President of AC Milan (1967–71) and Serie A (1973–6 and 1997–2001), he was head of CONI (1978–87) during the Moscow Olympics crisis, held executive roles in the Italian national airline Alitalia, and was a Socialist Minister of Tourism. Elected Mayor of Rome in 1989, his administration collapsed in a heap of corruption. In his second term as FIGC president (2001–6) he oversaw an incredible array of scandals and crises involving false passports, doping, false accounting and an underachieving national team, to name but a few. The Andreotti of Italian sport,[70] you might think trouble follows him.

As Mayor of Rome, Carraro met banker Cesare Geronzi, who had a passion for Lazio. Holding four prestigious advisory roles and four presidencies within Italian banking by the end of 2002, when the game's economic crisis struck Carraro was uniquely positioned to deal with it. With Lazio facing bankruptcy after the type of extravagant spending that had crippled Serie A, his accounting talents and relationship with Geronzi brokered an unprecedented deal that saved the club. Fiorentina, on the contrary, was financially asphyxiated. Sent down to Serie C2, the club re-formed and re-purchased its name at auction. Jumping a division, from Serie C2 to B, for 'sporting merit', its return to Serie A was remarkably quick under new president – JP Tod's owner – Diego Della Valle. However, Fiorentina's return to the big time was soon threatened by considerable bad luck and unfortunate refereeing decisions that drew it into the relegation mire. After two players were sent off in the first eight minutes of a match with Genoa, Della Valle was encouraged to contact the referee's secretary Paolo Bergamo. Following a convivial lunch, Fiorentina's fortunes improved and the club survived on a dramatic last day.

If Della Valle was discovering how matches and seasons could be unexpectedly determined, the authorities already knew. Investigations into the Juventus doping case had revealed an illegal gambling ring involving players, referees and the Neapolitan Mafia. Over 100,000 recorded phone calls were the basis of the evidence against those charged in the scandal that broke in May 2006. The system of favours and corruption that was found to be controlling football was a familiar one within everyday Italian life, where the power of *raccomandazione* (recommendation) counts and individuals accept often essential help. With Juventus at the centre of the storm, however, few were convinced that the outcome would be anything other than the usual lifting of carpets and the sound of furious sweeping. But this time there was clearly extra will, and recorded conversations from Luciano Moggi's phone.

A controversial figure in Italian football, Moggi brought success wherever he went, even Naples. As the accusations emerged, teams that had long complained about corrupt referees or 'institutionalized pressure' suddenly felt vindicated. Most notable was a goal scored by Parma's Fabio Cannavaro against Juventus, in the 1999–2000 season. Inexplicably cancelled by referee Massimo De Santis, telephone taps later revealed him to be Moggi's main man.[71] But this was no straightforward match-fixing scandal like that of 1982 in which players were bought and results arranged. It was almost the entire corruption of *calcio*. Involving over 50 people, the system had one objective: to ensure Juventus won. At its most simplistic, 'friendly' referees were not just allocated to Juventus matches but, most cunningly, they were selected for games involving teams that Moggi's club would meet in the following weeks. These were then lamed by excessive bookings and expulsions that would leave key players suspended.

There was also the role of the GEA World player agency.[72] While Juventus and Milan had consistently hoarded more players than they could ever need or want, in order to control the market and serve the *plus-valenze* system, GEA's most unsavoury aspect was its employees as much as its control of 20 per cent of Italian footballers. GEA's president was Moggi's son Alessandro, with directors including the television journalist Chiara Geronzi, daughter of Capitalia banker Cesare; Andrea Cragnotti, son of former Lazio president Sergio; Francesco Tanzi, son of the bankrupt, imprisoned former Parmalat and Parma owner Callisto; plus Giuseppe De Mita, son of the former DC prime minister Ciriaco.[73] It was the ultimate in Italy's sporting and political elite's self-serving exploitation of the national passion.[74] With Davide Lippi also a GEA agent, less than three weeks prior to the World Cup his father Marcello found himself rebuffing allegations that under pressure from Moggi he had selected players for the national team in order to increase their visibility, wages and value, with the added spin-offs for the player and agent.

One notable case was Juventus defender Giorgio Chiellini who, from 2004 to 2005, passed between Livorno, Roma, Fiorentina and Juventus.[75] Another was Fabrizio Miccoli, who protested against his proposed transfer to Lazio. Moggi 'let him know that he was only in the national team thanks to him and that could disappear from his horizons in a moment'.[76] Miccoli clearly didn't get the message, or maybe he did. He testified against GEA and Marcello Lippi never selected him again, even with the player in the form of his life in the run-up to the 2010 World Cup. Persona non grata. As it turned out, Moggi was also interfering in team selections, some of which were to protect Juventus players from injury. Equally bizarre, the FIGC president Franco Carraro was going through him to get a message to Lippi.[77]

But it didn't stop there. Most disturbing was Moggi's influence over one of Italy's TV football institutions, the appropriately named *'Il Processo del Lunedì'* – 'The Monday Trial'. In its 26th year under the control of veteran broadcaster Aldo Biscardi, it was renowned for slanging matches between journalists dissecting the weekend's most controversial incidents. With rumours circulating about Biscardi's involvement in the scandal, the septuagenarian offered his programme's introduction of the *super-moviola* (super slow motion) replay as evidence of its contribution to unveiling diving, cheating and general malpractice. Unfortunately, editorial control of the *super-moviola* was neither with Biscardi nor LA7's crew, but with Moggi.[78] One of many cited cases came after a 0-0 draw between Juve and Milan:

> Moggi: look, we need to fully absolve the referee!
> Biscardi: OK, I'll make sure there's little about it.
> Moggi: Nothing... no... nothing, nothing, nothing Aldo... Cut... cut... cut everything... you say the referee was right or you cut everything.[79]

Protesting his innocence, Biscardi left the show. He later returned as an eccentric match reporter on state television's RAI II football programme, '*Quelli che il calcio*'.

❂ ❂ ❂ ❂

Calcio's controlling caste was in disgrace. Seeking to limit the damage, Juventus accepted the resignations of its all-powerful leadership of Moggi, Giraudo and ex-player Roberto Bettega, with Giovanni Agnelli's nephew John Elkann taking control. As *La Gazzetta*'s editor Candido Cannavò commented: 'The death of Gianni [Agnelli] and his brother Umberto had freed Moggi of any aesthetic scruples: until the ruinous fall that he sees today... shut indoors with his six telephones that no longer ring.'[80]

Moggiopoli finally proved one disaster too many for Franco Carraro. Temporarily replaced as FIGC president by legal specialist Professor Guido Rossi, his first move was reassuringly controversial in appointing retired judge Francesco Saverio Borrelli to run the inquiry. Having led the 'Clean Hands' investigation, he had a nose for corruption and was unlikely to buckle under pressure, while unlike most leading figures in Italian society he claimed to support no team. Berlusconi's comparison of his appointment to the left selecting its own referee was unfortunate under the circumstances.

Borrelli's investigation revealed an intricate system of corruption; just what most people had suspected for years. As *La Gazzetta* explained:

> Moggiopoli functioned like this. The championship was controlled step by step: from the transfer market to the goal ruled out in the last minute, from the unseen offside to the red card given or not given, according to the level of protection enjoyed by the player.
> The controllers were... those who have emerged from the interceptions, Luciano Moggi above all. He tirelessly wove together the threads of the willing referee designators, dispensing favours to friendly squads and grief to the rebellious; along with his son he moved the pawns of the big game, the

players, coaches and in some cases the club presidents through an organization, GEA, that was much much more than a sporting agency.[81]

A sporting rather than criminal trial, the process was more streamlined, requiring only the establishment of the intent to corrupt rather than the actual corruption of matches, to determine guilt. Called in front of Neapolitan magistrates on 16 May, Moggi defended his innocence, claiming there was no 'Moggi system'. Two hours of probing reduced him to tears and truth. What he did was apparently to defend Juventus from the others, most notably Milan with its supportive television network and biased media. It was a strange but rather Italian defence.

On 19 May, national team captain Fabio Cannavaro's house and the Juventus offices were searched by investigating officers. *'Così fan tutti'* – Everybody's at it – as he later remarked to the disgust of *La Gazzetta*'s editor Candido Cannavò:

> Lovely, radiant, warrior. Cannavaro has been our standard. Now, with great unease, I ask how such an insensitive man can be captain of the national team. To a certain point I would have understood a silence like Lippi's. But this challenge to reason, morality, evidence and the magistracy is unacceptable.[82]

After early protestations of innocence, even Milan failed to stay out of the mire following the revelation of its 'referee attaché', Leandro Meani, who appeared to have been selecting linesmen for its matches. Having failed to lure Moggi in 2005, the club needed its own system to combat Juventus' which, according to Moggi, was there to combat Milan's.

A new broom that sweeps clean?

Berlusconi's sudden appearance on various television networks following Milan's defeat of Juventus, on 29 October 2005, smiling and magnanimous in victory, signalled the impending general election. During the 2006 campaign the prime minister and leader of the opposition, Romano Prodi, slugged it out old style, but in three live television debates there was surprise at how well Prodi combated the media master.[83] *La Gazzetta* played its part again, publishing full page adverts of Berlusconi, 'the president of the flags' and 'the president of spectacular football'.[84] Merely business? If any doubts remained, Carlo Verdelli's election-day editorial left little to interpretation: 'Silvio Berlusconi made his Milan great and his television empire even greater. Strong in this recognized capacity, he has already been called to run the country twice and today's vote will say if the majority will confirm its faith again.'[85]

✪ ✪ ✪ ✪

Early predictions of a heavy defeat for Berlusconi's *Casa delle Libertà* – House of Freedoms – coalition were mistaken. The election went to the wire and beyond, with Berlusconi's bitter contestation of the result and demands for an unprecedented re-count bringing an air of Florida 2000 to the contest, or Latin America more worryingly. For those already suspicious, it confirmed the ongoing slide from the second Republic to a banana one. More damagingly, it cast doubt over the legitimacy of Prodi's government, even before the prime minister had chosen his team and selected their shirt numbers. With a wafer thin majority in both houses, his administration appeared permanently on the verge of collapse.

Constantly talking of crisis while pouring doubt on the government's ability to survive, Berlusconi's sustained political pressure was intensified by his media outlets. Even 'friends' like the daily *La Repubblica* couldn't resist the easy copy and the national passion for a flutter on the government's survival. While this did not cause Prodi's ultimate demise, the persistent negative coverage and the government's inability to combat it made it far easier for a traitor to leave the team.

Inevitably, significant reform was hard to agree upon, with conflict of interests a vital issue. While legislation was prepared to reform radio and television, the administration's weaknesses, its internal divisions, plus the sensitivity of the issue that involved the leader of the opposition, created strong resistance that prevented its entry onto the statute book before the government collapsed. It was a grave error. Crucial to clip Berlusconi's wings, it was a lost opportunity to restore some credibility to Italy.

Prodi's government's achievements were certainly limited and, given its short, frail life couldn't realistically have been much else. Unlike Berlusconi, Prodi was not backed by the weight of the majority party within the coalition and, even if his leadership strength was his capacity to unite, he was unable to dictate terms and impose discipline. While his Achilles heel appeared to have been the significant presence of the Communists, the reality was that the hard left had nowhere to go. Sacrificing many principles to ensure the government's survival, it paid an enormous price in the 2008 elections when, for the first time in its history, no Communist deputies were returned to parliament, not even *Rifondazione Comunista*'s leader, Fausto Bertinotti.

Prodi's government was most damaged by its inability to communicate ideas and policies through the mass media and its sobriety that reflected its leader, both of which contrasted with Berlusconi's brash, polished image. As an active cyclist Prodi's physical participation differentiated him from his more sedentary rival, but he was an equally enthusiastic user of sporting metaphor to convey complex or unpopular policies. Unlike Berlusconi's promises of miracles however, his vision of Italy reflected the struggle and fatigue of his sport; *pedallare* – to pedal – returning to the political lexicon. Unquestionably realistic, rebuilding Italy with hard work and determination was hardly inspirational.

He also explained and justified serious, necessary, unpopular budget cuts in terms of the exploding football scandal, with his immediate ambitions 'not [designed] to bring Italy into a UEFA Cup place, but the middle of the league. We are starting... even further behind than Fiorentina.'[86] The Florentine club began the 2006–7 season with a 19-point deficit for its involvement in the scandal. It was far cry from Berlusconi's pledge to make Italy like AC Milan but, as the sage journalist Antonio Ghirelli proposed, his

> squad needed the look of a leader more than the friendliness of a Reggio Emilia parish priest. And Prodi, this time, vehemently turning to a sporting metaphor has made a good counterattack. The minus 26... is a familiar sporting formula to any Italian. From the perspective of communication, having used a common language is a good step forwards for a leader who is not outstanding in this area.[87]

Confronting his communication problems,[88] Prodi appeared more regularly on TV, embraced the internet, reacquainted the nation with his family, and wheeled out the bike. But it was not enough and, once again, he was brought down by his allies following the withdrawal of support from moderates who had every hope of finding new homes in the centre-right.[89] Given Berlusconi's media monopoly, Prodi's victory in 2006 was hugely impressive. But, once in power, he was undermined by opposition strikers and own goals, political constraints and expediencies. But it certainly wasn't a still-born administration, especially given its extraordinary good luck.

On 4 July 2006, only two months after his government had been sworn in, Italy won the football World Cup for the first time in 24 years, the victory rubbing kilos of salt into Berlusconi's gaping electoral wounds, even more so when Prodi hoisted the trophy alongside Cannavaro and the Minister for Sport. Unable to disguise his bitterness, Berlusconi again suggested that politics and sport really should be separate. For all of his money, connections and media, the greatest photo opportunity imaginable – Italy winning the World Cup – had eluded him by a whisker; his late mazy run and speculative shot had shaved the opposition's post. However, like Spadolini 24 years earlier, Prodi's team still had many difficult rounds to get through, but this time he couldn't play the football joker.

Figure 23: *Minister for youth and sport Giovanna Melandri (centre) and Prime Minister Romano Prodi (right) make political soup with Captain Cannavaro*

Déjà vu

Free from traditional juridical norms, the inquiry and trial into sporting justice progressed at an alarming rate for those involved, with a number of players forced to return from their training camp to give evidence. As the Juventus empire collapsed, coach Fabio Capello jumped ship, which cast further doubt on the futures of Gianluca Zambrotta, Fabio Cannavaro and goalkeeper Gianluigi Buffon, who might have been distracted by house hunting had he not found himself under investigation for betting on matches.[90]

The only positives were the similarities with 1982 and, for the millions of superstitious Italians, Italy's 12-year World Cup cabala predicted victory: 1974 – second, 1982 – winners, 1994 – second, 2006 – ? For completely different reasons to Enzo Bearzot in 1982, Marcello Lippi also employed a media silence. In arguably the toughest qualification group of the tournament, any mistakes and the *azzurri* would be home early to a demanding, unhappy public and press. Plan A was to stay in Germany as long as possible. Unlike 1982, the *azzurri*'s progress was solid if unspectacular; the perfect World Cup formula. With adversity forging a team spirit that had been missing for years, an eclectic group of individuals and egotists struggled and accepted substitutions with unknown good grace. Back home, flag sellers did a trade like never before, huge outdoor screens rose in cities and on beaches across the peninsula, and the nation downed tools at regular three-day intervals.

Italy's masterstroke was Germany's victory over Argentina, thereby eliminating the only team that really seemed insurmountable. It also brought the old foes together again. During the semi-final in Dortmund, where the hosts had never lost, Italy took the game to Germany. Completing the memories of 1982, Fabio Grosso followed his beautiful left-footed strike, which unblocked the match in the 119th minute, with a wide-eyed, disbelieving, dash to nowhere in particular. Had he not been the most unlikely player to break the deadlock, it might easily have been scripted so much did it evoke Marco Tardelli's iconic run and primal scream. Rejecting the negativity and insecurity that had permeated the team under Giovanni Trapattoni, Lippi broke with defensive tradition and threw on an extra attacker to administer the *colpo di grazia*. The goal of stunning movement and directness that followed appeared to signal a new dawn.

Italy's finest performance in years brought raucous crowds onto the streets of cities, towns and villages across the country, with Rome's thoroughfares choked until the early hours in a delirium of honking cars and scooters breaking every rule in the already flexible highway code. The large Italian ex-pat community in Germany also celebrated. Rooted in the transformation and mass emigration of the miracle years, Italy's poor performance in the 1974 World Cup in Germany had confirmed them as poor immigrants. Now, there was good reason to be noisily proud, even more so in the light of pre-match pizza jibes in the German daily *Der Bildt*: 'From us, our semi-final opponents will get what they know best: a pizza. But not any old pizza, rather the *Pizza Arriverderci*.'[91]

The Final itself was most memorable for Zinedine Zidane's chest butt on Marco Materazzi. Drawing 1-1 after extra time, it fell to the French Juventus striker David Trezeguet, who had condemned Italy to a European Championship Final defeat some six years earlier, to miss the decisive penalty. The best and hungriest side won, and Italy burst into another noisy night of celebration. Some confident fans carried prepared coffins of French football, ever-ready Neapolitans sold death notices announcing the passing of Signora Francia, and President Giorgio Napolitano drew upon his predecessor's antics, some 24 years earlier, to commune with the masses: 'They were fantastic and I am proud to have represented all the people of Italy with my presence in the stand... At the decisive penalty I jumped inside. I don't jump as well as Pertini.'[92] Exploiting the proven formula of humility and national representation, he confirmed the event's importance. 'I celebrated with the squad and am soaked. Partly sweat and partly orange juice. But in this moment I am sure I represent the pride and feelings of Italians... I must thank Lippi and the squad who have reinforced the national identity.'[93]

Everything must change if things are to stay the same

The homecoming celebrations in Rome's Circus Maximus were disappointing. With in the region of one million Romans packed into the ancient arena, nobody really seemed sure what to do other than wave flags and hum the White Stripes' 'Seven Nation Army' riff, which had become the unofficial anthem. As the players made their tortuous route from the airport via parliament, the event developed the feeling of a wet New Year's Eve with a bottle of Blue Nun and fireworks that just wouldn't light. Having fallen deliriously into bed with a game resembling Sophia Loren in her prime, the nation awoke only to find the ageing porn-star La Cicciolina by its side. With the results of the *calciopoli* trial due any day, the previous night's ecstasy was tainted by a bad smell and a strong sense of shame. It was questionable how many people agreed with Prodi's statement to the team: 'to Italian football that is experiencing an unprecedented storm, you have restored the dignity that it is worthy of'.[94]

With the feel-good factor running high, a campaign to amnesty those involved in the scandal began. Berlusconi also had an interesting take. Besides proposing that it was all yet another political conspiracy, he suggested that the individuals responsible should pay, not the clubs. The majority of Italians thought differently, even some fans of the clubs involved, although not many. To this day, the former *Lotta Continua* editor Giampiero Mughini, who remarketed himself in the 1990s as the thinking man's football pundit, continues to smart at the injustice of Juventus' persecution.

Twelve days after Italy scaled the heights of world football it plumbed the depths, as the sentences were released. Unequivocally punishing Moggi, who was recommended for a life ban from the game, Juventus was stripped of its last two league titles and relegated to Serie B, with a 30-point penalty to be imposed at the start of the following season. The club was to be joined by Fiorentina and Lazio, both with 12- and 7-point deductions. Milan survived in A, but had 44 points subtracted from its previous season's tally, thereby excluding it from the Champions League, in addition to a 15-point deficit at the beginning of the new campaign. Antonio Giraudo (Juventus), Diego and Andrea Della Valle (Fiorentina), Claudio Lotito (Lazio), Adriano Galliani and Leandro Meani (Milan) were suspended from football for three to five years, and Franco Carraro for four and a half.

As most of the nation cheered, finally believing the legal system had delivered justice, the incriminated appealed and the 'Big Sting'[95] soon became the 'Little Sting'.[96] Juventus remained in Serie B, but with a reduced penalty of −17 points, which raised the possibility of its return to A in one season. Fiorentina and Lazio were restored to Serie A, with respective penalties of −19 and −11 points, while Milan was the greatest beneficiary. Docked 30 points from the previous season, the *rossoneri* (red and blacks) were deducted a mere 8 from their next Serie A campaign and, most importantly, reinstated into the Champions League. They went on to win it. So light were the penalties that nobody was sure if anything had really happened at all and, if so, why weren't the guilty punished harder? Guido Rossi's earlier assertion that 'sporting justice would stop in front of nothing and nobody' rang somewhat hollow.[97] Written two months earlier, Claudio Verdelli's editorial seemed almost prophetic: 'Moggiopoli has only just been discovered and there is already a great desire to bury it. If that happens... Italian football will miss the last good chance to become a sport and thus a pleasure once again.'[98]

2006 was a year zero moment for Italy and *calcio* to finally say *basta* – enough! Instead, the old broom was brought out of the cupboard and the house tidied rather than scrubbed clean. As Giuseppe di Lampedusa suggested in his tale of the declining Sicilian aristocracy, *The Leopard*, perhaps everything did have to change if things were to remain the same? Writing in *La Repubblica*, Giuseppe D'Avanzo's argument was depressingly to the point.

> The wrongdoings of Moggi and his accomplices slams in our face how much 'at the lowest levels time changes nothing'. Despite the years that have passed, the pathologies of the system and our democracy are still there to be seen: intolerance of rules... laws ripped up, the lack of any sense of the State, obscure pacts between capitalism and government, the weaving of business and politics, an entrepreneurial class with no culture of the market and without any ethics of responsibility... And in the end – the reason of all reasons – the conflict of interests. A social habit. A metastasis that penetrates, lacerates and destroys the economic, political and institutional fabric.[99]

Awarding Inter the 2005–6 title was also farcical. Was it too much to leave it blank, so that future generations might ask why? It did little to appease Inter coach Roberto Mancini, but he certainly had a point in claiming that *calcio* would be more fun when we don't know the results in advance.

Not a normal country?

Sport's impact upon modern Italy has been significant and consistent, especially in terms of its national identity and almost permanent crisis of legitimacy. While it would be simplistic to suggest that the Piedmont-led unification, or annexation, was solely responsible for the nation-state's fundamental weaknesses, the alienation of many Italians from the new kingdom was worsened by the widespread absence of the state in any positive sense. Repression, corruption, high taxation and floundering reforms were compounded by unsuccessful nation-building strategies that included coercing citizens into the army to fight and lose obscure wars. Often blamed upon sub-standard military recruits, these failures established an important role for sport and physical fitness.

In the state's absence, the Church and Socialism shaped and politicized sport according to their needs, rather than those of Italy. Their ideological impediments, irresolvable doubts and reservations, however, prevented either from securing it as *their* sphere of influence and left Fascism to employ sport and recreation within its plan to revolutionize Italian society. Under the regime, the state's involvement in sport appears greater than at any point in the nation's history. However, organized by the Fascist Party organs of *Balilla*, the *Dopolavoro* and CONI, they acted very much as private bodies with the raison d'être of strengthening the regime's rule, even if publicly funded. Thus, in effect, through no fault of its own, the state was again effectively absented from sporting provision.

Despite Fascism's demonstration of sport's potential power, the draftsmen of the 1948 Italian Constitution failed to mention it, with CONI's fight for independence under Giulio Onesti evidencing its continuing politicization. Although the state thus assumed a supervisory role over CONI, which became an unofficial ministry for sport, its focus was upon the elite and national representation. Failing to provide for mass society created a vacuum in areas that might have been considered the state's preserve/duty, which were filled by 'political' agencies.

Having portrayed the state so negatively, it does have to be asked if its legitimacy crisis was necessarily all of its own doing, or were its weaknesses, inadequacies, corrupt and criminal tendencies really a representation of Italians themselves? For example, was the emergence of the Mafia in the immediate post-unification years a result of state weakness or, alternatively, was this a consequence of existing Mafia activity that prevented it from ever establishing control? If this logic is applied to sport, while the state's absence undoubtedly encouraged nationalists, the Church, and Socialists to exploit it, to what extent did their manipulation of sport prevent the state from developing a more balanced, neutral, hands-on approach?

Needing to create its own news, the sports press also politicized its product, *La Gazzetta* encouraging its readers to vote for candidates according to their sporting roles rather than party affiliations, prior to the 1948 elections. 'So, let's hope they get elected because this is their wish and being sportsmen, they are our friends... And we are sure that on reaching one of the Houses they will not forget the sport they have served.'[1] Repeating *Il Giornale dello Sport*'s 1921 message that implied the greater reliability of politicians with sporting links, it demonstrated sport's superior capacity to mobilize and generate support over pure politics.

Much work on Italian identity has defined the nation as an entity sharing common land, culture, values, language and history. But as John Dickie has argued, even the term nation is misleading: 'Firstly, it disguises the fact that not everyone in a nation has the same interests... Second, it is used to exclude certain groups from national status.'[2] Such a definition inevitably interprets post-unification history as a series of failed, state-based attempts to create Italians. Sport might support this, most notably in its use by the Lega Nord, which drew significant comment during the 2010 World Cup.

Even before the tournament had begun Umberto Bossi's son Renzo, a regional councillor, declared he would not support Italy. With the *azzurri* requiring a win over Slovakia to avoid elimination, Umberto was even more provocative: 'The national team? You'll see, it will pass the group because they will buy the match.'[3] Espousing the theory that the FIGC would pressure some Italian clubs into buying two or three Slovak players for the coming season on the understanding that their performance against Italy was suitably poor, it was not only offensive to the opposition but also extraordinary from a government minister responsible for constitutional reform. Italy's catastrophic 3-2 defeat supported *Il Messaggero*'s response to Bossi's comment: 'it wasn't the result of an unstoppable "Padanian hatred" for everything to do with the national flag but is evidently the synthesis of all he thinks about Italy and what it represents: a nation of thieves, conmen, corrupted and corrupters... In football as in life.'[4]

While the Lega Nord appears to demonstrate the failure of the Italian national project, this doesn't consider the complexity of identities within the national collective. More flexible, Benedict Anderson's concept of the nation as an imagined community better applies to Italy. Identifying the 'other' to define the nation by what it is not has been one of the few, consistent means by which Italians have tried to form some impression of who and what they are, which at times has resulted in considerable discrimination and racism.

The political left has also experienced long periods of otherness and exclusion, from the banning of the Socialist Party in Liberal Italy, its persecution under Fascism, post-war interpretations and memories of the Resistance through to the presentation of Red terrorism during the 'Years of Lead'. Less discriminated against but even more of an anti-nation has been the Catholic Church, which refused to participate in state activities and urged its supporters to do the same following its loss of lands to Italy. Contributing significantly to the state's legitimacy crisis, its cultural wing Catholic Action developed an alternative community that directly rivalled the Liberal state's nation-building initiatives. With the extent of 'otherness' also exaggerated by nationalists to serve their own agenda, the consequent confusion when attempting to define who is Italian, makes a strong case for the only real nation being that within the imagination.

While sport has contributed to this image of a fractious country, it has also provided arguably the only moments of unrestrained national unity that even the 1945 liberation did not achieve. As Carlo Verdelli asked, following the 2006 World Cup victory:

> What is football? An entire country united as if by magic: nobody or nothing else could aspire to such... And then how does a game reach where the passions of politics and religion, the gods of rock and cinema cannot even dream of? A nation that suddenly remembers it is one thanks to the national team, the blues of Germany: this is one of the many joyful mysteries of the moment.[5]

Pete Davies' observations during the 1990 World Cup further indicate sport's potential to mediate and celebrate difference:

> The San Siro in Milan was Ridley Scott science fiction, with a soundtrack from La Scala – but the Olympic in Rome was grand art all the way, with a

resonance of the most exuberant national pride. And though it often went manically overboard, I never felt overall, in Italy, that the nationalism that associates with football had that truly dangerous edge or undercurrent of desperation, of hysteric-pessimistic absolutism that comes with... well, with one other side one could think of.[6]

His lightly veiled reference to English football-patriotism also raises the question whether, rather than militarism and extreme nationalism, Italian sport and its heroes might have provided a more effective focus of collective identity. Davies' observations when Italy met Ireland in the 1990 World Cup quarter final in Rome are again worthy of note. The stadium was a

> roaring mass of red, white, and green, the colours waving in frenetic, lusting agitation. The naming of the new god Schilacci brought forth a boiling surge of apocalyptic noise... There were so many flags it was almost as if there were no people, as if the crowd had become one vast, frenzied sheet of national colours.[7]

Beyond unity and fissures, Italian sport has also reinforced national stereotypes/truths, most notably the presence of inherent illegality. Depressing as Moggiopoli was, arguably the worst thing was the general lack of surprise. Sadly, normal service appeared to have resumed as soon as possible. In November 2009 an anti-Mafia inquiry by the Potenza prosecutor's office revealed 'a clandestine gambling ring around *calcio*. Starting from the lowest divisions they reached the heart of Rome where – according to the accusation – the results of matches had been and would be decided.'[8] In March 2010 bookmakers also suspended betting on the Chievo–Catania match, after over two million pounds sterling were placed on the draw. The match finished 1-1. It barely raised a flicker of interest.

If gambling and corruption suggest that nothing changes in Italy, its athletes are evidence to the contrary. According to Mauro Valeri, the term 'Black Italians' was used to identify and discriminate against emigrant Italians, particularly in the US and Australia. 'At the same time, but so paradoxically, the same Italians haven't missed a chance to consider "black and mixed-race Italians" with as much contempt, above all those born and bred in the colonies.'[9] Having remained an almost totally homogeneous country for over one hundred years, waves of immigration from the 1980s onwards created tensions that have been fuelled by racist politicians, especially among the Northern League. Ironically, it was only the arrival of visible and audible outsiders that encouraged many

Italians to establish a sense of collective self. Sport has reflected this change and the racism that accompanies it.

The son of a Somali immigrant, Fabio Liverani's strong Roman accent discloses his youth spent in the capital's suburb of Torpignattara. On making his full international football debut, on 25 April 2001, Liverani became the first black Italian to represent the nation. Unfortunately, it was not the first time he had made the news. After he was bought by SS Lazio, in 2001, the walls of Rome and the club's training ground were daubed with the type of racist graffiti that had 'welcomed' the Dutchman Arron Winter, some eight years earlier.

One year prior to Liverani's debut for Italy, the black basketball star Carlton Myers, born in London to an Italian mother, carried the national flag at the Sydney Olympics. Myers suffered considerable abuse on the basketball court, one incident against Varese, in 2003, coming in the presence of Umberto Bossi who feigned ignorance. In response, Rome's mayor Walter Veltroni wrote a letter of solidarity to Myers:

> The idea that a minister of the Republic might have watched an explicit act of racism with indifference, perhaps even some pleasure, makes me shiver even if, unfortunately, it doesn't surprise me coming from somebody with his record and who only a few days ago referred to immigrants as 'Bingo Bongo'.[10]

Myers and Liverani nonetheless demonstrate a highly positive aspect of sport: its capacity to confront and challenge racism. Another high-profile black Italian athlete is Andrew Howe, who was born in Los Angeles and moved to Italy after his mother re-married. Naturalized Italian, the long jumper won gold at the European Championships in 2006 and silver at the World Championships the following year. He also joined the Italian Air Force and cut his plaited hair: 'it changed me for the better. I became more of a man, more mature. I didn't like [them] anymore because I seemed... an illegal immigrant.'[11] Although one can imagine that it wasn't the best look for the Italian military, it was a strange statement.

After the young black striker Mario Balotelli was insulted in a bar in Rome and bananas thrown at him, when on international duty in 2009, Howe jumped to his defence. But his support of Super-Mario indicated the problem:

> I don't believe it was a racist incident... I want to believe that it was only a gesture of football extremism... If I really must find a reason that isn't skin colour, it is in some of Balotelli's unfortunate gestures... I think black has nothing to do with it: if he had been Argentine for example, they would have insulted him in another way.[12]

Exactly!

The Under-21 manager Pierluigi Casiraghi concurred after Juventus fans chanted 'There are no black Italians', during Inter's visit to Turin in 2009.[13] 'It's his personality that's irritating, it's not racism... He has a big personality but sometimes exaggerates.'[14] National team coach Marcello Lippi went one step further, or too far, in asserting to 400 high-school students that 'cases of racism in football don't exist in Italy'.[15]

One wonders if Balotelli sees it quite the same way. A prodigious and precocious talent, whose northern accent disguises his birth in Palermo, his talent alone is enough to irritate opposition fans. But even if he is prone to the occasional cerebral short circuit, how can the unquestionable racism that he has experienced be his responsibility? There were similar explanations for the abuse of Carlton Myers, while presumably Messina's Ivory Coast defender Marco Andrè Kpolo Zoro had an equally bad attitude, hence the Inter fans' abuse of him on 27 November 2005. His response was to take the ball from the pitch in protest, before being persuaded to remain by his fellow professionals. But even they have not always been innocent. On 17 October 2000, then friend of Serbian war-criminal Arkan, Sinisa Mihajlovic abused Arsenal's Patrick Viera during a Champions League match. His public apology to the accompaniment of Lazio fans hissing and whistling was hardly surprising given their infamous banner exhibited during the April 2001 Rome derby: 'Squad of blacks, terrace of Jews'.

Serie A matches are preceded by warnings of sanctions against racist chanting, which few take seriously. Supporting the severest measures, the ex-CONI president Mario Pescante asked: 'The suspension of matches? Why not?'[16] Because there is no political will perhaps? In March 2010, Lazio fans' abuse of AC Milan's Clarence Seedorf almost forced authorities to suspend the match; but not quite. But for all its distastefulness, the Balotelli case has drawn huge attention to one of Italy's most pressing social issues. It remains to be seen if sport and its leading black figures are able to ease the country through its multi-racial growing pains or, alternatively, if it demonstrates how sections of the nation can only define themselves against images of the outsider, thereby exposing their own lack of commonality.

Despite various assertions to the contrary, racism is not just football's problem. As Il Venerdì di Repubblica's cover asked in June 2009: 'Is it not that you're racist and you don't know it?'[17] But Italy's stadiums do spotlight it, and never more so than the 28 April 1996 when Hellas Verona's notorious fans, one of which was apparently a parliamentary candidate for the extreme-right-wing Movimento Sociale Fiamma Tricolore, lynched a black effigy from the terraces in protest at their club's proposed purchase of the Dutchman Michel Ferrier.[18] Similarly, in celebration of Lazio going top of Serie A in 1999, the curva nord broke into a rendition of its old Fascist favourite 'Faccetta Nera' (little black face).[19]

Discrimination has long been a feature of Italian stadiums, with Napoli fans frequently greeted by chants of Africans and orders to wash, presumably in a fire-bath (*bagno di fuoco*) from the re-eruption of Vesuvius that extremist fans publicly long for. Certainly an area that would benefit from wider European comparison, a purely superficial glance suggests that Italy isn't alone in its racist stadiums. Where it may differ, however, is the degree to which racist/regionalist discrimination has been politically motivated.

For anybody who experienced English football in the 1970s and 1980s, the racist abuse, the chants, the bananas and the passing of the buck onto the game and the player is familiar. While racism has certainly not disappeared from English football, the strides made in the last two decades give hope for Italy. Great attention surrounded the first black England international in 1978, but since Viv Anderson's appearance roughly one in four England debutantes have been black. The first black captain, the former Inter player Paul Ince, was another key moment, while comment about Rio Ferdinand's recent appointment surrounded only his fitness and previous suspension for missing a dope test. Through educational programmes in conjunction with the Football Association and club community schemes, the 'Kick it out' campaign has had significant impact. Easy targets for anonymous, big mouths in the crowd, with enough support black players have become powerful forces in the campaign for racial equality.[20]

Yet successive Italian governments have shown little enthusiasm for learning from Britain, especially regarding Italian hooliganism. The inquiry following the riot at the Catania–Palermo derby in February 2007, which cost the 38-year-old police chief-inspector Filippo Raciti his life,[21] found that only six stadiums in Serie A and B met minimum standards.[22] Calcio stopped for 22 days before the show carried on. Laughable laws are put on the statute book and rarely implemented, Italian stadiums crumble and the politicians continue to wonder why.

Racism and violence are significant factors in *calcio*'s current sickness and growing loss of appeal. While ineffective 'anti-hooliganism' laws have made obtaining a ticket ridiculously difficult, the game's general malaise has seen crowds plummet. On the contrary, rugby union's popularity has swelled. The Italian Rugby Federation (FIR) was formed under Fascism in 1928, and the nation has participated in every World Cup since the tournament's creation, in 1987. Primarily a northern, minority sport up until Italy's entry into the Six Nations Championship, in 2000,[23] Rome's Flaminio Stadium is sold out for internationals, with the New Zealand All-Blacks visit, in 2009, filling Milan's San Siro. From modest beginnings and some heavy defeats, Italy's Six Nations performances have generally improved, with a fourth-place finish in 2007 its pinnacle so far.

Initially exploiting the International Rugby Board's rules on the selection of foreign born players with Italian ancestry, since 2004 the FIR restricted them to a maximum of three, to develop home-grown talent. Unusually for Italy, where sporting expectations are often destructively high, this seems less of a problem for rugby. While the national team's 2007 Six Nations success drew significant media attention, it was as much about the sport's image as a model of fair play. Despite losing the last game to Ireland, 10,000 plus fans congratulated the team in Rome's Piazza del Popolo. Contrasting with *calcio*'s violence and recriminations, on 18 March 2007 *La Gazzetta*'s headline declared: 'To lose like this is beautiful.' That said, defeating France for the first time in the Six Nations Championship and winning the Garibaldi Cup on 11 March 2011, was presumably even better.

✪ ✪ ✪ ✪

Following his purchase of AC Milan, Berlusconi's political programme and career has been more closely connected to sport than any modern, democratic politician. As Remo Bassetti proposes: 'in Italy the problem ha[s] become not of remembering that *sport isn't politics* but rather the opposite of underlining that *politics is not sport*'.[24] While not solely responsible, Berlusconi's role has been huge. The results have not always been edifying and when it has suited he has been the first to call for its separation from politics, despite his political use of football to break and enter Italian front rooms. His evasion of what few television restrictions remain can be contrasted with the BBC's refusal to allow the British Prime Minister Gordon Brown to appear on Match of the Day 2, in March 2010, so close to a general election.[25]

The natural reaction to Italy's example might be to argue against the politicization of sport, if that is at all possible. But it is equally hard to think of a more effective measure than the sporting boycott of South Africa in protest against apartheid, or the passage of the Olympic flame prior to the 2008 Beijing Games, which drew global attention to China's rule over Tibet. Thus, if Nelson Mandela is to pull on South Africa's rugby shirt to embody the rainbow nation, Berlusconi and the Northern League may well do so too. In his own special way, *calcio*'s heretic Paolo Sollier made a wonderful case not only in defence of the marriage between politics and sport, but also the need for it, for better or worse:

> Being apolitical doesn't exist, because who isn't political, who doesn't intervene, who is disinterested, is declaring they leave it to others. Thus, they support the authority.
>
> It's as if two people are fighting and you calmly watch, apolitical, inhuman, arsehole, without joining in to support the weakest. By doing nothing

you have, in fact, helped the strongest, you let him use his power, you let him massacre the other in the name of a false, cowardly, hypocritical neutrality. The same goes for the political struggle: being neutral is an even less credible alibi: if you don't take a position you are, in fact, an accomplice of the strongest, allied to the established power.

It's not by chance that those who continue to argue that sport is apolitical are Demochristians or declared reactionaries. For them it's ok if supporting a team closes the people's eyes: if they open them, who knows, they might get a kick up the arse.

As for me, the accusation is of using sport to make politics; only that I do politics independently from being a footballer. And in my way of doing politics there is an argument to discuss about sport, a critical and alternative argument...

I ask: if sport isn't political, why is it used politically... If sport isn't political, why is it always used by the priests to get children to go to mass? If sport isn't political, why does its framework faithfully mirror the political choices of the system in which we live?

The answer is easy: it's all smoke, support and rhetoric in the eyes.[26]

The remaining question is how unusual is this? How particular is Italy? From the evidence presented, the argument would seem quite conclusive. *Not a normal country* as one recent investigation put it.[27] Certainly, Italy is particular, with much of this originating in the peninsula's diverse history and people. Not naturally a country or a nation with strong ties of commonality, Italy's history has been one of constant nation-building, war, civil war and political extremes that expose its fractures and deep divisions. It also has a somewhat split character, especially towards the outside world. Almost always viewed as Mediterranean in terms of its social and family structures and agriculture, its modern, manufacturing sector is considered northern European. Having possessed the largest post-war Communist Party in Western Europe, with strong links to Stalin's Soviet Union, its position within the west was never questioned.

A country and people of extreme diversity, Italy's capacity to contest almost any definition of a nation has generated accusations of failure, which this book contests. As Daniele Marchesini suggested with regard to the post-war period:

If the motherland is reborn as a sporting sub species it is probably due to the transversal nature of the phenomenon sport, its capacity to overcome the plurality of different ways of feeling part of a national collective that are never definitively fixed but dynamic, perhaps even conflictual, yet still coexist.

> If there are many ways of feeling part of a nation... the criteria that unites them is the pride in belonging. Sport possesses this unifying quality at the highest level.[28]

There is, however, evidence to suggest this happened prior to the fall of Fascism. From its earliest manifestations in Liberal Italy, sport demonstrated its potential to accommodate all Italians, their contradictions and complexities included. Rather than a failure, *Sport Italia* presents an alternative view of a nation that has overcome adversity and diversity to represent itself through professional, amateur, group, individual, national, regional and local sporting activity. Exploited by all major opinion formers and cultural leaders, this representation has been multi-faceted and inclusive of Italy's micro communities and identities, more often than not. National sporting achievements, such as London 1908, Rome 1960, Mexico 1974 and Spain 1982, have provided Italy with some of its most solid moments of unity. Equally, it would be illogical to ignore how sport has spotlighted the fissures in the national character and nation-state but, even so, this still represents real rather than imagined Italy, where difference and diversity are pillars of the nation.

Only comparison with other nations can truly determine how 'abnormal' or otherwise Italy might be. But if it is not a normal country, to what should it be compared and which Italy should be presented? While it is to be hoped that sporting histories of other European nation states are written, thereby aiding any definition of normality, the suspicion remains that Italy might well still be out there on the extremity. As Donato Martucci, former head of CONI's press office, wrote in his analysis of Italians and sport in the late 1960s:

> By date the unification of our country is still recent, as it's still yet to reach a century. Problems... have made – and, in part, make even more difficult – general progress in our society. Sport is a socially valuable act, but it cannot consider itself decisive and a priority when compared to others. It must be recognised, in fact, that sport is conditioned by the evolution and development of other national activities. How can sport impose itself in a country of low economic revenue, tormented by employment, health, diet and education problems? A state that placed sport as the greatest necessity of social life would be defined, in the best of scenarios, a very strange one.[29]

Indeed!

Notes

Chapter 1

1   Davies, P., *All Played Out: The Full Story of Italia '90* (London, 1991), p.15.

2   According to Spanish tradition, they represent the victory of Aragon over the Moors at the Battle of Alcoraz in 1096, as the peninsula was reclaimed. The Sardinian version has the banner given by Pope Benedict II to the Pisans, in 1017, who were combating the Saracens (Moors).

3   '"Venite a prendermi, sono libero" finisce l'incubo di Titti Pinna', *La Repubblica*, 29 May 2007, p.14.

4   On the Rocco penal code see Foot, J., *Modern Italy* (Basingstoke, 2003), pp.73–5.

5   On this argument see Pavone, C., *Alle Origini della Repubblica: Scritti sul Fascismo, Antifascismo e Continuità dello Stato* (Turin, 1995), p.71.

6   Duggan, C., *The Force of Destiny: A History of Italy since 1796* (London, 2008); Ginsborg, P., *A History of Contemporary Italy: Society and Politics 1943–1988* (London, 1990); Ginsborg, P., *Italy And its Discontents: Family, Civil Society, State 1980–2001* (London, 2003); Mack Smith, D., *Modern Italy: A Political Italy* (New Haven, 1997).

7   Foot: *Modern Italy*, p.7.

8   For the debates on writing Italian history see Ben-Ghiat, R., Cafagna, L., Galli della Loggia, E., Ipsen, C., Kertzer, D.I. and Gilbert, M., 'History as it really wasn't: the myths of Italian historiography', *Journal of Modern Italian Studies*, 6, 3 (2001), pp.402–19.

9   Bosworth, R.J.B., 'The Italian Novecento and its Historians', *The Historical Journal*, 49, 1 (2006), p.318.

10   Jarvie lists the various explanations as: (i) a ritual sacrifice of human energy; (ii) providing a common cultural currency between peoples; (iii) a means of compensating for deficiencies in life; (iv) a mechanism for the affirmation of identity

and difference; (v) business rather than sport; (vi) a social product; (vii) a contested arena shaped by struggles both on and off the field of play and (viii) being a euphemism for Western or capitalist sport. Jarvie, G., *Sport, Culture and Society: An Introduction* (London, 2006), p.3.

11   For analyses of the variety of theories of sport see Cashmore, E., *Making Sense of Sports* (London, 2000); Houlihan, B., *Sport and Society: An Introduction* (London, 2003); Jarvie: *Sport, Culture and Society*; Jarvie, G. and Maguire, J., *Sport and Leisure in Social Thought* (London, 1994); Scambler, G., *Sport and Society: History, Power and Culture* (Maidenhead, 2005).

12   Huizinga, J., *Homo Ludens: A Study of the Play-Element in Culture* (London, 2003).

13   Elias, N., and Dunning, E., *Quest for Excitement: Sport and Leisure in the Civilizing Process* (Oxford, 1986).

14   See Gounot, A., 'Between revolutionary demands and diplomatic necessity. The uneasy relationship between Soviet sport and worker and bourgeois sport in Europe from 1920 to 1937', in P. Arnaud and J. Riordan (eds), *Sport and International Politics: The Impact of Fascism and Communism on Sport* (London, 1998); Gounot, A., 'Sport or political organization? Structures and characteristics of the Red Sport International, 1921–1937', *Journal of Sport History*, 28, 1 (2001), pp.23–39; Steinberg, D.A., 'The Workers' Sport Internationals 1920–28', *Journal of Contemporary History*, 13, 2 (1978), pp.233–51; Wheeler, R.F., 'Organized sport and organized labour: The Workers' Sports Movement source, *Journal of Contemporary History*, 13, 2 (1978), pp.191–210.

15   'Lo sport, I giovani e la coscienza rivoluzionaria', *Avanti!*, 11 October 2010, p.1.

16   See Bellamy, R. (ed.) *Antonio Gramsci: Pre-Prison Writings* (Cambridge, 1994); Forgacs, D. (ed.), *The Antonio Gramsci Reader* (New York, 2000); Hoare, Q. and Nowell Smith, G. (eds), *Selections From The Prison Notebooks of Antonio Gramsci* (London, 1971); Jarvie and Maguire: *Sport and Leisure in Social Thought*.

17   Keys, B., *Globalizing Sport: National Rivalry and International Community in the 1930s* (Cambridge, MA, 2006), p.17.

18   Cashmore: *Making Sense of Sports*, p.94; Hoch, P., *Rip off the Big Game: The Exploitation of Sports by the Power Elite* (Garden City, NY, 1972).

19   Cardoza, A., 'Cavour and Piedmont', in J.A. Davis (ed.), *Italy in the Nineteenth Century 1796–1900* (Oxford, 2006), p.112.

20   Cetorelli Schivo, G., *Lo Sport nell'Italia Antica: Sport e Ideale Atletico* (Milano, 2002); La Regina, A. (ed.), *Nike: Il Gioco e la Vittoria* (Milano, 2003); Harris, H., *Sport in Greece and Rome* (London, 1972); Kyle, D.G., *Sport and Spectacle in the Ancient World* (Oxford, 2007); Menotti, E.M,, *L'Atleta nell'Antichità* (Mantova, 2002); Newby, Z., *Greek Athletics in the Roman World: Victory and Virtue* (Oxford, 2005); Yegül, F., *Bathing in the Roman World* (Cambridge, 2010).

21   Kyle: *Sport and Spectacle in the Ancient World*, pp.300–1.

22   See Lanfranchi, P., 'I giochi con la palla all'epoca del calcio fiorentino e lo sport moderno', *Storia in Lombardia*, 1–2 (1995), pp.17–35.

23   Cashmore: *Making Sense of Sports*, p.104. See also Frasca, S., *Religio Athletae: Pierre de Coubertin e la Formazione dell'Uomo per la Società Complessa* (Roma, 2007); Guttmann, A., *From Ritual to Record: The Nature of Modern Sports* (New York, 1978); Overman, S.J., *The Influence of the Protestant Ethic on Sport and Recreation* (Aldershot, 1997).

24   Holt, R., 'Towards a general history of modern European sport. Some problems and possibilities', in A. Krüger and Teja, A. (eds), *La Comune Eredità dello Sport in Europa: Atti del 1° Seminario Europea di Storia dello Sport* (Roma, 1997), p.31.

25   For a more complete literature review of Italian sport in the last 20 years see S. Martin, 'Italy. A historiographical review', *Journal of Sport History* (2011).

26   Bassetti, R., *Storia e Storie dello Sport in Italia: Dall'Unità a Oggi* (Venezia, 1999); Fabrizio, F., *Storia dello Sport in Italia: Dalle Società Ginnastiche all'Associazionismo di Massa* (Firenze, 1978); Ferrara, P., *L'Italia in Palestra: Storia, Documenti e Immagini della Ginnastica dal 1833 al 1973* (Roma, 1992); Noto, A. and Rossi, L. (eds), *Coroginnica: Saggi Sulla Ginnastica, lo Sport e la Cultura del Corpo, 1861–1991* (Roma, 1992); Porro, N., *Identità, Nazione, Cittadinanza. Sport, Società e Sistema Politico nell'Italia Contemporanea* (Roma, 1995).

27   Teja, A., *Educazione Fisica al Femminile: Dai Primi Corsi di Torino di Ginnastica Educativa per le Maestre (1867) alla Ginnastica Moderna di Andreina Gotta Sacco (1904–1988)* (Roma, 1995).

28   Arnaud and Riordan: *Sport and International Politics*; Krüger, A. and Trangbaek, E., *The History of Physical Education & Sport From European Perspectives* (Copenhagen, 1996); Riordan, J. and Kruger, A. (eds), *The International Politics of Sport in the Twentieth Century* (London and New York, 1999).

29   Bianda, R., Leone, G., Rossi, G. and Urso, A., *Atleti in Camicia Nera: lo Sport nell'Italia di Mussolini* (Roma, 1983).

30   Canella, M. and Giuntini, S., *Sport e Fascismo* (Milano, 2009); Ponzio, A., *La Palestra del Littorio: L'Accademia della Farnesina: un'Esperimento di Pedagogia Totalitaria nell'Italia Fascista* (Milano, 2009).

31   De Grazia, V., *The Culture of Consent: Mass Organisation of Leisure in Fascist Italy* (Cambridge, 1981); Martin, S., *Football and Fascism: The National Game under Mussolini* (Oxford, 2004); Gori, G., *Female Bodies, Sport, Italian Fascism: Submissive Women and Strong Mothers* (London, 2004).

32   Marchesini, D., *Carnera* (Bologna, 2006); *Cuori e Motori: Storia della Mille Miglia 1927–1957* (Bologna, 2001); *L'Italia del Giro d'Italia* (Bologna, 1996).

33   Pivato, S., *La Bicicletta e il Sol dell'Avvenire: Sport e Tempo Libero nel Socialismo della Belle-Epoque* (Firenze, 1992); *Sia Lodato Bartali: Ideologia, Cultura e Miti dello Sport Cattolico (1936/1948)* (Roma, 1996).

34   Papa, A. and Panico, G., *Storia sociale del calcio in Italia. Dai Campionati del Dopoguerra alla Champions League (1945–2000)* (Bologna, 2000); *Storia sociale del*

calcio in Italia. Dai club dei pionieri alla nazione sportiva (1887–1945) (Bologna, 1993);
Foot, J., *Calcio: A History of Italian Football* (London, 2006); Agnew, P., *Forza Italia: A
Journey in Search of Italy and its Football* (London, 2006).

35 Ginsborg: *Italy and its Discontents*, p.113.

Chapter 2

1 For the various arguments regarding the Risorgimento see Riall, L., *The Italian
Risorgimento: State, Society and National Unification* (London, 1994).

2 Foot, J., *Modern Italy* (Basingstoke, 2003), p.194.

3 Duggan, C., *The Force of Destiny: A History of Italy since 1796* (London, 2008),
pp.292–3.

4 Teja, A. and Impiglia, M., 'Italy', in J. Riordan and A. Krüger (eds), *European Cultures
in Sport: Examining the Nations and Regions* (Bristol, 2003).

5 On the attempt to create identity in Liberal Italy see Córner, A., *Politics of Culture in
Liberal Italy: From Unification to Fascism* (London, 2008) and Duggan: *The Force of
Destiny*, pp.274–97.

6 Duggan: *The Force of Destiny*, p.272.

7 Conti, G., 'Il mito della "nazione armata"', *Storia Contemporanea. Rivista Bimestrale
di Studi Storici*, XXI, 6 (1990), p.1159.

8 Pivato, S., 'Far ginnastica e far nazioni', in A. Noto and L. Rossi (eds), *Coroginnica:
Saggi Sulla Ginnastica, lo Sport e la Cultura del Corpo, 1861–1991* (Roma, 1992), p.35.

9 'Ginnastica e repubblica', *La Educazione Politica*, 4, 89–90, 1–15 September 1902,
p.380.

10 Giuntini, S., 'Dalla ginnastica al calcio. L'esperienza piemontese tra otto e novecento',
Studi Piemontesi, XXVIII, fasc. 1, March (1999), p.158.

11 On the schism and creation of the National Gymnastics Federation see Giuntini, S.,
'Nascita di una Federazione', in Noto and Rossi: *Coroginnica*, pp.44–57.

12 Pécout, G., 'La nascita delle societa di tiro nell'Italia del Risorgimento, 1861–1865:
Fra volontariato e apprendistato civico', *Dimensioni e Problemi della Ricerca Società*,
1 (1992), pp.94–5.

13 Baratieri, O., 'I tiri a segno e le istituzioni militare', *Nuova Antologia*, 1 (1880),
pp.136–57. See also Mariotti, T., 'L'istituzioni del Tiro a segno in Italia', *Rivista Militare*,
April–June (1880), pp.30–55.

14 Teja, A., 'Educazione e addestramento militare', in Noto and Rossi, *Coroginnica*,
p.64.

15 Giuntini, S., 'Al servizio della Patria. Il tiro a segno dall'"Unità" alla "Grande Guerra"',
Lancillotto e Nausica. Critica e Storia dello Sport, 3 (1987), p.88.

16 Jacomuzzi, S., 'Gli sport', in AA.VV, *Storia d'Italia, Volume Quinto, I documenti*, I (Torino,
1973), p.921.

17   On the Touring Club see Bosworth, R.J.B., 'The Touring Club Italiano and the nationalization of the Italian bourgeoisie', *European History Quarterly*, 27 (1997), pp.371–410.

18   Papa, C., 'Borghesi in divisa. Sport e nazione nell'Italia liberale', *Zapruder. Rivista di Storia della Conflittualità Sociale*, 4 (2004), p.34.

19   'R. Istituto di Magistero per l'Educazione Fisica – Torino', *Il Ginnasta*, XXVII, 12, 15 December 1915, p.217.

20   Tarozzi, F., '"Far conoscere la montagna". Alle origini del Cai tra escursionismo ed esplorazione scientifica', *Il Risorgimento. Rivista di Storia del Risorgimento e di Storia Contemporanea*, XIV, 2 (1993), p.225.

21   CONI, *VII Giochi Olimpici Invernali. Rapporto Ufficiale* (Roma, 1956), p.77.

22   For further details on SUCAI activities see Papa, 'Borghesi in divisa...', *Zapruder*, pp.26–37.

23   Teja and Impiglia: 'Italy', pp.142–3.

24   AA.VV., *Storia d'Italia, Annali 15, L'Industria* (Torino, 1999), pp.27–28.

25   See Pivato, S., 'Associazionismo Sportivo e Associazionismo Politico nella Romagna d'Inizio Novecento', *Bolletino del Museo del Risorgimento* (1987–1988), pp.167–93.

26   'Velocità', *Lo Sport Illustrato*, 1, 25, 25 October 1937, p.1.

27   On the development of mass tourism see *Storia in Lombardia*, 1–2 (1995).

28   Triani, G., *Pelle di Luna pelle di Sole: Nascita e Storia della Civiltà Balneare 1700–1946* (Venezia, 1988), p.47.

29   Sorcinelli, P., 'Che pazzia affidarsi al mare! Per una storia del turismo balneare sull'Adriatico', *Il Risorgimento. Rivista di Storia del Risorgimento e di Storia Contemporanea*, XLV, 2 (1993), p.237.

30   Lombardo, A., 'Nuoto', in A. Lombardo (ed.), *Storia degli Sport in Italia, 1861–1960* (Cassino, 2004), p.237.

31   Papa, A. and Panico, G., *Storia Sociale del Calcio in Italia: Dai Club Pionieri alla Nazione Sportiva (1887–1945)* (Bologna, 1993), p.77.

32   Duggan: *The Force of Destiny*, p.360.

33   'Sport e... sport', *L'Avanguardia*, 1 August 1909, p.2. For reader responses see four consecutive editions from 22 October 1909.

34   Zibordi, G., 'Lo sport e I giovani. Una lettera di Zibordi', *Avanti!*, 4 October 1910, p.2.

35   Bassetti, R., *Storia e Storie dello Sport in Italia: Dall'Unità Oggi* (Venezia, 1999), p.64.

36   Zibordi, G., 'Sport, ginnastica e proletariato', *Avanti!*, 18 November 1909, p.3.

37   Bonomi, I., 'Lo "sport" e I giovani', *Avanti!*, 29 September 1910, p.2.

38   See Rossi, L., 'Per la Montagna Contro l'Alcool. Sei anni di alpinismo proletariato in Italia (1921–1926)', *Lancillotto e Nausica*, 2 (1988), pp.30–5.

39   See Lorenzini, A., 'I ciclisti rossi', *Avanti!*, 2 October 1912, p.3; S. Pivato, 'Le pigrizie dello storico. Lo sport fra ideologia, storia e rimozioni', *Italia Contemporanea*, 174, March (1989), pp.17–27.

40 'La magnifica riuscita del primo Convegno dei ciclisti rossi', *Avanti!*, 25 September 1912, p.2.

41 'Un convegno di "ciclisti rossi" a Imola', *Corriere della Sera*, 23 September 1912, p.7.

42 Lorenzini: 'I ciclisti rossi', p.3.

43 Semeria was one of the most well known Italian Catholics in this period. A talented orator, he participated in the First World War as a military chaplain of the Supreme command in the Udine area. See Istituto della Enciclopedia Italiana, *Enciclopedia Italiana di Scienze, Lettere ed Arti* (Roma, 1950).

44 Fabrizio, F., *Storia dello Sport in Italia: Dalle Società Ginnastiche all'Associazionismo di Massa* (Firenze, 1978), p.51.

45 Centro Sportivo Italiano, *Cent'Anni di Storia nella Realtà dello Sport Italiano: Dalla Federazione Associazione Sportive Cattoliche Italiane al Centro Sportivo Italiano* (Vol. I), (Bergamo, 2006), p.55.

46 Ferrara, P., *L'Italia in Palestra: Storia, Documenti e Immagini della Ginnastica dal 1833 al 1973* (Roma, 1992), p.186.

47 'Cronaca contemporanea', *Civiltà Cattolica*, IV (1905), p.211.

48 Centro Sportivo Italiano: *Cent'Anni di Storia nella Realtà dello Sport Italiano*, p.65.

49 'Commenti alla proibizione del corteo ginnastico cattolico', *Corriere della Sera*, 9 September 1913, p.2.

50 'Serata di dimostrazioni a Roma', *Corriere della Sera*, 9 September 1913, p.2.

51 See Catholic press of 8–9 September 1913.

52 'La violenza settaria degli anticlericali di Roma contro una tranquilla manifestazione di fede e di forza', *L'Italia*, 8 September 1913, p.1.

53 'Il ciclismo e la democrazia', *La Bicicletta*, 12–13 July 1894, p.3.

54 Piloni, R., 'L'industria della bicicletta a Milano dalla fine dell'Ottocento al 1914', *Storia in Lombardia*, IV, 2 (1985), p.88.

55 Pivato, S., 'The bicycle as a political symbol: Italy, 1885–1955', *The International Journal of the History of Sport*, 7, September (1990), p.173.

56 Bosworth: 'The Touring Club Italiano', pp.381–2.

57 Cappelli, V. (ed.), *Diario di un Cicloturista di Fine Ottocento: Da Reggio Calabria ad Eboli* (Castrovillari, 1989), p.iii.

58 Cappelli: *Diario di un Cicloturista di Fine Ottocento*, p.v.

59 Doglio, C., 'Lo sport in Italia', *Comunità: Rivista Trimestrale del Movimento Comunità*, VI, 13, January (1952), p.28.

60 Marchesini, D., *L'Italia del Giro d'Italia* (Bologna, 1996), p.69.

61 'L'onda invincibile', *La Gazzetta*, 24 August 1908, p.1.

62 Doglio: 'Lo Sport in Italia', p.28.

63 Quoted in Pivato, S., *La Bicicletta e il Sole dell'Avvenire: Sport e Tempo Libero nel Socialismo nella Belle-Epoque* (Firenze, 1992), p.95.

64 *La Gazzetta*, 31 May 1909, p.1.

65 'Diffondiamo le bellezze italiche', *La Gazzetta*, 8 March 1909, p.3.

66 'La Bicicletta e l'anarchia', *La Bicicletta*, 7–8 August 1894, p.2.

67 Lombroso, C., *Delitti Vecchi e Delitti Nuovi* (Torino, 1902), pp.293–305.

68 'CICLISTI ARMATEVI!', *La Bicicletta*, 31 August–1 September 1895, p.1.

69 'I Conquistati. Il Prof. Cesare Lombroso', *La Bicicletta: Giornale Popolare dello Sport*, I, 8, 10–11 May 1894, p.1.

70 'Ciclismo criminoso', *La Bicicletta*, 25–26 September 1894, p.2.

71 This and other examples cited in Marchesini: *L'Italia del Giro d'Italia*, pp.47–8.

72 'La donna e la bicicletta', *La Bicicletta*, 18–19 September 1894, p.2.

73 'FINALMENTE! I preti in bicicletta', *La Bicicletta*, 24–5 April 1897, p.1.

74 'I ciclofobi', *La Bicicletta*, 31 August–1 September 1894, p.1.

75 'Il velocipede e il sacerdote', *I Preti in Bicicletta. Supplemento al Giornale La Bicicletta*, 28 July 1894, p.1.

76 Piloni: 'L'industria della bicicletta a Milano...', p.97.

77 Pivato, S., 'Ginnastica e Risorgimento. Alle origini del rapporto sport/nazionalismo', *Ricerche Storiche*, XIX, 2 (1989), pp.257–61. On irredentism see Sabbatucci, G., 'Il problema dell'irredentismo e le origini del movimento nazionalista in Italia', *Storia Contemporanea*, 3 (1970), pp.467–502; 1 (1971), pp.53–106.

78 'Trieste Sportiva', *Lo Sport Fascista*, II, 6, 1929, p.65.

79 'Trieste Sportiva', *Lo Sport Fascista*, p.65.

80 Quoted in Toschi, L., 'Giovanni Raicevich, "il re della forza"', *Rassegna Storica del Risorgimento*, 90, 1 (2003), p.89.

81 'Un complotto d'odio contro Giovanni Raicevich', *La Gazzetta*, 4 December 1908, p.1.

82 'L'ultima solenne serata del campionato', *La Gazzetta*, 17 February 1909, p.2.

83 'L'ultima solenne serata...', *La Gazzetta*, p.2.

84 Grozio, R., 'Credono gli italiani alla Nazionale?', in R. Grozio (ed.), *Catenaccio e Contropiede: Materiali e Immaginari del Football Italiano* (Roma, 1990), p.118.

85 Gerosa, G., 'Brera l'incendario', *L'Europeo*, 2, April (2002), p.134.

86 Marchesini: *L'Italia del Giro d'Italia*, p.179.

87 'L'Italia ai Giuochi Olimpici 1908', *La Gazzetta*, 31 July 1908, p.1.

88 'La IV Olimpiade Internazionale', *La Gazzetta*, 27 July 1908, p.3.

89 'Risposta al "superfurbo" di Asor Rosa. L'Italiano di sempre', *La Repubblica*, 14 August 1984, p.6.

90 'L'educazione fisica e la legge del lavoro e della produzione', *Il Ginnasta. Organo Ufficiale della Federazione Ginnastica Italiana*, 14, 15 September 1902, p.49.

91 Reguzzoni, M., *Alberto Braglia: L'Uomo, il Ginnasta, il Mimo-Acrobata* (Modena, 1983), p.37.

92 'La IV Olimpiade Internazionale', *La Gazzetta*, 27 July 1908, p.3.

93 'La corsa di maratona', *Corriere della Sera*, 25 July 1908, p.5.

94 'Gli insegnamenti di una gloriosa sconfitta', *La Gazzetta*, 27 July 1908, p.3.

95 'Discussioni Olimpiche', *La Gazzetta*, 31 July 1908, p.5.

96 'Le Olimpiadi a Londra', *Corriere della Sera*, 26 July 1908, p.4.

97 'Il trionfo di Dorando Pietri', *Corriere della Sera*, 27 July 1908, p.5.

98 'La maratona', *L'Avanguardia*, 25 October 1908, p.3.

99 'L'Italia ai Giuochi Olimpici 1908', *La Gazzetta*, 31 July 1908, p.1.

100 Duggan: *The Force of Destiny*, p.290.

101 Ferrara: *L'Italia in Palestra*, p.200.

102 'Il dovere', *La Gazzetta*, 24 May 1915, p.1.

103 'L'ora di ricordare', *La Gazzetta*, 23 May 1915, p.1.

104 'Supremazia e superiorità dell'uomo dello sport pel "Grande Match"', *La Gazzetta*, 31 May 1915, p.1.

105 'Per la documentazione della diffusione al fronte de "Lo Sport Illustrato e la Guerra"', *Lo Sport Illustrato e la Guerra*, IV, 14, 15 July 1916, p.401.

106 'Gli abbonamenti per la Zona di Guerra', *La Gazzetta*, 2 January 1917, p.4.

107 'Nel decennio della Vittoria ricordiamo il contributo dato dallo sport alla guerra ed esaltiamo il sacrificio degli Sportivi caduti sul campo di battaglia', *Lo Sport Fascista*, 5, 1928, p.42.

108 Ferretti, L., *Lo Sport* (Rome, 1949), p.344.

109 'Prepariamo i futuri soldati', *La Gazzetta*, 6 September 1915, p.1. See also 'Dall'allenamento sportivo al getto delle bombe a mano', *Lo Sport Illustrato e Guerra*, 15 June 1915, p.343.

110 'Preparare', *La Gazzetta*, 24 May 1915, p.1.

111 'Lo Sport alla Patria', *La Gazzetta*, 17 May 1915, p.1.

112 'Per l'Italia', *La Gazzetta*, 23 May 1915, p.1.

113 'Velocipedismo militare', *La Bicicletta*, 30–31 January 1895, p.7.

114 'I ciclisti nel combattimento di notte', *La Bicicletta*, 26 September 1898, p.1.

115 Mack Smith, D., *Modern Italy: A Political Italy* (New Haven, 1997), p.222. John Foot quotes this figure as 90 per cent. Foot, J., *Calcio: A History of Italian Football* (London, 2006), p.40.

116 Marchesini: *L'Italia del Giro d'Italia*, p.81.

117 Fabrizio: *Storia dello Sport in Italia*, p.74.

118 'Lo Sport e le elezioni', *Il Giornale dello Sport*, 3 May 1921, p.1.

119 'I nostri deputati', *Il Giornale dello Sport*, 24 May 1921, p.1.

120 'Educazione Fisica', *Avanti!*, 22 August 1920, p.2.

121 'La questione dello sport', *La Battaglia Socialista: Settimanale della Federazione Provinciale Socialista Milanese*, 5, 53, 31 December 1921, p.2.

122 A leading revolutionary socialist, Serrati became director of *Avanti!* in 1913 after Mussolini's expulsion. See Istituto della Enciclopedia Italiana, *Lessico Universale Italiano di Lingua Lettere Arti Scienze e Tecnica Vol XX* (Roma, 1978), p.597.

123 'Lo Sport e la classe lavoratrice', *Sport e Proletariato*, 14 July 1923, p.3.

124 Bianchi, E., 'Sport (Dall'Italia)', *Giustizia e Libertà*, 10 February 1934, p.49.

125 On APEF see, Fabrizio: *Storia dello sport in Italia*, pp.80–3; 'L'esperienza di "Sport e Proletariato"', *Lancillotto e Nausica*, 3 (1986), pp.66–73.

126 'Vantaggi di una squadra ginnastica nell'Oratorio', *L'Eco degli Oratori*, 20, 18 October 1914, p.5.

127 Ghirelli, A., *Storia del Calcio in Italia* (Einaudi, 1990), p.93.

Chapter 3

1   On the Fascist rise to power, among the many options see Lyttelton, A., *The Seizure of Power: Fascism in Italy 1919–1929* (Princeton, 1987); Sassoon, D., *Mussolini and the Rise of Fascism* (London, 2008).

2   See, Martin, S., *Football and Fascism: The National Game under Mussolini* (Oxford, 2004), pp.130–3.

3   Ferretti, L., 'Lo sport problema di Stato', *Lo Sport Fascista*, II, 6, 1929, p.4.

4   'Dal Littoriale partono stanotte i messaggeri dell'augurio di tutta l'Italia sportive per gli Azzurri', *Il Resto del Carlino*, 25 May 1928, p.5.

5   'Lo sport è un'arma', *La Gazzetta*, 16 May 1940, p.1

6   Schnapp, J. (ed.), *A Primer of Italian Fascism* (Lincoln, 2000), p.308.

7   AA.VV., *Lo Sport in Regime Fascista 28 Ottobre 1922–I 28 Ottobre 1935–XIII* (Milano, 1935), p.6 and 'Mussolini, primo sportivo d'Italia', *Lo Sport Fascista*, VI, 1933, p.1.

8   For more details see Società Sportiva di Bologna (ed.), *Il Littoriale* (Bologna, 1931), pp.23–32.

9   AA.VV: *Lo Sport in Regime Fascista*, p.132.

10 'L'on. Arpinati per la razionalizzazione dello sport,' *Il Resto del Carlino*, 26 June 1928, p.3.

11 'Nel clima dell'Italia di Mussolini', *La Gazzetta*, 1 August 1938, p.1.

12 'E si vince!', *L'Ambrosiano*, 4 August 1924, p.1.

13 Camera dei Deputati, Seduta 18 Marzo 1933, in *Atti Parlamentari dell'Assemblea, Anno 1933, Volume VII, Discussioni* (Roma, 1934), p.8406.

14 Macellari, N., *Sport e Potenza* (Roma, 1940), p.36.

15 Cotronei, A., *Atleti e Eroi* (Milano, 1932), p.94.

16 For example, see 'L'educazione fisica della donna e del bambino', in AA.VV., *Almanacco della Donna Italiana* (Firenze, 1924), pp.189–220.

17 On Fascism, women and sport see De Giorgio, M., *Le Italiane dall'Unità a Oggi: Modelli Culturali e Comportamenti* (Bari, 1992); Gori, G., *Female Bodies, Sport, Italian Fascism: Submissive Women and Strong Mothers* (London, 2004); Teja, A., *Educazione Fisica al Femminile: Dai Primi Corsi di Torino di Ginnastica Educativa per la Maestre (1867) alla Ginnastica Moderna di Andreina Gotta Sacco (1904–1988)* (Roma, 1995).

18 Balilla is derived from the nickname of the Genoan Gian Battista Perasso, who launched an insurrection against the Austrian rulers in 1746.

19 AA.VV: *Lo Sport in Regime Fascista*, p.160.

20 Fantini, O., 'Sport e Turismo Potenza Nazionale', CONI, *L'Italia Turistica Annuario Generale. Sport – Turismo – Industrie Applicate* (Firenze, 1930), p.12.

21 Ferretti: *Lo Sport*, pp.87–8.

22 Marchesini, D., *L'Italia del Giro d'Italia* (Bologna, 1996), p.105.

23 'La triste fine di Ottavio Bottecchia', *La Gazzetta*, 2 October 1943, p.1.

24 Spitaleri, E., *Il Delitto Bottecchia* (Roma, 1987), p.67.

25 'La Gioia della bicicletta', *Lo Sport Fascista*, I, 6, 1928, p.50–4.

26 'Nel clima dell'Italia di Mussolini', *La Gazzetta*, p.1.

27 Minazzi, A., 'Il XVII Giro d'Italia', *Lo Sport Fascista*, II, 6, 1929, p.101.

28 Marchesini: *L'Italia del Giro d'Italia*, p.110.

29 Doglio, C., 'Lo Sport in Italia', *Comunità: Rivista Tremestrale del Movimento Comunità*, VI, 13 (January), 1952, p.29.

30 'Nel clima dell'Italia di Mussolini', *La Gazzetta*, p.1.

31 'Nel clima dell'Italia di Mussolini', *La Gazzetta*, p.8.

32 Cotronei: *Atleti e Eroi*, p.9.

33 Cannistraro, P.V. (ed.), *Historical Dictionary of Fascist Italy* (Westport, 1982), pp.339–40.

34 For this (p.161) and numerous other government orders to the press see Flora, F. (ed.), *Ritratto di un Ventennio: Stampa dell'Era Fascista* (Bologna, 1972). On government control of the press see Castronovo, V. and Tranfaglia, N. (eds), *La Stampa Italiana nell'Età Fascista* (Bari, 1980), pp.33–91.

35 See Ajello, N., 'Quando naquero le veline', *La Repubblica*, 1 May 2007, p.49.

36 For radio under the regime see Monteleone, F., *La Radio nel Periodo Fascista: Studi e Documenti 1922–1945* (Venezia, 1975); Isola, G., *Abbassa la Tua Radio per Favore… Storia dell'Ascolto Radiofonico dell'Italia Fascista* (Firenze, 1990).

37 Anderson, B., *Imagined Communities: Reflections on the Origin and Spread of Nationalism* (revised edition) (London, 1983), pp.45–6.

38 'Le direttive per la stampa', *Il Littoriale*, 11 October 1928, p.1.

39 Anderson: *Imagined Communities*, pp.45–6.

40 Macellari: *Sport e Potenza*, p.15.

41 'Mussolini, primo sportivo d'Italia', *Lo Sport Fascista*, VI, 1933, p.1.

42 Cotronei: *Atleti e Eroi*, p.12.

43 Macellari: *Sport e Potenza*, p.43.

44 AA.VV., *Mussolini e lo Sport* (Mantova, 1928), p.8.

45 'I calciatori italiani', *Il Popolo d'Italia*, 28 March 1928, p.3.

46 Bardi, P.M., *La Strada e il Volante* (Roma, 1936), p.126.

47 Hoberman, J., *Sport and Political Ideology* (Austin, 1984), pp.58–63.

48 See MINCULPOP order 28 July 1939 in Flora: *Ritratto di un Ventennio*, p.126 and 'Il Duce Sportivo', in AA.VV: *Lo Sport in Regime Fascista*, p.9.

49 AA.VV: *Lo Sport in Regime Fascista*, p.169.

50 Published in Lolli, L., *I Mondiali in Camicia Nera, 1934–38* (Roma, 1990).

51   Lanfranchi, P., 'Bologna: "The team that shook the world"', *International Journal of the History of Sport*, 8, 3 (1981), pp.336–46.

52   For detailed analysis of the takeover and restructure of football see, Martin: *Football and Fascism.*

53   For a short description of Arpinati's career in sport see Martin: *Football and Fascism*, pp.110–16.

54   'Epurare lo Sport', *Il Bargello*, 15 December 1929, p.2.

55   Pozzo, V., *Campioni del Mondo: Quarant'anni di Storia del Calcio Italiano* (Roma, 1960), p.10.

56   '"Per la bandiera"', *La Gazzetta*, 20 June 1938, p.1.

57   These players were the Uraguayans Orsi, Guaita, Cesarini, Monti, and the Brazilian Filo.

58   '32 Stati (ma saranno anche di più...) in lotta pei Campionati Mondiali di calcio', *Lo Sport Fascista*, 12, 1933, p.23.

59   Bianda, R., Leone, G., Rossi, G. and Urso, A., *Atleti in Camicia Nera: Lo Sport nell'Italia di Mussolini* (Roma, 1983), p.187.

60   'Il trionfo italiano nel Campionato mondiale di calcio', *Il Resto del Carlino*, 12 June 1934, p.4.

61   Gordon, R.S.C. and London, J., 'Italy 1934', in A. Tomlinson and C. Young, *National Identity and Global Sports Events. Culture, Politics, and Spectacle and the Football World Cup* (New York, 2006), p.43.

62   Papa, A. and Panico, G., *Storia Sociale del Calcio in Italia: Dai Club dei Pionieri alla Nazione Sportiva (1887–1945)* (Bologna, 1993), p.197.

63   See, 'Gli "azzurri" in Francia', *La Gazzetta*, 4 June 1938, p.5; 'Marsiglia avvampa d'entusiasmo per l'odierno duello italo-norvegese', *La Gazzetta*, 5–6 June 1938, p.5.

64   For other examples of anti-Fascist/Italian protests in France and the deteriorating relations between the respective countries, see Archivio del Ministero degli Affari Esteri (AdMAdE), AP, 1931–45 Francia, Busta 33/4, 'Rapporti Politici'.

65   Pozzo: *Campioni del Mondo*, p.266.

66   Ponzio, A., *La Palestra del Littorio. L'Accademia della Farnesina: un'Esperimento di Pedagogia Totalitarian nell'Italia Fascista* (Milano, 2009), p.12.

67   On Farnesina and physical education see Ponzio: *La Palestra del Littorio*; Bianda, Leone, Rossi, Urso: *Atleti in Camicia Nera*, pp.67–82; Martin: *Football and Fascism*, pp.32–40 and 93–4.

68   See, Ferrara, P., 'La "donna nuova" del fascismo e lo sport', in M. Canella and S. Giuntini (eds), *Sport e Fascismo* (Milano, 2009); Gori, G., *Italian Fascism and the Female Body* (London, 2004), pp.127–39.

69   Teja, A., 'Ondina e le Altre', *Zapruder. Rivista di Storia della Conflittualità Sociale*, May–August (2004), p.10.

70   AA.VV: *Almanacco della Donna Italiana*, p.298.

71 'Il mondo ci guarda', *La Gazzetta*, 2 November 1917, p.1.

72 'Note d'un profano', *La Gazzetta*, 11 May 1924, p.1.

73 'Note d'un profano', *La Gazzetta*, 14 May 1924, p.1.

74 Forgacs, D. and Gundle, S., *Mass Culture and Italian Society from Fascism to the Cold War* (Bloomington, 2007), p.81.

75 'Mentre Zanaga fugge...', *La Gazzetta*, 17 May 1921, p.4.

76 Facchinetti, *Gli Anni Ruggenti di Alfonsina Strada* (Portogruaro, 2004), p.78.

77 The Giro d'Italia winner's prize money from 1923 to 26, quoted as 100,000 lire, in Marchesini: *L'Italia del Giro d'Italia*, p.182.

78 'Note d'un profano', *La Gazzetta*, 14 May 24, p.1.

79 Saba, M.A. and Frasca Isidori, R., 'L'angelo della palestra', *Lancillotto e Nausica*, 1 (1986), p.60.

80 'Cronaca Contemporanea', *Civiltà Cattolica*, 2 (1928), pp.367–72.

81 Bianda, Leone, Rossi, Urso: *Atleti in Camicia Nera*, p.59.

82 Gedda, L., *Lo Sport* (Milano, 1931), pp.86–7.

83 Teja: 'Ondina e le Altre', p.18.

84 'Per voi, donne italiane, che non nuotate...', *Lo Sport Fascista*, II, 4, 1929, p.37.

85 'Per voi, donne italiane, che non nuotate...': *Lo Sport Fascista*, p.37.

86 'Basi e sviluppo dell'atletica femminile', *Lo Sport Fascista*, II, 7, 1929, pp.70–1.

87 'La donna e l'atletismo', *L'Osservatore Romano*, 16 May 1934, p.3.

88 'Sport e maternità', *Lo Sport Fascista*, II, 7, 1929, p.73.

89 'Mille di queste Mille Miglia', *Lo Sport Fascista*, II, 6, 1929, p.64.

90 Ferrara: 'La "donna nuova" del fascismo e lo sport', p.224.

91 'La signora del secolo scorso', *La Repubblica*, 17 October 2006, p.59.

92 Artom, S. and Calabrò, A.R., *Sorelle d'Italia: Quattordici Grandi Signore Raccontano la Loro (e la Nostra) Storia* (Milano, 1989), p.279.

93 'Nuovi aspetti dello sport femminile', *Lo Sport Fascista*, II, 7, 1930, p.54.

94 Teja: 'Ondina e le altre', pp.20–1.

95 'Sport e ginnastica per la salute e la bellezza della donna', *Lo Sport Fascista*, XII, 9, 1939, p.59.

96 Poggi-Longostrevi, G., *Medicina Sportiva* (Milano, 1940), p.100.

97 'Il fenomeno Carnera', *Lo Sport Fascista*, III, 12, 1930, p.5.

98 AA.VV: *Mussolini e lo Sport*, p.36.

99 'Carnera campione del mondo', *L'Illustrazione Italiana*, 9 July 1933, p.70.

100 Santini, A., *Primo Carnera: L'Uomo Più Forte del Mondo* (Milano, 2004), p.106.

101 'Il gigante e il divo', *Corriere della Sera*, 13 June 1934, p.4.

102 Santini: *Primo Carnera*, p.116.

103 'Intorno al ring di Piazza di Siena', *La Gazzetta*, 23 October 1932, p.2.

104 'Nella battaglia la celebrazione', *La Gazzetta*, 21–22 October 1933, p.1.

105 Valeri, M., *Nero di Roma: Storia di Leone Jacovacci l'Invincibile Mulatto Italiano* (Roma, 2008).

106 'Il Vinto', *La Gazzetta*, 25 June 1928, p.1.

107 'La discussa vittoria', *La Gazzetta*, 26 June 1928, p.1.

108 'Jacovacci, pugilatore imperfetto', *Lo Sport Fascista*, II, 1, 1929, p.83.

109 Flora: *Ritratto di un Ventennio*, p.140.

110 *La Gazzetta*, 24 September 1935, p.1.

111 'La F.P.I. inibisce a Carnera di combattere all'estero', *La Gazzetta*, 14 December 1937, p.1.

112 For descriptions of the idealized sporting Italian see Cotronei: *Atleti e Eroi*, pp.88–89; 94; 140; 257.

113 'Carnera non è più italiano', *Corriere della Sera*, 6 December 1929, p.4.

114 Santini: *Primo Carnera*, pp.27–28.

115 '"Esempi e idee per l'Italiano nuovo". L'eroe sportivo', *Lo Sport Fascista*, III, 5, 1930, p.47.

116 'Giochi olimpici ai tempi dell'Eliade e ai nostri', *La Stampa*, 18 April 1923, p.3.

117 'Come si organizza la "Mille Miglia"', *Lo Sport Fascista*, III, 6, 1930, p.32.

118 Following his demise in Sicily's 'Targa Florio', Giulio Masetti was declared a 'sporting hero' and perfect example of the 'new man'. '"Esempi e idee per l'Italiano nuovo"...', *Lo Sport Fascista*, p.48.

119 De Martino, E., *Mille Miglia* (Milano, 1940), p.176.

120 De Martino: *Mille Miglia*, p.188.

121 'Camicie nere. Tazio Nuvolari', *Il Popolo d'Italia*, 28 March 1928, p.3.

122 Marchesini, D., *Cuori e Motori: Storia della Mille Miglia 1927–1957* (Bologna, 2001), p.81.

123 'Automobilismo 1934–6', *Lo Sport Fascista*, III, 11, 1933, p.15.

124 'Borzacchini e Campari caduti per la causa dello sport', *Lo Sport Fascista*, III, 9, 1933, p.36.

125 Marchesini: *Cuori e Motori*, p.81.

126 '"Esempi e idee per l'Italiano nuovo"....', *Lo Sport Fascista*, p.48.

127 'Il Sindacato dei corridori automobilisti', *Lo Sport Fascista*, II, 3, 1929, p.52.

128 'La gemma che mancava', *La Gazzetta*, 9 April 1934, p.1.

129 Bardi: *La Strada e il Volante*, p.137. The Bonifiche were reclaimed marshes south of Rome that had been turned over to agriculture and new towns such as Sabaudia and Latina.

130 'L'opera del touring club italiano', *Lo Sport Fascista*, I, 4, 1928, p.41.

131 Bardi: *La Strada e il Volante*, p.123.

132 'L'opinione del Duce: l'automobile garanzia sociale', *Lo Sport Fascista*, I, 1, 1928, p.105.

133 'L'opinione del Duce', *Lo Sport Fascista*, p.105.

134 Bardi: *La Strada e il Volante*, p.129.

135 Marchesini: *Cuori e Motori*, p.109.

136 'Le corse d'una volta e quella d'adesso', *Lo Sport Fascista*, III, 6, 1930, p.33.

Chapter 4

1   'Sport Armato', *La Gazzetta*, 12 June 1940, p.1.

2   Mack Smith, D., *Modern Italy: A Political History* (New Haven, 1997), p.400.

3   'Il Tamburin Maggiore', *La Gazzetta*, 10 June 1940, p.1.

4   Ferretti, L., *Lo Sport* (Roma, 1949), p.339.

5   'Danao, il "millionario biondo" vince a San Siro il premio Monte Rosa', *La Gazzetta*, 26 July 1943, p.1.

6   Lepre, A., *La Storia della Prima Repubblica: L'Italia dal 1943 al 2003* (Bologna, 2004), pp.8–9.

7   'Lo sport per la Patria', *La Gazzetta*, 28 August 1943, p.1.

8   Lepre: *La Storia della Prima Repubblica*, p.12.

9   Lepre: *La Storia della Prima Repubblica*, p.37.

10   National Committee for the Liberation of Upper Italy (*Comitato di Liberazione per l'Alta Italia* – CLNAA) in the north and the Committee of National Liberation (*Comitato di Liberazione Nazionale* – CLN) in the south.

11   For concise analyses of PCI and DC strategies in this period see Ginsborg, P., *A History of Contemporary Italy: Society and Politics 1943–1988* (London, 1990), pp.42–52.

12   Pennacchia, M., *Il Calcio in Italia* (Torino, 1999), p.240.

13   Jones, W.R., *Un Programme di Educazione Fisica ad Uso dei Prigionieri di Guerra* (Locarno, 1942).

14   Papa, A. and Panico, G., *Storia Sociale del Calcio in Italia: Dai Club dei Pionieri alla Nazione Sportiva (1887–1945)* (Bologna, 1993), p.238.

15   Ginsborg: *A History of Contemporary Italy*, p.90.

16   Ginsborg: *A History of Contemporary Italy*, p.98.

17   Doglio, C., 'Lo sport in Italia', *Comunità. Rivista Trimestrale del Movimento Comunità*, VI, 13, January (1952), pp.22–31.

18   'Voti dei "reggenti" romani per uno sport nazionale e unitario', *La Gazzetta*, 20 July 1945, p.1.

19   Stadiums; income; physical education and sport; rules; funding and Allied relations.

20   'Lo straordinario Giulio. Quando un commissario diventa presidente, *Lancillotto e Nausica*', *Storia Critica dello Sport*, 2 (1986), p.73.

21   Teja, A. and Giuntini, S., *L'Addestramento Ginnico-Militare nell'Esercito Italiano (1946–1990)* (Roma, 2007), pp.19–22.

22   For Onesti's account of the measures taken see 'Lo straordinario Giulio...', *Lancillotto e Nausica*, pp.72–5.

23   Ferretti: *Lo Sport*, p.378.

24   For more details see Ginsborg: *A History of Contemporary Italy*, pp.92–3; Lepre: *Storia della Prima Repubblica*, pp.29–30.

25   'Un buon passo avanti', *La Gazzetta*, 27 July 1945, p.1.

26 'Cosa dovrà fare il CONI?', *La Gazzetta*, 20 August 1945, p.1.

27 'Un buon passo avanti': *La Gazzetta*, p.1.

28 'In alto mare e senza bussola', *La Gazzetta*, 9 October 1945, p.1.

29 'Lo sport agli sportivi', *Il Ginnasta*, 12, 30 June 1947, p.147.

30 Provvisionato, S., 'Invece di una liquidazione', *Lancillotto e Nausica. Storia Critica dello Sport*, III, 2, 1986, p.44.

31 Giuntini, S., *Pugni Chiusi e Cerchi Olimpici: Il lungo '68 dello Sport Italiano* (Roma, 2008), p.94.

32 Lombardo, A., 'Nuoto', in A. Lombardo, *Storia degli Sport in Italia, 1861–1960* (Cassino, 2004), p.249.

33 Fabrizio, F., *Storia dello Sport in Italia: Dalle Società Ginnastiche all'Associazionismo di Massa* (Firenze, 1978), p.173.

34 Ferrara, P., *L'Italia in Palestra: Storia, Documenti e Immagini della Ginnastica dal 1833 al 1973* (Roma, 1992), p.299.

35 Taken from a display of a Montante bike, Palermo airport, April 2009.

36 Brera, G., *Storia Critica del Calcio Italiano* (Milano, 1998), pp.193–4.

37 'Il trionfo di Villoresi', *La Gazzetta*, 24 April 1946, p.1.

38 Papa, A. and Panico, G., *Storia Sociale del Calcio in Italia: Dai Campionati del Dopoguerra alla Champions League (1945–2000)* (Bologna, 2000), p.13.

39 Papa and Panico: *Storia Sociale del Calcio in Italia... (1945–2000)*, pp.38–9.

40 'Vittorie nostre', *La Gazzetta*, 24 April 1946, p.1.

41 'Cosa dovrà fare il CONI?', *La Gazzetta*, 20 August 1945, p.1.

42 Bassetti, R., *Storia e Storie dello Sport in Italia: Dall'Unità a Oggi* (Venezia, 1999), p.133.

43 Papa and Panico: *Storia Sociale del Calcio in Italia... (1945–2000)*, p.16.

44 Quoted in Teja and Giuntini: *L'Addestramento Ginnico-Militare nell'Esercito Italiano*, p.23, note 139.

45 Marchesini, D., *L'Italia del Giro d'Italia* (Bologna, 1996), p.196.

46 Doglio: 'Lo sport in Italia', p.28.

47 'Si parla del "Giro"', *La Gazzetta*, 25 October 1945, p.1.

48 Marchesini: *L'Italia del Giro d'Italia*, p.186.

49 'Commozione profonda', *La Gazzetta*, 16 June 1946, p.1.

50 'Per tutti gli italiani', *La Gazzetta*, 18 June 1946, p.1.

51 Buzzati, D., *Dino Buzzati al Giro d'Italia* (Milano, 1981), p.35.

52 Ginsborg: *A History of Contemporary Italy*, p.79.

53 Arceri: 'Basket', in Lombardo: *Storia degli Sport in Italia*, p.65.

54 Arceri: 'Basket', in Lombardo: *Storia degli Sport in Italia*, p.79.

55 Known as the Foibe massacres after the deep pits into which the bodies were thrown, the incident was used as propaganda during the Cold War with the numbers of victims often exaggerated.

56 'Problemi e questioni sportive in terra irredenta', *La Gazzetta*, 5 May 1926, p.5.

57 Foot, J., *Calcio: A History of Italian Football* (London, 2006), p.359.

58   Pennacchia: *Il Calcio in Italia*, Vol. 1, pp.247–8.

59   Foot: *Calcio*, pp.360–1.

60   Reilly, E.J. (ed.), *Across the Diamond: Baseball and American Culture* (New York, 2003), pp.117–18. (From 1954–70, documents in the Bureau of Educational and Cultural Affairs (CU) History Office Collection at the University of Arkansas, Fayetteville, include tour reports and photographs of various college teams.)

61   'La promessa mantenuta', *La Gazzetta*, 1 July 1946, p.1.

62   'Commozione Profonda', *La Gazzetta*, 16 May 1946, p.1.

63   Facchinetti, P., *Quando Spararono al Giro d'Italia* (Arezzo, 2006), p.74.

64   'La promessa mantenuta', *La Gazzetta*, p.1.

65   Facchinetti: *Quando spararono al Giro d'Italia*, p.83.

66   'Al popolo italiano "la corsa del popolo", *La Gazzetta*, 8 July 1946, p.1.

67   'Per tutti gli italiani', *La Gazzetta*, 18 June 1946, p.1.

68   'Al popolo Italiano...', *La Gazzetta*, p.1.

69   Pio XII, *Discorsi e Radiomessaggi di Sua Santità Pio XII – Vol. VIII* (Roma, 1947), p.131.

70   Lepre: *Storia della Prima Repubblica*, p.18.

71   See, Sala, T., 'Un'offerta di collaborazione dell'ACI al governo Badoglio...', *Rivista di Storia Contemporanea*, IV (1972), pp.517–33.

72   Fabrizio: *Storia dello Sport in Italia*, pp.133–4; McCarthy, P., 'The Church in postwar Italy', in P. McCarthy (ed.), *Italy since 1945* (Oxford, 2000) p.136.

73   Pivato, S., 'Strumenti dell'egemonia cattolica', in S. Soldani e G. Turi (eds), *Fare gli Italiani: Scuola e Cultura nell'Italia Contemporanea. II. Una Società di Massa* (Bologna, 1993), p.381.

74   McCarthy: 'The Church in postwar Italy', p.136.

75   Pio XII, 'Il contributo della cultura fisica per la elevazione della gioventù', in Pio XII, *Discorsi e Radiomessaggi di Sua Santità Pio XII, Vol. VII* (Milano, 1946), p.60.

76   Gedda, L., *DIECI ANNI al Servizio dello Sport* (Roma, 1954), p.6.

77   Fabrizio: *Storia dello Sport in Italia*, p.141.

78   Fabrizio: *Storia dello Sport in Italia*, p.142.

79   Pio XII, 'Il contributo della cultura fisica per la elevazione della gioventù', in Pio XII: *Discorsi e Radiomessaggi... Vol VII*, pp.57–8 and 61.

80   On the left and mass culture see Gundle, S., *Between Hollywood and Moscow: The Italian Communists and the Challenge of Mass Culture, 1943–1991* (London, 2000).

81   Giuntini: *Pugni Chiusi e Cerchi Olimpici*, p.158.

82   Ginsborg: *A History of Contemporary Italy*, pp.104–5.

83   Ben-Ghiatt, R., 'The Italian cinema and the Italian working class', *International Labor and Working-Class History*, 59, Spring (2001), p.41.

84   Fabrizio: *Storia dello Sport in Italia*, p.155.

85   Fabrizio: *Storia dello Sport in Italia*, pp.156–7.

86   Ginsborg, P., *Italy and its Discontents: Family, Civil Society, State, 1980–2001* (London, 2001), pp.103–4.

87 'Coppi e Bartali: le due Italie di Curzio Malaparte', reprinted in *Corriere della Sera*, 12 May 2009, pp.38–9.

88 'Coppi e Bartali', *Corriere della Sera*, pp.38–9.

89 Marchesini: *L'Italia del Giro d'Italia*, pp.206–7.

90 *Stadium: Quindicinale del Centro Sportivo Italiano*, 7–8, October–November (1947).

91 Pratt, J., 'Catholic Culture', in D. Forgacs and R. Lumley (eds), *Italian Cultural Studies: An Introduction* (Oxford, 1996), p.135.

92 Pio was a Capuchin priest who received stigmata corresponding to the crucifixion wounds of Christ and experienced various supernatural phenomena throughout his lifetime. He was made a Saint on 16 June 2002.

93 Pratolini, V., *Cronache dal Giro d'Italia (Maggio-Giugno 1947)* (Milano, 1992), p.90.

94 Pivato: 'Sport', p.177.

95 For examples see Pratt: 'Catholic culture', p.135; McCarthy: 'The Church in postwar Italy', p.140.

96 'Discorso di S.S. Pio XII agli uomini di Azione Cattolica (7 settembre 1947)', *La Civiltà Cattolica*, 98, III, 1947, p.553.

97 Mack Smith: *Modern Italy*, p.437.

98 Lepre: *Storia della Prima Repubblica*, p.108.

99 Gozzini, G., 'L'attentato a Togliatti', in M. Isnenghi (ed.), *I luoghi della Memoria: Strutture ed Eventi dell'Italia Unita* (Bari, 1997), p.467.

100 Marchesini, D., *Coppi e Bartali* (Bologna, 1998), p.92; Turrini, T., *Bartali: L'Uomo che Salvò l'Italia Pedalando* (Milano, 2004), p.92.

101 Doglio: 'Lo sport in Italia', p.27.

102 Gozzini: 'L'attentato a Togliatti', p.477.

103 Pivato, S., *Clericalismo e Laicismo nella Cultura Popolare Italiana* (Milano, 1990), p.247.

104 Bertolotti, D., 'Bartali ha battuto Di Vittorio', *Gioventù*, 1 August 1948, in S. Pivato, *Sia Lodato Bartali: Ideologia, Cultura e Miti dello Sport Cattolico (1936/1948)* (Roma, 1996), p.129.

105 Pivato, S., 'Strumenti dell'egemonia cattolica', in Soldani and Turi (eds) *Fare gli Italiani... II*, p.386.

106 'Villari: nessuno allora seppe della telefonata che "salvo" il Paese', *Corriere della Sera*, 22 March 2006, p.43.

107 Goggioli, G., *I Grandi Campioni del Ciclismo Italiano* (Firenze, 1951), pp.82–4.

108 For an account of the 'passing of the bottle' see Marchesini: *Coppi e Bartali*, pp.106–10; Castelnoci, G., 'Un episodio quotidiano ormai diventato storia', *La Gazzetta*, 10 February 1993, p.22.

109 Turrini: *Bartali*, p.189.

110 For a full account see Manna A. and Gibbs, M., *The Day Italian Football Died: Torino and the Tragedy of Superga* (Derby, 2000); Foot: *Calcio*, pp.86–91.

111 Foot: *Calcio*, pp.86–91.

112 Foot: *Calcio*, p.90.

113 Foot: *Calcio*, p.95.

114 *La Gazzetta*, 5 May 1949, p.1.

115 Doglio: 'Lo sport in Italia', p.27.

116 Foot: *Calcio*, p.160.

117 Foot: *Calcio*, p.538

118 'Spalle nude di donna in una disputata alla Camera', *La Stampa*, 15 November 1950, p.1.

119 'Spalle nude di donna in una disputata alla Camera', *La Stampa*, p.1.

120 'Spalle nude di donna in una disputata alla Camera', *La Stampa*, p.1.

121 See Pinkus, K., *The Montesi Scandal: The Death of Wilma Montesi and the Birth of the Paparazzi in Fellini's Rome* (Chicago, 2003).

122 'La Turca desnuda', *L'Espresso*, 6 August 1998, pp.70–5.

123 Gorressio, V., 'Durante e dopo il boom: Sesso matrimonio famiglia', *I Problemi di Ulisse. Rivista di Cultura Internazionale*, XIV, 83–7 (1979), pp.33–4.

124 Gorressio: 'Durante e dopo il boom', p.35.

125 'Coppi uomo e atleta', *Stadium: Rassegna Mensile Illustrato di tutti gli Sport*, IV, 11, November (1949), p.6.

126 Marchesini: *Coppi e Bartali*, p.95.

127 Pivato: 'Sport', p.176.

128 Calabrese, O. (ed.), *Italia Moderna, Volume Terzo, 1939–1960: Guerra, Dopoguerra, Ricostruzione, Decollo* (Milano, 1984), p.309.

129 'Condannati con la condizionale...', *Corriere della Sera*, 15 March 1955, p.5.

130 'Fausto Coppi spiega in Tribunale perchè si allontanò dalla sua famiglia', *Corriere della Sera*, 13 March 1955, p.7.

131 'Fausto Coppi spiega in Tribunale...', *Corriere della Sera*, p.7.

132 'Fausto Coppi spiega in Tribunale...', *Corriere della Sera*, p.7.

133 Gorressio: 'Durante e dopo il boom', pp.36.

134 Stella, G.A., 'Coppi, il grande Airone che ha diviso il Paese', *Corriere della Sera*, 2 January 2010.

135 *La Gazzetta*, 7 January 1993, p.1.

136 On this topic see Seymour, M., *Debating Divorce in Italy: Marriage and the Making of Modern Italians, 1860–1974* (Basingstoke, 2006).

137 '2 Gennaio: Un anno fa moriva Coppi', *La Gazzetta*, 1 January 1961, p.9.

Chapter 5

1 Pennacchia, M., *Il Calcio in Italia*, Vol I (Torino, 1999), p.260.

2 Papa, A. and Panico, G., *Storia Sociale del Calcio in Italia: Dai Campionati del Dopoguerra alla Champions League (1945–2000)* (Bologna, 2000), p.22.

3 Pennacchia, *Il Calcio in Italia*, p.216.

4   Pennacchia: *Il Calcio in Italia*, p.217.

5   Imbucci, G., *Il Gioco: Lotto, Totocalcio, Lotterie. Storia dei Comportamenti Sociali* (Venezia, 1997), p.69.

6   Pivato, S., 'Sport', in P. McCarthy, *Italy since 1945* (Oxford, 2000), p.179.

7   Ginsborg, P., *A History of Contemporary Italy: Society and Politics 1943–1988* (London, 1990), p.210.

8   Ginsborg: *A History of Contemporary Italy*, p.214.

9   On consumption in this period see Livolsi, M. (ed.), *Il Consumo Culturale* (Padova, 1982); Sassatelli, R., *Consumo, Cultura e Società* (Bologna, 2004); Scarpellini, E., *L'Italia dei Consumi: Dalla Belle Epoque al Nuovo Millennio* (Bari, 2008); Scrivano, P., 'Signs of Americanization in Italian domestic life: Italy's postwar conversion to consumerism', *Journal of Contemporary History*, 40, 2 (2005), pp.317–40.

10   Calabrese, O., 'L'Italia di massa: prodotti e comportamenti collettivi nell'era del "boom" economico', O. Calabrese (ed.), *Italia Moderna, Volume terzo, 1939–1960: Guerra, Dopoguerra, Ricostruzione, Decollo* (Milano, 1984), p.467.

11   Ginsborg: *A History of Contemporary Italy*, p.239.

12   For further analyses of this period see Salvati, M., *Economia e Politica in Italia dal Dopoguerra ad Oggi* (Milano, Garzanti), 1984; Sassoon, D., *Contemporary Italy: Economy, Society and Politics since 1945* (London, 1986).

13   Ginsborg: *A History of Contemporary Italy*, p.240.

14   Castronovo, V., 'Premesse e attuazione del miracolo', in Calabrese: *Italia Moderna*, p.275.

15   On the launch of television and its early years see Chiarenza, A., *Il Cavallo Morente* (Milano, 1979); Colombo, F., 'La nascita della televisione', Calabrese: *Italia Moderna*, pp.485–504.

16   Severgnini, B., *La Bella Figura: A Field Guide to the Italian Mind* (New York, 2006), p.76.

17   Ginsborg: *A History of Contemporary Italy*, p.221–2.

18   Pivato: 'Sport', p.178.

19   Pivato: 'Sport', p.178.

20   Ginsborg: *A History of Contemporary Italy*, p.248.

21   Lepre, A., *La Storia della Prima Repubblica: L'Italia dal 1943 al 2003* (Bologna, 2004), p.148.

22   Livolsi, M., 'Behind the myth of the vespa', in O. Calabrese (ed.), *Italian Style: Forms of Creativity* (Milano, 1998), p.15.

23   Brandt, T., 'La Vespa negli Stati Uniti: il trasporto culturale di una merce italiana', *Memoria e Ricerca*, 23 (2006), p.131.

24   Livolsi: 'Behind the myth of the vespa', pp.28–9.

25   Fauri, F., 'The role of Fiat in the development of the Italian car industry in the 1950's', *The Business History Review*, 70, 2 (1996), pp.167–206.

26   Calabrese, O., 'The Italian utility car', Calabrese: *Italian Style*, p.78.

27   Scarpellini: *L'Italia dei Consumi*, p.143.

28   Dallaglio, M., 'La Riviera romagnola: un caso di sviluppo economico tra modelli elitari e turismo di massa', in R. Finzi (ed.), *Storia d'Italia: Le Regioni dall'Unità a Oggi. L'Emilia-Romagna* (Torino, 1997), p.467.

29   Calabrese: 'The Italian utility car', p.80.

30   Fante, J., *Tesoro, qui è Tutto una Follia: Lettere dall'Europa (1957–1960)* (Roma, 1999), p.22. From letter written in Naples 9 August 1957, the last year that the Mille Miglia was run.

31   Fante: *Tesoro, qui è Tutto una Follia*, p.22.

32   Abruzzese, A., 'Man and Machines', Calabrese: *Italian Style*, p.88.

33   Abruzzese, 'Man and Machines', Calabrese: *Italian Style*, p.89.

34   Williams, R., *Enzo Ferrari: A Life* (London, 2002), pp.175–6.

35   'Chi dice che il 13 porta sfortuna?', *La Gazzetta*, 13 May 1957, p.10.

36   'La scomparsa di De Portago', *La Gazzetta*, 13 May 1957, p.10.

37   'La settimana sportiva', *L'Osservatore Romano*, 7–8 July 1958, p.6.

38   Enzo Ferrari died on 14 August 1988 and FIAT took an immediate 90 per cent share of the company.

39   Forgacs, D., *Italian Culture in the Industrial Era 1880–1980: Cultural Industries, Politics and the Public* (Manchester, 1990), p.114.

40   See Foot, J., *Calcio: A History of Italian Football* (London, 2006), p.447.

41   Calabrese: *Italia Moderna*, p.529.

42   'Ungheria batte Italia 3–0', *L'Unità*, 18 May 1953, p.1.

43   'In centomila hanno applaudito la clamorosa vittoria ungherese', *L'Unità*, 18 May 1953, p.5.

44   Foot: *Calcio*, p.448.

45   Details of the various fights are covered in Foot: *Calcio*, 449–53; Ghirelli, A., *Storia del Calcio in Italia* (Torino, 1990), pp.264–5; Notarnicola, V., 'La grande corrida', *L'Europeo*, 2, April (2002), pp.76–80; Ormezzano, G.P., *Storia del Calcio* (Milano, 1986), p.138.

46   Foot: *Calcio*, p.458.

47   Papa and Panico: *Storia Sociale del Calcio in Italia... (1945–2000)*, p.48.

48   Allum, P., *Potere e Società a Napoli nel Dopoguerra* (Torino, 1975), pp.387–8.

49   Papa and Panico: *Storia Sociale del Calcio in Italia... (1945–2000)*, p.45.

50   Kühne, I., *Napoli Passione Mia* (Roma, 1985), p.38.

51   Milza, P., 'Il football italiano. Una storia lunga un secolo', *Italia Contemporanea*, 183, June (1991), p.254.

52   Wagstaff, C., 'Cinema', D. Forgacs and R. Lumley (eds), *Italian Cultural Studies: An Introduction* (Oxford, 1996), p.220.

53   Giving the Italian film industry control over the distribution of imports, the law enraged major Hollywood companies with their own distribution operations. Their subsequent withdrawal left a gap in the Italian market that was filled by domestic productions.

54   Forgacs: *Italian Culture in the Industrial Era*, p.116.

55   Forgacs: *Italian Culture in the Industrial Era*, p.121.

56   Nowell-Smith, G., *The Companion to Italian Cinema* (London, 1996), pp.4–5.

57   Gordon, R., *Bicycle Thieves* (London, 2008); Nowell-Smith: *The Companion to Italian Cinema*; Rohdie, S., *Rocco and his Brothers* (London, 2002).

58   Ben-Ghiatt, R., 'The Italian cinema and the Italian working class', *International Labor and Working-Class History*, 59, Spring (2002), p.43.

59   Wagstaff, C., 'Comic positions', *Sight and Sound*, 25, 7 (1992), p.27.

60   West, M., 'Holding hands with a bicycle thief', in H. Curle and S. Snyder (eds), *Vittorio De Sica: Contemporary Perspectives* (Toronto, 2000), p.146.

61   Wagstaff: 'Comic Positions', p.27.

62   Foot, J., 'Milan and Visconti's Rocco and his brothers', *Journal of Modern Italian Studies*, 2 (1999), p.211.

63   Ginsborg: *A History of Contemporary Italy*, p.222.

64   Miller, D.A., 'Rocco and his brothers', *Film Quarterly*, Fall 2008, p.14.

65   For a detailed description of Rome's various attempts to bid for the Games see Zauli, B., 'Roma finalmente Olimpica', *Lancillotto e Nausica: Storia Critica dello Sport*, 2 (1986), pp.76–9.

66   Provvisionato, S., 'Invece di una liquidazione', *Lancillotto e Nausica: Storia Critica dello Sport*, 2 (1986), p.46.

67   See Martin, S., 'Bikila's Aria: Rome 1960', in Tomlinson, A., Young, C. and Holt, R. (eds), *Sport and the Transformation of Modern Europe: States, Media and Markets 1950–2010* (London, 2011).

68   Kirk, T., *The Architecture of Modern Italy, Volume II: Visions of Utopia 1900–Present* (New York, 2005), pp.196–7.

69   The velodrome was demolished in 2008 due to inactivity and the need for costly structural works.

70   For the full debate see Camera dei Deputati, Seduta 6 Ottobre 1959, in *Atti Parlamentari dell'Assemblea, Anno 1959, III Legislatura, Discussioni* (Roma, 1960), pp.10612–18.

71   Modrey, E.M., 'Architecture as a mode of self representation at the Olympic Games in Rome (1960) and Munich (1972)', *European Review of History – Revue Européenne d'Histoire*, 15, 6 (2008), p.701.

72   Maraniss, D., *Rome 1960: The Olympics that Changed the World* (New York, 2008), p.29.

73   'Suore, preti e giovani di A.C. all'assalto degli olimpionici', *L'Unità*, 31 August 1960, p.10.

74   Maraniss: *Rome 1960*, p.375.

75   Cori, A., *Il Cinema di Romolo Marcellini: Tra Storia e Società dal Colonialismo agli Anni '70* (Recco, 2009).

76   Organizing Committee of the Games of the XVII Olympiad, *The Games of the XVII Olympiad. Rome 1960. The Official Report of the Organizing Committee, Volume One*, 1960, p.650.

77 Organizing Committee of the Games of the XVII Olympiad: *The Games of the XVII Olympiad*, p.199.

78 Organizing Committee of the Games of the XVII Olympiad, *The Games of the XVII Olympiad*, p.201.

79 The oldest bridge in Rome, built in 109 BC, the *Pons Milvius* had always served as the principal access to the city from the north and the *Via Flaminia*. It was here, in 312, that Constantine defeated Maxentius, paving the way for the Christianization of the Roman Empire.

80 Teja, A., 'Sport al Femimnile', in A. Lombardo (ed.), *Storia degli Sport in Italia, 1861–1960* (Cassino, 2004), p.324.

81 'Il successo dei Giochi di Roma in una intervista con Onesti', *Corriere della Sera*, 13 September 1960, p.13.

82 Bassetti, R., *Storia e Storie dello Sport in Italia: Dall'Unità a Oggi* (Venezia, 1999), p.172.

83 Bassetti: *Storia e Storie dello Sport*, p.174.

84 The obelisk was finally returned to Axum in 2005 and reopened in 2008.

85 'Un abissino dai piedi scalzi ha reincarnate Filippide', *Corriere della Sera*, 11 September 1960, p.14.

86 Marking the 50th anniversary of Bikila's win, the 2010 Rome marathon was dedicated to his memory. Fittingly, Ethiopia claimed a men's and women's double, with Ethiopian women finishing first, second and third. The men's race winner, Siraj Gena, also collected a €5,000 bonus for completing the last 300 metres barefoot.

87 'The editor speaks from Rome', *World Sports: Official Magazine of the British Olympic Association*, October (1960), p.27.

88 C. Levi, quoted in DVD of the Rome 1960 Games, CONI/LUCE, *La Grande Olimpiade*, 2001.

89 Pivato: 'Sport', p.179.

90 Bassetti: *Storia e Storie dello Sport*, p.177.

Chapter 6

1 Foot, J., *Calcio: A History of Italian Football* (London, 2006), p.214.

2 Papa, A. and Panico, G., *Storia Sociale del Calcio in Italia: Dai Campionati del Dopoguerra alla Champions League (1945–2000)* (Bologna, 2000), pp.87–8.

3 Dal Lago, A. and De Biasi, R., 'Italian football fans. Culture and organisation', in R. Giulianotti, N. Bonney and M. Hepworth (eds), *Football, Violence and Social Identity* (London, 1994), p.79.

4 Allum: *Potere e Società a Napoli*, p.319.

5 'La "Marcia" dei ventimila', *La Gazzetta*, 29 June 1964, p.5.

6   Ginsborg, P., *A History of Contemporary Italy: Society and Politics 1943–1988* (London, 1990), p.300.

7   Marsiglia, G., 'L'università di massa: espansione, crisi, trasformazione', in S. Soldani e G. Turi (eds), *Fare gli Italiani: Scuola e Cultura nell'Italia Contemporanea, II: Una Società di Massa* (Bologna, 1993), pp.134–5.

8   'ISEF in rivolta', *Il Discobolo*, March 1967, p.13.

9   'I fatti e le idee', *Il Discobolo*, 40, June–July 1968, p.4.

10   Berlinguer, E., 'Alleanze sociali e schieramenti politici', *Rinascita*, 40, 12 October 1973, p.5. See also preceding articles, 'Imperialismo e coesistenza alla luce dei fatti cileni', *Rinascita*, 38, 28 September 1973, pp.3–4; 'Via democratica e violenza reazionaria, *Rinascita*, 39, 5 October 1973, pp.3–4.

11   Ginsborg: *A History of Contemporary Italy*, p.356.

12   Pasquino, G., 'Political development', in P. McCarthy (ed.), *Italy since 1945* (Oxford, 2000), p.76.

13   On the history of the roots of Italian terrorism see Drake, R., 'Rethinking 1968: The United States and Western Europe', *South Central Review*, 16, 4 (1999–2000), pp.62–76.

14   'Si vis pacem...', *Lo Sport Fascista*, VII, 8, 1934, p.1.

15   Clark, M., *Modern Italy, 1871–1995* (London, 1996), pp.341–4.

16   Teja, A. and Giuntini, S., *L'Addestramento Ginnico-Militare nell'Esercito Italiano (1946–1990)* (Roma, 2007), p.23.

17   'Sport e forze armate', *Stadium: Rassegna Mensile Illustrata di Tutti gli Sport*, July 1950, p.12.

18   Teja and Giuntini: *L'Addestramento Ginnico-Militare nell'Esercito Italiano*, p.23.

19   Teja and Giuntini: *L'Addestramento Ginnico-Militare nell'Esercito Italiano*, p.23, note 139.

20   'Le voci del padrone', *Il Discobolo*, 40, June–July (1968), p.12.

21   'Chi risponde alla Confindustria', *Il Discobolo*, 40, June–July (1968), p.3.

22   From Supplemento di Sportgiovane, 'Giochi della gioventù: vent'anni, 1968', quoted in Giuntini, S., *Pugni Chiusi e Cerchi Olimpici. Il Lungo '68 dello Sport Italiano* (Odradek, 2008), p.120.

23   'I problemi post-olimpici', *Il Discobolo*, 42, November–December (1968), p.6.

24   'Da Roma a Monaco. Il Mercato Olimpico', *Il Discobolo*, 72–73, September–October (1971), p.15.

25   'I temi del VII Congresso Nazionale dell'UISP', *Il Discobolo*, 82, September (1972), p.8.

26   Zanetti, G. and Tornabuoni, G., *Il Giuoco del Calcio: Commento alla Legislazione della FIGC* (Milano, 1933), p.64.

27   See C. Doglio, 'Lo sport in Italia', *Comunità. Rivista Trimestrale del Movimento Comunità*, VI, 13, January (1952), pp.26–7.

28   Giuntini: *Pugni Chiusi e Cerchi Olimpici*, pp.105–6.

29   Papa and Panico: *Storia Sociale del Calcio in Italia... (1945–2000)*, p.100.

30   Ghirelli, A., *Storia del Calcio in Italia* (Torino, 1990), p.310.

31   'Hitchcock non poteva fare di meglio', *Il Giorno*, 19 June 70, p.1.

32   Dalla Chiesa, N., *La Partita del Secolo: Storia di Italia–Germania, 4–3* (Milano, 2001), pp.181 and 185.

33   Dalla Chiesa: *La Partita del Secolo*, p.169.

34   'Messico. Perché siamo impazziti', *Il Mondo*, 28 June 70, p.1.

35   Ghirelli: *Storia del Calcio in Italia*, p.310.

36   Dalla Chiesa: *La Partita del Secolo*, p.135.

37   Dalla Chiesa: *La Partita del Secolo*, pp.148–50.

38   'Sui colli di Roma', *L'Espresso*, 28 June 1970, p.18.

39   'È stata una fortuna per noi che il Brasile ci abbia battuti', *Domenica del Corriere*, 72, 27, 7 July 1970, p.4.

40   'Messico. Perché siamo impazziti', *Il Mondo*, 28 June 1970, p.1.

41   'Sui colli di Roma', *L'Espresso*, p.18.

42   Gerosa, G., 'Brera l'incendiario', *L'Europeo*, 2, April (2002), p.139.

43   'La caduta di Rivera', *Il Giorno*, 29 May 1970, p.13.

44   For more on the polemic and the press factions see *L'Europeo*, 2, April (2002), pp.130–55.

45   Brera, G., *Storia Critica del Calcio Italiano* (Milano, 1998), p.407.

46   'Sport e pratica sportiva', *Avanti!*, 23 June 1970, p.1.

47   Sannucci, C., 'In campo a sinistra. Intervista su calcio e impegno politico-sociale nell'Italia degli anni settanta', *Zapruder. Storie in Movimento*, May–August (2004), p.114.

48   'Il tennis si gioca su un campo rosso. Di sangue cileno', *Lotta Continua*, 1 October 1976, p.2.

49   'Discorso al lettore sul caso Italia-Cile', *La Gazzetta*, 15 December 1976, p.1.

50   'Sparate sul tennista', *Lotta Continua*, 29 September 1976, p.2.

51   'Davis 30 anni dopo', *La Repubblica*, 18 December 2006, pp.58–9.

52   'E Berlinguer disse: compagni, non boicottate la Davis', *Corriere della Sera*, 9 May 1996, p.43.

53   'Striscioni, slogan e proteste poi l'ok del Pci: andate pure', *La Repubblica*, 18 December 2006, p.59.

54   'Hanno toccato il fondo', *Lotta Continua*, 8 December 1976, p.1.

55   'Hanno toccato il fondo', *Lotta Continua*, p.1.

56   'Chi ha veramente vinto la Coppa Davis? Pinochet batte Italia: cinque a zero', *Lotta Continua*, 21 December 1976, p.5.

57   'Santiago: lo stadio degli aguzzini', *Lotta Continua*, 19–20 December 1976, p.5.

58   'No all'incontro Italia-Cile', *Lotta Continua*, 19 October 1976, p.2.

59   Hazan, B.A., *Olympic Sports and Propaganda Games. Moscow 1980* (New Jersey, 1982), p.84.

60 Coakley. J. and Dunning, E. (eds), *Handbook of Sports Studies* (London, 2002), p.219.

61 'Il CONI ha risposto con il suo documento', *Atletica Leggera*, June 1980, p.7.

62 'Quest'anno lo Yankee non corre', *Lotta Continua*, 15 April 1980, p.1.

63 'Quanti si ricordano degli atleti militari?', *Atletica Leggera*, August–September 1980, p.26.

64 'Così ha stabilito il nostro Governo', *Atletica Leggera*, June 1980, p.6.

65 'Il CONI ha risposto con il suo documento', *Atletica Leggera*, June 1980, p.7.

66 'Quanti si ricordano degli atleti militari?', *Atletica Leggera*, p.27.

67 Cited in Dal Lago and De Biasi: 'Italian football fans. Culture and organisation', Note 1, p.88.

68 Foot: *Calcio*, p.305.

69 Podaliri, C. and Balestri, C., 'The Ultràs, racism and football culture in Italy', in A. Brown (ed.), *Fanatics! Power, Identity and Fandom in Football* (London, 1999), p.91.

70 Roversi, A., *Calcio e Violenza in Europa: Inghilterra, Germania, Italia, Olanda, Belgio e Danimarca* (Bologna, 1990); Roversi. A. and Balestri, C., 'Gli ultras oggi', *POLIS. Ricerche e Studi su Società e Politica in Italia*, 3, 1999.

71 Triani, G., *Mal di Stadio: Storia del Tifo e della Passione per il Calcio* (Roma, 1990), pp.133–4.

72 'I club dei tifosi, il calcio violento ed altro: apriamo la discussione', *Lotta Continua*, 19 October 1976, p.2.

73 Foot: *Calcio*, p.375.

74 Sannucci: 'In campo a sinistra', p.112.

75 Giuntini: *Pugni Chiusi e Cerchi Olimpici*, p.108. This is refuted by Sollier in Sannucci: 'In campo a sinistra', p.113.

76 Sollier, P., *Calci e Sputi e Colpi di Testa: Riflessioni Autobiografiche di un Calciatore per Caso* (Milano, 1976), p.79.

77 Sollier: *Calci e Sputi e Colpi di Testa*, p.49.

78 Sollier: *Calci e Sputi e Colpi di Testa*, p.95.

79 Eco, U., *Travels in Hyper-Reality* (London, 1987), p.172.

80 'Sacrificare un uomo o perdere lo Stato', *La Repubblica*, 21 April 1978, p.1.

81 Ginsborg, P., *Silvio Berlusconi: Television, Power and Patrimony* (London, 2005), p.32.

82 Ginsborg: *A History of Contemporary Italy*, p.244.

83 McCarthy, P., 'The Church in postwar Italy', in McCarthy: *Italy since 1945*, p.144.

84 'Gli italiani non sono più quelli', *Corriere della Sera*, 10 June 1974, p.1.

Chapter 7

1 Ginsborg, P., *Italy and its Discontents: Family, Civil Society, State 1980–2001* (London, 2001), p. 108.

2 Severgnini, B., *La Bella Figura: A Field Guide to the Italian Mind* (New York, 2006), p.77.

3 Forgacs, D., *Italian Culture in the Industrial Era 1880–1980: Cultural Industries, Politics and the Public* (Manchester, 1990), p.183.

4 Ginsborg, *Italy and its Discontents*, pp.150–1.

5 CONI, *VII Giochi Olimpici Invernali: Rapporto Ufficiale* (Roma, 1956), p.77.

6 Garosci, A., 'La comunità ampezzana', *Comunità. Rivista Trimestrale del Movimento Comunità*, VI, 13 (January), 1952, p.10.

7 Bassetti, R., *Storia e Storie dello Sport in Italia: Dall'Unità a Oggi* (Venezia, 1999), p.238.

8 The World Cup is an annual circuit of skiing competitions held in Europe, North America and east Asia over the course of a season. Competitors attempt to achieve the best time in four disciplines: slalom, giant slalom, Super G and downhill. Combined events (calculated using results from selected downhill and slalom races) were included from 1974 to 1975.

9 Bassetti: *Storia e Storie dello Sport*, p.241.

10 'Montesi ha detto tutto...', *La Repubblica*, 4 March 80, p.13.

11 Foot, J., *Calcio: A History of Italian Football* (London, 2006), p.247.

12 For the full text of Cruciani's declaration to Rome's Public Prosecutor see: http://www.storiedicalcio.altervista.org/calcioscommesse_80.html

13 Lepre, A., *La Storia della Prima Repubblica. L'Italia dal 1943 al 2003* (Bologna, 2004), p.306.

14 Triani, G., *Bar Sport Italia: Quando la Politica va nel Pallone* (Milano, 1994), p.75.

15 'E Spadolini si è ritrovato in braccio un azzurro del Duemile', *La Gazzetta*, 7 July 1982, p.8

16 'Spadolini ai ministri. "Serve una squadra unita"', *La Repubblica*, 13 July 1982, p.5.

17 'È la vittoria dell'Italia leale', *La Gazzetta*, 10 July 2006, p.15.

18 Ghirelli, A., *Storia del Calcio in Italia* (Torino, 1990), p.337.

19 'Italiani, imparate dagli azzurri a superare le difficoltà!', *La Gazzetta*, 12 July 1982, p.8.

20 Ginsborg: *Italy and its Discontents*, p. 143.

21 'Italiani, imparate dagli azzurri...', *La Gazzetta*, p.8.

22 'Caro presidente...', *La Gazzetta*, 13 July 1982, p.1.

23 Milza, P., 'Il football italiano. Una storia lunga un secolo', *Italia Contemporanea*, 183 (June), 1991, p.253.

24 Ghirelli: *Storia del Calcio in Italia*, p.339.

25 'Ritorno trionfale', *La Gazzetta*, 13 July 1982, p.3.

26 'Italiani, imparate dagli azzurri...', *La Gazzetta*, p.8.

27 'Italiani, imparate dagli azzurri...', *La Gazzetta*, p.8.

28 'Spadolini: io vi ho portato fortuna, spero che adesso la portiate a me', *La Gazzetta*, 13 July 1982, p.4.

29 'Le regole del gioco', *La Repubblica*, 13 July 1982, p.1.

30 'Quando il cuore batte per il tricolore', *Gente*, 21 July 1982, p.52.

31 Eco, U., *Travels in Hyper-Reality* (London, 1987), p.163.

32 'Giocatori e società, interrompete i rapporti con gli ultrà', *La Gazzetta*, 5 February 2007, p.10.

33 Roversi, A., *Calcio e Violenza in Europa: Inghilterra, Germania, Italia, Olanda, Belgio e Danimarca* (Bologna, 1990), p.79.

34 Podaliri, C. and Balestri, C., 'The Ultràs, racism and football culture in Italy', in A. Brown (ed.), *Fanatics! Power, Identity and Fandom in Football* (London, 1999), p.89.

35 Onofri, M. and Ricci, M., 'I ragazzi della curva', *Il Mulino*, XXXIII, 5, 1984, p.828.

36 Dal Lago, A. and De Biasi, R., 'Italian football fans. Culture and organisation', in R. Giulianotti, N. Bonney and M. Hepworth (eds), *Football, Violence and Social Identity* (London, 1994), p.81.

37 Roversi, A. and Balestri, C., 'Gli ultras oggi', *POLIS. Ricerche e Studi su Società e Politica in Italia*, 3, 1999, p.457.

38 'L'estrema destra e l'identità ultrà', Il Messaggero, 8 February 2007, p.2.

39 Triani, G., 'Il campanile perduto', in R. Grozio, *Catenaccio e Contropiede: Materiali e Immaginari del Football Italiano* (Roma, 1990), p.137.

40 'Giocatori e società, interrompete i rapporti con gli ultrà', *La Gazzetta*, 5 February 2007, p.10. See also Scalia, V., 'Just a few rogues?: Football ultras, clubs and politics in contemporary Italy', *International Review for the Sociology of Sport*, 44, 41 (2009), pp.46–8.

41 Triani: 'Il campanile perduto', p.137.

42 On the scandals see Burns, J., *The Life of Maradona* (London, 1996); Petrini, C., *I Pallonari: Zone Grige, Fondi Neri e Luci Rosse: Vent'Anni di Calcio all'Italiana* (Milano, 2003), pp.123–33.

43 Papa, A. and Panico, G., *Storia Sociale del Calcio in Italia: Dai Campionati del Dopoguerra alla Champions League (1945–2000)* (Bologna, 2000), p.163.

44 P. Davies, *All Played Out: The Full Story of Italia '90* (London, 1991), pp.155–6.

45 Maglie, A., *La Disfatta: Come Hanno Sconfitto il Calcio Italiano* (Arezzo, 2004), p.vii.

46 Triani: *Bar Sport Italia*, p.81.

47 'Quel Mondiale in zona Cesarini', *La Gazzetta*, 16 May 1990, p.1.

48 Bassetti: *Storia e Storie dello Sport in Italia*, p.302. For example see, 'Lo stadio è costato due anni di lavoro, 5 morti e 42 miliardi', *La Gazzetta*, 30 May 1990, p.13.

49 Davies: *All Played Out*, p.48.

50 See Foot: *Calcio*, pp.473–4; Bassetti: *Storia e Storie dello Sport in Italia*, pp.300–4.

51 Ginsborg, P., *Silvio Berlusconi: Television, Power and Patrimony* (London, 2005), p.61.

52 Pasquino, G., 'Political development', in P. McCarthy (ed.), *Italy since 1945* (Oxford, 2000), p.86.

53 *Il Manifesto*, 27 January 1994, p.1.

54 Triani, G., 'Il mondo è uno stadio, la vita un derby', *L'Unità*, 10 February 1990, p.23.

55 'L'onorevole azzurro', *La Repubblica*, 22 April 1994, p.1.

56 'L'ANNUNCIO. Un discorso tv di otto minuti', *La Gazzetta*, 27 January 1994, p.8.

57   'Forza Italia!', *La Gazzetta*, 11 July 1982, p.1

58   'Bobbio liquida la nuova destra', *La Voce*, 20 May 1994, p.3.

59   Porro, N. and Russo, P., 'Berlusconi and other matters: the era of "football-politics"', *Journal of Modern Italian Studies*, 5, 3 (2000), p.356. See also, McCarthy, P., 'Forza Italia, the new politics and old values of a changing Italy', in S. Gundle and S. Parker (eds), *The New Italian Republic: From the Fall of the Berlin Wall to Berlusconi* (London, 1993), p.138.

60   De Biasi, R., '*Ultra*-political. Football culture in Italy', in V. Duke and L. Crolley (eds), *Football, Nationality and the State* (New York, 1996), p.125.

61   McCarthy: 'Forza Italia...', pp.135 and 142.

62   Poli, E., 'The revolution in the televised soccer market', *Journal of Modern Italian Studies*, 5, 3 (2000), p.376.

63   'Berlusconi: la palla a Scalfaro', *La Stampa*, 18 April 1994, p.2.

64   Triani: *Bar Sport Italia*, p.86.

65   Dal Lago, A., 'Il voto e il Circo', *Micromega*, 1 (1994), p.142.

66   Eco: *Travels in Hyper-Reality*, pp.170–1.

Chapter 8

1   From 1994 the MSI joined the National Alliance (*Alleanza Nazionale*) umbrella group led by Gianfranco Fini.

2   *Corriere dello Sport*, 20 May 1994, p.1.

3   'Berlusconi trionfa dal Senato ad Atene', *La Gazzetta*, 20 May 1994, p.5.

4   Rifondazione Comunista was formed in 1991 by a breakaway group of former PCI delegates unhappy at the party's name change to the *Partito Democratico Sinistra* (PDS).

5   On this metaphor see 'Duecento comitati in cerca di Prodi', *La Repubblica*, 25 February 1995, p.9.

6   '"Prodi, ci vediamo a Wembley"', *La Gazzetta*, 6 June 1996, p.3.

7   Duggan, C., *The Force of Destiny: A History of Italy since 1796* (London, 2008), p.586

8   Ginsborg, P., *Italy and its Discontents: Family, Civil Society, State 1980–2001* (London, 2003), p.175.

9   Triani, G., *Bar Sport Italia: Quando la Politica va nel Pallone* (Milano, 1994), p.85.

10   See Sema, A., 'Contro Roma Bossi Inventa lo Sport Padano', *Limes. Rivista Italiana di Geopolitica*, 1, 1998, p.139 and *La Padania*, 29 May 1997 and 1–2 June 1997, p.23.

11   'Maglia rosa in verde padano', *La Padania*, 3 June 1997, p.23.

12   'Italia, esplode il tifo "contro"', *La Padania*, 18–19 January 1998, p.23.

13   'Adotta la squadra del cuore', *La Padania*, 3 December 1997, p.23.

14   '15 September 96: nasce la Padania e la nazionale emigra al sud', *La Padania*, 28 January 1998, p.23.

15   'Ma perchè non facciamo come Catalunya?', *La Padania*, 8 January 1998, p.19.

16   The VIVA World Cup is a tournament for 'national' teams unrecognized by FIFA.

17   Smargiasse, A., 'Calcio, ultrà e ideologia', *Nuova Critica Marxista*, 1–2 (1993), p.70.

18   In the 2008 general election the Northern League made a dramatic comeback. Winning over 8 per cent of the national vote in both the upper and lower houses of parliament, it formed part of the government coalition holding important ministerial positions.

19   McCarthy, P., 'Forza Italia, the new politics and old values of a changing Italy', in S. Gundle and S. Parker (eds), *The New Italian Republic* (London, 1996), p.133.

20   'An Italian story', *The Economist*, 28 April–4 May 2001, pp.23–8.

21   Forza Italia, *Una Storia Italiana* (Milano, 2001), p.62.

22   'L'orgoglio ricucito', *La Gazzetta*, 24 May 2007, p.3.

23   McCarthy: 'Forza Italia… ', pp.134 and 136.

24   Forza Italia: *Una Storia Italiana*, p.62.

25   Forza Italia: *Una Storia Italiana*, p.64.

26   'Berlusconi, schiaffo a Zoff', *La Gazzetta*, 4 July 2000, p.1.

27   For the full controversy see various national press 4–8 July 2002.

28   'Oggi a lui domani a noi', *Il Manifesto*, 15 January 2001, p.1.

29   McCarthy: 'Forza Italia…', p.145.

30   Ginsborg: *Silvio Berlusconi*, p.146.

31   Foot, J., *Calcio: A History of Italian Football* (London, 2006), p.497.

32   For an excellent description of the confusing system see Foot: *Calcio*, pp.491–3.

33   'Berlusconi blinda Carraro', *La Gazzetta*, 12 August 2003, p.19.

34   *La Gazzetta*, 20 August 2003, p.1.

35   Bassetti, R., *Storia e Storie dello Sport in Italia: Dall'Unità a Oggi* (Venezia, 1999), p.323.

36   'Donati sgrida gli atleti "Confessate il doping"', *Corriere della Sera*, 18 January 2000, p.42.

37   On this argument see Hoberman, J., *Mortal Engines: The Science of Performance and the Dehumanization of Sport* (New York, 1992).

38   Houlihan, B., *Dying to Win: Doping in Sport and the Development of Anti-Doping* (Strasbourg, 2002), p.22.

39   Bassetti: *Storia e Storie dello Sport*, p.325.

40   Houlihan: *Dying to Win*, pp.33–4.

41   Rendell, M., *The Death of Marco Pantani: A Biography* (London, 2007), pp.291–2.

42   'Pantani come Coppi una leggenda al Tour', *La Repubblica*, 28 July 1998, p.1.

43   Pivato, S., 'Sport', in P. McCarthy, *Italy since 1945* (Oxford, 2000), p.178.

44   '"Io cavaliere?…"', *La Gazzetta*, 14 August 1998, p.18.

45   On revelations of Conconi inquiry see 'Conconi, ecco la lista choc', *La Repubblica*, 27 December 1999, p.43; 'Doping, un'altra lista segreta', *La Repubblica*, 28 December 1999, pp.1 and 15; 'Anche Pantani in quel computer', *La Repubblica*, 28 December

1999, p.53–4; 'Il fondo ai tempi dell'Epo "Chi non la usava era fuori"', *La Repubblica*, 31 December 1999, p.56.

46 Rendell: *The Death of Marco Pantani*, pp.167 and 173.

47 Rendell: *The Death of Marco Pantani*, p.170.

48 Rendell: *The Death of Marco Pantani*, p.115.

49 RAI3 documentary Sfide, 'L'ultima fuga di Marco Pantani', 25 July 2005.

50 See in particular Pantani, T., *Era mio Figlio* (Milano, 2008); Ronchi, M. and Josti, G., *Man on the Run: The Life and Death of Marco Pantani* (London, 2005).

51 Rendell: *The Death of Marco Pantani*, p.283.

52 Fondazione Marco Pantani: www.pantani.it

53 Quotation from Foundation's website, 13 January 2010.

54 'Gattuso: "Pantani? Mi faceva impazzire"', www.gazzetta.it, 13 January 2010.

55 See 'Anche il calcio ha il mal di Tour', *L'Espresso*, 13 August 1998, pp.68–71; 'Campionato da farmacia', *L'Espresso*, 20 August 1998, pp.52–4.

56 Zeman was not the only one to question Vialli's growth: 'Se Vialli diventa un peso', *La Gazzetta*, 9 February 1993, p.6.

57 Petrini, C., *I Pallonari: Zone Grige, Fondi Neri e Luci Rosse: Vent'Anni di Calcio all'Italiana* (Milano, 2003), p.109.

58 Petrini, C., *Nel Fango del Dio del Pallone* (Milano, 2000).

59 Petrini: *I Pallonari*, p.109.

60 Barletta, M., *Il Calcio in Farmacia: La Juventus e le Altre Squadre. Le Inchieste sul Doping. I Documenti. Le Testimonianze* (Torino, 2005), pp.87–93.

61 'Indagine Procura Sono morti 11 calciatori per sclerosi, *La Stampa*, 5 January 2001, p.29.

62 'La banda del doping', *La Repubblica*, 27 October 2000, pp.1 and 17 and '"Ecco il doping di Conconi"...' pp.12–13.

63 'Ma è la Juve oppure la Signora dei dopati?', *Panorama*, 1 July 2001, pp.68–71

64 Guariniello had previously locked horns with the FIAT management, in the 1970s, over the illegal retention of personnel records.

65 'Craxi: "Così fan tutti..."', *La Repubblica*, 4 July 1992, pp.1–2.

66 For a list of drugs see Barletta: *Il Calcio in Farmacia*, pp. 44–6; 213–17.

67 '"La Juve è leale: Esce a testa alta"', *La Gazzetta*, 27 November 2004, p.3.

68 'Giraudo assolto, Agricola condannato', *La Gazzetta*, 27 November 2004, p.2.

69 Foot: *Calcio*, p.269.

70 'Porto Franco', *L'Espresso*, 18 May 2006, p.85.

71 For this and a list of suspicious matches in the 1990s see 'L'Avvocato la cupola e sette scudetti', *L'Espresso*, 25 May 2006, pp.43–4.

72 For an organigram of the organization and futher detail on GEA see Hamil S., Morrow S., Idle C., Rossi G. and Faccendini S., 'The governance and regulation of Italian football', *Soccer and Society*, 11, 4 (2010), pp.373–413.

73 'I figli di Lippi, De Mita e Calleri tra gli indagati', *La Gazzetta*, 27 May 2006, p.2.

74 See 'Padri e business. Tutto inzia con la GEA dei tanti figli di papà', *La Gazzetta*, 25 May 2006, p.9.

75 'La piovra bianconera', *L'Espresso*, 25 May 2006, p.34. For more detail on Moggi's influence over the national team led by Marcello Lippi see: 'Marcello ora viene il bello', *L'Espresso*, 25 May 2006, pp.35–7.

76 'Luciano all'ultimo stadio', *L'Espresso*, 18 May 2006, p.83.

77 'Marcello ora viene il bello', *L'Espresso*, pp.35–7.

78 'Luciano all'ultimo stadio', *L'Espresso*, p.78.

79 '"Paparesta? L'ho chiuso dentro lo spogliatoio"', *La Gazzetta*, 13 May 2006, p.5; L'Espresso, *Il Libro Nero del Calcio Nero, Vol I* (Roma, 2006), p.266.

80 'Il metodo Moggi in prima pagina già otto anni fa', *La Gazzetta*, 20 May 2006, p.5.

81 'Moggiopoli, Italia', *La Gazzetta*, 24 May 2006, p.1.

82 'Capitano mio (?) capitano', *La Gazzetta*, 25 May 2006, p.3.

83 The final debate was reported in the style of a football match by Beppe Severgnini. 'Berlusconi–Prodi. Gol all'ultimo minuto', *La Gazzetta*, 4 April 2006, pp.1 and 17.

84 'Il presidente del calcio spettacolo', *La Gazzetta*, 1 April 2006, p.11; 'Il presidente delle bandiere', *La Gazzetta*, 4 April 2006, p.11.

85 'Promemoria per chi vince', *La Gazzetta*, 10 April 2006, p.1.

86 'Prodi agli industriali: la manovra vi favorisce', *La Repubblica*, 10 October 2006, p.9; 'Prodi: l'Italia? Una squadra che riparte da –26', *Il Messaggero*, 14 November 2006, p.5.

87 'Modello Juve, il Prof cerca il gol con le parole del calcio', *Il Messaggero*, 14 November 2006, p.5.

88 On this issue see, Roncarolo, F. and Belluati, M., 'Surfing and trying to keep afloat: The political communication process in a highly fragmented coalition led by a "Great Mediator"', *Modern Italy*, 13, 3 (2008), pp.333–48.

89 Paolucci, C. and Newell, J.L., 'The Prodi government of 2006 and 2007: A retrospective look', *Modern Italy*, 13, 3 (2008), p.287.

90 '"È vero, scommetevo: ma sono pulito"', *La Repubblica*, 14 May 2006, p.4; 'Buffon deve diffendersi. "Situazione delicata". Verifiche sulle date', *La Gazzetta*, 19 May 2006, p.11; 'Buffon libero di andare al Mondiale', *La Gazzetta*, 25 May 2006, p.6.

91 'Ricordi vintage, pizza a parte', *Il Manifesto*, 5 July 2006, p.5; 'Azzurri fra orgoglio e pregiudizi', *L'Espresso*, 22 June 2006, pp.86–91.

92 '"È la vittoria dell'Italia leale"', *La Gazzetta*, 10 July 2006, p.15.

93 'Napolitano: Orgoglioso di voi', *Corriere dello Sport*, 10 July 2006, p.10.

94 'Prodi: "Avete ridato dignità al calcio"', *La Gazzetta*, 11 July 2006, p.5.

95 'Stangatona', *La Gazzetta*, 15 July 2006, p.1.

96 'Stangatina', *La Gazzetta*, 26 July 2006, p.1.

97 'Guido Rossi: "Non finirà in una bola di sapone"', *La Gazzetta*, 27 May 2006, p.1.

98 'Moggiopoli, Italia', *La Gazzetta*, 24 May 2006, p.13.

99 'Tangentopoli e "Piedi puliti"', *La Repubblica*, 14 May 2006, p.11.

Chapter 9

1 'Nel solo nome dello sport', *La Gazzetta*, 13 April 1948, p.1.
2 Forgacs, D. and Lumley, R., *Italian Cultural Studies: An Introduction* (Oxford, 1996), p.20.
3 'Bossi provoca gli azzurri: si compreranno la partita', *Il Messaggero*, 23 June 2010, p.8.
4 'Bossi provoca gli azzurri', *Il Messaggero*, p.8.
5 'Lippi come Bearzot', *La Gazzetta*, 10 July 2006, p.2.
6 Davies, P., *All Played Out: The Full Story Italia '90* (London, 1991), p.270.
7 Davies: *All Played Out*, p.428.
8 'Scommesse, l'inchiesta fa paura', *La Repubblica*, 27 November 2009, p.68.
9 Valeri, M., *Black Italians: Atleti Neri in Maglia Azzurra. L'Italia Multirazziale* (Roma, 2006), Preface.
10 'Insulti a Myers, la vergogna di Varese', *La Repubblica*, 30 December 2003, p.48.
11 Valeri: *Black Italians*, p.234.
12 'Mario è solo un incompreso', *Il Messaggero*, 8 June 2009, p.35.
13 Roma, Fiorentina and Udinese were also fined in the 2008–9 season for racist chants against Balotelli. See *La Repubblica*, 21 April 2009, p.42.
14 'SOS razzismo...', *La Repubblica*, 27 November 2009, p.66.
15 'Razzismo, ecco la linea dura', *La Repubblica*, 1 December 2009, p.67
16 'Cori razzisti contro Seedorf match a un passo dallo stop', *La Repubblica*, 29 March 2010, p.47.
17 *Il Venerdì di Repubblica*, 26 June 2009.
18 'Pupazzo razzista', *Corriere della Sera*, 22 May 1996, p.13.
19 'E per far festa gli ultras cantano Faccetta Nera', *La Repubblica*, 20 December 1999, p.44.
20 See Hill, D., *Out of his Skin: The John Barnes Phenomenon* (London, 1989).
21 On the riot and death of Raciti see national newspapers from 3 February 2007. For photos of the 50 people killed in football stadiums since 1963 see 'Morti per una partita', *La Gazzetta*, 4 February 2007, p.5.
22 'Sono solo cinque gli stadi a norma San Siro non c'è', *La Gazzetta*, 5 February 2007, p.6.
23 For a brief history of Italian rugby see Bonini, G., 'Rugby – the game for "real Italian men"', in T.J.L. Chandler and J. Nauright (eds), *Making the Rugby World: Race, Gender and Commerce* (London, 1999).
24 Bassetti, R., *Storia e Storie dello Sport in Italia: Dall'Unità a Oggi* (Venezia, 1999), p.261.
25 'BBC turns down Gordon Brown as Match of the Day 2 guest', www.guardian.co.uk, 10 March 2010.
26 Sollier, P., *Calci e Sputi e Colpi di Testa* (Milano, 1976), pp.83–4.
27 Andrews, G., *Not a Normal Country: Italy after Berlusconi* (London, 2005).

28 Marchesini, D., 'Nazionalismo, patriottismo e simboli nazionali nello sport: tricolore e maglia azzurra', in F. Tarozzi and G. Vecchio (eds), *Gli Italiani e il Tricolore: Patriottismo, Identità Nazionale e Fratture Sociali Lungo Due Secoli di Storia* (Bologna, 1999), pp.314.

29 Martucci, D., *Gli Italiani e lo Sport* (Bologna, 1967), p.16.

Selected bibliography

This is a list of books cited in the Notes. The full details of academic articles, newspapers and other materials can be found in the notes themselves.

AA.VV., *Almanacco della Donna Italiana* (Firenze, 1924).

AA.VV., *Mussolini e lo Sport* (Mantova, 1928).

AA.VV., *Lo Sport in Regime Fascista 28 Ottobre 1922–I 28 Ottobre 1935–XIII* (Sport Fascista, Milano, 1935).

AA.VV., *Storia d'Italia* (Torino, 1973).

Agnew, P., *Forza Italia: A Journey in Search of Italy and its Football* (London, 2006).

Allum, P., *Potere e Società a Napoli nel Dopoguerra* (Torino, 1975).

Anderson, B., *Imagined Communities: Reflections on the Origin and Spread of Nationalism* (London, 1983).

Andrews, G., *Not a Normal Country: Italy after Berlusconi* (London, 2005).

Armstrong, G. and Giulianotti, R. (eds), *Entering the Field: New Perspectives on World Football* (Oxford, 1997).

Arnaud, P. and Riordan, J. (eds), *Sport and International Politics. The impact of Fascism and Communism on Sport* (London, 1998).

Artom, S. and Calabrò, A.R., *Sorelle d'Italia – Quattordici Signore Raccontano la Loro (e Nostra) Storia* (Milano, 1989).

Baransky, Z.G. and Lumley, R. (eds), *Culture and Conflict in Postwar Italy: Essays on Mass Popular Culture* (London, 1990).

Bardi, P.M., *La Strada e il Volante* (Roma, 1936).

Barletta, M., *Il Calcio in Farmacia: La Juventus e le Altre Squadre. Le Inchieste sul Doping. I Documenti. Le Testimonianze* (Torino, 2005).

Bassetti, R., *Storia e Storie dello Sport in Italia: Dall'Unità a Oggi* (Venezia, 1999).

Bellamy, R. (ed.), *Antonio Gramsci: Pre-Prison Writings* (Cambridge, 1994).

Bianda, R., Leone, G., Rossi, G., Urso, A., *Atleti in Camicia Nera: Lo Sport nell'Italia di Mussolini* (Firenze, 1983).

Brera, G., *Storia Critica del Calcio Italiano* (Milano, 1998).

Brown, A. (ed.), *Fanatics! Power, Identity & Fandom in Football* (London and New York, 1998).

Brunamonti, G., *50 Anni di Totocalcio tra Letteratura e Realtà* (Roma, 1996).

Buzzati, D., *Dino Buzzati al Giro d'Italia* (Milano, 1981).

Calabrese, O. (ed.), *Italia Moderna, Volume Terzo, 1939–1960: Guerra, Dopoguerra, Ricostruzione, Decollo* (Milano, 1984).

Calabrese, O., *Italian Style: Forms of Creativity* (Milano, 1998).

Camera dei Deputati, *Atti Parlamentari dell'Assemblea* (Roma, 1960).

Canella, M. and Giuntini, S. (eds), *Sport e Fascismo* (Milano, 2009).

Cannistraro, P.V., *La Fabbrica del Consenso: Fascismo e Mass Media* (Bari, 1975).

Cannistraro, P.V. (ed.), *Historical Dictionary of Fascist Italy* (Westport, 1982).

Cappelli, V. (ed.), *Diario di un Cicloturista di Fine Ottocento: Da Reggio Calabria ad Eboli* (Castrovillari, 1989).

Cashmore, E., *Making Sense of Sports* (London, 2000).

Castronovo, V. and Tranfaglia, N. (eds), *La Stampa Italiana del Neocapitalismo* (Bari, 1976).

Castronovo, V. and Tranfaglia, N. (eds), *La Stampa Italiana Nell'Età Fascista* (Bari, 1980).

Castronovo, V. and Tranfaglia, N. (eds), *La Stampa Italiana Nell'Età della TV* (Bari, 1994).

Centro Sportivo Italiano, *Cent'Anni di Storia nella Realtà dello Sport Italiano: Dalla Federazione Associazione Sportive Cattoliche Italiane al Centro Sportivo Italiano* (Bergamo, 2006).

Cetorelli Schivo, G., *Lo Sport nell'Italia Antica: Sport e Ideale Atletico* (Milano, 2002).

Clark, M., *Modern Italy 1871–1995* (London, 1996).

Coakley, J. and Dunning, E. (eds), *Handbook of Sports Studies* (London, 2002).

CONI, *L'Italia Turistica Annuario Generale: Sport – Turismo – Industrie Applicate* (Firenze, 1930).

CONI, *VII Giochi Olimpici Invernali: Rapporto Ufficiale* (Roma, 1956).

Cori, A., *Il Cinema di Romolo Marcellini: Tra Storia e Societa dal Colonialismo Agli Anni '70* (Recco, 2009).

Cörner, A., *Politics of Culture in Liberal Italy: From Unification to Fascism* (London, 2008).

Cotronei, A., *Atleti e Eroi* (Milano, 1932).

Dal Lago, A., *Descrizione di una Battaglia: I Rituali del Calcio* (Bologna, 1990).

D'Attorre, P.P. (ed.), *Nemici per la Pelle: Sogno Americano e Mito Sovietico nell'Italia Contemporanea* (Milano, 1991).

Davies, P., *All Played Out: The Full Story of Italia '90* (London, 1991).

Davis, J.A., *Italy in the Nineteenth Century 1796–1900* (Oxford, 2006).

De Giorgio, M., *Le Italiane dall'Unità a Oggi: Modelli Culturali e Comportamenti* (Bari, 1992).

De Grazia, V., *The Culture of Consent: Mass Organisation of Leisure in Fascist Italy* (Cambridge, 1981).

De Martino, E., *Mille Miglia* (Milano, 1940).

Duggan, C., *The Force of Destiny: A History of Italy since 1796* (London, 2008).

Duke, V. and Crolley, L., *Football, Nationality and the State* (New York, 1996).

Eco, U., *Travels in Hyper-Reality* (London, 1987).

Elias, N. and Dunning, E., *Quest for Excitement: Sport and Leisure in the Civilizing Process* (Oxford, 1986).

Fabrizio, F., *Sport e Fascismo: La Politica Sportiva del Regime 1924–1936* (Rimini/Firenze, 1976).

Fabrizio, F., *Storia dello Sport in Italia: Dalle Società Ginnastiche all'Associazionismo di Massa* (Firenze, 1978).

Facchinetti, P., *La Stampa Sportiva in Italia* (Bologna, 1967).

Facchinetti, P., *Gli Anni Ruggenti di Alfonsina Strada* (Portogruaro, 2004).

Facchinetti, P., *Quando Spararono al Giro d'Italia* (Arezzo, 2006).

Falasca-Zamponi, S., *Fascist Spectacle: The Aesthetics of Power in Mussolini's Italy* (Berkeley, 1997).

Fante, J., *Tesoro, qui è Tutto una Follia: Lettere dall'Europa (1957–1960)* (Roma, 1999).

Ferrara, P., *L'Italia in Palestra: Storia, Documenti e Immagini della Ginnastica dal 1833 al 1973* (Roma, 1992).

Ferretti, L., *Il Libro dello Sport* (Roma, 1928).

Ferretti, L., *Lo Sport* (Roma, 1949).

Finzi, R. (ed.), *Storia d'Italia: Le Regioni dall'Unità a Oggi. L'Emilia-Romagna* (Torino, 1997).

Flora, F. (ed.), *Ritratto di un Ventennio: Stampa dell'Era Fascista* (Bologna, 1972).

Foot, J., *Modern Italy* (Basingstoke, 2003).

Foot, J., *Calcio: A History of Italian Football* (London, 2006).

Forgacs, D. (ed.), *Rethinking Italian Fascism: Capitalism, Populism and Culture* (London, 1986).

Forgacs, D., *Italian Culture in the Industrial era 1880–1980: Cultural Industries, Politics and the Public* (Manchester, 1990).

Forgacs, D. (ed.), *The Antonio Gramsci Reader* (New York, 2000).

Forgacs, D. and Gundle, S., *Mass Culture and Italian Society from Fascism to the Cold War* (Bloomington, 2007).

Forgacs, D. and Lumley, R. (eds), *Italian Cultural Studies: An Introduction* (Oxford, 1996).

Frasca, S., *Religio Athletae: Pierre de Coubertin e la Formazione dell'Uomo per la Società Complessa* (Roma, 2007).

Gedda, L., *Lo Sport* (Milano, 1931).

Ghirelli, A., *Storia del Calcio in Italia* (Torino, 1990).

Ginsborg, P., *A History of Contemporary Italy: Society and Politics 1943–1988* (London, 1990).

Ginsborg, P., *Italy and its Discontents: Family, Civil Society, State 1980–2001* (London, 2003).

Ginsborg, P., *Silvio Berlusconi: Television, Power and Patrimony* (London, 2005).

Giulianotti, R., Bonney, N. and Hepworth, M., *Football, Violence and Social Identity* (London, 1994).

Giuntini, S., *Pugni Chiusi e Cechi Olimpici: Il Lungo '68 dello Sport Italiano* (Roma, 2008).

Goggioli, G., *I Grandi Campioni del Ciclismo Italiano* (Firenze, 1951).

Gordon, R., *Bicycle Thieves* (London, 2008).

Gori, G. (ed.), *Female Bodies, Sport, Italian Fascism: Submissive Women and Strong Mothers* (London, 2004).

Greganti, A. (ed.), *Cent'Anni di Storia nella Realtà dello Sport Italiano: Dalla Federazione Associazionie Sportive Cattoliche Italiane al Centro Sportivo Italiano* (Bergamo, 2006).

Grozio, R., *Catenaccio e Contropiede: Materiali e Immaginari del Football Italiano* (Roma, 1990).

Gundle, S., *Between Hollywood and Moscow: The Italian Communists and the Challenge of Mass Culture, 1943–1991* (London, 2000).

Gundle, S. and Parker, S. (eds), *The New Italian Republic* (London, 1996).

Guttmann, A., *From Ritual to Record: The Nature of Modern Sports* (New York, 1978).

Harris, H., *Sport in Greece and Rome* (London, 1972).

Hazan, B.A., *Olympic Sports and Propaganda Games: Moscow 1980* (New Jersey, 1982).

Hill, D., *Out of his Skin: the John Barnes Phenomenon* (London, 1989).

Hoare, Q. and Nowell Smith, G. (eds), *Selections from the Prison Notebooks of Antonio Gramsci* (London, 1971).

Hoberman, J., *Sport and Political Ideology* (Austin, 1984).

Hoberman, J., *Mortal Engines: The Science of Performance and the Dehumanization of Sport* (New York, 1992).

Hobsbawm, E., *Nations and Nationalism since 1870: Programme, Myth, Reality* (Cambridge, 1995).

Hoch, P., *Rip off the Big Game: The Exploitation of Sports by the Power Elite* (Garden City, NY, 1972).

Houlihan, B., *Dying to Win: Doping in Sport and the Development of Anti-Doping* (2nd edition), (Strasbourg, 2002).

Houlihan, B., *Sport and Society: An Introduction* (London, 2003).

Huizinga, J., *Homo Ludens: A Study of the Play-Element in Culture* (London, 2003).

Imbucci, G., *Il Gioco: Lotto, Totocalcio, Lotterie. Storia dei Comportamenti Sociali* (Venezia, 1997).

Isnenghi, M. (ed.), *I Luoghi della Memoria: Strutture ed Eventi dell'Italia Unita* (Bari, 1997).

Jarvie, G., *Sport, Culture and Society: An Introduction* (London, 2006).

Jarvie, G. and Maguire, J., *Sport and Leisure in Social Thought* (London, 1994).

Jones, W.R., *Un Programme di Educazione Fisica ad Uso dei Prigionieri di Guerra* (Locarno, 1942).

Keys, B., *Globalizing Sport: National Rivalry and International Community in the 1930s* (Cambridge, MA, 2006).

Kirk, T., *The Architecture of Modern Italy, Volume II: Visions of Utopia 1900–Present* (New York, 2005).

Koon, T.H., *Believe, Obey, Fight: Political Socialization of Youth in Fascist Italy 1922–1943* (Chapel Hill, 1985).

Krüger, A. and Teja, A. (eds), *La Comune Eredità dello Sport in Europa: Atti del 1° Seminario Europea di Storia dello Sport* (Roma, 1997).

Krüger, A. and Trangbaek, E., *The History of Physical Education & Sport From European Perspectives* (Copenhagen, 1996).

Kühne, I., *Napoli Passione Mia* (Roma, 1985).

Kyle, D.G., *Sport and Spectacle in the Ancient World* (Oxford, 2007).

La Regina, A. (ed.), *Nike: Il Gioco e la Vittoria* (Milano, 2003).

Leeden M.A., *West European Communism and American Foreign Policy* (New Brunswick/Oxford, 1987).

Lepre, A., *La Storia della Prima Repubblica: L'Italia dal 1943 al 2003* (Bologna, 2004).

Liguori, G. and Smargiasse, A., *Calcio e Neocalcio: Geopolitica e Prospettive del Football in Italia* (Roma, 2003).

Livolsi, M. (ed.), *Il Consumo Culturale* (Padova, 1982).

Lolli, L., *I Mondiali in Camicia Nera, 1934–38* (Roma, 1990).

Lombardo, A (ed.), *Storia degli Sport in Italia (1861–1960)* (Cassino, 2004).

Lombroso, C., *Delitti vecchi e delitti Nuovi* (Torino, 1902).

Lorenzini, A., *I Ciclisti Rossi: I Loro Scopi e la Loro Organizzazione* (Caravaggio, 1913).

Lumley, R., *States of Emergency: Cultures of Revolt in Italy from 1968 to 1978* (London, 1990).

Lyttelton, A., *The Seizure of Power: Fascism in Italy 1919–1929* (Princeton, 1987).

Mack Smith, D., *Modern Italy: A Political Italy* (New Haven, 1997).

Maglie, A., *La Disfatta: Come Hanno Sconfitto il Calcio Italiano* (Arezzo, 2004).

Manna A. and Gibbs, M., *The Day Italian Football Died: Torino and the Tragedy of Superga* (Derby, 2000).

Maraniss, D., *Rome 1960: The Olympics that Changed the World* (New York, 2008).

Marchesini, D., *L'Italia del Giro d'Italia* (Bologna, 1996).

Marchesini, D., *Coppi e Bartali* (Bologna, 1998).

Marchesini, D., *Cuori e Motori: Storia della Mille Miglia 1927–1957* (Bologna, 2001).

Marchesini, D., *Carnera* (Bologna, 2006).

Martin, S., *Football and Fascism: The National Game under Mussolini* (Oxford, 2004).

Martucci, D., *Gli Italiani e lo Sport* (Bologna, 1967).

McCarthy, P. (ed.), *Italy since 1945* (Oxford, 2000).

Menotti, E.M., *L'Atleta nell'Antichità* (Mantova, 2002).

Murialdi, P., *La Stampa nel Regime Fascista* (Bari, 1986).

Noto, A. and Rossi, L. (eds), *Coroginnica: Saggi Sulla Ginnastica, lo Sport e la Cultura del Corpo, 1861–1991* (Roma, 1992).

Nowell-Smith, G., *The Companion to Italian Cinema* (London, 1996).

Nowell-Smith, G., *Making Waves: Neorealism and the New Cinemas of the 1960s* (London, 2008).

Organizing Committee of the Games of the XVII Olympiad, *The Games of the XVII Olympiad: Rome 1960. The Official Report of the Organizing Committee* (Roma, 1960).

Ormezzano, G.P., *Storia del Calcio* (Milano, 1986).

Overman, S.J., *The Influence of the Protestant Ethic on Sport and Recreation* (Aldershot, 1997).

Pantani, T., *Era Mio Figlio* (Milano, 2008).

Papa, A. and Panico, G., *Storia Sociale del Calcio in Italia: Dai Campionati del Dopoguerra alla Champions League (1945–2000)* (Bologna, 2000).

Papa, A. and Panico, G., *Storia Sociale del Calcio in Italia: Dai Club dei Pionieri alla Nazione Sportiva (1887–1945)* (Bologna, 1993).

Pavone, C., *Alle Origini della Repubblica: Scritti sul Fascismo, Antifascismo e Continuità dello Stato* (Torino, 1995).

Pennacchia, M., *Il Calcio in Italia* (Torino, 1999).

Petrini, C., *I Pallonari: Zone Grige, Fondi Neri e Luci Rosse: Vent'Anni di Calcio all'Italiana* (Milano, 2003).

Pinkus, K., *The Montesi Scandal: The Death of Wilma Montesi and the Birth of the Paparazzi in Fellini's Rome* (Chicago, 2003).

Pio XII, *Discorsi e Radiomessaggi di Sua Santità Pio XII* (Roma, 1947).

Pivato, S., *Clericalismo e Laicismo nella Cultura Popolare Italiana* (Milano, 1990).

Pivato, S., *La Bicicletta e il Sol dell'Avvenire: Sport e Tempo Libero nel Socialismo della Belle-Epoque* (Firenze, 1992).

Pivato, S., *Sia Lodato Bartali: Ideologia, Cultura e Miti dello Sport Cattolico (1936/1948)* (Roma, 1996).

Poggi-Longostrevi, G., *Cultura Fisica della Donna: Linea Bellezza Salute* (Milano, 1938).

Pollard, J., *Catholicism in Modern Italy: Religion, Society and Politics since 1861* (London, 2008).

Ponzio, A., *La Palestra del Littorio: L'Accademia della Farnesina: un'Esperimento di Pedagogia Totalitaria nell'Italia Fascista* (Milano, 2009).

Porro, N., *Identità, Nazione, Cittadinanza. Sport, Società e Sistema Politico nell'Italia Contemporanea* (Roma, 1995).

Pozzo, V., *Campioni del Mondo: Quarant'Anni di Storia del Calcio Italiano* (Roma, 1960).

Pratolini, V., *Cronache dal Giro d'Italia (Maggio-Giugno 1947)* (Milano, 1992).

Reguzzoni, M., *Alberto Braglia: L'Uomo, il Ginnasta, il Mimo-Acrobata* (Modena, 1983).

Reilly, E.J. (ed.), *Across the Diamond: Baseball and American Culture* (New York, 2003).

Rendell, M., *The Death of Marco Pantani: A Biography* (London, 2007).

Riall, L., *The Italian Risorgimento: State, Society and National Unification* (London, 1994).

Riordan, J. and Kruger, A. (eds), *European Cultures in Sport: Examining the Nations and Regions* (Bristol, 2003).

Riordan, J. and Kruger, A. (eds), *The International Politics of Sport in the Twentieth Century* (London and New York, 1999).

Rohdie, S., *Rocco and his Brothers* (London, 2002).

Ronchi, M. and Josti, G., *Man on the Run: The Life and Death of Marco Pantani* (London, 2005).

Roversi, A., *Calcio e Violenza in Europa: Inghilterra, Germania, Italia, Olanda, Belgio e Danimarca* (Bologna, 1990).

Salvati, M., *Economia e Politica in Italia dal Dopoguerra ad Oggi* (Milano, 1984).

Santini, A., *Primo Carnera: L'Uomo Più Forte del Mondo* (Milano, 2004).

Sassatelli, R., *Consumo, Cultura e Società* (Bologna, 2004).

Sassoon, D., *Contemporary Italy: Economy, Society and Politics since 1945* (London, 1986).

Sassoon, D., *Mussolini and the Rise of Fascism* (London, 2008).

Scarpellini, E., *L'Italia dei Consumi: Dalla Belle Epoque al Nuovo Millennio* (Bari, 2008).

Schnapp, J. (ed.), *A Primer of Italian Fascism* (Lincoln, 2000).

Severgnini, B., *La Bella Figura: A Field Guide to the Italian Mind* (New York, 2006).

Seymour, M., *Debating Divorce in Italy: Marriage and the Making of Modern Italians, 1860–1974* (Basingstoke, 2006).

Soldani, S. and Turi, G., *Fare gli Italiani: Scuola e Cultura nell'Italia Contemporanea* (Bologna, 1993).

Sollier, P., *Calci e Sputi e Colpi di Testa: Riflessioni Autobiografiche di un Calciatore per Caso* (Milano, 1976).

Spitaleri, E., *Il Delitto Bottecchia* (Roma, 1987).

Tarozzi, F. and Vecchio, G. (eds), *Gli Italiani e il Tricolore: Patriottismo, Identità Nazionale e Fratture Sociali Lungo due Secoli di Storia* (Bologna, 1999).

Teja, A., *Educazione Fisica al Femminile: Dai Primi Corsi di Torino di Ginnastica Educative per le Maestre (1867) alle Ginnastica Moderna di Andreina Gotta Sacco (1904–1988)* (Roma, 1994).

Teja, A. and Giuntini, S., *L'Addestramento Ginnico-Militare nell'Esercito Italiano (1946–1990)* (Roma, 2007).

Tomlinson A. and Young, C., *National Identity and Global Sports Events: Culture, Politics, and Spectacle and the Football World Cup* (New York, 2006).

Tomlinson, A., Young, C. and Holt, R. (eds), *Sport and the Transformation of Modern Europe: States, Media and Markets 1950–2010* (London, 2011).

Triani, G., *Bar Sport Italia: Quando la Politica va nel Pallone* (Milano, 1994).

Triani, G., *Mal di Stadio: Storia del Tifo e della Passione per il Calcio* (Roma, 1990).

Triani, G., *Pelle di Luna Pelle di Sole: Nascita e Storia della Civiltà Balneare 1700–1946* (Venezia, 1988).

Turrini, L., *Bartali: L'Uomo che Salvò l'Italia Pedalando* (Milano, 2004).

Valeri, M., *Nero di Roma: Storia di Leone Jacovacci l'Invincibile Mulatto Italiano* (Roma, 2008).

Veltroni, W., *Il Calcio è una Scienza da Amare* (Milano, 1982).

Ventresca, R.A., *From Fascism to Democracy: Culture and Politics in the Italian Election of 1948* (Toronto, 2003).

Vergani, G. (ed.), *L'uomo a due Ruote, Avventura, Storia e Passione* (Milano, 1987).

Volpe, F. and Vecchierelli V., *2000 Italia in Meta: La Storia della Nazionale di Rugby dagli Albori al Sei Nazioni* (Santhià, 2000).

Wagg, S., *Giving the Game Away: Football, Politics and Culture on Five Continents* (Leicester, 1995).

Williams, R., *Enzo Ferrari: A Life* (London, 2002).

Yegül, F., *Bathing in the Roman World* (Cambridge, 2010).

Zanetti, G. and Tornabuoni, G., *Il Giuoco del Calcio: Commento alla Legislazione della FIGC* (Milano, 1933).

Index